DATE DUE

Private Wealth and Public Education

Private Wealth and Public Education

John E. Coons

William H. Clune III

Stephen D. Sugarman

The Belknap Press of

Harvard University Press

Cambridge, Massachusetts

1970

To nine old friends

of the children

Foreword

By James S. Coleman

THE HISTORY OF EDUCATION SINCE the industrial revolution shows a continual struggle between two forces: the desire by members of society to have educational opportunity for all children, and the desire of each family to provide the best education it can afford for its own children. Neither of these desires is to be despised; they both lead to investment by the older generation in the younger. But they can lead to quite different concrete actions. The conflict between the two forces is most evident in the decision about the means by which a child's education is to be financially supported. If there is to be educational opportunity for all children, then a child's education must not depend on his family's economic resources. But if a family is to be able to provide its children with the best education it can afford, then it must be able to employ its economic resources to do so. These two requirements are in direct opposition.

The educational systems of Europe have traditionally exhibited these dual forces through dual public school systems:

an academically-oriented set of secondary schools for an elite, and a set of schools terminating early for the masses. Another outcome of these forces has been the educational system of England: the state-supported schools were added in 1870 to a system of "voluntary" or privately supported schools. Thus the family with some financial means could satisfy both its aims by supporting the state system through taxes, providing one level of education, and sending its own children to private school, providing a higher level for them.

In the United States, a dual system never developed within public education, nor has the use of private schools been widespread. A common school has developed, beginning in the latter part of the nineteenth century, providing a single comprehensive public school system that covers the vast majority of children of school age.

It would appear, then, that the second of these forces, the desire of families to provide for their own children the best education they can afford, has been wholly submerged by the goal of educational opportunity for all children, or at least it has been implemented wholly through actions which achieved this latter goal.

This appearance, however, is quite misleading. In the United States, another means has arisen whereby persons with financial resources can employ them to their own children's benefit without having them spread thin over everyone else's children as well. This means is place of residence together with local financing in education. Modern technology, in particular the automobile, has allowed economic areas to become specialized and residential areas to become economically homogeneous. When this economic homogeneity coincides roughly with local school taxation boundaries, then the wealthy in one district can confine their expenditures to their own children and those of other families of similar wealth who are paying equally. The less wealthy in a neighboring district are left to finance their own children's education, with a reduced set of resources. If their resources are very small, then their children's education is very poorly financed.

Obviously, such a system is, at the extreme, wholly destructive of the goal of educational opportunity for all children, independent of their families' economic resources. The child's educational opportunity comes to be dependent on the economic resources of the local community — and those resources are coming to be more and more a reflection of his family's resources, as residential areas become more homogeneous.

States, which have responsibility under the Constitution for the provision of education, at the outset delegated this responsibility to their local subdivisions,[1] creating the possibility of gross inequality of financing. Subsequently, states have moved to repair some of the gross inequities in financing that this system produces, through partial state financing which supplements locally generated funds. State "formulas" for aid to local districts take several forms, but none of them eliminate the financial inequities produced by differing wealth per child in different localities, and some do not even begin to do so.

It is with this situation that Coons, Clune, and Sugarman begin. In Part I of this book, they examine the existing financial structure in a number of states and show how the various state aid formulas fail to eliminate the financial inequities caused by differences in taxable wealth per child in different localities. In Part II, they present a solution which will eliminate the inequities; and in Part III, they prepare the legal path to the adoption of such a solution by the courts.

Altogether, it is an extraordinary treatise, requiring an extraordinary combination of skills. To trace the history and current status of state aid formulas is in itself an achievement in educational economics. The authors have done this well,

1. That is, all states except Hawaii, which has a single statewide school system.

showing the sequence of attempts at solutions to inequities produced by local differences in wealth and showing how, in each case, the means for recreating inequities have crept in. To have devised a solution which retains local control over the degree of educational financing, without a resulting inequality of educational offering due to wealth, is an impressive intellectual feat, and they do just that. To bring together the legal history bearing on the Fourteenth Amendment to the Constitution (the equal protection clause), and bring that to bear on the inequities of school financing, is an important job of legal research. They have done this as well. Altogether, they have used with great skill a combination of social science and law in the service of a policy problem of great importance.

Coons, Clune, and Sugarman are not willing to sacrifice local decision-making about education in order to make the level of educational expenditures in a child's education independent of his parents' economic resources. They wish, rather, to preserve the locality's decision about how much education to provide, its decision about how much it is willing to tax itself to provide education for its children. They wish to preserve this local decision-making while freeing the resulting level of expenditure from the widely varying abilities of the localities to pay. The problem can be seen by three concepts they introduce: the educational *offering*, which is roughly the amount expended per child on education, educational *wealth*, which is roughly the wealth of the community per child in school, and educational *effort*, which is the rate at which wealth is taxed for education (ordinarily real wealth, taxed through the local property tax). If localities are purely self-financing in education, then offering to the children in that locality equals locality wealth times locality effort. Carried to the extreme, where the locality is a single family, this equation is purely private education, in which each family pays only for its own child's education — and the more that different school taxation districts differ in wealth, the closer to private education, where each child's education depends on his own family's expenditures on education, does the public system become. If financing of education is to be carried out equally within states, then the same equation, offering equals wealth times effort, holds, but at the state level. Such an equation equalizes educational expenditures throughout the state, but at the cost of local decision-making. Coons, Clune, and Sugarman want to maintain local decision-making — but they want to equalize the power that different localities have to realize their educational ends. Does it appear impossible? Not so; they have shown how it may be done, and the result is a principle they term "power equalizing."

Coons, Clune, and Sugarman argue convincingly that while the offering should depend on the locality's effort, it should depend also on the wealth of the state as a whole, rather than on the locality's own wealth; that is, districts in a state should have equal power to realize their educational interests. This would appear to be the intent of the constitutional vesting of responsibility for education in the states, but if so, it is an intent which has not been realized in practice. The result has been to make the educational offering dependent principally on the wealth of the district, rather than on its educational effort. It creates an incentive for all to live in wealthy districts with few children, and an incentive in those districts to keep out families with many children or low incomes or both. It drives those with high wealth living in low-wealth districts (for example, central cities) either out of those districts, if the taxes become high enough to allow educational expenditures that are competitive with high-wealth districts, or to private schools, if they do not. In short, it creates incentives to further homogenize residential areas and thus further intensify the inequality of educational expenditure due to wealth.

How Coons and his colleagues solve this puzzle without re-

sort to a centralized statewide system is their own story, and I
will leave it to them. The story is fascinating, and one is
tempted to comment on it at length — to raise detailed questions about how it might be implemented, to argue with them
about its consequences, to point out problems in its details,
to discuss further the possibilities of its being enacted by legislatures (a possibility that the authors view dismally, somewhat
more dismally than I would), and the possibilities of its being
realized through court action using the Fourteenth Amendment. I will resist these temptations, except for a few comments.

First, one must always ask of any method of public finance
what incentives it creates or destroys, and what the consequences of these incentives might be.

One beneficial incentive effect of the "power equalizing"
solution of the authors is that it destroys the incentive to move,
on educational finance grounds, out of poor areas and into
wealthy ones, because it frees the resources available for the
child's education from the locality's wealth. It thus removes
a portion of the vicious circle which increasingly concentrates
financial resources for education in homogeneous areas. This
effect, however, would probably not be strong, because parents'
decisions about what school district to live in probably depend
more on the other children in the schools than on the financial
resources of the school.

A second, not-so-beneficial, incentive effect, and one that
would likely grow in importance as the general level of real
income in families increases, is the incentive for the well-to-do
family to move its children from public school to private school
(since even by voting high local school taxes, the benefits of
these taxes would be low in a wealthy community) and its
residence to an area that votes low educational taxes. This is
very likely a serious incentive effect, one which in some areas,
even without "power equalizing," is already removing large

numbers of children from the public schools — children whose parents have more money, and are more interested in education, than the average parents. It appears likely that if upper middle class suburbs cease to be a semiprivate school refuge for families with money, they will resort to a final strategy — moving their children to private school.

It is a virtue of the "power equalizing" method of financing education proposed in this book that it does not entirely eliminate a family's ability to implement its desires to provide its own children with special educational benefits. For if it did so, as would a fully centralized system that not only equalized educational wealth across a state, but also educational effort, then those with sufficient wealth could and would send their children to private schools and vote against higher school taxes. In effect, the upper limit of a system in the direction of equality is imposed by this alternative. Any technique to create equality of financial resources for education in the presence of family income inequalities must have some means by which those with higher income can aid their child's education, or else they will use that income to do so outside the system of public education. Coons and his colleagues have devised such a means, while within a framework of equality of financial resources available for education. Whether it is sufficient depends largely on the parameters: on whether the financial power of a tax dollar in a wealthy community is still high enough that its members would not choose to substitute private education and low taxes for public education and high taxes.

There is, really, only one method of financing education which can bring about approximate equality of educational resources for children from families of different wealth without inducing strategies which would partially negate its effect, while still keeping the control of educational decisions localized. This is a return of resources to each family, in the form of tuition vouchers, so that each family has equal potential for obtaining its child's education, on an open market. Variations upon this method have been widely discussed in recent years, and Coons and his colleagues show how their principle of power equalizing may be realized by a type of modified voucher system. The result they term "family power equalizing" in contrast to "district power equalizing." They appear to feel it would be less likely of success as a principle the courts (or possibly legislatures) might adopt; but it may very well be more likely of success. The reason, of course, is that it frees the state from the responsibility and necessity of dictating that a given child attend school in a given district — a power that the court might rightly see as violating the Fourteenth Amendment at the same time that, following the authors' legal arguments, it saw the fiscal inequality of such a violation. For as my research and that of others has shown, the educational resources available to each child in a school include as an important component the educational backgrounds of the other children in the school — and any state which dictates the school or school district to which each child goes is unequally distributing those educational resources, however equally it is distributing finances.

As I indicated, the authors have in fact carried their principle of power equalizing to its nearly ultimate terminus, family power equalizing in education. Obviously, the application of this principle to all areas of consumption would do away in effect with income differences, destroying the whole system of incentives on which every society is founded. But education, they argue, is a special item of consumption, special because it fixes the child's chances to compete as an adult. Thus equalizing a family's power in *this* area is not really equalizing the adults' resources, but only those of the next generation. In providing the background of current economic inequalities in education, by providing the legal background for an elimination of these inequalities, and in providing a viable principle by which they can be eliminated, Coons, Clune and Sugarman have carried out an enormous service. This book may well speed by some years the achievement of equality of educational financing. Perhaps of even greater importance, it may influence the direction these policies will take, away from centralized control, toward a vesting of control in the family itself.

There is, of course, a broader sense of the term "equality of educational opportunity" which should be kept in mind: equality of *all* the effective resource inputs into education, not merely the financial ones. This equality can only be measured by equal effects for children of equal ability; but it clearly consists of a variety of input resources, not merely financial ones. The question about the state's provision of equal education opportunity becomes a difficult one: over which of these resources does the state have control, or should the state have control? Which of the resources can the state, through legal means, demand be redistributed equally? Certainly not the attentive help that some parents give their children in learning to read, nor the discipline some parents exert in enforcing the homework assignments of the school, nor the reinforcements by parents of the performance rewards given by the school. But the state has attempted to control the distribution of one educational resource, that is money — though, as Coons and his colleagues show, this distribution is currently far from equal — and recently it has, in what might be seen as a radical venture into resource redistribution, attempted to control the distribution of educational resources embodied in classmates. The means, of course, has been racial and social class integration. In this second area of resources, it has been even more ineffective than in its attempt to redistribute financial resources. This second kind of educational resource, in the form of other children in a school, Coons and his colleagues do not discuss. Yet the attempt of the state to effect a redistribution focuses attention on the fact that financial resources are not the only ones. More fundamentally, it raises the question of just how far the state can go, and how far it should go, in redistributing educational resources to provide equal protection to the young in the form of equal educational opportunity. It is not a question that is easily answered, and it is not a question raised in this book. Yet beyond the provision of equal financial resources for education, toward which this book provides a path, the larger question must be raised.

Preface

If you lived on this side, my friend, I should be an assassin,
and it would be unjust to slay you in this manner. But since
you live on the other side, I am a hero, and it is just.

Pascal, Pensees

COMMON OPINION HAS IT THAT INEQUALITY of educational opportunity is primarily a problem of racial segregation. The out-
pouring of literature devoted to proving the Negro school
inferior has become a mighty flood. Tributaries of this torrent
have explored the plight of the Appalachian white, the migrant
farm worker, and the Puerto Rican, but the mainstream is
racial, and at least until recently its message was clear. For
inequalities of education, integration has been the liberal's
patent medicine.

Integration is indeed a sound, long-run prescription for many
of the basic ailments of education and of our society — so long
as we don't, in the meantime, die of something else; but to

suppose that integration would itself produce equality of education is plainly naive. Where integration has existed, there has been inequality; integrated schools in our largest cities often, by any standard, have been grossly inferior to the district norm. Where there was segregation, at least sometimes there was equality in all other senses. Not only will quality education for all children not be guaranteed by integration, but there is danger that a holy war with this single objective will produce a Pyrrhic victory by neglecting and obscuring other important forms of discrimination in education against both white and black.

A brief tale of two schoolboys will illustrate. They could be any color, but suppose them white in a white neighborhood. One lives on 36th Street in Oakland, California; his friend lives across the street in Emeryville. Every weekday morning at 8:00 they separate, each to attend his assigned public school — one in the Oakland system, one in the Emeryville District. If the reader knows something of California public schools, this trivial event is worth recording. The separation is a fateful one for these children and the millions like them around the nation for whom the accidents of residence and boundary play a decisive role in the character of their formal education. The State of California, like most states, has provided a system guaranteeing to one child a superior education, while to the other it offers mediocrity or worse. Oakland will spend $600–700 on the first child; the Emeryville student will go first class at nearly three times that expense.[1] This example is neither extreme nor extraordinary. The spectrum of school districts in California includes expenditures both higher and considerably lower than these. Nor is the picture radically different in other states: expenditures in Illinois range from under $400 up to

1. The Oakland tax rate is nearly twice that of Emeryville; *California Public Schools Selected Statistics 1967–68*, 24 (Sacramento: Department of Education, 1969).

$1,600 or more per pupil, and the disparities in Ohio are similar.[2]

Differentials of these magnitudes in per-pupil expenditure within the same state should evoke nothing but outrage. Indeed, there is something incongruous about a differential of any magnitude the sole justification for which is an imaginary school district line between two children. It is the kind of phenomenon that forces its defenders into the dense refuge of "political realities" in search of a rationale. The plain fact is that our state governments have embraced the philosophy that, as a rule, the quality of public education should be in direct proportion to the wealth of the school district; in general this also means that the quality will be in inverse proportion to the needs of children. The primary dependence of public education upon the real property tax and the localization of that tax's administration and expenditure have combined to make the public school into an educator for the educated rich and a keeper for the uneducated poor. There exists no more powerful force for rigidity of social class and the frustration of natural potential than the modern public school system with its systematic discrimination against poor districts.

The remedy is not obvious. Political forces supporting the status quo no doubt vary in strength from state to state, but educational systems themselves are so structured as to be naturally protected from legislative drift toward an egalitarian

2. Something of the national picture can be gathered from Appendix F, Tables 1–3. Table 1 shows the range of interquartile school district expenditures per classroom within those states with the widest and narrowest bands. Because the median expenditure of the states varies significantly, it is more appropriate to state this range as a ratio. Table 2 shows the national extremes in the ratio of the interquartile range of expenditure. Table 3 shows the national extremes in the ratio of the 98th percentile of district expenditure within the state to the 2nd percentile (eliminating "freaks" at either end). Expenditure figures of this kind are suggestive of the endemic problem but do little to explain the underlying causes until coupled with data on district wealth and tax effort. See Part I.

form. Districts favored by a superior tax base are likely to be opposed to change on all grounds; districts of average affluence are apathetic but can also be opposed to change because they fear potential loss of local control. Poor districts alone have a clear stake in change, but their case is supported only by justice. Hence the persuasiveness of the argument from "reality." Little is to be expected from the political process in its legislative mode.

What, if anything, can be expected from the judicial process? The lawyer's instinct is to recoil from judicial intrusion into the structure of state government. The instinct is sound; but, like most instincts, it can also mislead. Its solid core lies in the mistrust of political change through nonmajoritarian decision-making. It is at ground a democratic impulse which prefers that questions of structure be submitted at least indirectly to the popular will. Under certain conditions its essential benevolence is self-defeating. Legislative malapportionment is a historic instance in which vox populi was simply unavailable in any effective form. The will of the majority required not judicial restraint but judicial rescue.

The goal of equal education may justify heroic judicial measures on a rationale similar in two respects to the reapportionment theme. First, as noted, the deprived child and his subsociety may be and frequently are in a position of political impotence, not because of limited numbers but because of districting structure and other factors organic to the system. Second, education shares with voting the quality of being logically and practically anterior to all other values in democratic society. In fact, as between the two, education arguably deserves precedence as the indispensable preamble of political life.

But there is a third and independent rationale for equality in public education in any capitalist society. At the pinnacle of our economic temple still flies the standard of universal access to the levers of opulence and mobility. Beyond argument, the prime mover in the modern labor market is education. In a free-enterprise system its differential provision by the public school marks the intrusion of economic (if not legal) heresy, for it means that certain participants in the economic race are hobbled at the gate — and hobbled by the *public* handicapper.

In assessing the propriety of judicial intervention under the Fourteenth Amendment these three factors and others will be elaborated in more detail. They are noted at this preliminary stage to suggest both that systematic discrimination in quality of public education may be viewed as a realistic constitutional issue and that the objection to it is in many respects an intensely conservative one. This latter observation is useful here to parry or at least postpone the natural reaction that equality is once more to become the leveler's stalking horse. The truth is not so simple. The case for equality in public education is a schizophrenic medley of Karl Marx and Barry Goldwater, St. Thomas and Saint-Simon. Reservation of judgment is all that can be asked, but nothing less will do.

The problem is complicated principally by the value that Americans place on local decision-making—a value we shall label "subsidiarity." Few would object in theory to equality of educational opportunity if that result did not seem necessarily to cast out local choice. Some argue simplistically that equality of educational opportunity is flatly inconsistent with local authority.[3] We are convinced that this supposed antithesis be-

3. See, e.g., Phillip Kurland, "Equal Educational Opportunity: The Limits of Constitutional Jurisprudence Undefined," *University of Chicago Law Review*, 35:583 (1968). This article appears also in the collection of papers from a 1968 conference; G. U. Daly, ed., *The Quality of Inequality: Suburban and Urban Public Schools* (Chicago: University of Chicago Press, 1968). Kurland's exaggerated pessimism may be a product both of the general shortage of intelligible analysis of existing school finance structures and of the deplorable bent of aspiring school reformers for uniform — and often federal — solutions. The other contributions in the volume noted are not calculated to allay such fears.

tween equality and subsidiarity is overdrawn: that both values can be preserved if only one is willing to struggle with the complexities and fine tuning required of any balanced system. Much of this book involves an analysis of the relation between the two values and of structures designed to achieve such a balance. A moment's reflection will suggest the significance of such structures for the movement toward greater decentralization of control in public education. Until it descends to the level of the family, the drift toward smaller units in education has no natural limit other than the ability of such units to finance themselves.

This book, then, is about the value systems, including the law, that affect the distribution of educational resources. It is not comprehensive in the sense of exposing the character and magnitude of dollar discrimination in every state. Rather it is analytic, suggestive, heuristic. It is also argumentative and, in certain respects, not particularly objective. We have a strong preference, and that preference is for balance. We find grossly offensive the existing discrimination against poor school districts; we find equally offensive the current efforts to use the Constitution as a battering ram for uniformity or even for compensatory education.[4] There are less polarized and destructive ways to approach the problem of fiscal equity through the courts, but these can only appear after someone has made a serious effort to analyze existing statutory systems and to delineate the alternatives available to the legislatures once the

---

See also A. E. Wise, *Rich Schools, Poor Schools: The Promise of Equal Educational Opportunity* (Chicago: University of Chicago Press, 1968), a former dissertation manifesting an education specialist's fascination with the law in the form of equal protection decisions of the Supreme Court. One can speculate whether our heavier emphasis on the character of school finance is a shorter path to wisdom; perhaps both books only confirm the insecurities of the professional concerning his own discipline.

4. See, e.g., McInnis v. Shapiro, 293 F. Supp. 327 (N.D. Ill. 1968), aff'd *mem. sub nom.* McInnis v. Ogilvie, 394 U.S. 322 (1969). The *McInnis* and similar cases are discussed extensively in Part III.

courts have set them free. So far as we can determine that effort has not yet been made; hence this book.

We wish to express profound thanks for the support — financial and professional — given us by the Program in Law and the Social Sciences at Northwestern University and its sponsor, The Russell Sage Foundation. We are proud to have played a role in this unique undertaking at what is surely the finest of the great Midwestern law schools.

The individual acknowledgments should — but will not be — legion. The law faculties at Northwestern and Berkeley who have suffered nearly en masse are thanked hereby in that same manner. This is a form of collectivism well suited to begin a book so much concerned with equality. This rule is designed for lawyers only, however, leaving us free to confess specifically our debt to Professor Charles Benson of the School of Education at Berkeley. All we need say of Benson is that he is such a professional he is not afraid to encourage amateurs.

Ted and Linda Akulian demonstrated that a nice sense of the absurd can make even cite-checking tolerable, and Pat Brudney's elegant typing maintained an esthetic atmosphere in the struggle. For both we are grateful. As for those of us with wives and children, considering the last three years it is surprising.

John E. Coons
William H. Clune III
Stephen D. Sugarman

August, 1969

Contents

Part III. The Cutting Edge

Private Wealth and Public Education

A certain balance is necessary between equality and
inequality. . . . If no matter who can attain the social rank
corresponding to the function he is capable of filling, and if
education is sufficiently generalized so that no one is
prevented from developing any capacity simply on account
of his birth, the prospects are the same for every child. In
this way, the prospects for each man are the same as for any
other man, both as regards himself when young, and as
regards his children later on.

Simone Weil, *The Need for Roots*

Introduction: Values in Collision

> *. . . in theory . . . every sane man admits a perfect equality*
> *between himself and others; but in practice, in his feelings*
> *and dealings, he is ever affirming the immeasurable difference,*
> *the fundamental dissimilarity between himself and them.*
> *Soloviev,* The Meaning of Love

THIS BOOK IS ABOUT EQUALITY of educational opportunity.
Nearly every American — and we include ourselves — endorses
it, often with fine unconcern for the serious difficulties of definition. For sheer ambiguity each of its terms would be hard to
improve upon: equality and opportunity alike elude description. Taken together they cloak the most diverse and conflicting philosophies. There is here even a suggestion of contradiction; perhaps equality and opportunity can coexist, but theirs
is a mixed marriage that requires accommodation.

Despite such reservations, there will be much use of these
terms, especially equality, in ensuing chapters. This could be
misleading. The frequent use of "equal," "equality," "equaliz-

1

ing," and the like may give the impression of an underlying design more egalitarian than is intended. Our central motif emphasizes opportunity as much as equality, for there is a subtle harmony between those egalitarian and individualistic values that simultaneously inform our "free-enterprise democracy."

But this places us slightly ahead of our story, and indeed it is a story much more than it is a philosophy. It has its heroes and villains, and, as we come upon the scene, the villains are in the ascendancy. The states are dispensing public education according to the wealth of school districts. Children who live in poor districts — children rich and poor, white and black alike — are being injured. This story, which anyone can understand, is an existing condition that needs an alternative more than it needs philosophy. We would like to frame a different plot for the tale and render it less a tragedy.

The new theme is a simple formula with modest aspirations — one designed to reach the specific evil in the system and no more: *The quality of public education may not be a function of wealth other than the wealth of the state as a whole.* It will be evident from this precept that we do not aim to effect equality of educational opportunity in all its possible senses. But to lapse briefly into philosophy, it should be asked, why do we care at all? Whence the sense of injustice? What is intelligible and sound in "equality of educational opportunity," first, that makes it worth seeking at all, and second, that is offended by the specific existing systems that dispense public education by wealth?

ON HAVING THE SAME POOR ALWAYS WITH US: MOBILITY, EQUALITY, AND EDUCATION

There is an enduring tension of purposes in American public education that is nicely syncretized and obscured in "equality of educational opportunity." Notions of equality, in the senses both of uniformity of schools and of their products, must compete for allegiance with the often contrasting values of individualism and social mobility. All these views must be harmonized; thus, to the extent that equality might imply sameness, our ethos rejects it. To be sure, our consciences may be troubled by permanent inequalities (for example, in the sense of inherited burdens from poverty or race); but the remedy sought is never that of regimented uniformity. Our folklore easily abides the descent of the rich man's son to poverty so long as his grandson may reascend. The Negro's continuing poverty might be tolerable if we could be persuaded that he deserves it. The crucial value to be preserved is the opportunity to succeed, not the uniformity of success. It is the philosophy of contest — free enterprise in the broadest sense. This is not to be construed as an exclusive emphasis on business success, on competition for money or on enterprise in its narrow sense. It is rather a label for the maximizing of individual choice, of flexibility in life roles, of alternatives for participation in the social system.

But, however broadly the prize is defined, the newborn are incompetent to seek it, and they remain dependent until pushed from the nest into the struggle for place. The mere lapse of time hardly prepares them for entry into the competitive world; when they do enter the contest, they must be reasonably fit, considering their natural limitations. In short, the sine qua non of a fair contest system — of equality of opportunity — is equality of training. And that training is what public education is primarily about. There are, we hope, loftier views of education that coexist, but in a competitive democracy those views represent dependent goals that can be realized only upon a foundation of training for basic competence in the market.

Such a view tolerates gross differences in outcome, if the contest is fair. Native ability and effort must in this view account for relative success, and the marketplace serves as the impartial judge. But because the market can distinguish only competence it cannot decide if the contest itself is just; it neither knows nor cares how competence was achieved. If Stephen cannot read, the market will not ask whether his father could read or whether Stephen had a father. The search for excellence is ruthlessly impartial, but the opportunity to train for excellence may be less so.

Here from the viewpoint of equality we find the soft spot in the system: in practice, the market effectively sustains a competence which is inherited or may even be nourished by governmental privilege but which in either case is unmerited. For many of us competence effectively is "inherited" because our society, organized in large part about the family, stimulates the transference of advantages and disadvantages from parent to child. Democracy can stand certain kinds and amounts of this; there are enormous gains from moderate dynastic stimuli such as the laws of inheritance and wills. Unmerited success can be viewed in such cases as the end product of a fair contest, a legitimate reason for trying to get ahead in the first place. What democracy cannot tolerate is an aristocracy padded and protected by the state itself from competition from below, while an underclass coexists that is largely excluded from hope of success. Members of the new generation of contestants must not be bound by the state to the failure or sucess of their ancestors, for this is the hallmark of an unfair contest.

Insofar as public education seeks in theory to counter this "inherited incompetence" it is informed by more than egalitarian values. It strives to make room for the deserving children of the poor and the foolish not merely in the middle but at the top. Social mobility as a value plays a potent role here, and public education must be seen in its special relation to the underclasses to whom it is the strongest hope for rising in the social scale. The public school was designed to permit the poor to compete; it was explicitly a response to their fate in a pay-as-you-go educational system. The intended relation of the public school to the problem of permanent social inequality is vivid in this excerpt from an address by Thaddeus Stevens to the Pennsylvania legislature, in which he pleaded for the continued existence of the school law:

> This law is often objected to, because its benefits are shared by the children of the profligate spendthrift equally with those of the most industrious and economical habits. It ought to be remembered, that the benefit is bestowed, not on the erring parents, but the innocent children. Carry out this objection and you punish children for the crimes or misfortunes of their parents. You virtually establish castes and grades founded on no merit of the particular generation, but on the demerits of their ancestors; an aristocracy of the most odious and insolent kind — the aristocracy of wealth and power.[1]

Stevens and other nineteenth-century reformers saw the tension in the social order between equality and opportunity.[2]

1. Thaddeus Stevens, "An Appeal for Tax-Supported Schools," in C. H. Gross and C. C. Chandler, eds., *The History of American Education through Readings* (Boston, 1964), pp. 114–115.

2. The idea that merit alone should determine wealth and power is actually very old. Plato's education system was intended to apply to a very small group — magistrates and military men — excluding businessmen, farmers, and, of course, slaves. Yet within the military and magistrate classes, all privilege of birth was to be abolished in favor of physical, moral, and intellectual excellence. As for the excluded classes, it is misleading to apply the contemporary model of mass democracy; there is abundant evidence that, within the limitations of political reality, Plato's egalitarian sentiments extended to those classes as well (except for slaves). See R. C. Lodge, *Plato's Theory of Education* (London, 1947), pp. 234–259. Dewey observes that Plato had no perception of men as individuals, however: education would determine which class an individual should enter, rather than liberate unique capacities; John Dewey, *Democracy and Education* (New York, 1963), pp. 89–90. Plato's idea may since have gained a curious renascence through our heightened awareness of the link between education and social class. See also F. A. Hayek, *The Constitution of Liberty* (Chicago, 1960), pp. 92–93. See generally M. M. Tumin, *Social Stratification* (Englewood Cliffs, 1967), pp. 1–4, for a brief discussion of the

They saw in "free-enterprise democracy" the potential contradiction between preferment for the excellent and control
by the majority.[3] These men were not levelers. They accepted
the tension and contradiction, but they did so on condition:
equality of opportunity through education. Dewey later put it
this way:

> Obviously a society to which stratification into separate
> classes would be fatal, must see to it that intellectual op-
> portunities are accessible to all on equable and easy terms.
> A society marked off into classes need be specially atten-
> tive only to the education of its ruling elements. A society
> which is mobile, which is full of channels for the distribu-
> tion of a change occurring anywhere, must see to it that its
> members are educated to personal initiative and adaptabil-
> ity. Otherwise, they will be overwhelmed by the changes
> in which they are caught and whose significance and con-
> nections they do not perceive. The result will be a confu-
> sion in which a few will appropriate to themselves the
> results of the blind and externally directed activities of
> others.[4]

To the extent that public education is designed for mobility,
the present fiscal discriminations are especially absurd and ag-
gravating. The existing systems represent the very worst basis
upon which to distribute public education, if our hope is to
increase the mobility of the poor. At least this is true to the
degree that poor people live in poor districts.

Obviously nonmonetary factors endemic to poor men and
poor districts also have an enormous impact on how well prepared for life a child will be upon completion of his formal

ubiquity in Western culture of the proposition that equality of opportunity
refers to stratification by merit rather than by birth.

3. See, e.g., The Rockefeller Brothers Fund, "Excellence and Equality Are
Not Incompatible," in Gross and Chandler, *History*, p. 420.

4. Dewey, *Democracy and Education*, pp. 87–88.

education. These factors will remain even after the economic unfairness in the education system is eliminated. Poverty is not eradicated by ending its effect upon the quality of public education a child receives, and its influence will continue to be significant in his life inside and outside of the classroom. The poor will not be saved by equality of opportunity in education; they merely cannot be saved without it.

There is, however, an important difference between discrimination in public education and most of those other social ills we tend to associate with poverty. Crime, slum housing, illness, and bad nutrition are not the anticipated consequence of government planning. Discrimination in education, on the other hand, is precisely the anticipated consequence of the legislated structure of public education. Far from striving to overcome poverty's effects upon education, the state, in structuring the system, has taken that poverty itself as the measure of quality in education. Such a system bears the appearance of calculated unfairness.

Equality and the Nonpoor

It would be wrong to suppose that social mobility is the only value competing with equality in public education or to suppose that public education is designed for the poor alone. This is so clear as to need no argument — at least not from those hundred millions of Americans who are not poor but who have used the public schools. It would be tiresome to try to list every purpose of such persons in choosing public education. They are as numerous as the reasons for choosing to be educated at all plus some others peculiar to the American middle class. We might encapsulate them in the general idea that such children, like all others, must be prepared to function in a competitive society. Perhaps the additional value that this suggests may simply be labeled "preparedness." [5]

5. Education's importance in this regard has been greatly magnified by the

What, then, is the objection, if any, of the nonpoor to the present systems of distribution of public education? For those nonpoor (or, for that matter, those poor) who live in school districts which are themselves wealthy there is no objection whatsoever; they enjoy the privileges of the system, and their children are in general the best prepared. But for the nonpoor living in a poor district the objection is much the same as that of the poor man. To the extent that quality of public education affects preparedness, each is injured by the system. The complaint of the nonpoor student is less poignant, for he can escape to private schools, protect his mobility, and achieve his other purposes. Nevertheless, quite aside from objecting to the double cost of private education, he may ask the more fundamental question, by what rationale does the state dispense education in such a manner? For him the ultimate value question can be put this way: To what extent may the state be arbitrary in its provision of public education, and is a wealth-determined system of distribution anything but arbitrary? [6]

----

modern economy. As the economy becomes more specialized and the work environment more bureaucratized, technological, and national, the quality and level of education become increasingly determinative of success in life. At whatever earlier occasion sheer "adaptability" as the focus of training might have sufficed as a kind of universal success factor, and however desirable it remains, it is today an insufficient qualification for success in most areas of the economy. We have indeed witnessed the death of the salesman, and if the "sales engineer" is his legitimate progeny, he is not a chip off the old block. Training, even for the pseudo-engineer, unmistakably implies formal education of a substantial character. See C. S. Benson, *The Economics of Public Education* (Boston, 1961), pp. 220–221.

6. From earliest times the state has perceived its interest in education: Aristotle, *Politics*, v, 9, in *Great Issues in Education* (Chicago, 1956), I, 87; Stevens, in Gross and Chandler, *History*, pp. 111–114, 119; Horace Mann, "An Educator Speaks on Education," *ibid.*, pp. 94, 101. This interest may be in preserving a stable and perceptive constituency, as suggested by Aristotle, Stevens, and Mann, or in economic prosperity. See articles by H. M. Groves, Theodore Schulz, R. D. Baldwin, H. P. Clark, and Edward Denison, in C. S. Benson, ed., *Readings on the Economics of Education* (Boston, 1963), pp. 7–41.

Whatever the lure, it is fascinating to observe the onesidedness of this point

With respect to the nonpoor another point should be borne in mind. When persons are distinguished from one another by their relative wealth, irrelevancy is risked, for the subject then has become not school children, but their parents. Children in a true sense are all poor. It is difficult to perceive how children residing in poor districts, either of poor or nonpoor families, deserve less in terms of public education. If government is to educate at all, these children should be as prepared to participate and compete in our society as their peers, rich and poor, who live in wealthy neighborhoods.

If we believe all this, why have we so narrowed our focus? Why, for example, have we left out private schools, and why is the proposition we promote so conservative? If equality of opportunity in education is desirable, why not strike at anything whatsoever that impedes it? The answer is not that we have no constitutional handle upon private education — though we don't — or that we do not approve compensatory education, which we do. Rather it is twofold: first, to us the state's moral and legal imperative extends no further than those inequalities created by government itself. Discrimination by the state is our sole object; this excludes the duty to ameliorate cultural or natural disadvantages. It is important to cast this in terms of absence of the state's *duty:* we do not suggest that the state is forbidden to compensate for such disadvantages.

as it is made in educational literature: The state is seen to have an *interest* in demanding a minimum of education from everyone but to have no corresponding *duty,* having entered the field, to dispense the service fairly. See Sidney Webb in Benson, *Economics of Public Education,* p. 218. This is in spite of the fact that the same underlying "neighborhood effects" support both the right and the duty. If an ignorant man has wide social and economic impact he is also widely impacted by society and economy. See Milton Friedman, "The Role of Government in Education," in Benson, *Perspectives on the Economics of Education,* pp. 132–134. By some legerdemain it seems the state can enter the field of education because of interlocking social and economic effects, intensify the necessity of education a la Sputnik, and then without challenge apply differential pushes to its trainees on the basis of wealth!

Yet, if the standard were put in terms of a duty to establish pure equality of schooling, we would be forced either to forbid compensatory education or else to define equality in a most peculiar fashion. Thus we have chosen to employ a negative proposition which reaches the important state-created discrimination (that by wealth) but leaves the way open for rational dispensation of resources according to educational need, if that appears desirable to the legislatures of the states. Let us add that this is not merely a device. We accept in most respects the statement of relevant principles delineated by Hayek:

> A hundred years ago, at the height of the classical liberal movement, the demand was generally expressed by the phrase *la carrière ouverte aux talents*. It was a demand that all man-made obstacles to the rise of some should be removed, that all privileges of individuals should be abolished, and that what the state contributed to the chance of improving one's conditions should be the same for all. That so long as people are different and grow up in different families this could not assure an equal start was fairly generally accepted. It was understood that the duty of government was not to ensure that everybody had the same prospect of reaching a given position but merely to make available to all on equal terms those facilities which in their nature depended on government action. That the results were bound to be different, not only because the individuals were different, but also because only a small part of the relevant circumstances depended on government action, was taken for granted.
>
> This conception that all should be allowed to try has been largely replaced by the altogether different conception that all must be assured an equal start and the same prospects. This means little less than that the government, instead of providing the same circumstances for all, should aim at controlling all conditions relevant to a particular individual's prospects and so adjust them to his capacities as

to assure him of the same prospects as everybody else. Such deliberate adaptation of opportunities to individual aims and capacities would, of course, be the opposite of freedom.[7]

Our proposition, of course, is more limited than Hayek's statement insofar as we would forbid only such state discrimination as depends upon wealth. (The rationale for this limitation is simply the lawyer's fetish for sticking to the facts of his case; when the state begins to discriminate by the color of one's hair, it will be time to consider broadening the principle.) Further, unlike Hayek, we would confine the prohibition to education (a limitation which requires the more elaborate explanation offered in Part III). We are more "liberal" than Hayek, however, in the sense that we would permit and promote, though not require, prudent expenditure according to such criteria as need or gifts.

Equality of opportunity represents the defining rhetoric of American free-enterprise democracy; the public school is charged with its realization. This renders the distribution of quality of public education according to wealth an incongruity in need either of powerful justification or speedy elimination. That is the bedrock judgment in this book, and we believe that it is supported by an American consensus.

Measuring Opportunity

The analysis now is threatened by an ambiguity that is inevitable in any discussion of equality of educational opportu-

7. Hayek, *Constitution of Liberty*, pp. 92–93. Here Hayek is curiously reminiscent of the words of President Jackson's veto of the bank bill: "There are no necessary evils in government. Its evils exist only in its abuses. If it would confine itself to equal protection, and, as Heaven does its rains, shower its favors alike on the high and the low, the rich and the poor, it would be an unqualified blessing" (J. D. Richardson, ed., *A Compilation of the Messages and Papers of the Presidents, 1787–1887* [Washington, D.C.: U.S. Government Printing Office, 1896–1899], II, 590).

nity: the confusion between two competing measures of excellence in education. This is an issue we have already settled by implication, but one we had best make clear before proceeding further. One measure of education focuses upon the *child* and the effects of education upon him. How is he actually changing as a consequence of the process? How is he being prepared for the contest? The other measure focuses upon the *school* and, thus, the objective characteristics of the education process. We might call one the *child concept* and the other the *school concept* of opportunity. When measuring opportunity, the question may be either: (1) are children graduated from schools A and B equally prepared for life, or (2) are schools A and B providing equal programs of instruction? Another simple way to phrase the problem is this: Are schools to be equal or are they to be equalizers? The distinction corresponds to that between state-created inequalities (unequal schools) and inequalities generated by other sources (unequal children).

Neither view of opportunity can be entirely rejected; both influence policy and will continue to do so. The "child concept," however, involves implications that, at the extreme, approach the whimsical. Setting aside all questions of the proper measure of a child's general competence for life and even allowing for all the "natural" inequalities of intelligence and physique, it remains grossly improbable that public education can compensate for cultural deprivation. In order for the schools to produce children equipped equally except for their natural differences it would be necessary for them to overcome the congeries of forces operating outside the classroom which contribute to the inequality. The school would have to reverse the whole pattern of social stratification and in so doing perform tasks such as improving family life, housing, and protection from crime. It is quite clear that the remedy of formal education is simply not directly relevant to many of these needs, or, if relevant, not adequate.

Yet we have already said and we now reaffirm that, as a matter of policy, the state may choose unequal schools to compensate to the extent possible for environmental burdens; there is nothing in democratic theory to impede this and everything to applaud it, so long as the resources for compensation are reasonably allocated. (If experience shows that it takes $25,000 a year for 10 years to raise an intelligence quotient from 70 to 80, priorities must be carefully evaluated, especially when that $25,000 must be drawn from other educational or social uses.) Others would argue that, rather than providing in-school compensation, the money would be better spent in special programs outside the system of formal education. A few perhaps would raise this to an imperative and state that compensatory education is antidemocratic in its violation of formal equality.

While we are much concerned with sound educational policy, we are first concerned with *what the state must do or not do* under the organic law of our society. As a constitutional standard, the child concept is excessively vague. It is difficult to imagine the most sympathetic court deciding that unequal education is *required*, if only because the standards of appropriate inequality under a child performance concept are almost totally subjective and incommunicable.

On the other hand, the concept of school equality is objective and could pass muster for clarity in a constitutional contest. It is not entirely quixotic to suppose a duty that the state refrain from operating educational systems that guarantee inferior schools to identifiable classes of persons. We have chosen to formulate that duty in terms of forbidding the state to dispense education by wealth. That standard is as objective as one reasonably can wish; indeed it is measurable in terms of dollars. However, it is not precisely equivalent to "school equality," for it would permit differences in quality springing from sources other than wealth.

Subsidiarity and Education

The competing values of equality and mobility have found dynamic balance through their absorption into the complex concept of equal opportunity; and that concept in turn has become the theoretical cornerstone of a democratic educational system. It follows that the imposition of inferior schools upon the residents of poor districts simply because of their district's poverty is offensive to American values. But it is clear that this does not imply the impropriety of every variation in quality within a state. We have already suggested that children with certain needs or certain abilities might well be preferred by the state, as they sometimes are, in its distribution of resources. Equality of opportunity cannot be insulated completely from competition with other values.

Historically, its most constant competition — its nemesis, in fact — has been that slightly eccentric emphasis upon local government which is the scandal of foreign visitors and the pride of the pioneer. There is no adequate name for it. "Federalism" is a label for what is merely one domestic example of the principle; the terms "provincialism" and "localism" both overemphasize the whimsical aspects of the matter and conjure the image of a town meeting featuring spittoons and grass-chewing farmers. There is nothing simpleminded or bizarre about the principle that government should ordinarily leave decision-making and administration to the smallest unit of society competent to handle them. Neither Congress nor the city council should decide when a man's children shall go to bed. On the whole, indeed, we leave decision-making to the individual. Even the family's recognized sector of power over its minor children stands as an exception to the rule, and the rule is self-determination of the individual.

This preference for low level decision-making has furnished the common coin of political discourse in America since 1789.

It speaks with many voices on many levels but, for present purposes, its most important application lies in the petty federalisms of local government. The parceling out of the state's powers to its created subentities has provided the incubator for a cultural localism reminiscent of the respect accorded the federal system itself. The citizen who is jealous of state prerogatives under the Constitution is likely also to cherish the "prerogatives" of school district 52 over and against the state. The attitude is not only understandable but, within limits, laudable. It is usually supported upon the rationale noted above: local people should support and run their own schools.

This principle is as old as Aristotle. Like his scholastic successors, we shall give it the ungainly label *subsidiarity*. It is not a word found in Webster's *Unabridged*, but it should be. There is need for it.[8] Subsidiarity embodied in local control of taxation is the apparent stake in the coming struggle for fiscal

8. The principle is of course imprecise and is often invoked in support of conflicting positions on the proper location of responsibility and power in a specific case. It is expressed thus in *Quadragesimo Anno*, an encyclical of Pope Pius XI, par. 79: "It is gravely wrong to take from individuals what they can accomplish by their own initiative and industry and give it to the community. It is also an injustice . . . to assign to a greater and higher association what a lesser and subordinate organization can do." See also Austin Fagothey, *Right and Reason* (St. Louis: C. V. Mosby, 1967), pp. 319, 421–422; John XXIII, *Pacem in Terris*, pt. IV (New York: Paulist Press, 1963); J. Messner, *Das Naturrecht* (Innsbruck, 1966), pp. 294–304. The primary value that the principle purports to guard is independence. In scholastic thought dependence, whether imposed or voluntary, is an imperfection in man's nature; J. F. Kenney, "The Principle of Subsidiarity," *The American Catholic Sociological Review*, 16:31–36 (March 1955). The pervasiveness of the principle in American thought is illustrated by the Ninth Amendment, "the enumeration in the Constitution, of certain rights, shall not be construed to deny or disparage others retained by the people," and the Tenth Amendment, "the powers not delegated to the United States by the Constitution, nor prohibited by it to the States, are reserved to the States respectively, or to the people." The concept is not to be confused with "pluralism," which is concerned with the interrelation of social, cultural, and religious groups in a factually differentiated society. Subsidiarity can be satisfied in a homogeneous culture; pluralism cannot. Pluralism can be used either in a descriptive or normative sense; subsidiarity is purely normative.

equity. Our conviction that equality and subsidiarity are compatible values will require elaborate defense and demonstration, a task that will consume a fair portion of this book.

Of all the decisions that have to be made about education, perhaps the most significant is the level of effort that will be made for its financial support. And when we talk about public education, that decision is one about taxation. The decision can be made at a number of levels. Public education is presently financed by taxes set and levied in large part at the school district level; that is, decisions are delegated to and made by units smaller than, and included in, the states whose reserved powers include that to maintain public schools.

To have significant choice at the local level, more is necessary than mere local collection and local expenditure of money, for under such a system all decisions concerning the level and type of tax and expenditures could be made centrally. Subsidiarity means more: it implies at least the power of localities to decide (a) how much education they desire (perhaps within minimums and maximums set by the state) and (b) how much they are willing to spend to reach their goals. It is this outlook toward public education which permits some localities to spend more than others; it is a source of one kind of inequality.

Let us assume for the moment that this kind of inequality is undesirable. To offset the bad effect the special advantages of local decision-making will have to be identified and weighed against equality. Many of the advantages are obvious,[9] starting with sheer satisfaction with schools; a variety of local decisions means that the personal choices of more people are likely to be reflected in the schools. Further, a degree of freedom is gained for the dissatisfied constituents in one school district who at least can move to another; under a system of statewide decision-making there is only one choice. Perhaps the point seems ele-

9. See generally Benson, *Economics of Public Education*, pp. 226–229.

mentary, but in our experience persons seeking better schools through centralized "equality" often overlook the fact that the achievement of such an equality guarantees not better but only similar schools.

The educational needs of children differ widely, and various educational services require differential efforts from district to district. It is plausible that persons on the local scene are in general better able to evaluate what must be spent and what measures are required to achieve an acceptable education in their district. At least, there exists no body of experience demonstrating the superiority of the insights of state-level administrators. Furthermore, one district may simply be more efficient than another: it should be allowed to enjoy the benefits of good husbandry, but its neighbor, on the other hand, should not be constrained to poorer schools by a rigid standard of equality. In general, the combination of better information and stronger motivation of those who are affected by decisions assures a better fit of local services to local needs. Virtually any criterion of "equality" dictated from above (equal dollars per pupil, for example) would have to be grossly general and necessarily gloss over one or all of these dimensions.

A similar advantage of local choice lies in the possible desirability of some "inequality" of schools. Schools, after all, are not an end in themselves; much of their purpose is fixed by the general goals of society. When the state permits variation in local commitment to schools, by minimum and maximum tax rates, the local community has discretion to adjust the blend of its total services, educational and otherwise, so as to achieve better these broader goals. Thus $50,000 extra in social services may be more effective in achieving the broader goals of "education" in a general sense than $50,000 in schools. It is also possible that the extra $50,000 is better kept in the taxpayers' pockets; clearly at some point the marginal utility to the community in question of extra money in schools must be too small to justify another dollar.[10] Similar considerations may apply to the diverse needs of subcultures within the general society. Computers and closed circuit television imparting knowledge of calculus and oriental languages will best meet the needs of one district, Montessori and vocational schools another.

There are other, more diffuse advantages of subsidiarity. While it is possible for a community under a local option system to undervalue education, it is also possible — even likely — that the plurality of independent and self-interested decision-makers will stimulate competition, thus constantly increasing the total commitment of the state to education. Further, local freedom may well mean local creativeness. As with the "grand experiment" of federalism, this may mean more trial and error than experiment, but even this is, for us, preferable to bland monotony. Looking at the same argument from the lower level, subsidiarity in education forms (literally) a school for democracy, providing experience in government for the maximum number of people; also, the persons really affected in the constituency are infinitely more likely to come into face-to-face contact with local decision-makers than with centrally located ones. It means, too, an additional political option for the citizen. His participation in local decisions never forecloses his involvement at state levels. To complete the sketch, it can be said that there are also real advantages in amateurism. Educational administration is not noticeably overpopulated with philosopher kings. Even if it were, education is too important to be left to professionals whose plenary control under a centralized system would be difficult to avoid.

In recent years, the historic subsidiarity of state systems of

10. There is a philosophy of local government, sometimes called the "political economy" school, which holds that a community has a "right" to poor services so long as its taxes are at a low level to compensate the residents; see Benson, *Economics of Public Education*, p. 241, referring to the words of James M. Buchanan and Kjeld Phillips.

education has come under attack for at least two good reasons. One is the difficulty of lessening racial segregation in our great city school systems in the absence of an interdistrict authority that can order the use of facilities in accessible suburbs. This is not our subject (though we may observe that special-purpose interdistrict authorities are not necessarily inconsistent with a general district system). The other reason for the attack on subsidiarity is its apparent incompatibility with equality of opportunity in the fiscal sense. The poor districts have begun to awaken to the fact that the autonomous district system has something to do with the financial inferiority of their schools. But even while subsidiarity has been under this attack from fanciers of uniform solutions, it has ironically been given a new lease on life by some of its most prominent victims. Black community groups have begun to press, sometimes with success, for something resembling the very "autonomy" which heretofore has crippled the poor districts.[11] These groups appear willing to risk equality of opportunity for the sake of greater local control; and a risk it is, for they are not typically wealthy communities and are dependent upon continued outside toleration and support. The stage seems set for a curious struggle for a community "freedom" that in fact can only remain an intolerable bondage to the financing authority until community solvency accompanies community autonomy. No way yet has been perceived to harmonize subsidiarity and equal opportunity; there is still a real possibility that centralization and uniformity of fiscal policy will be seen as the only "solution." We think a policy answer can be suggested that will save both values. That answer has the further virtue of being complicated and expensive and is, consequently, an ideal reform.

11. See generally Martin Mayer, The Teachers Strike: New York, 1968 (New York, 1969); Reconnection for Learning: A Community School System for New York City (Report of the Mayor's Advisory Panel, 1967).

Preliminarily, however, there are two elementary points to be clarified. First, it must be apparent by now that we have focused upon the state instead of the federal government as the primary source for reform in public education. This is not because federal power is irrelevant; it is simply that the constitutional responsibility we seek to establish is more easily fastened upon the state and, also, that we think the proper federal role is ancillary and remedial in character, even if it is crucial and extensive. That role will be elaborated in Part II, but it should be stated here that the federal role cannot begin to make sense until the states put their own houses in order. It is clear from the data in Appendix A that the states, because of their varying wealth, stand to one another much as school districts do within states; but it will only be when the states have ceased to discriminate by wealth *inside* the state that the federal government can begin intelligibly to ameliorate the effects of differences in wealth among them.

The other point to be clarified is the wider implication of subsidiarity. Examples given of its application thus far have all involved school districts and their powers and duties; but there is nothing to prevent extension of our analysis to the level of the family. It is quite possible to argue that the locus of decision about the financing of public education could and therefore should fall on the family, and we will eventually outline a system harmonizing equality and subsidiarity at the family level.

Juggling the Values

To understand the apparent conflict between equality of opportunity and subsidiarity, something must be said of the form and effects of a district system of education. Some kind of local support necessarily is involved in the application of subsidiarity to school finance. When it is said that communities must evaluate how much education is worth to them, financial sacrifice is implied. If all the money earmarked by the state for education comes from outside the district just for the asking, local choice is effectively removed. Voters in general would elect the best education available. If subsidiarity is to make any sense, the acquisition of more education must cost the district, just as all other market choices cost, and there should be fewer dollars left for other things.

Allocating wealth among needs, the purchaser (the district) is guided by the totality of everything that is needed and that can be afforded. In the abstract, except for the inequality proceeding from free choice, there is nothing in this kind of local tax support that must produce inequality — a fact which helps explain why the practical effects of existing systems are widely misunderstood. If all districts were equally wealthy in proportion to the amount of education to be provided, inequalities of expenditure might be tolerable. But wealth is not evenly distributed. Indeed, distribution is very uneven, with some districts rich and others poor. The resulting inequities are the source, stimulus, and subject of this book.

The consequence of uneven distribution of wealth is wide variation in the sacrifice necessary to produce the same amount of money. As a result, the multitude of decisions that are made by districts regarding commitment to education is everywhere weighted by wealth. In order for a poor district to procure a school as good as its thrice rich neighbor it must be willing to tax three times as hard; even then it may well be prevented from doing so by state-mandated tax maximums. But in either case it is ordinarily left behind in the race for superior schools, for, clearly, the rich district can always stay ahead if it decides to.

Of course, this systematic hobbling of poor districts in the race for good schools is precisely the condition that conflicts with basic democratic values. The public school system has taken on the evils of the private school system it replaced. In a race for better schools that is fueled by the kudos and hard cash offered by colleges to the best educated students and then reintensified by comparisons of college entrance test scores, the poor districts are doomed to failure by their poverty.

It is group poverty produced by distinctive residential and wealth patterns which is determinative rather than individual poverty, but for most children the outcome is the same. To the extent that extra dollars can purchase educational resources, the people in richer districts can afford to keep their children ahead of those in poorer ones. Often poorer districts tax themselves at higher rates than richer districts, only to garner significantly lower yields. The difference in ability to pay is thus taken out on the children in quality of schools, as well as out of the depleted tax base of the district. Subsidiarity under such circumstances is not only unserviceable; it is hard to see how it can be invoked as a supporting value in the first place, if one of its presuppositions is the uniform — or at least general — competence of the decision-making unit to perform the particular function. We have ceased to depend upon the family alone to teach the child precisely because of the gross differences in educative capacity among families. Our society has decided that the value of educational "home rule" is outweighed by the homes' differential ability to perform the task, and public education has come to replace the family with larger economic and administrative units. But if for variations in family ability we have substituted a similar crazy quilt of district abilities, it is hard to see that we have satisfied the assumption underlying the preference for subsidiarity.

It is of absolutely vital importance to understand that *between the values of equality and subsidiarity, as we have defined them, there is no direct conflict such that choice of one implies abandonment of the other.* Recall that the standard for equality of educational opportunity was framed in the negative.

That proposition is satisfied when decisions regarding commitment to education are free of local wealth determinants: to make them so, in the purchase of education it should "hurt" as much for a poor district to raise an extra dollar as a rich one, but it should hurt no more. The mechanism by which proportionality of sacrifice can be obtained will be explored briefly at the end of this chapter and in detail in Part II. To prepare for its explanation a brief section on terminology is in order.

Basic Factors in School District Finance

The discussion of equality and subsidiarity has thus far proceeded on an abstract level. As the focus shifts increasingly to the existential, it will be necessary to discuss at some length the process of purchasing education in order to render intelligible the reforms that can assure the harmonizing of equality and subsidiarity. The reality of school financing is sufficiently complex and difficult to describe that we must set out some of the major potential sources of misunderstanding and indicate some of the assumptions we will be making later. Though most clarification will be reserved for Chapter 1, three points should be stated here.

First, equality of school districts has no meaning unless we can state the amount of education that must be accomplished in the district ("educational task"); the existence of an equal number of identical school buildings and teachers in every district in the state would obviously leave districts with more students relatively pressed. Equality must be measured according to some unit of educational task; for the moment, and throughout, unless otherwise specified, the task unit we will employ is the individual student. If we say that school districts are spending the same amount on education, we mean that they are spending the same amount *per student*.

Second, there are technical and, within limits, arbitrary

decisions to be made by the state. What is "education" and what is not? In some districts, unrelated community services may be appended to the school; financing of these would not have to be free from local wealth determinants to satisfy our principle. The distinction between current and capital expenditures might be more troublesome. Educational quality is often measured simply by current expenditures because it is thought that these have the most direct impact on the true quality of the school;[12] also, there are formidable problems which inhere in the accounting of capital expenditures. Nevertheless, many modern proposals for reform include capital expenditures.[13] In general these conundrums are no problem for us. We are less interested in the specific substance of education than in its distribution; all we assume (unless otherwise indicated) is that, whatever standards the state is using, they are the same for each district.

Third, there is another basic limitation to the debate. We are interested in the problem of *inter*district discrimination, not in the duty of the school district to distribute its resources to its own constituents according to some standard of rationality or justice. Others have treated of the latter issue,[14] and more surely will follow. The issue for us is not whether a specific school fails to meet some criterion or other, but whether

12. This was the method chosen in an excellent study of the cost-quality relationship; H. H. Woollatt, *The Cost-Quality Relationship in the Growing Edge* (New York, 1949), pp. 32–33, reviewed by P. R. Mort, "Cost-Quality Relationship in Education," in R. L. Johns and E. L. Morphet, eds., *Problems and Issues in Public School Finance* (New York, 1952), pp. 15–17.

13. The late Paul R. Mort not only recommended to the New York State legislature that the current debt services be included in determining state aid, but he advocated the dissolution of excessive accumulated debt principal as well. Seventy-five percent of the total accumulated debt which could not be redeemed by a 2-mill tax was to be redeemed by the State. P. R. Mort, "Unification of Fiscal Policy in New York State," in C. S. Benson, ed., *Perspectives on the Economics of Education* (Boston, 1963), pp. 342–343.

14. Harold Horowitz, "Unseparate But Unequal — The Emerging Fourteenth Amendment Issue in Public School Education," *U.C.L.A. Law Review*, 13:1147 (1966).

the children of school *district* 124 are being cheated because of something about the district taken as a whole in comparison to other districts. Thus, ironically, the question of an "equal school" does not concern us except as one potential side effect of reform of the state structure; the actual quality of the individual child's education is technically irrelevant, and the existing wrong he suffers is perceived, for our purposes, solely in the state's treatment of the child's district. To invert the irony, the child may in fact receive a splendid education and yet be cheated by discrimination against his district. We deal, then, in collectives. Further, and crucially, by accepting local decision-making *we permit differences in per pupil expenditures from district to district*. Again, our formula for equality of opportunity is satisfied by the insulation of quality from the influence of wealth, other than the total wealth of the state. All that need be done to purify the district system is to bestow equal power upon the districts to generate dollars — though, of course, many other solutions also would be consistent with the principle.

The Cost-quality Question

If we are to speak of equality, we must first reckon with quality. There must be some standard for judging whether education is better in one district than in another. We have already distinguished two basic views of equal opportunity — the objective school concept and the subjective child-performance concept — and the difference is relevant here. Having chosen the objective standard, the measure of quality becomes not what is achieved but *what is available*. This way of stating the issue very nearly dictates the answer. What is available becomes whatever goods and services are purchased by school districts to perform their task of education. Quality is the sum of district expenditures per pupil; quality is money.

This approach may appear excessively formal, but it has significant advantages. Its employment reduces the problem of quality to manageable simplicity. Money is the only measure applicable to every element in the educational process — salaries, plant, equipment, and so on: all educational goods and services are objects of purchase. Consider the alternative measures necessary to cope with fifty state systems, each of whose districts exercises a wide administrative discretion in spending. Should the question be whether two hours of folk singing equal one of history? Or whether four teachers with B.A.'s equal three with M.A.'s? We have no stomach for such an imbroglio. Ultimately we will need a standard appropriate to the rigors of judicial proof, and the only convincingly quantifiable item in the spectrum is money available for the general task of education in each district.

The statutes creating district authority to tax and spend are the legal embodiment of the principle that money is quality in education. The power to raise dollars by taxation is the very source of education as far as the state is concerned. By regulating the rates of taxation, typically from a minimum to a maximum, the state is in effect stating that dollars count (at least within this range) and that the district has some freedom to choose better or worse education. If dollars are not assumed to buy education, whence the justification for the tax?

The formal dollar standard for measuring quality would suffice as a basis for our central theme, that wealth must not determine the quality of public education; indeed, it is an integral part of that theme. Suppose, however, it could be shown that those objects which education is designed to promote — knowledge, skills, personal development — would be served equally by forbidding the operation of all schools, public and private. If in fact dollars for schools have no positive effect upon those objects, this book is largely a sterile exercise and all the excitement over the school finance question is a mere distraction. Indeed, something more than merely "some positive effect" would be needed to justify the costs borne by the taxpayer in the name of education. Legislators have assumed, the courts have assumed, society has assumed that spending for education in fact purchases some effect worth having and that more spending will purchase more of that effect. Historically, educators, with near unanimity, have asserted a powerful cost-quality relation in education.[15] Suburban "light house" districts have built their reputations (and their swimming pools) on that foundation. Paul Mort, a leader in this field for forty years, suggested that the cost-quality relation may even be an accelerating one — that the last dollar spent in the district of highest expenditure may be the most productive of all expenditures.[16]

Of course, all of this could be sheer fantasy fired by the self-interest of educators, and America may have wasted all or a fair share of the hundreds of billions it has poured into schools; such heretical notions have received a certain ambiguous support in recent years. This has been the unlikely fallout from massive efforts of social science to explore the effects of racial segregation. The Coleman Report on equality of educational opportunity ironically has been the source of certain of these doubts.[17] Our sole concern with this very complex document centers in its hesitant suggestion that, for certain classes of students, per-pupil expenditures show little relation to achievement if social background and attitudes of individual

15. See, e.g., C. S. Benson, *The Cheerful Prospect: A Statement on the Future of Public Education* (Boston, 1965), pp. 22–26; W. D. Firmon, "The Relationship of Cost to Quality in Education," in National School Finance Conference, Committee on Educational Finance, ed., *Long Range Planning in School Finance* (Washington, D.C., 1963), pp. 101, 107; H. J. James, J. A. Thomas, and H. J. Dyck, *Wealth, Expenditure and Decision-Making for Education* (Palo Alto, 1963), p. 125.

16. Mort, in Johns and Morphet, *Problems and Issues*, pp. 9–10 (review of studies).

17. J. S. Coleman et al., *Equality of Educational Opportunity* (Washington, D.C.: U.S. Government Printing Office, 1966).

students and their classmates are held constant.[18] This "conclusion" has been used as ammunition in the sometimes nasty debate over the relation between the goals of racial integration and compensatory education. Some integrationists (not Coleman) seem to adopt the position that the poor — at least the black poor — are incapable of academic improvement except in integrated schools. We find this particular use of the Report difficult to understand and risky in its implications; even the authors themselves hedged the conclusion in several respects, and the Report's authority on the point is uncertain. Bowles and Levin recently have argued that the research design employed by Coleman was "biased in a direction that would dampen the importance of school characteristics. . . ." [19] The Report, for example, was not designed to take into account such arguably cognate factors as class size; further, it used only gross district expenditure figures although individual schools within districts vary widely in per-pupil cost. Nevertheless, even utilizing data in the Report itself, Bowles and Levin found that "some school inputs appear to have significant effects on achievement." [20] Teacher salaries are probably the most significant factor:

> . . . the same teacher characteristics that account [in the Report] for significant variations in achievement relate directly to instructional expenditures. In a multiple regres-

18. *Ibid.*, p. 325.
19. Samuel Bowles and Henry Levin, "The Determinants of Scholastic Achievement — An Appraisal of Some Recent Evidence," *Journal of Human Resources*, 3:3 (1968). According to Bowles and Levin a fundamental bias was the introduction of a background variable in the regression analysis before the resources variable. Since expenditures were highly correlated with background, the variable first introduced would "wash out" the other. While this choice was based upon the proposition that background precedes school spending in time, the authors of the Report in fact offer no time analysis of the mutual influence, if any, of child resource and school resource. *Ibid.*, pp. 13–16 and n. 24. But see Coleman's reply, *Journal of Human Resources*, 3:237, 240–244 (1968).
20. *Ibid.*, p. 9.

sion analysis using the survey data, teachers' characteristics explain about three-quarters of the variance in teachers' salaries.

The implication of this evidence is that higher expenditure on teachers' salaries does indeed lead to higher achievement levels among students.[21]

A more recent study by Thomas Ribich has attempted to evaluate the cost-benefit relation in those few "compensatory" programs which have collected data in anything approaching a systematic fashion.[22] Ribich's painstaking analyses suggest, if anything, a variety of sometimes conflicting relationships between cost and purely economic benefits from added dollar increments. His analysis seems to show, as one would expect, that a good deal depends on what kind of education, for whom, at what level, with how many extra dollars added to what base, and so on. The relationships that did appear were relatively mild.

Ribich concludes, and we repeat, that all efforts at measuring expenditure efficiency risk the objection that there is no agreement on just what effects schools are intended to have. If one is concerned only with reading scores or I.Q.'s, one kind of conclusion may be drawn; but there are countless ways to state the benefits of education.[23] Ribich's analysis was set largely in terms of fighting poverty: that is, of calculating economic benefits only, and not of assessing quality in the sense of the child's personal development or of the total increase of his opportunities for a useful and happy life as a consequence of his education. Nonetheless, Ribich concludes candidly that, even within the limited compass of his study:

21. *Ibid.*, p. 10.
22. Thomas Ribich, *Education and Poverty* (Washington, D.C., 1968).
23. *Ibid.*, pp. 100–132. That the problem of defining output poses an almost insuperable barrier to establishing an input (money)-output relationship, see Jesse Burkhead, *Public School Finance* (Syracuse, 1964), pp. 76–77, 92 (chapter based on materials prepared by Harold F. Clark).

"It is at best questionable . . . whether these first-round projects are truly representative of what large scale, broadly based programs can do to fight poverty." [24]

There are similar studies suggesting stronger positive consequences from dollar increments, and there are others suggesting only trivial consequences,[25] but the basic lesson to be drawn from the experts at this point is the curent inadequacy of social science to delineate with any clarity the relation between cost and quality. We are unwilling to postpone reform while we await the hoped-for refinements in methodology which will settle the issue. We regard the fierce resistance by rich districts to reform as adequate testimonial to the relevance of money. Whatever it is that money may be thought to contribute to the education of children, that commodity is something highly prized by those who enjoy the greatest measure of it. If money is inadequate to improve education, the residents of poor districts should at least have an equal opportunity to be disappointed by its failure.

Of course one might assert that, though money may be a good measure of quality, this could hold true for rich districts

24. Ribich, *Education and Poverty*, p. 62.
25. For evaluation of a number of studies, see Henry Dyer, "School Factors and Equal Educational Opportunity," *Harvard Educational Review*, 38:38 (1968); James Guthrie and J. A. Kelly, "Compensatory Education — Some Answers for a Skeptic," in E. Keach, R. Fulton, and W. Gardner, eds., *Education and Social Crisis* (New York, 1967). The most recent major report is the "preliminary draft" of the evaluation of Head Start programs, "The Impact of Head Start," mimeographed (Westinghouse Learning Corp., 1969). Its report of minuscule lasting gains already has caused at least one of its consultants to denounce its methodology and withdraw the use of his name. Another rather gloomy report is that based on data from the More Effective Schools Program in New York City. Here students showed minimal achievement gains from large increases in expenditure; but the increases went mostly for smaller teaching units. The MES data suggests the limited value of the particular technique used alone, but not the hopelessness of every program which might cost more money. See David Cohen, "Policy for the Public Schools: Compensation and Integration," *Harvard Education Review*, 38:114 (1968); "Defining Racial Equality in Education," *U.C.L.A. Law Review*, 16:255 (1969).

only. Such a notion might require us to assume falsely that nonpoor families seldom inhabit poor districts or that children of the rich are homogeneous; nevertheless, let us suppose for the moment that such is the case. According to the thesis, these children of poor districts (especially those of rural and urban lower class minority families) can absorb only the most rudimentary and (hence?) inexpensive instruction because of environmental or genetic misfortune: the three R's are hard enough to get across without trying anything tougher. Rich children, on the other hand, prepared and motivated, are capable of soaking up the most esoteric offering. Hence it is proper to prefer them in spending. The gross condescension of this argument should be enough to condemn it, but it is regrettably persistent in important private circles. The simple factual responses to it are two. It may be true that, on the average, the educational needs of various groups differ, so that instruction effective for one group would be wasted on another;[26] but it is not necessarily true that costs will differ in a uniform manner between the different kinds of instruction required by each group. Part of this ambiguity arises from differing goals, vocational versus college preparatory for example, and part from differing techniques to reach the same goals. Even the relation between cost and the level of education is quite ambiguous. For all we know, it may be more expensive to teach monkeys to do somersaults than to teach human children to read; nothing in the sheer academic level of the educational job reveals anything about its cost. Historically, in fact, vocational training has been among the most costly. In any event, even assuming that you "get less for your money" with poor children, this doesn't mean such children haven't the right to equal schools. We concede that equal opportunity across the board will not

26. Arthur Jensen, "How Much Can We Boost IQ and Scholastic Achievement," *Harvard Education Review*, 39:1 (1969). See also the critiques of the Jensen article in *Harvard Education Review*, 39:273–356 (1969).

produce equality in a performance sense; still, one doesn't force a losing baseball team to play with seven men.

But there is an even more fundamental difficulty with the uneducable poor argument which renders some of the above needlessly elaborate. Would it not be miraculously coincidental if capacity to use money efficiently were distributed precisely as is school district wealth? Does it seem likely that a system with its historical roots in fiscal considerations would "happen" also to take on a structure related to educational need? The obvious answer to these questions indicates something very fundamental about the uneducable poor argument: it is a rationalization. There is no "educability" standard to debate, there is only a rich-poor standard.

False Issues Concerning Money and Quality. The cost-quality question is occasionally obscured by two arguments that are essentially irrelevant. The first is that schools cannot cure society's ills even with fiscal equity (or, that equal schools will not result in equality of opportunity) and that, therefore, reform elsewhere is more appropriate. We concede the premise, but the conclusion is a non sequitur. Fiscal reform in education concededly is not the sufficient condition of a utopian tomorrow, it is only one of many steps necessary if we expect to realize the societal goals we preach. But it is a step, and the objection is not germane. The children of poor districts have a right to equality of treatment, notwithstanding the impotence of schools to solve all their problems.

The second objection, somewhat closer to the mark, insists that administrative reforms must accompany fiscal reform if money is to achieve maximum effect.[27] More money, it is said, will not increase quality so long as and to the extent that the structure of the educational bureaucracy frustrates its efficient application to needs. For example, even if it were assumed that poor urban districts could afford salaries and class sizes equal to

27. See Benson, *Cheerful Prospect,* pp. 71–74, 117–118.

suburban districts, equality would not be guaranteed; slums are dangerous, slum children are hard to teach, and few teachers would wish to live within easy commuting distance. Yet the administrative system continues to permit experienced teachers to elect safer neighborhoods and superior young teachers to choose the suburbs in the first place. Equal money power could help to alter this pattern, but administrative changes permitting state control of assignment of teachers to districts might be equally important. Again, however, there is no incompatibility. Fiscal equality will be the answer to some problems; administrative reform to others; both to still others.

A Preview of the Solution to Inequality of Educational Opportunity

There are a number of ways to satisfy the basic principle that wealth should not determine the quality of public education. One, of course, is the abolition of public education. Another is the abandonment of subsidiarity by the creation of a completely centralized state system with expenditures either equalized on a per-pupil basis or rationalized according to need and/or other criteria. As we proceed laboriously to lay bare the existing extent and mechanisms of discrimination against the poor, the reader may begin to despair of any middle path that can preserve the subsidiarity built into the existing system while satisfying the principle of fiscal equity. It may therefore be useful in these next few pages to delineate in skeletal form the solution we propose, not as required by the Constitution, but simply as the most desirable social and educational policy. The description will evoke a dozen objections besides those we will raise ourselves; but we trust that the reader will eventually pursue possible answers to the objections in the denser thickets of Part II.

Our approach depends for its practical effect upon manipulation of tax systems. Equal district power is the key. The concrete financing proposal may be stated thus: equal tax rates should provide equal spendable dollars. That is, the local unit would be empowerd to fix the tax rate (effort) to be imposed upon a specific class of local wealth. For every level of local tax effort permitted by statute, the state would have fixed the number of dollars per task unit (probably per pupil) that the district would be empowered to spend. The state also guarantees that this number of dollars will be available to the district. Assume, for example, that by statute a fifteen-mill district tax rate makes $600 per pupil available to the district. If the local levy raises less than $600, the state makes up the difference from a fund generated by taxation of general state wealth. If the local tax produces an excess (it can be set so that it never does), that excess is redistributed to poorer districts within the system.

The local share would come probably from a levy on real property, though income would be superior as a fair measure of the district's ability. Whatever the source, it must be a reasonably accurate measure of wealth, and it must be reasonably local in its incidence, for the aim is to provide a measure of the district's sacrifice.

The state tax that supplements insufficient district collections in theory should be progressive to the degree that the decisions of individual taxing units about their appropriate sacrifice for school expenditures are all made on an economic parity. Such a fine adjustment may be too much to expect, but in any event it should not be a regressive tax.

A highly oversimplified example may help.[28] Imagine a state divided into two school districts, A and B, each with 100 pupils. District A has a total wealth of $10,000 ($100 per pupil). Dis-

28. See the closely similar Table 7.1 in Benson, *Economics of Public Education*, p. 243. Benson's demonstration of the evenhandedness of this type of grant provided a primary clue to the more general solution we have adopted as our own.

trict B has a total of $90,000, or $900 per pupil. Each decides to tax its wealth at the rate of 10 percent for schools, yielding respectively $10 and $90 per pupil. Under our basic value judgment, district A is $80 short — it tried just as hard, so it should be able to buy just as good a school. The $80 must come from a state tax. Since the total wealth of the state is $100,000, in order to raise the $80 per pupil for district A the state chooses to levy a flat 8-percent tax, producing $72 per pupil from district B and $8 from district A. Now look at the example from the other side. In *gross taxes* per pupil district A has paid $10 (local) plus $8 (state), or $18. District B has paid $90 (local) plus $72 (state), or $162. *As a percentage of local wealth, each total tax is exactly the same,* while the redistribution of wealth has produced equal expenditures. Each is taxed at 10 percent locally and 18 percent totally, each has $90 to spend — from each according to his ability, to each according to his effort.

We call the scheme "power equalizing." Eventually we will show that it may be used to equalize either governmental units such as school districts or that it may be applied to families. It is imperfect; it is probably feasible; it is vastly superior to any existing system; it preserves most of the present systems. It takes advantage of an interesting phenomenon that will emerge in Part I: poor districts show a tendency to tax themselves as hard as or harder than rich. Under existing systems this sacrifice by the poor is unrewarded, for it is imposed on an inferior tax base and produces inferior education. The solution suggested would sacrifice nothing but the right of the rich to have superior public schools with less effort. It would insist that if you want to be number one, rich or poor, you must try hardest.

Part I · The Apparatus of Privilege

> . . . seeking an advantage over the many is by convention
> said to be wrong and shameful, and they call it injustice. But
> in my view, nature herself makes it plain that it is right for
> the better to have the advantage over the worse, the more
> able over the less.
>
> Callicles in Gorgias, Plato

1 · How the System Grew: The Good as Enemy of the Best

The best is the enemy of the good.

Voltaire, Art Dramatique

Our first task is to demonstrate the manner in which states have designed their educational systems to favor rich districts. To this end, the next five chapters will be devoted to the background of the American system of education finance; its mainstreams of development in the twentieth century; a method for empirical analysis of state systems; the disappointing inadequacy of even the most recent reforms. We conclude that, although the states have formally chosen subsidiarity as the cornerstone of public education, in reality they have structured home rule to withhold the advantages of subsidiarity from the poor district.

To be sure, the states have not been completely insensitive to the unfairness to children that results from leaving public education financing entirely to the resources of local school districts. Over time the district wealth imbalance has been redressed in varying degrees through state financial participation in public education; the states have turned to a combination of local fund raising and state subvention[1] to pay for public education. Nonetheless, the complex ways in which the states have attempted to account and adjust for wealth and poverty, are structurally incapable of providing children equal opportu-

1. "Subvention" is the technical term for state aid to a subsidiary economic unit. C. S. Benson, *The Economics of Public Education* (Boston, 1961), p. 187.

nity, whether or not they are so intended. Despite political rhetoric, compromise has merely kept poor districts from disaster — though this has not always been true — while keeping them from meaningful equality as well. Small reforms have warred against full solutions. We intend to grapple with the complexities of these systems of state aid to the districts. Mies van der Rohe once remarked that "God is in the details." We shall see.

TERMINOLOGY

The analysis of schemes for state aid to local districts requires reasonably sharp descriptive tools, some of which will be defined here and others along the way. These tools are pure constructs, an unexciting but necessary shorthand for gauging and expressing the impact of mathematical formulas imbedded in the state systems.

Educational offering has already been simplified by adopting a money standard: it means the number of dollars available to spend per student (or other convenient unit of task, such as a classroom). More important and difficult is the description of the causes of variation in offering. These are a function of variations in *educational task, educational effort* and *educational ability*.

Gross educational task refers simply to the total educational job assigned to the district. Determination of a district's task requires, first, a count of the number of pupils it must educate. Hence, task will vary from district to district not only on the basis of total population differences, but also because of the characteristics of the population: the proportion of older people without school-age children, college-age youths and young couples, parents who send their children to private school, the size of families, and so on.

Second, even this simple nose count requires careful definition, and a decision must be made as to how pupils are to be tallied. First-day registration (enrollment), year-round registration (average membership), and year-round seats filled (average attendance) are three choices, each of which may be argued as reasonable. Variation among districts in factors such as truancy and migrant population means that the yardstick chosen may yield important differences in the relative task from one district to the next.

Third, sheer numbers of students, however calculated, do not tell the whole story of educational task and may be adjusted in one or both of two respects. In the first place, the performance of precisely the same objective educational acts costs different numbers of dollars in different districts. For example, the cost of getting the children to a school and heating that school will differ with population density, size of the school, climate, and so on.[2] Secondly, and more subtly, the measure of task depends upon whether one includes *child-oriented policy objectives* in defining task. Once the question becomes the cost of making the school adequate to achieve a desired result with a specific type of student, the objectivity of the measure largely disappears. The policymaker may speak of special "needs," but the seeming objectivity is misleading. The real import of such discourse is largely that the state has objectives for particular children — a certain level of performance on standard tests, for example. Two senses of "adjusted" cost thus emerge: the cost of doing the same thing for different pupils and the cost of doing different things for pupils because of achievement objectives. Note that even the notion of doing the same thing does not exclude all consideration of individual differences. It may cost more to transport a handicapped child

2. The fundamental problem is to determine how real costs vary around the per-pupil core. F. G. Cornell and W. P. McLure, "The Foundation Program and the Measurement of Educational Need," in R. L. Johns and E. L. Morphet, eds., *Problems and Issues in Public School Finance* (New York, 1952), pp. 195, 208.

to school so that the "same thing" may be done for him there as for other children.

In this book, unless otherwise specified, the term *task* will mean sheer numbers of students; however, it should be clear from what we have just said that task is a complex notion and may, for many purposes, reflect the extra cost of education caused by other than an increase in mere numbers of students or class units. When we come to speak of why it may cost more to educate one child than another we will need to employ an *adjustment of task* to reflect this reality. A more detailed analysis of factors that can be taken into account in evaluating a district's task in such a manner will be made later.

Educational effort means the manifested willingness of the district to sacrifice (that is, to tax itself) for education. When the states turned the responsibility for public school finance over to local districts, they were giving the districts the power to tax themselves. Although there were notable early exceptions, some of which still have slight importance today, the fundamental resource which the district was allowed to tap was the value of real property inside its borders.[3] Thus, the real property tax has long been the base upon which school finance is established.[4] Economic theory might state the issue as the share of its current income a district is willing to spend for education, or perhaps even as the marginal utility it is willing to give up. But because of the standard method of money collecting involved, effort is most conveniently measured, and will be considered here (initially, at least) in terms of the

3. See P. R. Mort and W. C. Ruesser, *Public School Finance*, 2nd ed. (New York, 1951), p. 3; U.S. Department of Health, Education and Welfare, *Revenue Programs for the Public Schools in the United States, 1959–60* (Washington, D.C., 1960).

4. See generally R. A. Freeman, *Taxes for the Schools* (Washington, D.C., 1960), pp. 102–104, 222–232. Some feeling for the widespread use of the property tax can be gained from Appendix F, Table 4, which presents data from selected states, many of which will be further analyzed later.

rate of property tax levied for educational purposes in the district.[5]

Gross educational ability, measured independently of task, is the total of permanent assets and current income of the community; if the district is to finance its own schools, obviously it is more able to do so the more resources it has to draw upon. Although gross ability might be best measured by some other device, again, because of the common method of resource collection, it is initially examined here in terms of the total real property in the district. Devising an acceptable means of measuring taxable wealth is an undertaking of no mean complexity and has been the subject of extensive study.[6]

5. For consideration of the accuracy of the tax on property as a measure of percentage of income taxed, see Jesse Burkhead, *State and Local Taxes for Public Education* (Syracuse, 1963), pp. 28–31. The property tax is under attack from many quarters as an inadequate measure of ability or benefits, as a useless comparative device, and as an improper instrument of taxation in practice. The basic objections are that (1) its incidence is generally regressive and also unfair to real property owners, though its actual incidence is uncertain; (2) the methods of assessment are unfair and inconsistent; (3) its unevenness in application makes national comparisons impossible. Nonetheless, property taxes accounted for 53% of all our spending on education in 1965–66 and in 1964 property taxes accounted for 15.4% of our total nationwide tax collections. It is the one tax which, under present policies, is an important local revenue-producing device. Property has been adopted by the states as a measure of wealth in school finance formulas, as we shall see. The property tax rate is the state employed guide to local effort.

6. See generally A. J. Burke, "Measurement of Taxpaying Ability," in C. S. Benson, ed., *Perspectives on the Economics of Education* (Boston, 1963), p. 363; R. L. Johns, "Local Ability and Effort to Support Schools," in Johns and Morphet, *Problems and Issues,* p. 219. Defining ability in terms of value of real property implies that if there is high property value in the district the district is better able to afford education than a counterpart district with lower property valuation. As a further point, economists tell us that a given level of effort will be more easily supported by a district with greater gross ability than by a poor one because of marginal utilities operating between them. See generally Benson, *Economics of Public Education,* pp. 78–111. It is easier to give 5% of one's income to charity if one earns $100,000 a year than if $1,000. Even though the dollar sacrifice is proportional (and in absolute terms much greater for the richer person), the demands on the other 95% are less

There are several problems in this area which bear on the issue of equality; for example, is the measure of wealth — assessed valuation — applied uniformly from place to place (property valuations of course may be jockeyed for self-interest)?

Education wealth. In order to compare districts we need to combine the factors of *gross task* and *gross ability* into one concept relating ability to the task assigned the district. Relative ability will vary as both the gross task and the gross ability of the district vary. This factor of relative ability we label *wealth:* it is simply ability per unit of task or, cast in its traditional tax framework, district assessed property valuation per pupil or classroom. Since all finance theories have been formulated in terms of this concept, that approach will be employed here as well. It will be seen eventually how any factors that money can influence can be considered by adjustments within this framework.[7]

In terms of wealth, effort, and offering, then, we can easily construct a simple model of performance that can be understood by reference to a hypothetical state with two districts and local financing. If *wealth* and *effort* are the same in the two districts (equal assessed valuation per pupil and equal tax rate), their *offering* will be the same. If wealth is the same, then variation in local incentive which yields differences in tax effort will lead to different offerings. But if wealth differs, then the same effort will yield different offerings, so that the poorer

---

for the richer man. He must give up fewer necessities — food, clothing, shelter — to make the contribution. The distorting effect of this factor will be further discussed in Part II.

7. For example, differential weighting of those pupils with a greater educational need can be represented as a larger or adjusted task. Note, however, that definitional problems cut across these abstract variables; e.g., in comparing the quality of schools through the use of expenditure data — the offering — it may be considered more accurate to include only operational expenditures and exclude debt services. These differences can be accommodated without affecting the basic categories.

district will have to exert a greater effort if it is to provide the same offering as the richer one. If one of the three factors in the equation differs as between two districts, obviously the other two factors cannot both be the same for the two districts. Hence the equation: offering is a function of wealth and effort. In the real world of school finance with its property tax and its geographic boundaries wealth variance is endemic. It is a pattern which shows no signs of disappearing;[8] it is the reason that an unadjusted local system of finance must contain inequality.

The Original Compromise in Public Education

By the turn of the century the pattern of American life had already been deeply affected by the industrial revolution. One crucial consequence was the dramatic variation in wealth between geographic regions. As a secondary and less visible result, the then fledgling institution of locally financed public education was in danger of being turned into an engine for oppression of the poor, as pernicious in its effects as the exclusive private education of earlier days which it had begun to replace. Localism by itself already was failing spectacularly to provide the needed solution.

Given this setting, a revolution might have been expected aimed at forcing education to become a centralized state function so that the dramatic unevenness of wealth throughout the states would no longer determine the relative quality of education provided in the various districts. But the forces for localism and the value of subsidiarity had already become too solidified. Either the virtues of pseudo-subsidiarity were perceived as preponderant over equality, or the wealthy were too

8. Within Cook County, Illinois, the wealth of the richest elementary school district is almost 35 times that of the poorest. This dramatic relation is the effect of a bizarrely rich industrial district, but even the second richest is 12 times richer than the poorest. See the detailed discussion of Illinois in Chapter 4.

entrenched in their favored enclaves, or perhaps both. In any event, would-be reformers achieved little significant change. The story of public education for the first sixty-nine years of the twentieth century is not one of basic reform, but merely that of increasing marginal state aid to local schools. An egalitarian philosophy has been enunciated repeatedly in the formulas of subvention, but the limitation of district wealth as the criterion of quality has made only haphazard and relatively trivial progress. It is understandable that legislators have put the self-interest of their constituents ahead of the value of equality for all; what is surprising is that the theoretical works of the reformers themselves have been but half-measures. Perhaps it is not irrelevant that the theoretical contributions to reform have been made by scholars with at least one foot in the practical affairs of the public schools. Limited by inadequate theory and a keen sense of the politically possible, boldness has rarely been a distinguishing feature of their systems. A fair distribution of resources has never been seen as more than one value among many to be balanced and compromised in deference to the voting power of the wealthier half of society.

In order to appreciate the first state aid movements that consolidated in about 1906, we must examine briefly the early character of public education and the clash of philosophies in which it was born. The spirit of that clash is difficult to recreate. For us today the appellation "public" may suggest merely the contrast with "private"; it does not necessarily suggest the nineteenth-century perspective that "public" meant for all the people and not merely the privileged few. Even seeing this does not expose the precise character of the struggle; it is hard to set aside our preoccupation today with the parochial-public school contrast. The real issue in the nineteenth century common school movement was the finance question: in short, taxes. The great school debate concerned whether it was moral, right, democratic, and constitutional to make schools a function of government, thereby forcing non-consenting, nonusing taxpayers to support them.

Prior to the great reform, education was a private affair for both rich and poor. The elite went to truly private schools and the poor were left essentially with the charity school (financed by the rich) and the rate-bill school (the rate-bill was a tuition-like device which "taxed" the parents of attending children).[9] Not only were both inadequate, they became infamous — an ideal debating example for reforming argument and propaganda. The system of private education had become closely identified with a stratified, elitist society, essentially an aristocracy. What was urgently needed was a redistribution of educational resource, from taxpayers without school children to those with and from rich to poor. A true tax, a general tax, was called for; education, to the reformers, had to become a public function.

From the outset the change was resisted by property owners whose steady counter-force was reflected in the shape and implementation of the reforms, which were grudging and gradual.[10] One of the first concessions by state governments was to permit local communities to organize schools which would have the power to tax consenting residents. Fortune did not

9. E. P. Cubberley, *School Funds and Their Apportionment* (New York, 1905), p. 15; W. E. Drake, *The American School in Transition* (Englewood Cliffs, 1955), pp. 196–202; Newton Edwards and H. G. Richey, *The School in the American Social Order*, 2nd ed. (Boston, 1963), pp. 291–295, 326–337; Richard Hofstader, William Miller, and Daniel Aarun, *The American Republic* (Englewood Cliffs: Prentice-Hall, 1959), I, 455; S. G. Noble, *A History of American Education* (New York, 1954), pp. 166–167.

10. "Needless to say, the struggle for free schools was not won overnight; a generation was to pass before the idea became generally acceptable in the North. In the almost entirely agricultural South progress was even slower. Although rapid improvement was to be noted in all sections, particularly in the urban areas, the implementation of the ideal of free schools was largely the accomplishment of the last half of the nineteenth century." Edwards and Richey, *School*, p. 299.

bless this experiment in moral suasion; nor did the early forms of state aid, collected from such sources as lotteries and dog taxes, notably advance the cause.[11] The first crisp and meaningful step was to permit localities to organize districts to tax nonconsenting adults; and finally, of course, to *require* the districts to be organized and to commence taxing.[12]

What is instructive in this process is the unwillingness of the state government to assume the function of education. The reformers' plea was made directly to the state — the entity with power to organize a school system; but the response came in the form of delegation of primary responsibility to the smallest possible local unit — first the individual and then the local community. This vigorous buck-passing was in substantial degree ideological at root. Education was thought to be the sphere of the individual and every related act of government a potential intrusion. Pressed to take on the function of education, but strongly opposed by powerful citizens espousing an individualistic philosophy, the legislatures sought and found the smallest workable unit for the task — a solution perhaps dictated by subsidiarity.

At that point, the systems stabilized in a compromise between subsidiarity and equality — a compromise that was expressed in the balance of the school districts' relative autonomy

11. The funds from sale of public lands, escheats, liquor licenses, marriage fees, dog taxes, and lottery licenses are all properly termed "endowment funds." Noble, *History*, p. 184.

12. Just as "private" devices (which in fact were often creatures of the law) were varied, the history of taxes for schools showed considerable variety. Cubberley elaborated the techniques employed: (1) Permission granted to communities so desiring to organize a school taxing district, and to tax for school support the property of those consenting residing therein. (2) General taxation of all property in the taxing district permitted by vote, regardless of individual consent. (3) State aid to taxing districts, from the income from permanent school funds or from the proceeds of a small state tax or appropriation. (4) Compulsory local taxation to supplement the state aid received. (5) Township or county taxation, often added to supplement state and district sources. E. P. Cubberley, *State School Administration* (Boston, 1927), p. 35.

on one hand and its duty to educate all children on the other. Given a relative uniformity of wealth and population distribution, the system was tolerable.[13] Economic revolution swiftly turned the compromise into a Frankenstein. What the individualist had surrendered to government was to remain lost; what the egalitarian had gained from government was to be eliminated. What remained was accidental and haphazard privilege.

The Segregation of Wealth and the Beginnings of Its Redistribution for Education

The effect of the economic revolution was not merely that some localities grew richer faster than others; many districts remained unaffected by the changes in the economy, and many more actually grew poorer.[14] Yet education became many times more expensive and extensive as it responded to the increased costs and demands of the new economy.[15] The result was that many localities found themselves wholly unable to finance adequate education.

The extent of this underfinancing can be seen from statistics gathered by this century's first great reformer, Ellwood P. Cubberley.[16] Poor districts were forced to tax their wealth at

13. In the middle of the nineteenth century, wealth and population were relatively evenly distributed with respect to each other. Cubberley, *School Funds*, p. 21.

14. Cubberley quotes an 1871 report of Mr. Joseph White, secretary of the Massachusetts Board of Education, to the effect that of 37 Massachusetts towns of less than $300,000 valuation, 22 had decreased in valuation between the years 1865 and 1871. *Ibid.*, p. 29.

15. According to Cubberley, the cost of education almost doubled between 1870 and 1900; *ibid.*, p. 34. Rapidly expanding costs have continued to strain the ability of the state to provide equality of educational opportunity. See, e.g., P. R. Mort, "Unification of Fiscal Policy in New York State," in Benson, *Perspectives*, p. 340.

16. Cubberley was both an eminent historian of education and a theoretician of educational finance. His work in the area of state aid to education was continued by Paul R. Mort and his associates. See E. P. Cubberley, *Public Education in the United States: A Study and Interpretation of American Edu-*

many times the rate of rich districts but gleaned only a fraction of what their neighbors produced with a lighter burden. According to the custom of the early part of this century, when funds dried up the poor districts simply closed their meager schools.[17] The vast discrepancies of wealth which developed can be seen from a comparison made by Cubberley of the seven wealthiest and seven poorest (of twenty-three) towns in Connecticut at the turn of the century. The seven wealthy towns taxed at an average rate of 2.76 mills to produce an average per-pupil offering of $24.65, while the poor taxed at 4.37 mills (about 60 percent higher) to produce $20.87. As Cubberley observed, the disparities were greater in less densely settled areas. In Wisconsin, the highest taxing (and the poorest) county of those reported taxed at a rate sixteen times that of the lowest (and richest), while even the average tax rate of the five richest counties was one-sixth that of the four poorest.[18]

The reformers who have come forward in this century to point out the inadequacy of the state financial commitment to public education were and are primarily technicians in the field of educational finance. Their work, far more technical and pedestrian than that of nineteenth-century enthusiasts, has taken the form of an increasingly sophisticated, but scarcely urgent, call for a gradual erosion of inequality of wealth among districts. These new reformers have succeeded in evoking modest steps by state governments toward the ideal of redistributing educational resources. Their solutions are always measures superimposed upon the old system, the new commitment of

cational History (Boston, 1919); Readings in Public Education in the United States: A Collection of Sources and Readings to Illustrate the History of Educational Practice and Progress in the United States (Boston, 1934); and the frequently cited School Funds. See generally Jesse Sears and Adin Henderson, Cubberley of Stanford (Palo Alto, 1957).

17. Cubberley reported widespread inability of localities to support the burden of the minimum required by the state government. Cubberley, School Funds, pp. 25–27.

18. Ibid., pp. 44–48.

the state coming in the form of state aid, generally gathered from statewide taxes, to supplement the revenues of localities unable to support adequate public schools on their own.

Since 1900 the pace of change has been glacial. The first state distributions were very small and uneven. Revenues were collected from the sale or rent of public lands, or from the proceeds of miscellaneous taxes, to be distributed when an amount had accumulated that made distribution worthwhile.[19] Later, more stable tax bases were substituted; and the amount to be distributed was determined in advance and independently of the yield of a given source. Recently the method of distribution among districts has become increasingly the center of attention, with emphasis shifted to equalizing the district's ability to pay. But the result has not been satisfactory. Take, for example, this summary of the outcome of one state's effort today to correct the inequities produced by the system of local finance:

> According to the United States Office of Education, 70 per cent of state aid in Massachusetts is distributed under an "equalizing formula," i.e., under a formula . . . which purports to give more dollars to poor districts than to rich. Yet, a recent study of subventions of education in Massachusetts concluded ". . . the correlation between the rate of state support and local ability was so slight that the state could actually have done as well if it had made no attempt to relate its support program and distributed its largesse in a completely random fashion, as by the State Treasurer throwing checks from an airplane and allowing the vagaries of the elements to distribute them among the different communities."[20]

19. At one time there was great optimism concerning the possibility of financing education through endowment funds. Edwards and Richey, *School*, pp. 326–327. But by Cubberley's time these funds were understood to be entirely inadequate. Cubberley, *School Funds*, p. 65.

20. C. S. Benson, *The Cheerful Prospect: A Statement on the Future of Public Education* (Boston, 1965), pp. 85–86.

The ultimate failure of the states' original choice of a quasi-private means of financing, that is, unadjusted localism, is attacked today in terms which embody and echo the original criticisms that Horace Mann, Henry Barnard, and Thaddeus Stevens leveled at the wholly private system of financing public education:

> As we all know, the concern with inequalities of opportunity has reached the headlines across the land. It is now a good liberal position to support programs to improve slum schools, and the slum schools which rightly attract attention are those found in our dense urban areas. But this, I submit, implies a Peace Corps attitude toward our fellow citizens, many of whom, under our regressive system of local taxation, pay a higher proportion of their household incomes for education than do the liberal spokesmen for urban school betterment. What the confident liberal might better do is push for such controls of local educational expenditure that our economically favored districts can no longer claim the privilege of commanding an undue proportion of educational resources for the exclusive benefit of their resident pupils.[21]

THE FLAT GRANT FORM OF STATE AID

Cubberley's principal empirical demonstration was that wealth among districts varied radically and that this variance determined their relative ability to provide for education. Ironically, his practical proposals would improve the wealth imbalance only incidentally. His avowed goals were the extension of basic education through state aid to all, irrespective of wealth,[22] and the establishment of new educational services

---

21. *Ibid.*, p. 3.
22. The basic problem as seen by Cubberley was inability of the poor communities to maintain schools; Cubberley, *School Funds*, pp. 18, 25, 83–87.

(trade schools, high schools, kindergarten) on a wide scale.[23] Unfortunately, he did not much concern himself in his concrete proposals with payments by the state to localities according to their wealth.[24] Neither did he desire to change the way taxes were levied (on property),[25] nor the source of state aid (except that he predicted the eventual insufficiency of the endowment funds then in use).[26] Rather, he adopted a threshold goal of insuring that a poor community could, with a maximum effort on its part and a minimum effort by the state, maintain an adequate offering for the full school term.[27] He seemed to visualize increased state aid, in whatever minimal form necessary, as the solution to local underfinancing.

Cubberley emphasized the use of what are called "flat grants" today: money is paid to every district directly on the basis of the number of units of task in the district and not on the basis of need. In fact, his major concern, and in turn one of his major contributions, was evaluation of the unit best reflecting educational task; that is, once the state chooses to distribute

23. *Ibid.*, pp. 224–249.

24. Cubberley did recommend some extra aid for very poor districts, at one point suggesting that 5% of state aid be distributed on an equalizing (ability to pay) basis. Aside from the small amount of such aid on a percentage basis, his perspective on the purpose of grants of this character is illustrated by the formidable array of limitations which circumscribed his recommendation: (a) "[I]t should clearly be understood that the purpose is not to equalize taxes throughout the state but only to equalize them down to a determined maximum rate." (b) The "bona fides" of the community in representing unusual need should be carefully investigated. (c) The task unit chosen for distribution of the extra money should reward effort and insure that the poor districts are expanding their facilities. (d) The equalization aid should be temporary, ceasing when the community no longer requires it. For example, Cubberley approved a Connecticut plan whereby aid ceased when a property tax of 4 mills produced a specific return per student. See Cubberley, *School Funds*, pp. 219–220.

25. *Ibid.*, p. 18.

26. *Ibid.*, p. 65. Cubberley also discussed the existing practices of general taxation for education by the states and lucidly expounded the principles of distribution that should pertain thereto (pp. 66–79).

27. *Ibid.*, p. 219.

money to the districts, the criteria upon which the aid is to be based are of crucial importance. His efforts established the philosophy that aid should in some way be related to the job to be done — the number of task units. Appendix B reveals that the criteria in use in Cubberley's time were woefully lacking from that point of view. It is crucial to understand this problem he grappled with, to which he brought the beginnings of order. If any coherent scheme to prevent wealth from determining the quality of a child's education is to be possible in a system emphasizing subsidiarity, then some standard by which to compare accurately the relative tasks of the districts is essential. As demonstrated earlier in this chapter, under the existing local finance model, offering is a function of wealth and effort. If wealth is to be removed from the equation, then an adequate accounting as regards both its aspects — ability and task — is essential.

In his practical proposals Cubberley chose to represent the task of educating pupils indirectly by focusing upon the size of the staff needed to instruct them. He suggested the distribution of aid on the basis of the number of teachers employed by the district. This standard is superficially appealing: state money can both assure that all districts can afford enough teachers to provide a basic education and stimulate districts to hire more teachers because of the carrot of more aid. Unfortunately, a flat grant per unit is not based upon the relative need of the poorer districts; at best its effect is what we will later call *nonequalizing*. It merely assists all districts by paying for their task unit costs.[28]

28. As to how the district may use the proceeds: Many state grants are "earmarked," i.e., the locality must use them for some designated purpose or purposes; such funds are called "specific grants"; nonearmarked funds are "general purpose grants." As might be suspected, these categories can be somewhat artificial; "specific grants" can be broad enough to be functionally indistinguishable. Consider, e.g., "operational expenditures," or "for any purpose but the buying of textbooks." In any event, this test has nothing to do with whether

Consider what this means for actual operation of the school system. Rich districts raise money for spending *in addition* to this uniform grant more easily than do poor. The program offers little hope of bringing the offering provided by the poor much closer to that provided by the rich under a purely local finance scheme. If the state provides so many dollars per pupil (or teacher) for each district under the Cubberley method, but if a desirable educational offering requires an additional amount of dollars per pupil, poorer districts must submit to a much greater local tax burden (effort) to achieve that level. In practice, the poor districts in fact could not produce dollars in numbers which, when added to state aid, would achieve anywhere near the quantity available to the rich districts. In our judgment such a system is defective if only because *it is not fair to tell poor districts that the way to prevent wealth from being an obstacle to equal opportunity is for them to try harder.*

A full analysis of the flat grant requires consideration of the general impact of state taxes which generate the state aid funds. In part, a flat grant plan can be seen as a mere reshuffling of dollars through seemingly unnecessary channels, for much of the money is repaid to the districts whose constituents raise it. On the other hand, it does produce money that otherwise might not be raised for all districts, particularly since state taxes are less visible to the taxpayer than local ones.[29]

But the important point to see here is that, through the flat grant plan, the poor district might well be indirectly assisted if the state were to return more money than the district pays in.

or not the grant is aimed at relieving the problem of wealth disparity. Flat grants may be of either the general or specific sort; so may equalizing grants — those which account for ability to pay — which are discussed in later chapters.

29. Actually, both state and local taxes seem to be in a residual category compared to federal taxes; Burkhead, *State and Local Taxes*, p. 16. Perhaps this means simply that taxes are more visible the more "local" they become.

Many kinds of progressive taxing plans could have this impact. Cubberley, however, did not address himself to the appropriate state source of money. For him, at least, broadening of the tax base was merely an ancillary benefit. We should therefore be alert to the possibility that state money might in fact come from a regressive source.

The flat grant plan can help poorer districts but is inadequate as typically conceived. Imagine a state with ten districts, each with one pupil (or teacher) and each with $100, $200, $300, respectively at $100 intervals up to $1,000 in total ability. The wealth (ability/unit) of the richest is ten times that of the poorest. The state task units number ten and the state total ability is $5,500. If the state wants to provide flat grant aid of $55 per unit, it will have to tax 10 percent of its assets (ability) to raise the needed $550. But if the richest and poorest districts each want to spend $100 per unit they will each have to raise $45 locally, which will require the poorest district to tax 45 percent of its assets while the richest can get the money from but 4.5 percent of its assets. Almost surely the poor district will not be able to afford such a burden and will not keep up with its rich neighbor. If it taxes only at the rate of its rich neighbor, however, it will have but $59.50 to spend, compared with the latter's $100. In any case, it can be seen that the flat grant, since it was awarded on the basis of task alone, had no impact on the relative ability of the poor district to raise money. A local decision to raise $45 still takes the same sacrifice as before.

If we look to the state aid again we can see that some relief from wealth variation may have been accomplished. If the state taxed at 10 percent across the board (proportional) to obtain the $550, then the richest district paid $100 and the poorest $10. Thus, if this kind of state fund raising is used, there is a kind of equalizing of sacrifice and money raised in regard to state aid — each district paid 10 percent, each received $55. But when the whole $100 program is considered,

Relation of ability, effort, and offering in a hypothetical flat grant plan

District	Total ability ($)	State aid unit ($)	State taxes paid with 10% tax ($)	Local rate (%) to raise $45/unit locally	Total taxes paid ($)	Total tax (%) to yield $100/unit	$ available for education if each taxed at 4.5% and had $55 flat grant	Rate needed (%) to raise full $100/unit locally
1	100	55	10	45.00	55	55.00	59.50	100.
2	200	55	20	22.5	65	32.5	64	50.
3	300	55	30	15.	75	25.	68.50	33.3
4	400	55	40	11.25	85	21.25	73	25.
5	500	55	50	9.	95	19.	77.50	20.
6	600	55	60	7.5	105	17.5	82	16.7
7	700	55	70	6.43	115	16.43	86.50	14.3
8	800	55	80	5.63	125	15.63	9.	12.5
9	900	55	90	5.	135	15.	95.50	11.1
10	1000	55	100	4.5	145	14.5	100	10.
All districts	5500	550	550	–	1000	–	–	–

the poorest still would have to bear taxes of 55 percent to keep up with the richest, which is bearing but 14.5 percent.

In sum, flat grant aid to supplement local spending can be seen today as a minuscule advance toward the removal of local wealth as the determinant of the quality of education a child receives. But it must be noted that this criticism holds only so long as the grant is merely supplementary. Because the flat grant is related to task only rather than to task *and* ability to pay, as it comes closer to paying 100 percent of the expenditure level desired by the most ambitious districts the system itself approaches statewide uniform treatment of children. Thus, if the state ended subsidiarity and paid all the costs of education through flat grants, all moneys could be collected through a statewide tax (hopefully proportional if not progressive), while funds could be distributed on some task basis. Put into our terminology, when local effort is not necessary local ability loses importance. But since flat grants are seldom as high as 50 percent of the total budget of even a poor district (let alone the 55 percent used in the example), this program is never more than a halfway house.

Another major criticism of Cubberley's suggested system of distributing state aid is that the "teachers employed" basis permits the amount of state aid received by any one district to be affected by local spending. It might be said that he failed adequately to consider the behavioral response to aid plans. He was correct in locating teachers' salaries as the major cost of education (at least of current expenses); but his choice of a *revenue unit* (number of teachers), rather than a *load unit*, (number of pupils or classrooms of thirty) to represent this reality produces unfortunate results. The very expenditures which are supposed to be offset by state aid themselves become the criteria for state aid. Poor districts, whose educational task should require more teachers, cannot afford to hire them in the first place; rich districts which can afford to employ additional teachers now have the state defray part of the costs. Whenever the state agrees, in effect, to pay part of an additional service, thus making it cheaper to purchase, rich schools will buy more "units" than poor schools. As a result, aid distributed over a revenue unit system, despite its otherwise nonequalizing attributes, is actually *anti-equalizing*: poor districts tend to receive relatively less, not more, than rich districts. Cubberley's choice of a revenue unit may have been intentional because of his conviction that state aid ought to stimulate local expenditures; nevertheless, he did not seem to appreciate the selective impact of the stimulation, a misperception preserved in certain contemporary plans.

Some states still pay the districts a certain number of supplemental aid dollars for each educational task unit that exists in the district. Although the task units may be based simply upon pupils in attendance, or may be adjusted to reflect size of districts or salaries of teachers, or may even be cast in a sophisticated classroom-unit concept, nonetheless the amount of money raised locally and the local ability to raise it are effectively ignored in determining amount of state aid. As a result, state assistance is designed to do practically nothing to eliminate the effects of wealth variations among the districts. Therefore, under such plans, to the extent of district wealth variation, there is systematic discrimination on the basis of wealth. Perhaps the one major positive effect of significant state flat (or fixed) grant aid is an increased total spending for education in the state, although, once again, even this depends upon the visibility of the state taxes which compose the state school aid fund and the degree to which local decision making is influenced by such state collections.

South Carolina is one of the eleven states listed by the United States Office of Education as basically a fixed-grant state and is a good example of a Cubberley approach to state subvention.[30] Its varied method of allocation illustrates a range of characteristics typical in "flat" systems. The basic package of state aid to local school districts has five parts. As amended by the 1966 legislative session they were (1) teacher salary support on a sliding scale; (2) $5 per pupil for supervision and overhead; (3) $10 per pupil for maintenance and operation; (4) $20 per pupil for physical facilities; (5) from a general fund, aid of undetermined amount based upon any state excess of revenue over expenditure.[31]

The first observation to be made is the obvious: aid is awarded irrespective of district ability to support schools with local property taxes. Second, South Carolina's flat grants are *special* rather than *general*, for the dollars are earmarked for specific purposes. Of course, the categories of purpose are the broad ones for which all schools must spend. It is doubtful, therefore, that the districts find either the limitations very confining or the meager assistance very helpful.

Third, the teacher salary aid program is a *revenue* task unit form of subvention. Dollars are awarded on the basis of education and years of service of the employees in the district; support ranges from $1,749 for a nondegree-holding newcomer to $7,221 for a teacher with a Ph.D. and fourteen years' experience.[32] Of course, as suggested earlier, richer districts are better able to attract better educated personnel and, with the ability to pay more, keep them longer. Thus the funding tends to flow, not to those who need it, but to those who have it. It is

30. U.S. Department of Health, Education and Welfare, *State Programs for Public School Support* (1965), p. 3. The eleven states are Alaska, Arizona, Connecticut, Delaware, Hawaii, Nebraska, New Mexico, North Carolina, South Carolina, South Dakota, and Vermont. Yet the classification used seldom gives a clear picture; many states — Arizona, for example — have both "flat" and "equalizing" aid programs. As Chapter 3 illustrates, these labels can lie. Hawaii, too, is rather a special case, as will be noted later.

31. CODE OF LAWS OF SOUTH CAROLINA, tit. 21, §§ 258, 260, 261, 272, 293 (Supp. 1968).

32. *Ibid.*, at § 258.

stimulation of the improper kind, as it is anti-equalizing. This kind of stimulation policy can be proper only after districts are put on an even footing in regard to wealth.

Fourth, inasmuch as the districts (and counties) have local levies as their major source of revenue for education,[33] the aid plan is of use to poor districts only in its incidental aspect of spreading the tax base for the collection of state aid revenues. Hence, for the children of the poor South Carolina districts it can be confidently predicted that the offerings they receive will be of lower quality because of the wealth handicap under which their provider must operate. Even if the cost (and standard) of living is relatively low in South Carolina, a flat grant of something in the neighborhood of $200 per pupil (which the five programs appear typically to yield, assuming a classroom of thirty) will simply not suffice to boost the poor areas into any kind of competition with the rich for relative quality of public education.

33. *Ibid.*, at §§ 911, 913.

2 · Equalization for Basic Education: The Foundation Plan

The prophets prophesy falsely, and the priests bear rule by their means; and my people love to have it so. . . .

Jeremiah 5:31

The Foundation Plan Philosophy:
The Equalization Myth

THE PIONEER EFFORT TO TRANSLATE the philosophy of equal educational opportunity into a viable state finance program adjusting for district wealth variation was made by George D. Strayer and Robert M. Haig[1] in 1923 and later refined and developed by Paul R. Mort.[2] The program came to be known as the foundation plan. Modified, scrutinized, criticized as it was, the program remained the paradigm of state aid to education until after 1960. The philosophy of the movement that produced it is described in its extreme version by the authors of the plan: "[T]he state should insure equal educational facilities to every-

1. G. D. Strayer and R. M. Haig, *Financing of Education in the State of New York* (New York, 1923). Their contribution to state aid for education dates from the work of the Educational Finance Inquiry Commission (1921–1924). "As Professor Mort has written, there were two pages 'almost hidden' toward the end of the Commission's study for New York State, prepared by George D. Strayer and Robert M. Haig that contain the 'conceptual basis' of much of the present-day practice in equalization"; C. S. Benson, *The Economics of Public Education* (Boston, 1961), p. 201.

2. Mort participated in study and recommendation for reform in state aid to education as well as numerous other subjects of interest for over 40 years. In 1926 he published his book *State Support for Public Schools* (New York, 1926). Thereafter he developed and refined the foundation program until after 1960 when he switched to the percentage equalizing grant to be analyzed in Chapter 4. Of his prolific writings, the best known is P. R. Mort, W. C. Reusser, and J. W. Polley, *Public School Finance*, 3d ed. (New York, 1960).

one within its borders at a uniform rate throughout the state in terms of the burden of taxation. The tax burden of education should throughout the state be uniform in relation to taxpaying ability, and the provision of the schools should be uniform in relation to the educable population desiring education." [3] The goals expressed are similar to Cubberley's; the practical program — like Cubberley's — deliberately falls far short of the rhetoric. The gap between description and deed exercised a pernicious influence for two generations. The failure to articulate the fact that the "solution" in reality permits wealthy districts to perpetuate their advantage left the erroneous impression among education amateurs that the problem had been solved. The allure of an ornamental equalizing grant formula that still permitted local incentive for better schools captured the loyalty of the average reformer with little time for technicalities and provided the basis for what can only be described as the equalization myth. Historical materials in Appendix C illustrate development of the myth.

Shortly we will examine the mechanics of the foundation plan and observe it in operation in several states. Its operation can be complex, and we will proceed with accelerating sophistication. Starting at the beginning, simply put, under the Strayer-Haig scheme the state establishes a dollar level (foundation) of spending per pupil which it guarantees to every district; this can be set hypothetically at $500 per pupil. To qualify for the guarantee a district must tax at a certain minimum property tax rate, hypothetically 1 percent. The amount raised by a district at that tax rate will be supplemented by state aid to the extent necessary to insure the district the foundation level offering. Thus if a 1-percent tax in a given district raises $400 per pupil, state aid will come to $100. To preserve incentive, the district is allowed to tax more than the minimum rate whenever it wants additional local revenues.

3. Strayer and Haig, *Financing of Education*, p. 173.

It was Charles S. Benson, in his book, *The Economics of Public Education*, published in 1961, who finally rallied the arguments against the foundation program and began to dismantle the myth that it provided equal educational opportunity.[4] Benson saw that the crux of the problem lies within that part of the formula which guarantees local incentive. The foundation plan has never provided that all districts can have the same offering if they make the same effort; the state will not equalize local ability to tax above the foundation level. Rich districts can turn out a better offering at every level of local effort above the minimum rate. The effect, of course, is to radically exacerbate disparities between rich and poor with every tax increment above the foundation level. Local incentive — subsidiarity — is useful only to the rich. Furthermore, what is empirically demonstrable is that in most states nearly all districts, rich and poor, do tax at a level above the minimum, so that the foundation program is indeed but a foundation upon which the districts with richer tax bases continue to build much finer houses than do poor districts. Under this plan, equal opportunity in terms of balancing offering, wealth, and effort is a hoax.

Unfortunately, rather than concentrating on its structural inadequacy, for many years reformers worked merely within the parameters of the foundation plan. Their attention focused upon (1) refining the measures employed in the Strayer-Haig scheme and (2) detailing the shortcomings which beset the plan, even within its own modest goals, when put into practice by the states. These two efforts provide concepts which are useful to an understanding of any sophisticated school financing plan, and they illustrate how for many years the reforming zeal was dissipated in confrontation with minutiae.

4. Benson, *Economics of Public Education*, pp. 201–210.

Implementing the Myth

Mort was principally responsible for clarifying the three basic steps in the formulation of the foundation plan;[5] the analysis which follows is based upon his work.

Determine the Unit Cost of the Minimum Program. The first step in the foundation plan is the legislature's determination of the minimum level of education that all districts will be guaranteed if they tax at some minimum rate. This minimum education must be phrased in terms of number of dollars per task unit. Mort, however, felt that describing the program in dollars per pupils in average daily attendance (ADA) was too crude an approach; there had to be additional refinements of control to assure that the districts would be judged by the same standards. Thus, one very important criterion for state aid was the universality of a program. If almost every school has a kindergarten, kindergarten should be part of the minimum program. Secondly, there should be adjustments for those additional undertakings, such as transportation in rural districts, which are necessary to make the basic program possible. This approach sought to standardize the dimensions of the program.

Then Mort focused on refining the task unit. For the foundation scheme his approach was to divide school costs into two groups, classroom costs and all other costs. He noted that classroom costs tend to vary greatly from place to place depending on the kind of factors identified by Cubberley, whereas other costs remain fairly constantly related to number of pupils. Mort's solution was the "weighted pupil," a system for multiplying the number of students in a school by a certain factor depending upon the size of the school.[6] He also

5. Mort, *State Support*, pp. 6–34, 47–97.

6. For example, a school with 0–27 students would be weighted by multiplying the number of students in average daily attendance by 1.48 and adding 14.47; *ibid.*, p. 56.

devised a technique for including the cost of transportation in the weighted pupil measure; this, too, was computed by multiplying the number of students in average daily attendance by some factor. The result of this first step in constructing the minimum foundation program then, is a *unit cost per weighted pupil* which purports to cover the real costs of a certain level of education throughout the state. Granting that these adjustments are difficult to make with precision, their attractiveness is clear. Many states have nevertheless continued to base their plans on a simple per-pupil formula; on the other hand, some of the same states have adopted special grants to help defray costs arising from diversity of districts, for example, a special transportation fund.

Determine the Nature of the State-local Financing Partnership. Establishment of the level of fiscal obligation which must be undertaken by a district in order to participate is next in order. As noted earlier, insofar as the minimum foundation program achieves equalization, it does so by supplementing what is raised locally by a minimum tax rate. Of course some districts may be so rich that, at the minimum tax rate, they raise as many or more dollars than the foundation plan guarantees and are therefore entirely out of the aid plan. The original planners did not seem to intend this to happen often; they typically set the minimum rate so that none or only a few districts would exceed the foundation level.

One peculiarity of Mort's proposal was that existing state flat grants were to be subtracted from the basic program in order to determine the state share under the equalizing grant. Thus, if the state were already supplying $2 per pupil for textbooks, that amount would be subtracted from whatever the state aid otherwise happened to be.[7] If a district, under the formula, were to receive $50 per pupil under the foundation program, it

7. Mort called this process "The Optimum Combination of Large and Small Fund Methods when Old Grants are Continued"; *ibid.*, pp. 27–33.

would not, in effect, receive the flat grant as well. This made
some sense from the standpoint of the pure philosophy of the
program. State aid purported to assure payment of the full
costs of a "basic" education, so why should it support a greater
level? Nonetheless, even within the foundation philosophy,
from the point of view of equalization the flat grants should
have been eliminated and textbook aid supported through the
equalizing fund. Otherwise this combination of state forms of
aid has an undesirable impact, as appears later. In any case,
Mort's refinement was made meaningless; the states typically
did not support the unit cost of even a basic education, let
alone a substantial one.

Determine Ability to Pay. As the third step, the equalizing of
sacrifice at the foundation level requires a rational measurement of local ability. Assessed valuation of property (often
realty only) is nearly everywhere the measure of ability, and,
in turn, the tax rate on that ability is the measure of sacrifice.
Refinement in this case meant the acquisition of standardized
ability data and was difficult because of the varying local assessment practices.

These then are the three chief elements of the foundation
plan; but their adoption has not been uniform. Too often the
admonitions of Mort and others regarding meaningful implementation of the plan are ignored, rendering individual programs almost complete shams. It is possible to particularize the
kinds of inadequacies which contributed to the failure of the
foundation to reduce inequalities even to a respectable minimum level. They include:

(1) Political compromise — task unit distribution. An important weakness of the Strayer-Haig system is the political
sensitivity of the foundation level. The theoretical goal of the
foundation program is to determine and support the real cost
of some basic and substantial educational offering. The structure of the guarantee — usually simply a certain number of

dollars per pupil — lends itself from the outset to political compromise. The support level always remained below the real costs of any substantial level of education and became an index merely of the available resources and the educational politics of the particular state legislature, not of any job to be done.[8]

(2) Static nature of the support level. The needs of education have steadily outgained support levels. There are two reasons for this, one the fast-growing cost of education. Mort admitted in one of his last publications: "The level of support used in the State Aid formula did not rise automatically with the cost increases. Only population increase was in any degree reflected in the formula." [9] Second, school expenditures have shown great "expansibility" (a tendency to branch into new areas), far beyond what Mort had anticipated.[10] Hindsight makes it obvious that the political process has been ill-suited to produce the continually strengthened support required.

(3) Lack of flexibility in meeeting local needs. A foundation program tends to produce uniformities of two kinds among poor districts: one is uniformity of expenditures because of the great burden of raising additional funds, the other is the related uniformity of educational style.[11] At the "basic" level of spending the districts are far less free to experiment and diversify. Their meager resource is largely consumed merely in the strug-

8. A good example of the kind of compromise that has always plagued the Strayer-Haig device occurred when it was first adopted in New York. Paul Mort determined at that time that a satisfactory offering would cost $70 per pupil, or $1,900 per teacher. However, this amount "was judged by both professional workers and laymen to be unreasonably high. Twelve hundred dollars per typical teacher was considered a proper level. This is somewhat in advance of the present actual minimum found in the state" (Mort, *State Support*, p. 23).

9. P. R. Mort, "Unification of Fiscal Policy in New York State," in C. S. Benson, ed., *Perspectives on the Economics of Education* (Boston, 1963), p. 341.

10. Benson, *Economics of Public Education*, pp. 209–210, 242–246.

11. *Ibid.*

gle to meet state standards, including the traditional starting point of any system, teachers' salaries. Experimental or light house programs become such by virtue of the dollars available above the educational subsistence level: light house districts are invariably rich districts.

(4) Continued presence of flat grants. Most states use the Strayer-Haig distribution and employ flat grants of the specific or general purpose type as well. These grants often reduce the equalizing nature of the foundation program, usually obscure the realities of district needs, and always contribute to the vulnerability of the program to political compromise.[12]

(5) The minimum rate — reducing state support from below. The technical machinery of the plan, by which it achieves whatever equalization occurs, has also been an obstacle to the achievement of equalization. This point requires some elaboration.

The minimum foundation rate is usually chosen with reference to some district in the state in which the minimum rate will produce enough local money to meet the foundation program. That district would represent the level of wealth at which state aid would cease. Thus, assume that the foundation level is $1,000 and that the richest district in the state is assessed at $100,000 per pupil. A 1-percent tax would then produce the minimum program in the richest district; and if 1

12. As stated by Paul Mort:

Inflation, rising living standards, the pressure upon teachers' salaries, rapid expansion in facilities, and the fever for improving the schools were dealt with piecemeal. They were attacked as small independent fires without recognition of the fact that they were manifestations of a single pervading conflagration. The result was a multiplicity of modifications of the law and special provisions to correct specific aspects of the weaknesses. The result has been high local tax rates or curtailment of school quality in many school districts.

The piecemeal modifications and special laws have reached a level of complexity where they have overshadowed the idea that a basic statewide fiscal policy does in fact exist (Mort, "Unification," in Benson, Perspectives, p. 341).

percent were chosen for the participation tax, every district in the state would have to work equally hard to produce the $1,000. In fact, it was never seriously urged that the richest district be used as the standard for the participation rate, for often it was freakishly wealthy; rather, it was recommended that a "key" rich district be chosen.[13] In practice, however, the average district more often became the "key." If the average district were assessed at $50,000, a 2-percent tax would have to be chosen as the participation rate (the rate necessary to raise $1,000 in that district), and equalizing grants would be distributed only to districts below the state average valuation. Superficially, one might think it is more equalizing *not* to give any state aid to districts richer than average. Unfortunately this result is achieved by giving the poorer districts less, because the minimum rate must be set higher (2 percent instead of 1 percent) in order to produce the guaranteed amount in the average district.

This means that, even within the foundation plan itself (that is, at the participation tax level), districts richer than the "key" district can exploit wealth. If all districts sacrifice at the participation level, there will not be equal offerings. Only the poorer ones will have the same dollars, because the richer half even at that tax rate will exceed the guaranteed minimum. Of course, beyond the foundation tax level there is *no equalization* for any district. What is produced by a given tax effort is precisely relative to wealth at all levels above the average. Thus we may say that choice of the average district as key does not even ameliorate the problem of wealth variations — except as to the lower half of the districts, and then only up to the minimum participation rate.

The problem with characterizing inadequacies of the foundation plan this way — from within the framework of the theory — is that it fails to focus upon the behavioral response of the

13. Mort, *State Support*, p. 27.

districts. Let us therefore assume a state without these inadequacies, in which the foundation level is continually adjusted
upward, in which only foundation aid and no flat grants are
employed, in which the plan is keyed to a rich district, and, most
importantly, in which the support level is sufficient to provide a
substantial educational offering. Consider the probable behavior of districts in response; if the foundation is still inadequate to satisfy the objectives of local educators, school board
authorities, and local citizens in a number of districts, some
will tax locally above the participation rate to supplement the
state guarantee. The wealthier districts, of course, will have a
far easier time raising the additional money, and it is inevitable
that they in fact will raise more. This is the typical result in
even the most progressive states. On the other hand, if few districts had aspirations to exceed the foundation level, there
would be less tendency for individual districts to raise significant amounts of additional funds locally. That is, local variation in wealth diminishes in importance to the extent that
local incentive disappears. Still, so long as any two districts desire to exercise local incentive, the richer will have an advantage
over the poorer. To avoid this, revisions would have to be built
into the Strayer-Haig approach which would change its very
nature. Districts would have to be prohibited from spending
more than the foundation amount. To effect this, either that
amount must be high enough so that no district will want to
exceed it with local collections, or any excess collections must
be rebated to the state.

With a fixed effort level and fixed expenditure level the
foundation plan would be transformed to a centralized system,
and statewide incentive would become the sole source of educational betterment. This is not what the foundation program
contemplates: it would then no longer be a foundation, but a
ceiling. Nor is it the solution we urge. It is not necessary to
eliminate local decision-making concerning the level of the

child's offering in order to terminate variation by wealth among districts.

TYPICAL FOUNDATION PLANS IN ACTION: OHIO AND NEVADA

"The General Assembly shall make provision [for] a thorough and efficient system of common schools throughout the State" (Constitution of the State of Ohio, Art. VI, Sec. 2). "The legislature declares that the proper objective of state financial aid to public education is to insure each Nevada child a reasonably equal educational opportunity. Recognizing wide local variations in wealth and costs per pupil, the state should supplement local financial ability to whatever extent necessary in each school district to provide a minimum program of education" (Chapter 387 Nevada Rev. Stats., Sec. 2).

Ohio and Nevada have been selected for analysis because (1) they finance schools with more or less traditional Strayer-Haig foundation plans and (2) both have altered their foundation programs in recent years, making their impact somewhat less invidious.

The Ohio Plan

The Ohio support program represents a very traditional application of a Mort-adjusted Strayer-Haig system.[14] The state support level is not fixed in terms of so many dollars per pupil in ADA, but rather is cast in terms of "classroom units." This concept is a modern example of a basic process we have already seen — a way of adjusting the task unit so that instructional, administrative, and other burdens, which fall on districts differently because of size, location, and other characteristics, might be fairly taken into consideration in the aid formula. The

14. OHIO REV. CODE ANN. §§ 3317.01–.02 (Supp. 1967). See generally Ch. 3317.

program remains based on an equalized guaranteed dollar minimum of support for each student in average daily membership (ADM). Of course, if the district wants to spend more on its schools, it simply taxes at more than the minimum. (Or in cases of the very rich, more dollars are raised even at the foundation rate.)

The Ohio aid program has been altered in amount a number of times in recent years, although the approach has remained fundamentally the same. Details of the plan adopted in 1967 to govern future school terms are worth explaining. Classroom units for each district are awarded (a) one for every sixty kindergarten pupils, (b) one for every thirty elementary and high school pupils, (c) some for vocational and special education burdens, then (d) one additional unit for each eight units in order to compensate for administrative and operational demands, plus (e) some other minor adjustments.

The foundation level under the plan is variable but tends to be upwards of $8,000 per classroom unit; fundamentally it is calculated as the sum of (1) a sliding salary schedule amount for certified teaching employees and (2) $2,425 per classroom unit. On the basis of these two factors, for example, a district would be supported up to the level of $7,625 for a classroom unit if it had a certified employee with a B.A. and one year's experience ($5,200 plus $2,425). The amount of state aid is determined by the difference between the foundation amount and the amount raised locally by a levy of 17.5 mills. The Ohio program also includes a guarantee that no district will receive aid from the state of less than $3,050 per classroom unit.

Note that the sliding salary part of the Ohio aid program is anti-equalizing. It is an allowance based on a revenue task unit which stimulates districts to hire teachers with advanced educational training. Thus, for example, the state will support a higher foundation for a unit in which the teacher has an M.A.

Richer districts, of course, can more easily take advantage of this aid.

The 1967 version of the Ohio aid plan is a marked dollar improvement over the previous plan: that is, the foundation level has been substantially raised (along with the participation rate). Impetus for this change seems to have come in part from the proposals made by a committee of education experts for the Ohio Foundation in 1966.[15] The program represents a change in degree, if not in kind; the committee proposed more sweeping changes than were adopted, including a shifting of the entire Ohio focus away from the foundation system,[16] but the general structure remained intact. The data to be generated for the 1969–70 school year should manifest fewer and less dramatic differentials than those we are about to examine from the 1965–66 year, but the differences will be there and they will be substantial. The system makes them inevitable.

Spending and Wealth in Ohio

Analysis was made of the 162 city school districts in the state in terms of their expenditures per pupil in average daily membership for 1965–66 (including state aid).[17] The range of current expenditures was a high of $806.93 to a low of $329.40. The weighted mean was $457.41 and the mean $448.80. Table 1 indicates roughly the distribution of the districts according to

15. The Ohio Foundation, *Achieving Equality of Educational Opportunity* (pamphlet, May, 1966).

16. The consultants (including Charles Benson) suggested adoption of the "percentage equalizing" grant to be discussed in Chapter 4, plus a shift to a statewide fund to support a substantial "foundation," which would have been similar to the Utah system discussed later in this chapter.

17. Ohio State Division of Computer Services and Statistical Reports, *Cost Per Pupil in Average Daily Membership in Ohio's City, Exempt Village and County School Districts, 1966*, provided the raw data from which the figures employed were selected. Although aid is distributed on a teacher unit basis, Ohio spending data is collected on a pupil basis.

Table 1

Ohio city districts: frequency distribution of current expenditures (dollars)

Expenditure per pupil in ADM	Number of districts	Expenditure per pupil in ADM	Number of districts
325–350	8	575–600	2
350–375	19	600–625	1
375–400	24	625–650	2
400–425	24	650–675	2
425–450	22	675–700	2
450–475	15	700–725	1
475–500	18	725–750	1
500–525	14	750–775	0
525–550	2	775–800	0
550–575	4	800–825	1

their spending. Figure 2-1 pictures the spending distribution more vividly.

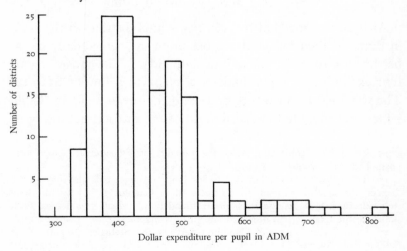

Dollar expenditure per pupil in ADM

FIGURE 2-1

What is striking about this distribution is not only that 18 of the cities represent the long tail of the curve, thereby far surpassing their fellow cities in expenditure, but also that even in the bunched group of cities (the remaining 144), the range is nearly $200 (or more than 60 percent of the lowest expenditure district). Even the middle 50 percent has a range offering of almost $100. This great disparity of spending among cities reflects a failure of the Ohio "equalizing" program to produce much of a dent in Ohio inequality of offering.

A look at the state's big cities further demonstrates significant, if diminished, discrepancy in terms of the average amount of money spent on each child depending upon where he lives:

City	Expenditure per pupil in ADM
Cincinnati	$501.84
Cleveland	481.90
Dayton	479.44
Akron	441.19
Toledo	412.30
Columbus	410.68

Accounting for the variation in expenditure per pupil in the 162 Ohio city districts requires analysis of the ability of the local district to do its own financing. The Ohio plan in effect until recently is a good test of the tendencies of the Strayer-Haig approach to tie educational opportunity to wealth: it presents a relatively simple Strayer-Haig state aid pattern plus state participation at a relatively low level (that is, the foundation support level is clearly not adequate by itself to operate the school system).

The results of wealth-expenditure analysis clearly link what is produced with ability to pay.[18] The wealth measurement used was the district's assessed property valuation per pupil. The

18. Informal examination of the exempted village and county districts indicates that the amount of inequality is at least as large or larger in the smaller (on a pupil count basis) districts. Thus, these conclusions about the city districts apply a fortiori to the others.

Table 2

Ohio city districts: wealth and spending comparison by number of districts in each spending quartile

Wealth status	Spending quartiles[a]			
	Q1(40)	Q2(41)	Q3(40)	Q4(41)
Above average wealth	38	24	17	2
Among 20 wealthiest	16	3	1	0
Among 10 wealthiest	9	0	1	0
Among 20 poorest	0	1	3	16
Among 10 poorest	0	0	0	10

[a] Includes state and federal aid; Q1 is highest.

Table 3

Ohio city districts: numbers of districts ranked by spending and wealth

Wealth status	Districts in terms of spending per pupil (state and federal aid included)		
	Top 10% (90–100 centile) (total 16)	Middle 20% (40–60 centile) (total 32)	Low 10% (0–10 centile) (total 16)
Districts with wealth above median	16	17	0
Districts with wealth below median	0	15	16
Districts ranking among 20 wealthiest	12	0	0
Districts ranking among 20 poorest	0	0	8

162 cities, ranked in terms of expenditure per pupil, were divided into quartiles and analyzed, and the assessed valuation per pupil for the median district was found to be $13,300. Table 2 portrays the relation of expenditure to wealth; 38 of the 40 best offerings are by districts with above-average wealth and of the ten wealthiest all but one have offerings in the top quarter. When we consider the extremities of the wealth spectrum in Table 3 we see an even more dramatic contrast.

The dominating impact of the wealth factor could hardly be made clearer; but another perspective can be gained by looking at the wealth and spending figures for the 5 largest city school systems in the state (Table 4), which account for more than 20 percent of the total number of Ohio school pupils. The wealthier the community the better education for the children, consistently. Of course the correlation is not perfect, and other factors may exert some influence, including cost of living differences (likely not to be large among these big cities), economies of scale (also probably not a differentiating factor among large systems) and willingness to support schools through tax effort. Thus, for example, Toledo, the sixth largest district, while third in terms of wealth is fifth in expenditure among the top six.

Table 4

Spending and wealth of five largest Ohio cities

City	Expenditure (dollars) per pupil in ADM [a]	Assessed valuation per pupil (dollars)	ADM
Cincinnati	501.84	20,514.56	87,681.28
Cleveland	481.90	18,555.34	151,986.24
Dayton	479.44	16,126.50	59,658.17
Akron	441.19	14,801.14	58,297.95
Columbus	410.68	13,087.93	103,550.09

[a] State and federal aid included.

The range of assessed valuation among Ohio city districts is from $5,358.27 to $85,174.20 per pupil. Some extremes are naturally to be expected. More important is the range of $8,500 to $25,000 — approximately a 3–1 ratio — which separates the richest and poorest of the middle 80 percent of the districts (cutting off, that is, the extreme 10 percent at each end so as to eliminate "freaks"). Given such polarization of wealth, no matter how hard a poor district tries it is not likely to catch up with the rich one without more state help.

The Ohio legislature, by delegating the financial responsibility to local districts and by engaging only in tokenism from the state treasury, transmuted the proper private advantage of the rich into a public institution having the essential economic characteristics of a private system. The new plan will do little to change this. In Ohio, a child's public education is dependent for its quality upon the private wealth of his district. It is as simple as that.

The Nevada Plan

Nevada is another example of the Strayer-Haig approach.[19] The state guarantees a minimum support level, subtracting from that figure the amount raised by a mandatory local taxing effort in order to determine state contributions to a district. If they wish to exceed the guaranteed minimum, districts may tax more heavily locally. In the main, the Nevada plan discussed here is that which has been in effect for some time and for which data is available. The new Nevada plan referred to from time to time embodies no significant change in philosophy. Although the core of the foundation program in Nevada has been based upon the concepts of certified employees and of pupils in ADA, once again this is but a different way of approaching the task units; as in Ohio, it is an attempt to employ

19. The plan for 1966–67 is set out in old § 387.125 NEV. REV. STATS., replaced in April, 1967, by §§ 387.121–387.126, NEV. REV. STATS.

modern educational accounting to adjust for variations among districts in the cost of education.[20] Under the new plan, a variable ADA pupil is the task unit used.

Under the plan in operation for 1966–67, the foundation level was basically geared to the sum of $5,100 per "allowable certified employee" plus $100 per pupil in ADA (additional adjustments were made for transportation and special education). Under the old plan the state board of education was empowered to establish rules for determining how many certified employees each district is allowed for this purpose; hereafter the legislature apparently intends to carry out this responsibility itself. The calculation is in large part based upon ADA pupils. Once the task unit adjustment has been made, the aid to each district is reconverted to a per-pupil basis called "basic need." Thus, each district has a different foundation level per pupil that the state will support — this is true under both the new and the old plans. Because the board of education, as an agency for constant re-evaluation of the needs of the state school system, has been in a position through its rule-making power to influence the effective support level, and because the legislature too has been sensitive to change, the foundation in Nevada tends to approach what by today's standards represents the full cost of a good education. This constitutes a more significant state commitment than obtained in Ohio at least under the old Ohio plan. It is also notable that, for short-term purposes, Nevada has been providing emergency education funds on top of "basic need" funds that are allocated for districts with unusual financial difficulties. Lincoln County, which has suffered from declining assessed valuation while the other counties are rising, has been the object of extraordinary aid for the past four years.

20. Under the old plan, among the 14 significant Nevada districts (the other 3 are very small systems) the ratio ranged in 1966–67 between 15.50 and 18.40 pupils in ADA for each allowable certified employee.

Nevertheless, there is still significant unequalized local spending generated through local taxes above the minimum qualifying level. The mandatory participation rate is seven mills, and districts are allowed to tax up to fifteen mills. To the degree that such additional taxing is exercised, quality is a function of wealth; the rich produce more than the poor with the extra levy. Further, it is a fact that the Nevada minimum aid program, generous perhaps, is not adequate today by the standards of Nevada citizens. Eleven of the 17 districts are now taxing at the 15-mill level, and all but one (at 11.6) are above 12.5.[21]

Nevada Wealth and Spending

Tables 5 and 6 illustrate in further detail Nevada's taxing and spending in all districts for 1966–67. Clear-cut comparisons are made difficult because of the distribution of Nevada's public school pupils among the seventeen districts. Whereas about three-fourths of the state's 120,000 pupils are in two of the districts (Clark and Washoe), three small districts (Eureka, Esmeralda, Storey) have fewer than 200 pupils each (Table 5 col. 1). These three have the greatest wealth (Table 5 col. 2 and Table 6 col. 1) and are at the top in terms of available offering (Table 5 col. 5 and Table 6 col. 3), but conclusions must not be drawn too quickly because of the obvious problems of scale faced by such small systems.[22] This point is reinforced by the fact that, under the state's allowable certified employee formula, these three districts have by far the lowest pupil-per-employee ratios and in turn the highest foundation levels or basic need (Table 5 col. 6).

21. Nevada Department of Education, Division of Finance and Retirement, *Comparisons of State and Local District Contributions to School Financing, 1966*, and the *Biennial Report of the Superintendent of Public Instruction, 1966*, provided the raw data on which the Nevada analysis is based.

22. Districts with small populations tend not only to have the transportation problem, but also to have the problem of too few pupils to support efficient instructional, administrative, and physical structures.

Table 5

Nevada, 1966-67: wealth, offering, effort, and district size

	(1)	(2)	(3)	(4)	(5)	(6)	(7)	(8)	(9)
County district	Size (ADA best 6 mo)	Wealth ($/pupil)	Locally raised $/pupil	State aid $/pupil	Available offering/ pupil [(3)+(4)]	Foundation/ pupil	$/ pupil from un-equalized local tax	$/ pupil in excess of foundation [(5)−(6)]	Effort (tax in mills)
Churchill	2,405	9,507	157	367	524	426	80	98	15
Clark	56,863	11,607	187	309	496	385	90	111	15
Douglas	1,274	30,052	371	208	579	394	140	185	11.6
Elko	3,723	17,072	251	290	541	407	120	134	14
Esmeralda	45	62,222	978	423	1,400	777	500	623	15
Eureka	184	72,991	985	301	1,286	569	430	717	15
Humboldt	1,682	18,459	273	274	547	395	130	152	12.9
Lander	547	18,435	296	343	639	425	150	214	13.9
Lincoln	750	10,933	180	512	692	460	90	232	15
Lyon	2,012	18,520	297	299	596	418	150	168	15
Mineral	1,806	4,582	76	389	465	465	30	0	15
Nye	991	19,778	317	307	624	440	160	184	15
Ormsby	3,487	8,979	123	404	527	390	50	137	12.6
Pershing	666	30,631	475	221	696	416	240	280	14.7
Storey	110	31,306	496	256	752	484	250	268	15
Washoe	23,379	16,254	262	286	548	385	130	163	15
White Pine	2,491	13,007	208	395	603	428	100	175	15

Table 6

Nevada district rankings based upon data from Table 5

City	(1) District wealth	(2) Locally raised dollars	(3) Available offering	(4) Offering in Excess of Foundation	(5) Dollars from unequalized local tax
Eureka	1	1	2	1	2
Esmeralda	2	2	1	2	1
Storey	3	3	3	4	3
Pershing	4	4	4	3	4
Douglas	5	5	10	7	8
Nye	6	6	7	8	5
Lyon	7	7	9	10	7
Lander	8	8	6	6	6
Humboldt	9	9	12	12	9
Elko	10	11	13	14	11
Washoe	11	10	11	11	10
White Pine	12	12	8	9	12
Clark	13	13	16	15	13
Lincoln	14	14	5	5	14
Churchill	15	15	15	16	15
Ormsby	16	16	14	13	16
Mineral	17	17	17	17	17

But before one dismisses these three districts as freaks, mention must also be made of their financing power. Their high wealth per student is advantageous because of the supplementary taxing power they exercise. They are the top three districts in number of unequalized dollars per pupil raised by supplementary taxes (Table 6 col. 5). This tends to boost them above the adjusted state foundation further and more easily than their sister districts. As a result, because the supplemental taxing part of the program is not equalized, it is no surprise that they rank as three of the top four districts when measured by that sum by which the available offering exceeds the foundation (Table 5 col. 8 and Table 6 col. 5).

For a more balanced view of the Nevada system we will cease to concentrate on the extremes of wealth and look across the board to the relation between district wealth and money raised locally for schools (Table 5 cols. 2, 3 and Table 6 cols. 1, 2). Obviously the relation between wealth and local output becomes simple and very positive when the state sets a tax ceiling and the statewide pattern is to tax at or near that maximum. The rank order correlation between wealth and money *locally* raised will be and, for Nevada, is nearly perfect. (Table 6 cols. 1, 2). What must now be examined is what the state aid program is doing to offset these obvious effects of differentials in ability.

The district's total available offering, including state aid (Table 5 col. 5) can be compared initially with the amount generated locally (Table 5 col. 3). There is some equalizing effect: the *range* of difference in amounts available per pupil, which was $399 based upon local funds only (not including the three small districts), is now reduced to $231 with state aid. Moreover, if we eliminate the three districts which raise the least locally (there is no special reason to do so except to eliminate any objection that "freak" data is being used), the range is reduced from $295 before state assistance to $200 with it. Even with these gross comparisons, it is clear that equalizing is by no means achieved.

Perhaps we should be more sophisticated and take account of the unequal costs of education facing districts that are physically different. The state board has recognized them in its formula for state aid. It is true that each of the districts has state money available to spend, at least at the level to which the state basic formula declares the district will be guaranteed. But even excluding the three districts smallest in population, the money available in excess of that which the state guarantees is of great significance, for it ranges from none to $280 (Table 5 col. 8). Why have some districts exceeded the foundation set for their needs by amounts greater than their sister districts? The basic answer, once again, is that the Nevada system is not effective in eliminating the effects of wealth variation.

If we compare that amount of money which the local districts raise per pupil via the supplementary local tax (the unequalized share — that part of the tax amounting to eight mills in most districts) with districts' wealth, we see that the richest eight districts are the eight most succesful in raising extra local revenue; the nine poorest are the nine least successful, naturally. (Compare Table 6 cols. 1 and 5.) On a dollar basis, we see that, although there are motor vehicle revenues and federal revenues, which get involved and distort things somewhat, the amount of money raised by this supplementary tax is basically the amount that allows each district to exceed the foundation. (Compare Table 5 cols. 7 and 8 and note the general dollar relationship.) Seven of the eight districts raising the most unequalized local funds rank in the top eight in terms of amount the districts exceed the foundation (Table 6 cols. 4, 5). Again, the significant discrepancy from this pattern — Lincoln County — can be explained by the emergency extra funds allocated to it. But the emergency funds do not seem to be given out in a formula fashion and are not designed to equalize; rather, they are used for some immediate and particular problem.

When we cut through the data, we see that the Nevada plan operates as the theory says it will — that is, everyone gets at least the state supported amount (politically determined) and local incentive must do the rest. This in turn means that pupils in rich districts get more than their poor counterparts even with less or equivalent effort (Table 5 col. 9). Further, Nevada's ceiling upon the spending level in effect forbids the poor to catch up. A top-quality educational opportunity is not available to the children of poor districts even if their parents want to give it to them. This is clearly *not* to say that the absence of a maximum rate would in fact give the poor that chance and that it therefore is the appropriate solution.

The new Nevada plan is no revolutionary advance; as in Ohio, it is simply an increase in the degree to which the state will equalize local wealth through foundation plan subventions. Rather than have an agency calculate the foundation for each district, the state has made legislative judgments in this regard and built them directly into the statute. Instead of an administrative finding for 1966–67, therefore, of a basic need per pupil ranging from $385 to $777 at the extremes (see Table 5 col. 6), the statute itself spells out support levels which vary from a low of $474 to a high of $1,101. Thus, while Nevada has made another step toward state support of the full cost of public education, the same inequalities from voluntary local taxing which historically have benefited rich districts will continue to affect its school finance picture.

UTAH: THE FOUNDATION PLAN AT ITS INADEQUATE BEST

The Utah system discriminates perhaps as little as possible in a state using the Strayer-Haig approach.[23] The reason is simply that Utah state foundation support level is high enough that few districts voluntarily exceed the equalized amount to any significant extent; consequently, the offerings tend to be uniform. Thus, although in overall design the terms of the Utah plan do not differ greatly from the Ohio/Nevada model, its effects are less invidious. There is an interesting further Utah variation, a departure which in theory, though not yet in practice, could render the foundation program even more nearly equalizing in effect.

The state formula in Utah is built around task elements

23. UTAH CODE ANN. tit. 53, ch. 7, § 16 (1967 Supp.). See also *The Book of Mormon*, 16 Alma 16 (Salt Lake City, 1920).

entitled "distribution units." Once again, however, this task unit is simply an adjusted ADA figure which takes into account cost variations. As the details are explained, it can be seen how the drafters again had the classroom in mind as the measure of their foundation level.[24] A distribution unit is awarded for every twenty-seven ADA pupils, for every fifty kindergarten pupils, for factors of small schools, special education, special summer terms, and vocational programs, and then one more unit is awarded for each nine distribution units otherwise calculated (for supervisory personnel).

The state has a three-part finance program, the effects of which range from highly equalizing to nonequalizing and, simultaneously, from emphasis on uniform local effort to local initiative. Utah has taken a very sound and modern approach insofar as that is possible within the Strayer-Haig principles. Its program makes clearer what the limits of a foundation plan must be.

The Three-Part Utah Plan

The Basic Plan. The basic Utah program involves the bulk of current cost of the Utah school system, estimated at $94 million of the total of $122 million in 1967–68 and $101 of $129 million in 1968–69.[25] For those two school years the state support level is at $7,400 and $7,700 per distribution unit, respectively. (For convenience, reference will be confined to

24. One can appreciate how the classroom concept can be more meaningful from the viewpoint of determining the dollar level of state support than the frequently employed ADA pupil concept can be. By focusing upon the classroom the state can first consider costs in terms of the teacher, giving it a much better appreciation of actual cost; also, supplies and supporting personnel can be perceived much better as supplementing a class than as supplementing individual students.

25. The raw data on which the Utah analysis is based comes from an unpublished paper prepared by Dr. Maurice N. Barnett, of the Utah State Board of Education ("School Finance Program," unpub. paper on file at School of Law, University of California, Berkeley), and from the *Utah State Board of Education Annual Report, 1965–66* (Salt Lake City, 1966).

the 1967–68 year.) Each district is required to levy sixteen mills as the local share, and the state equalizes up to the support level noted. It is most interesting from the viewpoint of theory that the basic program also requires any district which raises *more* than the support level through the sixteen-mill local levy to *turn any excess over to the state for redistribution to other districts.*[26] This is the important new wrinkle in Strayer-Haig referred to above. As a practical matter, however, only one district is now wealthy enough to locally surpass the support level through its financing at the sixteen-mill figure (San Juan, with a $112,858 assessed valuation per pupil estimated for 1967–68). This basic part of the program is fully equalizing: it is mandatory, uniform, and without local leeway.

The Board Leeway Program. A second and separate aspect of the Utah picture is the state supported board leeway program, which combines local incentive and equalization and begins to give Utah the unequalizing characteristics of traditional Strayer-Haig. The district school board is allowed to impose an additional levy of up to twelve mills; for each mill authorized, the state will guarantee up to $140 per distribution unit. Thus, if the full twelve mills is levied, there will be a support level of $1,680 per DU (distribution unit). At this point, full participation in both the basic and board leeway programs guarantees a district a minimum of $9,080 (1967–68) per distribution unit at a twenty-eight-mill tax rate. All but two of Utah's forty districts are levying at the full twenty-eight-mill rate. But if the extra twelve mills of the board leeway program generates locally any excess above the $140 per distribution unit, this can be retained by the local district. Fourteen districts in fact generate such an excess and thus participate in, but get no state aid under, the state-supported leeway scheme.

To the extent that an excess is raised locally, richer districts

26. UTAH CODE ANN. tit. 53, ch. 7, § 18 (1967 Supp.).

do produce better school systems for their children with the same effort on the part of the taxpayers. However, because the wealth pattern (with isolated exceptions) seems not to be as dramatically disparate as elsewhere, and because the rate of $140 per mill is relatively high, it is not common for districts to raise far more than the full amount locally; thus the advantage of the rich is, as a practical matter, kept to a minimum. In theory, if full equalization were the goal (and particularly because the "leeway" program in fact includes all but two districts and is thus a uniform rate for almost everybody), Utah would require the full twenty-eight mills for everyone, equalize up to the $9,080 level, and continue to require the excess raised to be paid to the state.

The Referendum Program. A third major program of revenue-raising within the Utah package is the state-supported voted leeway program, or referendum program, which maximizes local incentive, allowing up to a ten-mill addition by district referendum.[27] There is again some carrot of state matching for poor districts, in that the state will guarantee up to an additional $110 per distribution unit for each mill taxed over twenty-eight. If the full amount were taken advantage of (although no district now taxes more than seven mills under this referendum program), the level of state support would be raised to $10,180 per distribution unit. Here again wealthy districts can tax without being equalized and they keep the excess they raise over the "equalized amount."

It is interesting to note the behavior of rich and poor districts under the third or referendum plan. Three of the fourteen wealthier districts which do not qualify for any state equalizing under the board leeway program have voluntarily imposed an additional levy on themselves through local initiative under the referendum plan. Voters in eight of the twenty-six other districts — those poor enough to be equalized under the state-

27. *Ibid.*, at § 24.

supported board leeway program — have also voluntarily imposed further taxes by referendum. It should be noted that of these eight, five were equalized under the referendum scheme but three were not (they were rich enough to exceed the $110 locally under the referendum plan, but not the $140 locally under the board leeway plan). Whether rich or poor tries harder may be unclear, but the negative is clear: the rich districts are producing better offerings, but not because of greater effort.

Wealth and Offering in Utah

The educational offering of the forty Utah districts does not display dramatic variation because two of the three taxing programs — the basic program up to sixteen mills and the board leeway program from sixteen to twenty-eight mills — satisfy the desires of the bulk of the districts. Further, the dollars generated by these two programs do not vary significantly in amount among the districts. Still, the more that districts begin to generate dollars beyond the guaranteed $1,680 per distribution unit with their 16–28 mill levy under the board leeway plan and the more that districts (particularly the rich ones) participate in the third taxing scheme — the extra ten-mill referendum program — the more the Utah scheme will represent in fact a system of discrimination. There is nothing in the system itself to prevent it; the relative equality seems rather the product of unusually uniform district aspirations which rarely exceed the more equalized levels of the program.

Table 7 presents Utah data on wealth, effort, and offering available for the 1967–68 term on the basis of the three-stage foundation plan (transportation funds removed). For convenience, the districts are numbered 1–40. Districts numbered 1–11 participate in all three financing programs; those numbered 12–40, with two exceptions, participate fully (tax at twenty-eight mills) in the first two programs; those marked

Table 7

Available offering, wealth, and extra effort for the 40 districts
in Utah 1967–68

District	Available offering ($/distribution unit)	Wealth (rich = X [a])	Extra effort in excess of 28 mills
Tintic	9800		6.40
Granite	9700		5.71
Salt Lake City	10900	X	5.50
Murray	9600		4.94
Ogden	9600		4.91
Park City	9600		4.70
Beaver	9600		4.51
Carbon	9900	X	4.22
Grand	10500	X	3.99
Provo	9500		3.58
Wasatch	9500		3.42
San Juan	13900	X	0
North Summit	10300	X	0
Iron	10100	X	0
Joroan	10000	X	0
Morgan	9700	X	0
Rich	9600	X	0
South Summit	9500	X	0
Unitah	9500	X	0
Box Elder	9200	X	0
Juab	9100	X	0
Millard	9100	X	0
Alpine	9080		0
Cache	9080		0
Daggett	9080		0
Davis	9080		0
Duchesne	9080		0
Emery	9080		0
Garfield	9080		0
Kane	9080		0
Logan	9080		0
Nebo	9080		0
North Sanpete	9080		0

Table 7 (continued)

District	Available offering ($/distribution unit)	Wealth (rich = X [a])	Extra effort in excess of 28 mills
Piute	9080		0
Sevier	9080		0
South Sanpete	9080		0
Tooele	9080		0
Washington	9080		0
Wayne	9080		0
Weber	9080		0

[a] A district is "rich" if it receives no equalization aid when participating in the "state supported (board) leeway plan."

with an X are rich enough to receive no equalization money under the second or board leeway plan.

Notice first the 29 districts (12–40) taxing at the 28-mill level — that is, participating in the basic and leeway programs. (The table assumes that San Juan, which has been taxing at 19.9 mills, and Tooele, at 24, will participate fully; this seems proper because the latter is of little importance and the former's wealth in context appears freakish and should be ignored.) It is clear that the variation in local wealth which is allowed to come into play permits the richer districts to generate an offering of up to more than $1,000 per DU above the foundation level on the same effort. To be more precise, North Summit's offering based upon this program can be thirteen percent larger than that of its twenty-eight poorer brethren without greater effort.

Of the eleven referendum districts listed in order of effort, the three which can offer the highest dollar programs are the three richest. Another way of understanding the small but systematic wealth-offering correlation is to compare the eight poorer districts of greater effort with the ten (San Juan excluded) rich districts of no extra effort. The eight still are not able to provide an offering comparable to many of the ten even with their manifest initiative and even, in five cases, with additional state support.

Another way to appreciate the Utah scene is by reference to Table 8, which exposes the wealth-effort inversion for the

Table 8

Wealth and effort comparison: Utah districts above $9,080 in offering

Offering	Number	Wealth		Extra effort	
		Rich[a]	Poor	Rich	Poor
$9,100–9,600	12	6	6	0	6
$9,700 and above	10	8	2	3	2
	22	14	8	3	8

[a] As definited in Table 7.

districts with offerings available in excess of the $9,080 foundation provided by the first two plans. For this purpose San Juan can be properly included.

Let us divide roughly in half, by level of offering, those twenty-two districts with better than the foundation offerings which are guaranteed at a twenty-eight-mill tax rate (the first two programs). It can be observed from Table 8 that, of the twelve in the first or lower group, as many members are poor as rich; but it should be noted that, while all the poor must make extra effort to get into the group (this is so by our definition), none of the rich need make the attempt. Only two poor districts (of greater effort, of course) are able to break into the second group of ten, where they join eight rich colleagues making no more than the minimum (twenty-eight-mill) effort.

For a specific example of unfairness, contrast Granite with Morgan.

The following conclusions emerge from the Utah plan. It is still quite obviously designed to allow the rich to take advantage of their wealth. Its three-part format includes programs that are fully, partly, and slightly equalizing. It reflects the belief that local incentive is a value to be promoted by the scheme, but, as the plan has been designed, the local incentive principle operates so that local incentive is more meaningful to the rich. However, in the total picture, local incentive is less stimulated than in most foundation systems. In fact, subsidiarity tends to be sacrificed in order to make the school system fairly equalizing. Instead of producing the widely varied efforts and offerings of the usual Strayer-Haig programs, the outcome for Utah is similar effort (twenty-eight mills) and similar offering. Yet, if the basic program amount of support were increased to $10,000 at approximately thirty-five mills, the outcome in the state, given present aspirations and costs, would be expected to be almost fully equalized with about the same participation by the state from other sources but with more districts having to pay excess into the state fund. Such a solution would represent a greater commitment to equality but would mean a correlative sacrifice of subsidiarity. In short, as Utah illustrates, no foundation plan is capable of satisfying both values simultaneously.

3 · Models for the Empirical Description of State Systems

. . . thinking thus, in nicer terms,
with nicer tools of thought,
you pull the issue into clarity
. . . unambiguously, because
your terms are unambiguous.

Llewellyn, The Bramble Bush

THAT FOUNDATION PLANS ARE INADEQUATE to eliminate wealth factors is sufficiently clear; yet, it is important for many purposes that a system be developed for analyzing and describing the true effects of these systems with greater precision than we have essayed so far. A concise demonstration of the invidious character of a given system may affect the outcome of a judicial test. It is one thing to recognize the theoretical faults of a system, another to specify in detail the incidence and quantum of the injury. Lawyers, lobbyists, journalists, and school economists need a reasonably simple set of analytical and descriptive tools; the degree and character, if not the fact, of inequity are somewhat esoteric. This is especially true where the foundation plan is combined with flat grants in systems that differ greatly from one another in form and consequence.

At this point we will discuss a technique for separating the impact of state aid into what we define as its equalizing, non-equalizing, and anti-equalizing aspects, employing the Arizona system to illustrate. In Chapter 4 we shall apply some rather simple mathematical analysis to the Illinois system to illustrate a method by which any state's data can be evaluated to show in detail wealth, effort, and offering relations. A brief description of some fairly isolated and more simplified approaches to financing than have yet been examined and some miscellaneous cautionary points and measurement problems will close the chapter; this is designed to clear the ground for an evaluation of an approach to education finance called "percentage equalizing" that has gained popularity recently.

THE PROBLEM OF MISLABELING

At last count, forty-three states could be said to have systems in which both the local share and state subvention significantly contribute toward the funding of public education.[1] These mixed financing schemes create a panorama of state subvention style, and terminology is needed both to categorize systems of state aid to the districts and then to evaluate them against the criterion that wealth be eliminated as a determinant of quality.

The three most useful terms are equalizing, anti-equalizing, and nonequalizing, words already used to some extent. With them it can be stated whether and in what ways state aid programs are designed in fact (1) to help poor districts overcome their poverty barrier (equalizing); (2) to assist the rich in exploiting their wealth advantage (anti-equalizing); or (3) to function indifferently to the wealth of the districts (nonequalizing).

It is what the plan does, and not its general type or types, that counts; its label may be important but must be treated with great care. That there has been misbranding will be made apparent. In this regard the Office of Education has contributed to the confusion by dividing the forty-three mixed financing states into those with predominantly flat grants, those with predominantly equalizing grants (foundation plans or some

1. For national analysis, see generally U.S. Department of Health, Education and Welfare, *State Programs for Public School Support* (1965); F. W. Harrison and E. P. McLoone, *Profiles in School Support: A Decennial Overview* (Washington, D.C., 1965); U.S. Department of Health, Education and Welfare, *Revenue Programs for the Public Schools in the United States, 1959–60*; U.S. Department of Health, Education and Welfare, *Public School Finance Programs of the United States, 1957–58*.

modern improvements thereon), and those with both types in significant proportions. This taxonomy helps little to clarify the important qualities of equalizing, nonequalizing, and anti-equalizing. The Office of Education's analysis is crudely based upon the share of state funds given under a label attached by the state; no inquiry is made into the plan's actual operation or even into its formal structure. We have already seen in Chapter 1 how misleading such a simplistic approach can be with respect to flat grants. On the surface it appears simply nonequalizing. But if the grant is supported by a progressive tax, it may indirectly be equalizing; on the other hand, if its award is geared to a revenue unit it may be received more by the rich than the poor and thus be anti-equalizing.

There are two inter-related problems of mislabeling. The first is that foundation plan "equalizing" aid may be in part non-equalizing. The second is that flat grant aid, when found in a subtle (and common) combination with foundation plan aid, may be anti-equalizing. Throughout this discussion the relevance of our value orientation should be kept clearly in mind: the granting of any state aid which is not equalizing, whether labeled properly or not, represents a deliberate decision to promote something other than fiscal equity;[2] further, equal-

2. One is forced to the conclusion that fiscal *inequity* is the objective. Almost any other policy objective of state aid can be achieved most fully in an equalizing context (e.g., the relief of local tax burdens on the guarantee of a minimum education). Fully equalizing aid is sometimes resisted on grounds that large grants to poor districts sap their local prerogatives and, under a percentage equalizing scheme, distort the local budget by drawing disproportionately large allocations into education as distinct from other, non-equalized, services. We regard such noble sentiments on behalf of the poor as paternalistic at best. A more enduring objection is that large grants erode fiscal responsibility because the community spends, predominantly, other people's money. It is overlooked that, as long as the proportion of local wealth expended is the same in any two districts, the motivation to economize very likely will be the same; further, we question the philosophical origins of the criticism, for which there is no empirical evidence. Even if its validity were demonstrated, it could be argued that the districts should be given a choice between their present condition and the larger grants with additional state

izing aid is inadequate until it has eliminated the effects of district wealth variations.

Nonequalizing Foundation Aid

Foundation aid can be nonequalizing. Abstractly, this phenomenon can be said to occur whenever foundation plan aid is given to the richest district in the state; quantitatively, the amount of foundation aid which is nonequalizing is measured by that which the richest district receives.

Assume a state with a foundation guarantee of $500 per task unit. Suppose that, at the participation rate of effort, the richest district raises $400 per task unit and the poorest $100. Under the plan, the former would receive aid of $100 per task unit and the latter $400. The bar graphs in Figure 3-1 show

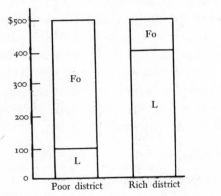

Fo, foundation aid; L, local share

FIGURE 3-1

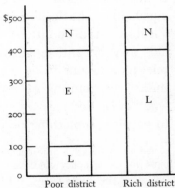

L, local share; E, equalizing state aid; N, nonequalizing state aid

FIGURE 3-2

sources of the dollars for offerings at the participation rate of effort for the richest and poorest districts.

Not all of the aid in this case is equalizing aid. Since the

supervision. See C. S. Benson, *The Economics of Public Education* (Boston: Houghton Mifflin, 1961), pp. 231–232, and the 2nd ed. of the same book (1968), p. 185.

rich district gets $100, only $300 of the $400 that the poor district gets is equalizing. Above $300 the two are already equalized at this rate of effort, and the additional $100 to each is nonequalizing or indifferent to wealth. The bar graphs in Figure 3-2 analyze the offering into its component parts. Since the mislabeling exists to the extent of aid to the rich district, it disappears when, at the participation rate, the richest district raises as much or more than the foundation amount. For example (see Figure 3-3), all aid is equalizing when the foundation level is $500 and the richest raises $500 (or more) locally at the participation level rate.

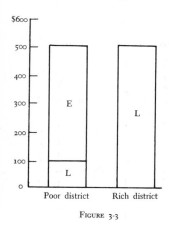

FIGURE 3-3

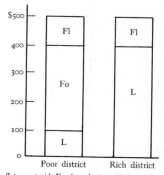

Fl, flat grant aid; Fo, foundation aid; L, local share

FIGURE 3-4

Using the basic example from Figure 3-1, the phenomenon that foundation aid may be nonequalizing as well as equalizing can be described in another way. The Figure 3-1 example has been treated as a foundation plan with a $500 foundation level. It can as easily be considered a combination of two plans — one a foundation plan with a $400 support level, the other a $100 flat grant plan on top of the foundation. Figure 3-1 would be altered thus to Figure 3-4.

Assuming an even rate of increase in wealth (assessed valuation per pupil) from poor to rich districts Figure 3-5 demonstrates the full picture of the foundation aid given in our basic hypothetical (with the $500 foundation level).

In a sense, all districts are supported to above the wealth of the richest district based on the participation rate of taxation; that is, because of state aid all districts at the participation rate have more dollars to spend than even the richest could raise

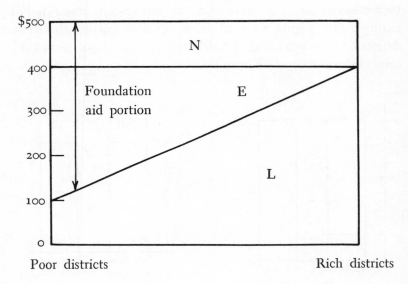

FIGURE 3-5

locally. Or, put another way, the "key" district is an imaginary district richer than the richest. The problem, of course, is that, as such plans are set today, we can expect the districts to tax locally far in excess of the participation rate. Figure 3-6 demonstrates the total range of offerings, assuming that all districts tax at a uniform rate equal to twice the participation rate. Figure 3-7 is like Figure 3-6 except that all funds raised locally are lumped together.

The evil of foundation plan dollars that are nonequalizing

should now be clear. If this foundation plan were to distribute *all* its dollars in an equalizing manner it could more nearly approach a fair system while using the same amount of state money; state aid which is nonequalizing in its effect could be redistributed so that it is equalizing under a plan with a higher foundation level and a higher participation rate. The label of

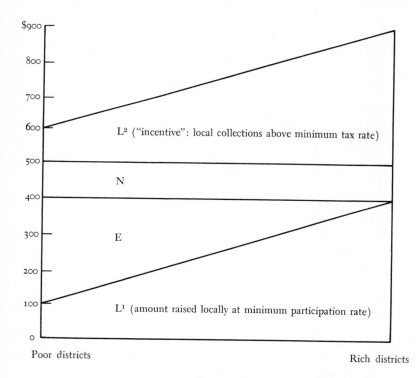

FIGURE 3-6

the plan would be the same, but its operation far different. Putting all those state aid dollars to work in an equalizing plan which functions as its label suggests might produce the picture in Figure 3-8. That is, the state might be able to equalize up to a foundation level of $750 per unit so that at the participation rate of effort (now twice that set in the previous examples), the offerings would be far more uniform. Of course, the actual picture — the extent to which a foundation level could be supported with the same state funds — depends on a variety of factors. In any event, as structured in Figure 3-6 the foundation plan clearly is doing far less for the poor than

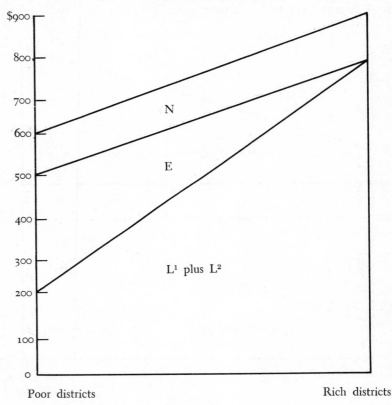

FIGURE 3-7

could a redesigned plan with the *same amount* of state money invested. But as long as only the foundation plan label is attached, this fact cannot be discovered until the workings of the program are carefully analyzed.

It is useful to contrast this example and the earlier point

that one of the principal ingredients of the foundation plan is the choice of the "key" district — that is, the district in which the participation rate of local tax effort by itself produces the foundation amount per child. We have noted that if this key district is below the richest in wealth (average, for example),

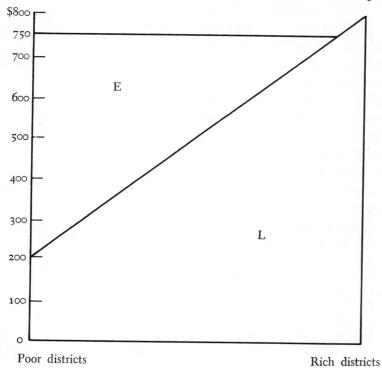

Poor districts   Rich districts

FIGURE 3-8

then by necessity the state financing plan cannot be fully equalizing unless the rich districts pay into the state a portion of the funds raised locally. Contrariwise, the effect of selecting a key *above* the richest district is to hurt poor districts in another way: by diverting state aid to nonequalizing purposes.

By knowing whether or not the key district is below or above the richest, we know what remedy to apply. If the key is above the richest, the state should raise both the participation rate and the foundation level so as to achieve more equalizing with the same money. If the key is below, the state must require that the richer districts pay back the amount of money in excess of the foundation level produced by the participation tax (as in the Utah basic plan) in order to increase equalization and still employ the same amount of "state source" funds. Otherwise improvement will have to come from increased state commitment.

Of course, these refinements in the foundation plan do not eliminate wealth determinants of quality except at the participation rate. Above that rate each tax increment produces dollars precisely in proportion to district wealth. In order to eliminate this basic flaw the paticipation rate would have to be the maximum rate permitted, or else it would have to be set so high that none would wish to exceed it. In either case the effective consequence is a uniform and centralized system of finance utterly foreign to the philosophy of the "foundation" plan.

Anti-equalizing Flat Grants

In some cases flat grant aid can be anti-equalizing when combined with a foundation plan. This phenomenon is but an interrelated variant of the one just examined. First, it must be explained that the many states with combined flat and foundation plans use one of two methods of combination. The fundamental difference lies in whether the flat grant is *supplementary to* or *included in* the amount of foundation aid.

Type 1 (supplementary). If the foundation level is, for example, $400 and the flat aid is $100, districts will first be equalized up to $400 (the foundation part) and then all districts will be given $100 of additional aid (the flat grant). Thus the state contributes: ($400 minus L) plus $100.

Type 2 (inclusive). Here, assume the foundation level at

$500 and the flat aid is $150. The districts first will be given $150 (the flat grant part) and then equalized up to $500 (after counting both the local share and the flat grant). Thus the state contributes: $150 plus ($500 minus [L plus $150]).

Consider Type 1 first. Assume (a) a plan with a $400 foundation level and a $100 supplementary flat grant and (b) the amount raised locally by the richest and poorest districts as $400 and $100, respectively, at the participation rate of effort. Then the offerings at the participation rate would be, as Figure 3-9 explains, $500 for each. This result is exactly that of our foundation plan basic hypothetical (see Figure 3-1), except that in Figure 3-9 there are formally two plans and

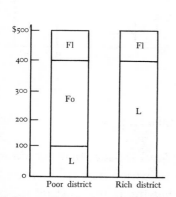

Fl, flat grant aid; Fo, foundation aid; L, local share

FIGURE 3-9

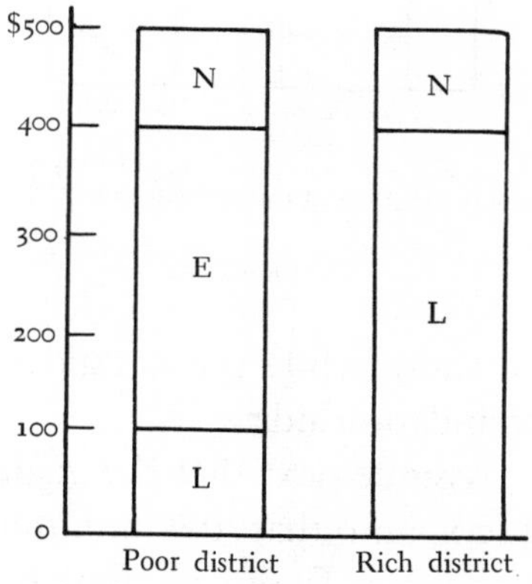

FIGURE 3-10

thus two labels. In this particular example the flat grant aid is nonequalizing; the foundation plan aid is equalizing. The labels of the two plans are, in this fact situation, good ones. Analyzing the plan in the terms we have used before, the now familiar graph again appears in the form of Figure 3-10.

Assume next that the participation rate is lowered (or that the districts are less wealthy, which is the same for these purposes). Under a Type 1 program, the aid would be distributed as Figure 3-11 demonstrates. These facts show again the operation of the earlier described "foundation aid can be nonequalizing" phenomenon. The reader should quickly be able to see that the true nature of the aid is as illustrated in Figure 3-12.

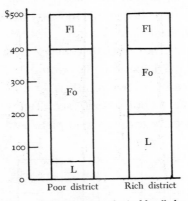

$50 and $200 are assumed raised locally by the two districts at the participation rate.

FIGURE 3-11   FIGURE 3-12

In short, while the flat aid is nonequalizing, so is some of the foundation aid.

Assume next that the guaranteed level is $400, that flat aid is $100, and that the minimum participation rate is increased under the Type 1 combination so that the richest district raises $500 as the local share. Figure 3-13 on state aid to rich and poor shows the result. In terms of our analysis, Figure 3-14 explains the combined plan. The plan starts dispensing nonequalizing aid before it has equalized even at the participation rate of effort. The offerings are not uniform even at this tax rate, and state aid is to blame. It is bad enough when the rich end up ahead of the poor when both tax at an equal level of effort above the participation rate, but it is outrageous that they do so even at the participation rate with the state giving money to the rich district. Figure 3-15 shows the combination at work in this setting for districts of varying wealth.

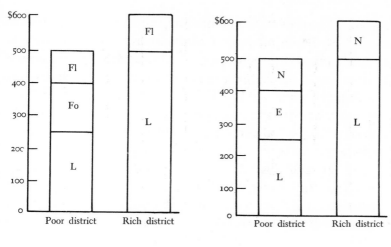

FIGURE 3-13

FIGURE 3-14

Even more offensive is the Type 2 combination which under certain circumstances is blatant in its anti-equalizing effect. That is, under Type 1, while poor districts can object to the state's attitude, they would not be helped if the nonequalizing

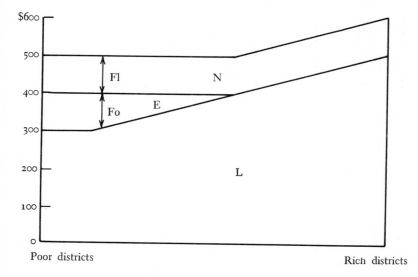

FIGURE 3-15

(flat grant) part of the combination were scrapped; for them to be relatively better off it would be necessary for the money to be redirected into an equalizing plan. Under Type 2, however, the poor would be relatively better off, at least in some circumstances, if the whole flat grant plan simply did not exist.

Assume the hypothetical Type 2 plan; assume also that the poorest district raised $100 locally and the richest $300 locally. Since the guarantee level is $500, the poor district will receive $400 in state aid. That is, 150 plus (500 minus [100 plus 150]) equals 400. But if only the foundation plan existed, the poor district would get the same amount of aid through *that* program. That is, 500 minus 100 equals 400. In short, though under the combined plan it is entitled to $150 as the flat grant part, to the extent that it gets such aid the poor district must give up foundation aid. The flat aid means nothing, as Figure 3-16 illustrates.

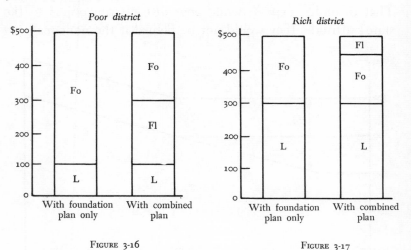

FIGURE 3-16   FIGURE 3-17

The hypothetical rich district under these facts is in a similar position. It would receive $200 in foundation aid if that plan alone existed: that is, 500 minus 300 equals 200. Under the combined plan it gets the same $200: $150 as flat aid and $50 as foundation aid. That is, 150 plus (500 minus [300 plus 150]) equals 200, as illustrated by Figure 3-17. Figure 3-18 shows the ultimate nature of aid the districts are receiving under these facts — which, of course, is the same regardless of the label or labels on the program from which it comes.

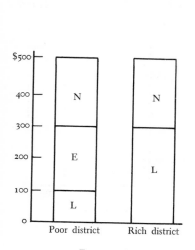

FIGURE 3-18

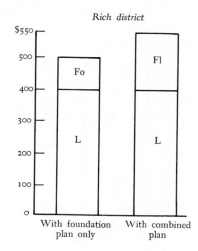

FIGURE 3-19

Thus far the Type 2 method of combining flat and foundation aid is no more invidious than any other aid package analyzed here. In fact, the flat part of the program is simply meaningless under these facts; the program operates just as a foundation plan with some non-equalizing effect, as we have earlier described, would operate.

Assume now, however, that the rich district under the Type 2 plan generates $400 locally at the participation rate. If only the foundation part of the program existed, it would receive $100 in aid; that is, 500 minus 400 equals 100. But because of the flat grant plan it gets the minimum $150 and of course is entitled to no additional aid under the foundation part. Figure 3-19 illustrates; and Figure 3-20 compares the rich and poor districts under these facts.

In short, the $50 greater offering that the rich district has at the participation rate of effort is due solely to the flat grant plan, which now can be vividly seen as operating for its benefit only. Because under this aspect of the combined plan some aid goes to the wealthier districts only, it can justly be termed anti-equalizing — a subsidy for the rich — as Figure 3-21 shows.

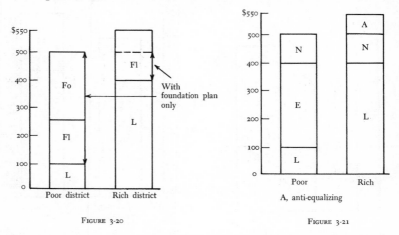

FIGURE 3-20   FIGURE 3-21

Figure 3-22 illustrates the same unfairness at work when the whole spectrum of districts is observed (assuming an even rate of increase in wealth from poor to rich districts). Recall that the assumed foundation level is $500, that the flat grant is $150, and that this is a Type 2 plan.

The evil is even more pronounced if, for example, the following assumptions are made for a Type 2 plan: (1) the amount raised locally by the richest and poorest districts is $400 and $100, respectively, (2) the foundation level is $400, (3) the flat grant aid is $200 (see Figure 3-23). In this setting the flat grant is seen as fully anti-equalizing. This effect can be explained in another way: the Type 2 combination says to the districts, "You will be equalized up to $X (foundation aid), but in no case will you be given less than $Y (flat aid)." Stated

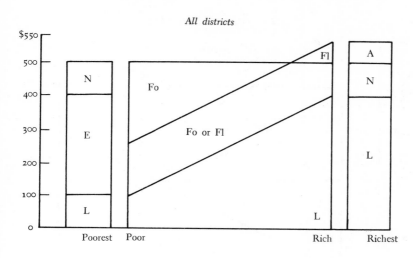

FIGURE 3-22

thus, in this context, it is obvious that the "in no case" provision is intended for the rich alone. The minimum promise is
useful only to them.

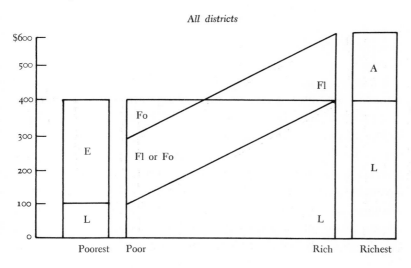

FIGURE 3-23

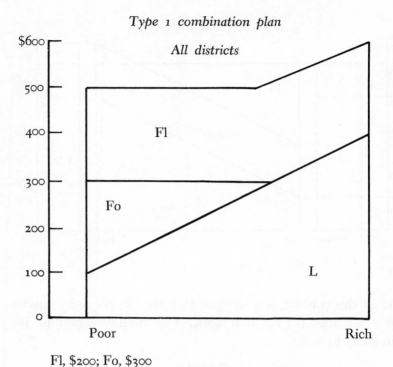

Type 1 combination plan

Fl, $200; Fo, $300

FIGURE 3-24

Figures 3-24 and 3-25 contrast hypothetical Type 1 and Type 2 plans and reveal an interesting inter-relation. Assume in each case that the poorest raises $100 and the richest $400 locally at a given participation rate of effort, but with the foundation level at $300 in the Type 1 and $500 in the Type 2 plan. Assume also a $200 flat grant. Simply put, it is evident because the charts are the same that a Type 2 plan which formally sets the foundation support at $500 is nothing but a Type 1 plan with a foundation support of but $300, assuming the flat aid is $200. Therefore, the Type 2 state is supporting the poor district to a woefully low level while taking credit for what might appear to be a progressive and equalizing system.

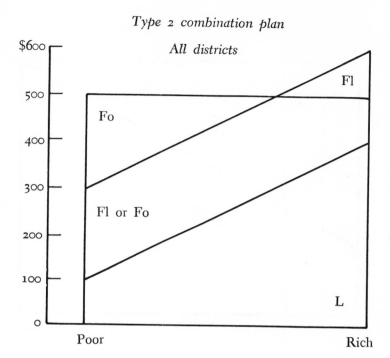

Type 2 combination plan

Fl, $200; Fo, $500

FIGURE 3-25

This is especially distressing when it could do significantly more with the same money.

By using the same state funds used in Figure 3-25, but distributing all of them as true equalizing dollars, the state could support a much higher foundation plan, assuming an increased participation rate. Thus, if the participation effort is doubled an $800 foundation could be supported. The local shares raised by the richest and poorest districts would be $800 and $200 respectively, and the state aid would be distributed so that at this tax rate all would have the same offering (Figure 3-26).

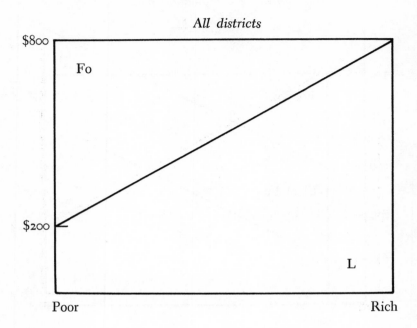

FIGURE 3-26

Compare this outcome with that of the effectively identical Type 1 and Type 2 plans described in Figures 3-24 and 3-25, assuming that districts tax uniformly locally at twice the participation rate (the rate used in Figure 3-26 as the participation rate for an $800 foundation plan). Instead of $800 for each district, we have a range from $600 to $1,000 (Fig. 3-27). For a state to credit itself with equalizing when it has a combination flat-foundation plan of this character — especially when there are available alternatives costing the same money — is sheer hypocrisy.

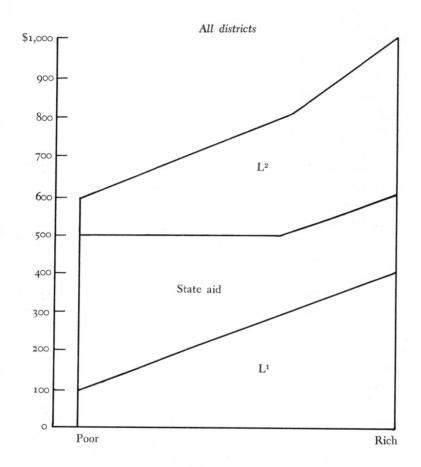

FIGURE 3-27

ARIZONA: LABELS CAN LIE

The Arizona plan helps illustrate the problems of mislabeling by reference to a specific set of facts. Nearly $59 million of the almost $79 million in state school aid which was distributed by Arizona to county districts in 1965–66 [3] was in form a simple

3. The Arizona analysis is based upon raw data found in the Office of the State Superintendent of Education, Division of Research and Finance, Arizona

flat grant of $170 per pupil in ADA.[4] Arizona also has a foundation plan which guarantees an offering of $320 per common school pupil in ADA, and $445 per high school pupil in ADA;[5] $12 million was paid by the state to local districts under its provisions. On the basis of these gross facts, Arizona was labeled a flat grant state by the Office of Education. But this barely scratches the surface in describing what Arizona actually is doing.

In Arizona, the basis for awarding foundation aid may be simplified as follows. (We will focus on the common school part of the plan.) Common school districts are given the difference, if any, between $320 per pupil in ADA and the sum of (1) the amount raised locally per pupil in ADA at the participation level of taxation and (2) $170 per pupil in ADA, which is the amount awarded under the flat grant scheme.[6] Arizona thus has a Type 2 combination plan, but of course that label tells little unless the plan is seen in operation.

Recall our basic conclusions as regards the flat and foundation labels. (1) To the extent that the foundation plan awards money to all districts, then for each district an amount equal to that received by the richest district is really a nonequalizing grant; in other words, only dollars which are awarded solely to poorer districts are equalizing. (2) Where plans are combined in the manner that Arizona's are, and to the extent that some districts do not receive foundation money, the amount of aid those districts get solely by virtue of the flat plan is anti-equalizing.

The critical facts determining characteristics of the Arizona

---

Annual Report of the Superintendent of Public Instruction, 1965–66 (Phoenix, 1967).

4. Ariz. Rev. Stat. Ann. § 15-1211 (1967 Supp.).

5. Ariz. Rev. Stat. Ann. §§ 15-1221–1225 (1967 Supp.).

6. This is simplified; actually flat aid plus the local share plus special federal Indian education funds are deducted from $320 in common school districts and from $445 in high school districts in calculating the equalizing amount.

scheme in operation are that: (1) all districts in 1965–66 received *some* foundation aid and that (2) the richest received an amount of foundation aid which is nearly *de minimis*.[7] It should be clear that these results are not inherent in the program; for, depending upon the details of the complicated relaation between levels of foundation and flat aid, the required local participation rate, and the wealth of the districts, it might happen that all districts get a significant amount of foundation aid or that a significant number get only the flat aid.

The upshot, ironically, is that in Arizona the labels on the program in fact are fairly accurate indications of the operation of the aid plan, at least insofar as it operated for 1965–66; the amount of state aid in Arizona for 1965–66 was very nearly $59 million in nonequalizing (from the flat plan) and $12 million in equalizing (from the foundation plan). This can be determined because we know who gets foundation aid and how much.

Consider, as a first hypothetical, what would occur if there were no flat grant plan in Arizona at all, and all $71 million were awarded under a foundation plan with a $320 foundation. Each district would still get the very same number of total aid dollars from the state, except that all the money would then come in the form of foundation plan dollars instead of being split among foundation and flat grant dollars. The reason is clear: it will be recalled that, if there were no $170 per ADA pupil aid to add to the local share in calculating the foundation level of aid, then each district would be eligible for up to $170 per ADA pupil more in foundation money. Moreover, since in fact each district already qualifies for some foundation money, then all would get the full extra $170 per ADA pupil as foundation money if flat aid were eliminated.

7. Mohave, the most meaningful district upon which to focus because it is effectively the richest and receives effectively the least aid for this purpose, was awarded $3,867.48 in equalizing aid for its common school children and had 2,337 pupils in ADA: i.e., less than $2/pupil.

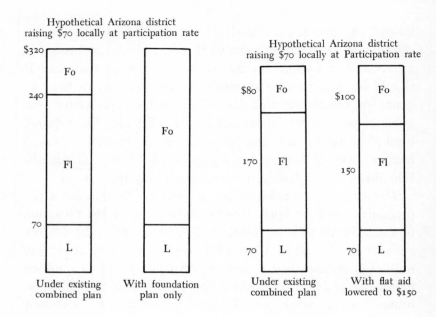

FIGURE 3-28   FIGURE 3-29

Figure 3-28 uses a hypothetical Arizona district as an example. Under such an assumed plan Arizona might well be *labeled* an equalizing grant state because all of its state aid money would now be passed out under a plan which is based on a theory of equalizing, the foundation plan. But, as the pattern of total state aid fund distribution would remain the same as occurs under the combined plan, we know that all the dollars would not in fact be equalizing dollars. At least the part which is labeled flat under the actual combined plan would remain, at best, not equalizing; $170 per ADA pupil surely is not paid inversely to wealth.

As a second hypothetical, consider what would happen if the Arizona flat aid were set at $150 per ADA pupil instead of $170. Once again the same money would be distributed as it is distributed today, but again under a different proportion for each label (see the hypothetical district in Figure 3-29). Because the

$170 is still not equalizing, it is clearly neither the type of plan nor the size of the flat aid which dictates how much is equalizing. Rather, we must divide up the foundation part into the part which is equalizing and the part which is not. Since the richest begins to get foundation aid (but barely), all the foundation aid (practically) is equalizing and the flat aid is nonequalizing. Figure 3-30 illustrates by showing the plan's operation at the foundation rate of effort for all districts in terms of both sources and effect.

Consider as a third hypothetical what would happen if the flat aid of $170 per ADA pupil were retained but the foundation amount raised from $320 to $500 per ADA pupil. In such a case, each district would get $180 per ADA pupil more than now. The money would come from the foundation plan, but because all districts receive it the aid would be nonequalizing. Figure 3-31 shows that the increased foundation aid is given indifferently to wealth: rich and poor are recipients of the same sum.

The two basic aid plans in Arizona combined in 1965–66 to yield in fact $171 of state money per ADA pupil for each district. This much was nonequalizing money. As the flat aid is $170, it turns out to be a good guide to the amount of nonequalizing aid given. Similarly, because the richest district received only about $1 per ADA pupil from the foundation plan, the foundation aid money was almost all equalizing, and the plan label was a good guide to the amount of equalizing aid given. Yet, as can be seen from the hypothetical situations, it is only by the accidental combination of factors that the labels are appropriate. Were the facts to be changed in any of the three supposed ways, then the foundation label would be too generous in indicating how much of the plan's funds were equalizing; always there will be more nonequalizing aid than one might assume from labels.

Likewise, the labels could be misleading in another sense if

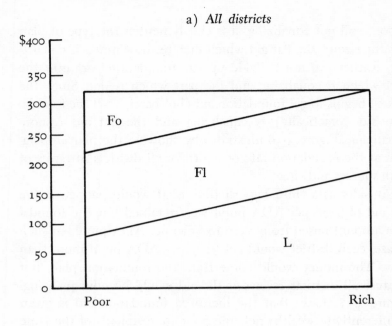

a) *All districts*

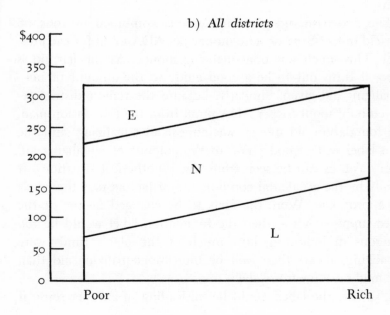

b) *All districts*

FIGURE 3-30

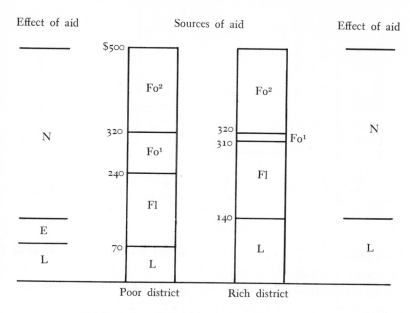

Fo¹ $320 foundation guarantee
Fo² Hypothetical increase of foundation to $500

FIGURE 3-31

one assumes the facts of a fourth hypothetical in which there is anti-equalizing flat aid. Imagine the richer districts in Arizona even richer, so that, when they tax at the participation level, the money they raise when added to the flat aid of $170 per ADA pupil exceeds the foundation plan guarantee of $320 per ADA pupil. Then anti-equalizing would occur. This is understood when it is remembered that the poorer districts would get the same total amount of dollars under the mechanics of the foundation plan even if the flat grant part of the plan were eliminated. The minimum of $170 per ADA pupil which the state guarantees to all districts has no impact on the poor. Yet, for our hypothetical rich districts, the amount of aid received depends heavily on the flat part of the plan; the guarantee of $170 per ADA pupil is a bonus to them. With it they end up

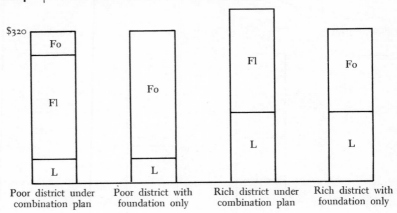

FIGURE 3-32

with more than $320 per ADA pupil (at the participation level of taxing); clearly these richer districts alone benefit from the flat grant program. In short, the money paid to them, to the degree that it pushes them over $320 per ADA (at the foundation participation rate of effort) is anti-equalizing; it is paid, in effect, as a reward for wealth (see Figure 3–32). The effect of the aid in our familiar terms is indicated in Figure 3-33. Al-

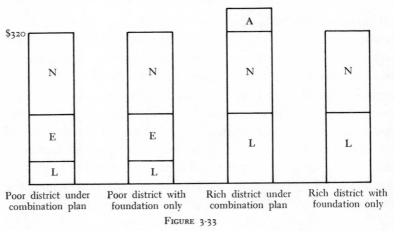

FIGURE 3-33

though this anti-equalizing phenomenon was not operative in Arizona in 1965–66, it could occur under the formula with a slight shift in wealth; it is in fact happening in Illinois elementary districts.

To comment briefly about the Arizona scheme on its merits: the combined facts that (1) all of Arizona's districts received some equalizing aid, (2) all received $170 per ADA pupil in flat grant aid, and (3) no district received in 1965–66 more than $100 per ADA pupil under the foundation plan indicate the most important characteristic of the Arizona school finance picture. This is, simply, that wealth variation among Arizona school districts is not as large as elsewhere. On a comparative basis one would not expect Arizona to evidence as much inequality as most states.

It is unfortunate that this state, which has a relatively small equalization task, has done so little. Why are states such as Arizona, with both kinds of grants, reluctant to shift to grants which are really only of an equalizing nature? Why are any dollars given to rich districts when the poor districts are not yet equalized? The answer must lie in expedience, as it surely does not lie in fairness.

4 · Application and Criticism of the Method: Complex and Simple Systems

Yossarian marveled that children could suffer such barbaric sacrifice without evincing the slightest hint of fear or pain. He took it for granted that they did submit so stoically. If not, he reasoned, the custom would certainly have died, for no craving for wealth or immortality could be so great, he felt, as to subsist on the sorrow of children.

Joseph Heller, Catch-22

NOWHERE DO WE ATTEMPT AN EXHAUSTIVE ANALYSIS of a complex system; it would be unduly cumbersome and quite unnecessary, considering the heuristic purpose of this book. What must be shown is merely that complex state systems can be tested convincingly for wealth discrimination; it will also be useful if the method for doing so proves reasonably simple. Having probed in an exploratory fashion several foundation programs, we will now examine in a more comprehensive way the veritable thicket that is the Illinois system. In doing so we will add to the empirical dimension with a more substantial set of district figures.

THE ILLINOIS LABYRINTH

Illinois relies upon locally administered real property taxes, supplemented by a mixture of state aids in flat grant and foundation plan form — providing from the state level about thirty percent of total state current educational expenditures. Article 8, Sec. 1, of the Illinois Constitution reads: "The General Assembly shall provide a thorough and efficient system of free schools, whereby all children of this state may receive a good common school education." [1] To the extent, if any, that this

1. Considering the grim realities of the Illinois system, it is ironic that the Illinois Education Association starts with this as the premise on which its discussion of state subvention is founded. See Illinois Education Association, *Lessons in Illinois Public School Finance* (February, 1952).

command directs the general assembly to create equality of educational opportunity, the assembly clearly has failed to live up to its mandate. Because of (1) the very limited state participation in the financing of its schools and (2) the aid structure, Illinois will be seen to rank among the worst of the states in terms of eliminating the relation between wealth and offering; and that relation is acute because of the great range of district wealth.

Illinois has a great variety of minor state aid programs of dubious value which operate on a special project basis,[2] but the bulk of the funds and the heart of the program center in two general grant schemes.[3] Some dollars are distributed on a unit cost basis and are made available to districts regardless of local wealth or effort;[4] other dollars are also distributed on a unit cost basis, but a local contribution is demanded and wealth is taken into account in determining the local share.[5] In sum, Illinois has a combination of flat grant and foundation aid.

Table 9 shows the increased level of state participation in educational finance in Illinois through both the flat grant and foundation grant programs at intervals over the past forty years.[6] Despite this increase, the share of state aid in the total Illinois school finance picture remains small.[7] In 1956–66, total state aid from the two basic programs was $256 million. Grants from the flat grant plan totaled $89 million (35 percent) and foundation plan grants totaled $167 million (65 percent).[8] By

2. U.S. Department of Health, Education and Welfare, *State Programs for Public School Support* (Washington, D.C., 1965), p. 33; U.S. Department of Health, Education and Welfare, *Public School Finance Program 1962–63* (Washington, D.C., 1965).

3. See generally ILL. STAT. ANN. ch. 122, § 18 (Smith-Hurd Supp. 1967).

4. ILL. STAT. ANN. ch. 122, § 18-8(1) (Smith-Hurd Supp. 1967).

5. ILL. STAT. ANN. ch. 122, § 18-8(2) (Smith-Hurd Supp. 1967).

6. See Illinois Education Association, *Common School Aid in Illinois* (December, 1963).

7. U.S. Department of Health, Education and Welfare, *State Programs*, p. 33.

8. Superintendent of Public Instruction, Division of Finance and Statistics,

Table 9

Illinois aid dollars per ADA pupil

Year	Flat grant All districts	Foundation Guarantee
1927	9	34
1935	11	41
1939	11	51
1941	11	56
1943	13	52
1945	19	80
1947	22	90
1949	22	160
1953	22	173
1955	22	200
1959	47[a]	252
1965	47	330
1967	47[b]	400

[a] 32, high school pupils
[b] 54.05, high school pupils

1968–69, total aid had reached $357 million, $98 million in flat grants (27 percent), and $259 million in foundation plain aid (73 percent).[9] Of course, the reader should be skeptical about whether the change in proportion has really meant increased equalization. In fact, it has.

Illinois has a plethora of school districts. Not only are there frequent divisions between high school and elementary bases, but the districts are small: the total number was 1,336 for 1967–68.[10] This pattern remains despite efforts through state

Illinois Amended State Aid Claim Statistics: Illinois Public Schools 1965–1966 School Year, Circular Series A, no. 196, 1967.

9. Superintendent of Public Instruction, Division of Finance and Statistics, Annual State Aid Claim Statistics: Illinois Public Schools 1967–68, Circular Series A, no. 231, 1968.

10. Superintendent of Public Instruction, Division of Finance and Statistics, 1965 Assessed Valuations and 1966 Tax Rates in Descending Order of Illinois Public Schools, Circular Series A, no. 198, 1967.

legislation to stimulate consolidation. The state scheme contemplates elementary (kindergarten through eighth grade), high school (grades 9–12), and unit districts (kindergarten–12). The state aid plan, moreover, makes it possible generally for districts to obtain more state funds as unit districts rather than as separate high school and elementary districts.[11] Nevertheless, even in geographically coextensive situations the separate district structure has remained.[12]

The large number of districts is important because, given the limited state aid commitment, it is a major source of inequality in terms of educational offering. The smaller the districts, the more widely the wealth among them will vary; and where the system, as in Illinois, adjusts so little for wealth, the disparity is devastating. This accounts, perhaps, for the eagerness of Illinois educators to promote larger districts as one segment of financial reform. However, when the rich are able to exploit their wealth better by remaining in smaller districts, a permissive state approach is unlikely to produce voluntary consolidation of geographically separate districts of unequal wealth, except in rare instances of significant economies of scale.

The flat grant portion of the aid is given to every district that meets certain nonfinancial requirements. In 1968–69 it was in the amount of $47 per ADA elementary pupil and $54.05 per ADA high school pupil.[13] The district does not have to tax at any particular level of effort to receive this money, and of course, by its nature, this form of aid is unrelated to other funds the district can raise locally because of its own wealth. Flat

11. See R. N. Puffer, "A Private Study," unpub. paper (1967) on file in the author's office at Northwestern University.

12. Part of the reason may be the debt limitations which apply to school districts. Thus, while receiving less aid, a community may be able to at least double its potential bond funding by having separate high school and elementary districts. See generally ILLINOIS SCHOOL CODE art. 19.

13. ILL. STAT. ANN. ch. 122, § 18-8 (Smith-Hurd Supp. 1967).

grant and foundation aid are both given for the district to spend in meeting current expenses only.

The foundation portion of the state aid plan is programmed as follows. Elementary and high school districts must tax at 8.4 mills and unit districts at 10 mills to participate. Adding the amount of funds raised by that local assessment to the amount of funds available to the district through the flat grant plan, the state subsidizes the district up to the foundation level of $400 per ADA elementary pupil and, by special provision, effectively $452 per ADA high school pupil; whether this higher level for high school is more than a temporary legislative departure is unclear. As to the mechanics of the plan: if, for example, an elementary school district raises $200 per pupil through the 8.4-mill local tax, this, combined with the $47 flat grant, gives it $247 of the $400, and the state will add $153. If the amount raised locally were $500 through the 8.4 mills there will be no foundation aid, in which case the district might choose not to levy at the 8.4-mill rate at all, depending upon what its overall educational aspirations are. For such a district, local effort is unrelated to state support and the $47 flat grant aid would be forthcoming anyway.

In short, Illinois employs a Type 2 combination plan, and under the present facts some of the flat grant aid is anti-equalizing in the manner suggested in Chapter 3. Recall that in the absence of any flat grants, but given the same $400 equalizing level, all those districts which now receive *anything* in state equalizing aid would still receive the same *total* grant they do now from the state. This, of course, is because the flat grant aid is counted as part of the local share in the equalizing formula. The upshot is that flat grants are only meaningful for those elementary districts which produce $353 per ADA pupil ($400, the foundation amount, minus $47, the flat grant) or more at the participation rate. That is, such districts get outright at least $47 per ADA pupil, which is more than they would get under the equalizing plan taken alone. Clearly, then, to the extent that there are such rich districts, this part of the state aid plan is anti-equalizing. The incidence of this anti-equalizing effect is mainly in high school districts, but it exists in the other two types of districts as well. This being the case, it should be understood that all the foundation aid is equalizing — not equalizing enough, clearly, but "equalizing" describes whatever the foundation part of the plan provides. This, again, is because at the participation rate in all three kinds of districts none of the foundation aid goes to the richest districts.

Two further features should be noted. First, the Illinois formula takes little account of major differences in the cost of educating high school and elementary school pupils (there is a difference of about $50 per pupil in state aid if a possibly temporary fourteen-percent extra high school support is included in the foundation plan); it is, therefore, a throwback to the most simple Strayer-Haig model. Secondly there are typically about seven elementary school pupils for every three high school pupils. Hence, where two districts occupy the same geographic area the high school district has the same tax base for many fewer pupils than the elementary district; as a result it has a much greater assessed valuation per pupil. In Illinois, at the minimum rate required for participation in the foundation program, few of the high school districts would raise less than the amount which a high school district can raise and still get foundation aid. Further, the cost of high school education for pupils in almost all districts is well beyond the guarantee level of the foundation plan. Therefore, except for flat grants, high school districts by and large function apart from the aid program altogether.

Figure 4-1 represents the range of offerings for high school districts in Illinois if all were to tax at the participation rate of 8.4 mills. (Using $400 as the foundation guarantee and $54 as

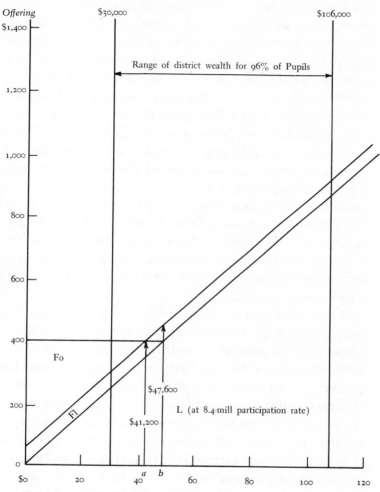

Illinois high school districts (wealth in $1,000's AVPP)

Fl, flat grant aid; Fo, foundation aid; L, local share

FIGURE 4-1

the flat aid, the horizontal line should be raised about $50 if the special 14-percent bonus high school aid plan is to remain.) Districts with wealth up to point a ($41,200 per ADA pupil) would receive foundation aid; using 1968–69 figures[14] those districts contain but 10 percent of all high school pupils, or 25,000 of 250,000. These districts would receive the same total aid with only a foundation plan, as discussed earlier. Districts with wealth between points a and b ($41,200 per ADA pupil and $47,600 per ADA pupil) are poor enough so that if there were no flat grant they would get some foundation aid; but they are rich enough so that they raise more than $346 per ADA pupil at 8.4 mills and hence would receive only flat aid under the Illinois Type 2 plan. Districts with wealth above point b (greater than $47,600 per ADA pupil) would receive flat aid but would get no aid if only the foundation plan were in operation; nearly 80 percent of the students attending public high school are in such districts.

Hence, some of the aid given above a and all given above b is anti-equalizing. Considering, for convenience, those high school districts with 96 percent of the pupils, this can be illustrated with the kind of charts used previously (see Figures 4-2 and 4-3). In short, while all the foundation aid is equalizing (therefore, raising the level from $330 to $400 without changing the participation rate meant that all increased money given through the plan was equalizing money), it is trivial in amount. It goes exclusively to districts with only 10 percent of the pupils and helps them hardly at all. In 1966–67 high school districts together received $600,000 in foundation aid and $11,100,000 in flat grant aid. From the dramatic range of offering yielded at the participation rate, $306–$944 per ADA pupil, it should be no surprise that the range of effort is also large —

14. Data supplied by Illinois Superintendent of Public Instruction, on file with the authors. All subsequent statewide figures are from this source.

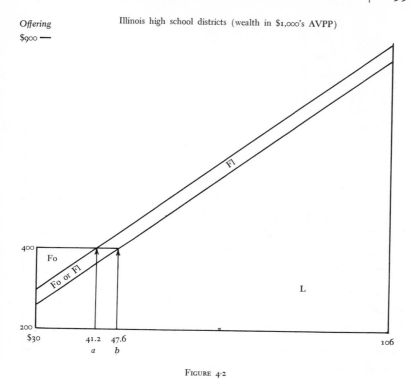

Offering

$900 —

Illinois high school districts (wealth in $1,000's AVPP)

Fl

400

Fo

Fo or Fl

L

200

$30   41.2   47.6   106
             a   *b*

FIGURE 4-2

many districts tax at less than the participation rate (72 percent of 211 in 1967) and many at substantially more.

Elementary school districts, typically with more than twice the pupils but the same gross valuation as counterpart high school districts, are less wealthy and are thus more frequently equalized. Still, a number of the elementary districts are rich enough to raise more than $353 per ADA pupil ($400 — $47) thereby making some of the flat aid anti-equalizing. Figure 4-4 portrays the elementary district situation. Elementary districts with wealth of more than $47,600 per ADA pupil are receiving flat aid but generate $400 per pupil locally at 8.4 mills and hence would receive no aid if there were no flat grant. Everything they get is anti-equalizing. Yet the elementary districts

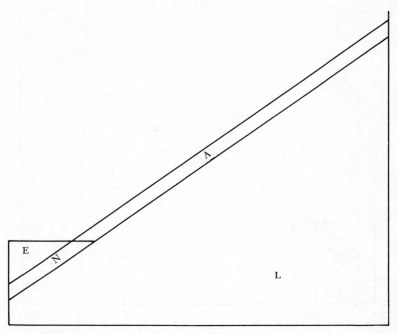

A, anti-equalizing; E, equalizing; N, nonequalizing; L, local

FIGURE 4-3

with wealth of $47,600 per ADA pupil and less have about 95 percent of the pupils (573,000 of 606,000); thus a relative few are substantially better off at the participation rate. In 1968, however, 612 of 723 elementary districts taxed above the participation rate; at higher levels of taxation the sloped line which always represents the result of local effort takes over and dominates the picture. Most elementary districts want programs above the $400 level, but the poorer districts have a significantly harder time getting them. If all districts taxed at 11 mills, for example, Figure 4-5 would demonstrate the offering/wealth relationship for those districts with the middle 96 percent of the pupils.

Illinois Elementary districts (wealth in $1,000's AVPP)

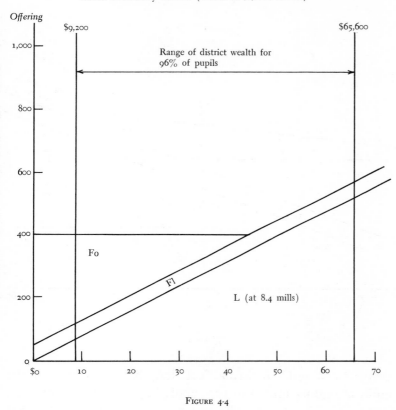

FIGURE 4-4

The foundation aid is quite helpful to the elementary districts. Of the $88 million in state aid received by elementary districts in 1966–67, $61 million was from the foundation plan. Still, it is disappointing that, so long as many districts wish to tax above the participation rate, the other $27 million is distributed in a nonequalizing or even anti-equalizing fashion. Ultimately, of course, the disappointment lies in the very use of the foundation/flat plan.

Finally, consider the unit districts. Those with wealth of $40,000 per pupil in ADA will raise enough money locally at the participation rate ($400 per pupil) for any flat aid they

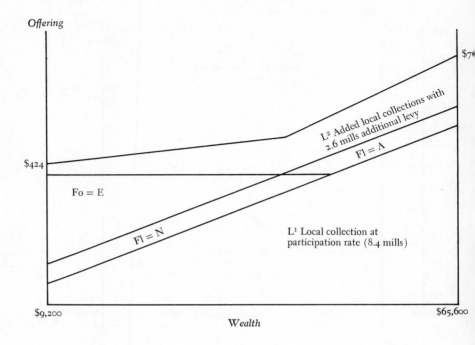

FIGURE 4-5

receive to be anti-equalizing. Yet, less than 1 percent of the pupils attending unit district schools live in districts that rich (11,000 of 1,160,000 pupils). Of the $174 million in aid that the unit districts received in 1966–67 from all state funds, the districts too rich to receive foundation aid received but $1.5 million. This latter figure includes all the aid to the districts which would have begun to receive foundation aid if there were no flat aid; in 1966–67 the foundation level was only at $330 rather than $400. Hence, today the amount of the anti-equalizing aid to unit districts is less than $1.5 million; a good estimate is about $600,000.

This relatively good news about anti-equalizing does not mean that the whole picture is bright. In 1966–67, $53 million of the $174 million total was given as flat, nonequalizing aid.

This would not be so objectionable if unit districts were content to tax at the 10-mill participating rate; but the facts are that in 1968 only 2 of 383 unit districts taxed at below the participation rate, while 244 unit districts taxed above 15 mills. Hence, as in the elementary districts, effort above the participating rate far more easily boosts richer unit districts into the better offerings than it does the poorer. Consider Figure 4-6,

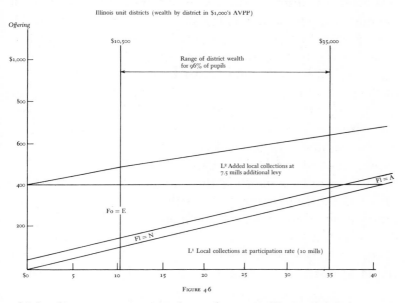

FIGURE 4-6

which shows money raised at the 10-mill participation rate (L_1), the flat aid (fl), the foundation aid (fo), and money raised at an extra effort of 7.5 mills (L_2). Assuming a uniform local 17.5-mill effort (close to today's average unit district effort), the offerings (including state aid) for the 96 percent of the pupils in the middle range would vary from $480 to $660, the rich getting over one-third more dollars without higher effort. The reader is invited to speculate about what might be purchased with this $180 per pupil — in a classroom of 30 students it represents $5,400 a year, more than a teacher earns in some parts of Illinois. If 30 students per class were the rule at $480 per pupil, then one choice at $660 per pupil could be to lower the class size to perhaps 22 pupils. In such a setting to disburse more than $50 million in nonequalizing rather than equalizing aid is indefensible.

Following this analytical view of the Illinois system as it operates in each of the three kinds of districts, some general data about the districts will help to illustrate the magnitude of the problem. The wealth range, using the most recent data, is from $4,748 to $416,401 per pupil for elementary districts; from $27,409 to $292,166 for high school districts; and from $3,976 to $107,703 for unit districts. If districts attended by the 80 per cent of pupils in the middle range are examined, the spread, of course, is considerably narrowed: for elementary districts, from $12,573 to $40,584 per pupil; high school, $41,253 to $85,372; unit, $13,391 to $24,294. Still, for this bulk of the pupils, those at the high end are supported by what is often twice the wealth supporting those at the low end. In such a situation the foundation plan, with or without a flat plan, simply cannot bring justice to the poor districts until the foundation level is raised to the level of the district with the best offering — at which time the program will have been converted in effect into a uniform, centralized system of finance.

Cook County, Illinois: Elementary Districts

As a special experiment, the results of the Illinois Type 2 foundation plan will be considered as manifested in Tables 10, 11, and 12 depicting the relations between wealth, effort, and offering in the 119 elementary districts in Cook County (Chicago itself has a unit district and is excluded) using the 1966–67 data.[15] These districts were selected in part because of the

15. The raw data upon which the Cook County analysis was made appear in a series of papers prepared by the Illinois Office of the Superintendent of Public Instruction, on file in the School of Law, University of California, Berkeley.

Table 10

Joint distribution of wealth and offering in Cook County
elementary districts by quartile (Q-1 is highest)

		Wealth				
		Q-1	Q-2	Q-3	Q-4	Total
Offering	Q-1	20	8	1	0	29
	Q-2	7	15	7	1	30
	Q-3	3	5	16	6	30
	Q-4	0	2	6	22	30
	Total	30	30	30	29	

Table 11

Cook County, Illinois, elementary districts: matrix of numbers of
districts by wealth and effort (local property tax rate)

		Wealth				
		Q-1	Q-2	Q-3	Q-4	Total
Effort	Q-1	2	12	12	5	31
	Q-2	3	8	9	10	30
	Q-3	7	5	6	11	29
	Q-4	18	5	3	3	29
	Total	30	30	30	29	

Table 12

Cook County, Illinois, elementary districts: matrix of numbers
of districts by offering and effort

		Offering				
		Q-1	Q-2	Q-3	Q-4	Total
Effort	Q-1	8	11	10	2	31
	Q-2	5	6	9	10	30
	Q-3	3	8	6	12	29
	Q-4	13	5	5	6	29
	Total	29	30	30	30	

assumed similar cost of living throughout the Chicago metropolitan area and in part because of their general suburban nature, so that the sample contains somewhat comparable items. The districts were analyzed by quartiles. Q-1 represents the highest quartile, that is, it includes the top 30 (approximately) districts of the 119. A matrix chart comparing wealth and offering thus will show how many of the wealthier districts (that is, Q-1) also had the best offering (Q-1), the next best category (Q-2), and so on; and, similarly, how many of the districts with the best offering were the wealthiest, poorest, and so on. If there is no relation between the factors we can expect the quantity to be uniformly 7 or 8 (7-1/2 times 4 equals 30). "Offering" includes local, state, and federal contributions. Tables 10 to 12 illustrate the propositions that, for the districts sampled under the Illinois plan, *a good offering is primarily the result of wealth, not effort,* and that *greater effort tends to be expended by those with less wealth.*

These conclusions should be examined in greater detail, starting with wealth and offering. The good offering is highly associated with wealth. In Table 10, of the 29 best offerings (read across from Q-1 offering), 20 are in the wealthiest districts (Q-1 wealth) and 8 in other districts also of above-average (Q-2) wealth. Similarly, a poor offering is well correlated with low wealth; of the 30 worst offerings (read across from Q-4 offering) 22 were from the poorest (Q-4 wealth) districts, 6 from the next poorest (Q-3 wealth). Hence, despite state aid and the impact, if any, of higher effort examined below, poor districts come out on the short end of the offering stick. Little has been accomplished to overcome a purely local-finance model in which wealth and offering are perfectly correlated: the upper left to lower right diagonal through the matrix contains 73 of the 119 entries, while the reverse diagonal (upper right to lower left) contains but 12.

Consider the relationship from the perspective of wealth in

Table 10. Not only do 20 of the 30 wealthiest districts provide offerings in the highest category, but 7 more produce the offerings in the next best quartile; none are among the lowest quartile in offering. At the other end, of the 29 poorest districts, only one provides an offering above average. Next, notice that offering does not show any particularly significant relation to effort. In Table 12 the best offerings (Q-1 down) are most often the product of the least effort (13 of 29). On the other hand, wealth and effort show a strong inverse relation, as seen in Table 11. The wealthier districts simply tax themselves less than the poorer ones do. From Table 11 it is seen that, of the 30 wealthiest districts, only 2 were in the top quartile in terms of effort but 18 were in the bottom quartile. Similarly, of the 61 below average wealth districts, 36 were above average in effort while 23 were below average.

Putting this relationship of effort and wealth (inverse if anything) together with the one manifested by offering and wealth (strong), the conclusion forcefully appears that it is wealth alone which means good offering, and that even though the poor districts characteristically tax high they are unable to catch up, so great is their relative poverty. It might be noted that the same experiment was run with 1964–65 data and yielded the same conclusions with the same clarity. At that time the relative number of ADA pupils (the "size" of the district) was also evaluated for any impact or correlation that might be revealed, but no important relation to the size of the district was discovered.[16]

What is the magnitude of the problem of inequality for Cook County elementary districts? One index is the range and distribution of offering, effort, and wealth involved. For 1966–67, in terms of wealth, the overall range on an assessed valuation per-pupil basis was from a low of $8,066 to a high of $231,203. Even eliminating the one incredibly wealthy dis-

16. The data and relations are set out in Appendix D.

trict, the next highest was $101,739 per pupil, which makes it a full 12 times wealthier than the poorest district in the county. At the quartiles, the assessed valuations were: Q-1 equals over $40,000, Q-2 over $25,000, Q-3 over $15,300, Q-4 under $15,-300 — so that the district in the 75th percentile (bottom of Q-1) has wealth which is 261 percent of that in the 25th percentile. Herein, of course, is the root of the problem.

Having shown that, if anything, the poor districts tend to make greater effort, the offering range is important because it illustrates in numbers what the tables show only generally: offering remains quite varied, just as it would if there were no state aid and uniform effort. For the Cook County elementary districts in 1966–67, offering ranges from a high of $1,106 (actually $1,469 in the one especially rich district) to a low of $407. This is a disparity of more than two and a half to one. Also consider the quartile variations: Q-1 equals more than $695 per ADA pupil, Q-2 more than $580, Q-3 more than $495, and Q-4 less than $495. Therefore, the district in the 75th percentile has an offering, measured in terms of dollars spent per ADA pupil, 140 percent that of the district at the 25th percentile. In the elementary districts, the Illinois version of the foundation plan cannot and does not effect equality from any angle.

Cook County, Illinois: High School Districts

A similar study was made of the high school districts in Cook County, using 1966–67 data. This was an examination of a system of almost pure local finance. As emphasized earlier, these districts have a great enough tax base so that equalization aid is almost never available to them. Of course, all receive flat grants. But as this support for high school districts is only $54.05 per ADA pupil even now it is nearly inconsequential.

The dimensions of variation among the districts were again enormous. Wealth ranged from $31,000 to $108,200 per pupil — a ratio of more than 3 to 1. The quartile figures were: Q-1 equals $73,900 or more, Q-2 61,900 to $73,500, Q-3 $47,200 to $60,500, Q-4 $41,700 and less. Property tax rates varied from 7.9 to 15.7 mills, a 2 to 1 ratio. Expenditures ranged from $716 to $1,400 per ADA pupil: nearly twice the offering in the best district compared with the worst. The middle 50 percent of the districts spent between $875 and $1,055, which meant that the better provided over 20 percent more than the worse.

An examination of offering, effort, and wealth demonstrates that the same relations between these factors are present in the high school districts as those that appeared in the elementary ones, and that they are perhaps stronger. Consider Tables 13, 14, and 15, which compare wealth, effort and offering on

Table 13

Cook County, Illinois, high school districts: matrix of number of districts by wealth and offering

| | | Wealth | | | | |
		Q-1	Q-2	Q-3	Q-4	Total
Offering	Q-1	5	2	0	0	7
	Q-2	2	2	2	1	7
	Q-3	0	2	4	1	7
	Q-4	0	1	1	5	7
	Total	7	7	7	7	

Table 14

Cook County, Illinois, high school districts: matrix of numbers of districts by effort and wealth

| | | Effort | | | | |
		Q-1	Q-2	Q-3	Q-4	Total
Wealth	Q-1	1	0	2	4	7
	Q-2	1	1	2	3	7
	Q-3	1	4	2	0	7
	Q-4	4	2	1	0	7
	Total	7	7	7	7	

Table 15

Cook County, Illinois, high school districts: matrix of numbers
of districts by effort and offering

| | | Effort | | | | |
		Q-1	Q-2	Q-3	Q-4	Total
Offering	Q-1	2	0	2	3	7
	Q-2	2	0	2	3	7
	Q-3	0	5	1	1	7
	Q-4	3	2	2	0	7
	Total	7	7	7	7	

a quartile basis for the Cook County high school districts. The
absence of a relation shows as a 1, 2, or 3; the average is 1.75.

The pattern is clear. Wealth is highly related to offering, as
five of the seven best offerings are produced by the seven
wealthiest districts and five of the seven poorest offerings come
from the seven poorest districts. The relation between wealth
and effort is equally striking. Only one of the wealthiest districts (Q-1) applied more than average effort, and all but one
of the poorest districts (Q-4) more than average. Finally, it can
be stated fairly that the offering/effort relationship is nonexistent. The upshot is that wealth and offering are strongly
related, and wealth and effort are strongly inversely related.

Since wealth distribution among Cook County districts is
similar to that throughout the state as a whole, it can be expected that the inequalities operating generally in Illinois will
be similar to those exposed here. For example, as a final test
consider Table 16, in which the one hundred high school districts with more than a thousand pupils each in ADA are categorized for comparison of wealth and effort, using 1964–65
data. The table demonstrates once again that the poorest districts, generally, must pay greater property tax rates than the
rich ones.

Table 16

*Illinois high school districts with more than 1,000 ADA pupils:
matrix of numbers of districts by wealth and effort*

		Wealth				
		Q-1	Q-2	Q-3	Q-4	Total
Effort	Q-1	1	5	8	11	25
	Q-2	4	8	6	7	25
	Q-3	4	8	7	6	25
	Q-4	16	4	4	1	25
	Total	25	25	25	25	

A final point: the major source of the money used by the
State of Illinois for distribution to the various districts was the
state sales tax. It is important at least to raise the question of
the impact such a collection program might have on equal
educational opportunity. Can equality be produced solely by
adjustment at the level of state funds? Does it matter if the
sales tax generally falls proportionately on Illinois citizens? No
answer will be given for the moment, but the fact that there
are a number of complexities involved in addition to wealth,
effort, and offering should be remembered when proposed
solutions to existing inequality are evaluated.

The general conclusions to be drawn about the Illinois system are:

(1) In *elementary* districts, the flat grant part of the program is largely inoperative (although in part it is anti-equalizing), and the "equalizing" portion is woefully inadequate to
produce any kind of equality; consequently the rich enjoy substantial wealth advantages.

(2) In *high school* districts, the equalizing program is hardly
operative. The flat grant part is largely anti-equalizing but is
altogether so small as to make these districts almost wholly

dependent upon local finance. Hence, dramatic wealth/offering and poverty/effort relations appear. In these crucial precollege years, the rich districts have a tremendous advantage.

(3) *Unit districts* are much like elementary districts, and correlation studies should illustrate a wealth/offering relation of the same magnitude. In any event, as so many unit districts tax well above the participation rate, the syndrome of greater dollars to the rich for similar effort is clearly repeated.

(4) In *all three kinds of districts*, the school system which Illinois has set up must produce inequality; it is designed to discriminate against the poor districts because of their poverty.

(5) The analysis of complex state systems in terms of wealth discrimination can be made convincing without esoteric economics or statistics.

SIMPLER STATE SYSTEMS

At last count, only seven states do not have what can be termed a state-local partnership in the financing of education. The decentralized states, first, provide so little state aid that school finance becomes almost entirely a matter of local responsibility in the manner of the 1800's. The states thus categorized by the Office of Education are Iowa, Nebraska, New Hampshire, and South Dakota.[17] The labels are somewhat misleading. Although state aid given in New Hampshire is only about ten percent of the total statewide spending for education, it is all at least intended to be of an equalizing sort. On the other hand, state aid in Nebraska and South Dakota is in the form of flat grants, which puts them perhaps even closer to being models of the early days of school finance. These systems are designed systematically to discriminate on the basis of wealth. Nevertheless, on a *comparative* basis, the states with decentralized financing will not necessarily show up worst in terms of in-

17. U.S. Department of Health, Education and Welfare, *State Programs*.

equality of offering or effort. A condition of unusually low variation in wealth may exist among the state's school districts that may even partially explain the failure to change to a modern system.

The centralized jurisdictions represent an extreme of an entirely different sort. Three states fit this model according to the Office of Education, Delaware, Hawaii, and North Carolina.[18] But even they must be placed in two categories: Hawaii is fully centralized in that there is but one school district operated by the state Department of Education,[19] whereas in the other two financing is still on a state aid to local district basis. Hawaii minimizes subsidiarity — the approach many observers might choose in attempting to eliminate the evil of local wealth as a determinant of quality. Of course, it is neither the necessary solution nor the one we advocate.

The Hawaii model is not necessarily fully destructive of subsidiarity. Even where centralized funding is adopted, management sciences often may dictate considerable decentralization of the supervision of public education; willingness to let the decentralized units try differing approaches with their allotted funds would be likely. (In Hawaii each county submits a budget for school expenditure to the state.) Much of today's district approach would remain even if stripped of local variation in available funds — if, for example, the state took over the property tax, levied uniformly, returned dollars to the districts based upon task, and prohibited added local tax-raising effort. Functionally, this is what would occur under a fully equalized foundation plan where the foundation is higher than any district wants to or is allowed to go, so that all districts offer education at the "maximum."

Thus the centralized "Hawaii model" easily includes local administrative decision-making. It would be subsidiarity to a

18. *Ibid.*
19. See generally HAWAII REV. LAWS tit. 6 (Supp. 1965).

degree, but it strips subsidiarity of its crucial attribute, *local determination of the degree of commitment* for education. It eliminates more than wealth as a factor, for it destroys incentive. If a state wants to keep this aspect of subsidiarity alive (we think it is a good idea, and constitutionally permissible if properly structured), then the Hawaii approach is inadequate. A more sophisticated method would have as its goal achievement of both equality of financial power and local incentive; such a method is, indeed, possible.

Although Delaware[20] and North Carolina[21] combine local administration with generally centralized finance, they both allow local supplementary financing and it is generally employed by the districts. Therefore, although the state pays for more than eighty percent of the cost of education in these jurisdictions, state aid analytically is no more than a flat grant; but as a practical matter inequality will not be too large, because, so long as the flat amount remains high enough to satisfy most felt needs of most districts, the amount of extra money which the districts spend will not be so very large. Moreover, the general spreading of the tax base becomes more important as the state share rises. Hence, there is clearly a tendency toward an equalization of sorts. Nonetheless, surely the Utah equalizing approach, which also involves a large state proportion, is a more satisfactory one than is the Delaware-North Carolina approach.

20. See DEL. CODE ANN. tit. 14, ch. 13 (State Supported Salary Schedule for School Employees), ch. 15 (Fiscal Provisions), ch. 17 (State Appropriations), and ch. 19 (Local School Taxes) (1953 and Supp. 1966). See also *Annual Report, 1965–66*, Statistical Section, Delaware Department of Public Instruction (Dover, 1966).

21. See N.C. GEN. STAT. ch. 115 (1966 and Supp. 1967). For an analysis of the North Carolina plan, consult Office of the State Superintendent of Public Instruction, *Current Expenditures by Source of Funds, 1965–66* (Raleigh, 1966).

REFINEMENTS OF THE MEASURE

At this point the tools for analysis of school financing require some further clarifications. The first has to do with the distinction between current and capital expenditures. Among various states the notion of current expenses differs. The basic demarcation is, most commonly, between administrative, instructional, and operating expenses on the one hand, and capital outlay, debt retirement, and debt service on the other. What is crucial is that most state aid programs give funds only for current expenses, variously defined, and thus do little or nothing to adjust for the ability of districts to provide physical plant. That ability is clearly related to local wealth.

Why, then, does this book focus upon school financing for current expenditures only and not for capital outlay (primarily physical plant)? There are a number of reasons; but note first that, to the extent that we neglect to subject the capital expenditure problems to a wealth determinant analysis, we have spared our easiest target. If we demonstrate inequality under systems that have been created to diminish wealth discrimination, the capital expenditures case is a fortiori, for "equalizing" programs have rarely extended to capital costs. In the second place, most experts agree that current expenses are much more clearly related to the kind of education provided than are physical facilities, particularly once the school has overcome the minimum requirement of sufficient classrooms. Third, the total spending for current expenditures greatly exceeds that for physical plant. Finally, it is in the area of current expenditures that the historic conflict over wealth and equal opportunity has been fought and that the educational ideology at stake has grown up and is most clearly articulated.

A simpler point involves the definition of education: we have been concerned primarily with what might be called the "vertical" shortcomings of public school finance and state aid —

the effect of the wealth ladder. Obviously, equalization can also be blocked by stingy horizontal definitions and mechanisms. A fully equalized state aid program which supports library books but nothing else does not remove wealth determinants from quality of education.

A broader issue is posed by the assumption so far that the measures employed by the state for wealth, effort, and offering are a sufficient index of discrimination by wealth in education. In fact, there are some difficulties in this regard that deserve at least passing attention before the discussion of traditional systems is concluded. The general question is: to what extent is it possible to determine who is being hurt by the system, and to what extent should that knowledge shape our attitude toward the system? Given this focus, inquiry will first be into the extent that discrimination against poor districts entails discrimination against poor people.

What is at stake in such an inquiry is merely a better understanding of the complexity of the relation of district and individual poverty. Our position does not depend upon the existence of such a relation. A strong preference for educational systems freed of wealth determinants (and specifically our own scheme for "power-equalizing" — see Chapter 6) would continue even if the victims of the present systems were not the children of the poor or even if they were random with respect to individual wealth. Our concern is as much for the children of middle-class and wealthy parents as for those of poor; it may appear that we have been casual about their interests simply because we see fewer threats within the system to their personal fulfillment. So far in this book the common-sense identification of district poverty with the poor family living in the ghetto of Newark or on the wrong side of the tracks in a dying coal town or on a corner of land in rural America has been accepted. But there are nonpoor living in poor districts and their children, too, are cheated. To purify our purposes, we could go even further — as we will when we come to speak of the law — and concede that concern about poor families and poor people can become excessive and misleading. Distinctions between children that are based upon wealth are problematic because, after all, every child is poor; it is parents among whom wealth differs. Even a distribution of resources *favoring* children of poor families on the basis of their poverty would be questionable, for it would discriminate against the poor children of nonpoor families. Why should any child be discriminated against in his *public* education by reason of anybody's wealth, including that of his parents? This view is not complicated by the fascinating general question of when the interest of the child should be assimilated to and identified with the interest of the parent. The state has prescinded from this issue by making education compulsory: children with rich parents, poor parents, or no parents at all must attend school, making the child and not the parent the proper focus.

In short, we think it wrong for the state to make any child's education a function of district wealth; it is merely more vicious when the victims are children of the poor. But, setting aside commitments of this sort, let us consider briefly the factual relation between the collective poverty of the district and the individual poverty of its residents.

Even before the individual victim can be identified with particularity, an injured district must be defined. This has not quite yet been settled; what we have established is the relative truth that the poorer the district, the more injured it is. But if the intention is to announce a relation between being poor and being injured, we should have a standard for inclusion and exclusion of districts. In a system of wealth discrimination with a wide spectrum of wealth this is not an easy task. In one sense the disadvantaged districts are all those in the state except the richest; compared with the richest, every other district is saddled with the second-class status of relative poverty.

But, in another sense, as compared with the poorest district every other district is advantaged because of its relative affluence. A third perspective could focus on who stands to gain and who stands to be hurt by the elimination of wealth variation from the system. One is tempted to say simply that those with below-average wealth will benefit at the expense of those with above-average wealth. Yet it is difficult to ignore the possibility that some districts with wealth somewhat above average would feel themselves gainers if they were able to stand on a par with the super-rich, even if it also means standing beside everybody else. In short, from the view of any particular district except the richest, a claim that the system is discriminating against it is plausible or at least intelligible.

The problem becomes even more complex when the queston of who the specific victims of the system are is added to the identification of a poor district. Some of the potential perspectives can be illustrated here.

The correlation of district and individual poverty seems high as a matter of common sense, yet it is by no means factually clear; but this very lack of clarity is adequate to condemn the system. To the extent that poor districts in fact contain poor families and rich districts rich, the policy of favoring rich districts is merely intolerable. To the extent that there is a jumble in the rich-people/rich-district and poor-people/poor-district pattern, the policy is utterly irrational. Only if reality is topsy-turvy from appearances, and the character of the districts is in fact fully inversely related to the character of the residents, could the present state programs be defended. In that case, although we would not favor it, the system would be defensible, for the state would be aiding upward mobility by giving the children of the poor a chance at better education. But, of course, this view of the facts is insupportable; the present systems are to some undefined extent systematically hurting children of poverty families unfairly and children of both the rich and poor arbitrarily.

Furthermore, however doubtful the general relation, one can always pick out a district whose poverty in taxable wealth corresponds to and may be caused by the poverty of its residents, and, similarly, one can point to some rich district whose rich population parallels or is the source of its taxable wealth. This comparison, whether representative of an entire state or not, is in itself enough to damn the system. Regardless of how children in any other districts are affected, these children in a certain district when compared with another district are victimized because of collective wealth differences that are rendered all the more poignant by their own family's poverty. They may not care how the state policy influences other poor and rich people; plainly, they can argue that it is wealth-based decision-making which is destroying their chance of equal educational opportunity. Of course, some poor families do live in the same communities as the rich and therefore benefit from the current system, just as the children of wealthy families living in a poor district are being harmed to the extent of devaluation of their public school option. But this hardly makes the state policy seem fairer to the complaining parties in poor districts who cannot understand why the poor who live near wealth should get ahead more than those who do not.

Another factor that confounds full understanding of the system's effects is inclusion in the tax base of industrial and commercial property. This kind of wealth, located in districts of poor people, can allow them a greater share of state wealth than would be available to them on a personal-wealth basis alone. In fact this is what often makes industrial and commercial centers with large numbers of poor people living in them relatively rich. Nonetheless, since by no means all districts which would otherwise be poor are fortunate enough to have this nonresidential property sitting within their geographic boundaries to be taxed, its sometime presence is clearly no justification for the present scheme. By allowing districts to tax local industrial and commercial property the state is really supplementing the personal local wealth of the people of that district just as it does through state aid; but, if the appropriate principle is that wealth variation should cease to affect public education, the adventitious location of nonresidential property in poor districts can scarcely be cited as a rational equalizing device. It should be noted too that many districts with rich residents also have sizable amounts of commercial and industrial property within them, boosting them even further ahead in the education race. Our data would be far more reliable and convincing, and the system as a whole more rationalized (but possibly worse), if industrial and commercial property were taken off the local tax roles for education purposes, leaving other elements as is. Then the rich-people/high-offering, poor-people/low-offering relationship would be more dramatically exposed.

Another, quite different, consideration must be faced: the adequacy of property as an index of wealth. This raises the issues of incidence and regressiveness of taxes to be analyzed in Chapter 6. The matter is particularly important here as applied to real property, inasmuch as most states include only this kind of accumulated wealth in the property tax base. To the extent that one socioeconomic class more than another tends to tie up its wealth in realty, this form of wealth measure is biased.[22] Superficially, one could suggest that poor people

---

22. The evidence on this point is inconclusive: "Although property tax revenues correlate very highly with personal income in a given county or region, the correlation among individuals is very imperfect"; Jesse Burkhead, *State and Local Taxes for Public Education* (Syracuse: Syracuse University Press, 1963), p. 32. We do not know whether school districts are as well correlated as counties or regions. The evidence presented in Chapter 6 that

tend to have none of their property held as realty; that middle class homeowners tend to have a great deal committed thus; and that wealthy people have a relatively small proportion so involved in that they tend to hold intangibles (stocks and bonds) and personalty (jewelry and boats) in larger amounts. Nevertheless, at least in regard to the poor, this superficial analysis could be misleading: to the extent that they rent living accommodations, they may well suffer part of the impact of the property tax on their apartment building or house through rent payments. The question is disputed,[23] but, assuming that such taxes are passed on in full to the poor man, he has perhaps a greater part of his wealth involved in the object of the tax than any other class in that twenty-five percent or more of his income will likely go toward paying for shelter. The problem of shifting tax incidence probably does not exist so significantly in the case of the homeowner or landowner who keeps his property for noncommercial purposes. The upshot is that the use of real property valuation as the wealth measure may make districts with numerous poor residents appear somewhat richer than they really are. This, if we focus on it alone, makes our general argument a fortiori.

Since, in general, districts that *appear* poor in assessed valuation tend to have cheaper offerings, and vice versa, it is difficult to believe that the relation between property valuation and "true" wealth is really universally inverted or even merely unreliable. The fact that all the famed high-offering schools are in districts both rich in assessed value and rich in family wealth (New Trier, Scarsdale, and so on) may not be proof, but it is

---

the tax is at least mildly regressive suggests that where there are groups of poor people there will be some overvaluation of wealth (current income). See J. A. Thomas, *School Finance and Educational Opportunity in Michigan* (Lansing: Michigan Department of Education, 1968), p. 183.

23. The Thomas study quoted above assumes that 75% of real property taxes on rental property is borne by renters; *ibid.*, pp. 185–186. See generally Chapter 6, below.

scarcely accident. The probability is overwhelming that property valuation in general is a good measure of relative ability to provide education. Nevertheless, a selective inaccuracy in the wealth/property valuation relationship could still mean that the real picture is different from what the evidence shows.

If only *some* districts are relatively richer in reality than their property valuation shows, and if this undervaluation is combined with an interest in education which is the same as that of districts with similar actual wealth, the undervalued districts will presumably have higher rates in order to generate the same kinds of offerings. They would show up in our data as the poor taxing more, when they are simply the rich taxing as hard as other rich. If they are the exceptions we find to the rule of poor districts and low offerings, does this mean that the poor district and poor offering relation is really *better* confirmed or does it mean that there is *less* of a poor-district/high-effort relation than we had found? Or both? Or neither? It is hard to tell.

Likewise, some poor districts may be overvalued if they have a relatively low percent of real property as compared to current income. If they are interested in education in the same way as other poor-in-fact districts, they will only need lower rates to generate the same kinds of offerings. To the extent that these phenomena exist, it is difficult to tell either who the high- and low-effort districts are or what the economic character of the high- and low-offering districts is. When the realities of wealth distribution are not known we cannot meaningfully assess its influence on offering. To the extent that the relationship the state relies upon is jumbled, not only is the equalization fund passed out incoherently, but the whole structure of the scheme is randomly and arbitrarily discriminatory. In sum, the unreliability of the state-selected measure of wealth, while it makes special criticism less reliable, on the other hand makes it impossible for the state to justify a plan founded on wealth.

Common experience by itself indicates that some school districts are richer than others, and the existence of state equalizing plans confirms that the states are convinced that wealth varies. Furthermore, since the avowed purpose of the foundation (equalizing) plans is to help poor districts, and because state funds are geared to local property valuation, it is clear that all existing government action is grounded on the assumption that the property valuation of a district is a good measure of its wealth. The assumption could be wrong; the more it is, the more difficult it is to identify children of the poor as victims of wealth discrimination receiving low-quality offerings, but the more capricious the whole aid plan becomes as well.

By concentrating on local decision-making and by letting local wealth determine the offering, the state has frustrated systematic evaluation of the plan in terms of wealth discrimination. Moreover, because the state's contribution is often relatively trivial and mainly sedative in effect, it can afford to be careless (it may prefer to be so) in the devices it employs to judge where and how state funds are to be disbursed. In passing judgment upon the systems, the state should either be bound to its own selected measures of wealth and offering — and thus damned — or be conceded their irrationality and twice damned. The state can clear itself only by adopting a policy designed to make wealth variation neutral. Only then will the burden shift to the critics to disprove that neutrality.

In the end, one can get too bogged down in worrying over the degree to which children of poor people are the ones receiving the lower-quality offerings. Once we lose confidence in the property valuation we also have no confidence in location of the poor. But it is absurd to insist upon apodictic certainty, when data from the conventional measure are in accord with general experience. Thus the following conclusions: various children do in fact get the worst offerings, and as to those with the worst offerings we are sufficiently confident that (1) although the impact of district effort on this plight could be more than previously thought, wealth is still the significant factor and (2) for whatever it is worth, most of them are children of poor families. All the difficulties with the unreliability of measures the state has adopted still cannot cancel out the evil it has created. Not until a system is adopted which purports to take wealth out of public education can the question of whether or not the indicators of wealth, effort, and offering are accurate be tested definitively.

5 · New Directions and Old Pitfalls

Partiality and selectivity that favor any child at the expense
of another, or deny any youngster an opportunity available
to his neighbor have no longer any place in our schools. They
never did, in principle, but now we mean to bring our
practices abreast of our principles. And the task of reconcil-
ing practice with precept is the central task of those who lead
our schools.

> Fischer, "Our Schools:
> Battleground of Conflicting Interests"

THE SMALL FRATERNITY OF THEORISTS who worry about such technical matters as subvention formulas has offered a variety of remedies for the sea of troubles left by existing programs. The modern method most frequently proposed for distribution of funds is generally referred to as the *percentage equalizing grant*; it was endorsed by Paul R. Mort shortly before his death and owes most of its success to the efforts of Charles S. Benson.[1]

The driving principle of the percentage equalizing grant is its abandonment of the unit cost method of measuring educational task. In its stead the state simply pays part of the local budget; that part is inversely related to local wealth so that the grant is equalizing. Hence, the label "percentage equalizing" refers to that percentage of the local budget which is paid by the state to adjust for the district's relative poverty. The budget can be designed to include debt service, expenditures like transportation (now often financed by specific grants), and the like, as well as traditional current operational expenditures.

1. C. S. Benson, *The Economics of Public Education* (Boston, 1961), pp. 242–246; C. S. Benson, *The Cheerful Prospect: A Statement on the Future of Public Education* (Boston, 1965), pp. 90–94; C. S. Benson, "State Aid Patterns," in Jesse Burkhead, *Public School Finance* (Syracuse, 1964), pp. 214–232. See also P. R. Mort, "Unification of Fiscal Policy in New York State," in C. S. Benson, ed., *Perspectives on the Economics of Education* (Boston, 1963), p. 340; and D. Lees, "Percentage Versus Unit Grants," *ibid.*, p. 354.

In turn, the state aid share can be calculated to include federal money (for which the state acts as intermediary), if this is desired. In addition to providing a potential for real equalization, the program encourages simplification of the present tangle of overlaid grants.

This approach has resulted from dramatically increased understanding of the economics of school finance and some hard thinking about what equal educational opportunity must necessarily require. Although not all of the concepts are Benson's, it was his book *The Economics of Public Education* which first effectively rallied the ideas. Properly implemented, the formula can be equalizing in the finalistic sense, rejecting mere equalization up to a foundation level.[2] Although there are sophistications in any concrete application, a look at the general idea from the viewpoint of the district as it receives money removes most of the complexity. The simple beauty of the plan is this: by focusing on the local budget it preserves local incentive but ties the results solely to extra effort rather than greater wealth. In a nutshell, it eliminates variation in district wealth as a factor in determining the offering, at all levels of effort.

As a result, high levels of effort by poor districts will be made much more significant for quality of education than they now are. Agreeing to commit one percent of its wealth to education, the poor district will, after state aid, end up with as many total dollars per student to work with as will a rich district which commits one percent of its money. In the more familiar terminology of the property tax, if all districts tax themselves at fifteen mills, each will have the same total dollars per pupil (or per any selected task unit) to spend, regard-

2. Actually, this is giving Benson the benefit of the doubt. While the formula can be fully equalizing in terms of its elimination of wealth, as will be seen in the next chapter, Benson has not unequivocally endorsed this logical conclusion.

less of how much it raises locally through the fifteen-mill levy. A rich district will have fewer dollars available if it taxes at fourteen mills than will a poor one which taxes at fifteen mills. Local incentive can be preserved to the extent desired; the districts may be given great or little leeway in the level of effort they will exert.

Such an approach equates equal opportunity with equalized taxable wealth for each district. It aims to create clusters of equal financing power, not a utopian equality of persons. The theory is aimed directly at the historic problem: since the old plans systematically discriminate against the poor districts on account of their poverty, the way to relieve that problem for educational purposes is in effect to remove that poverty insofar as it affects public education. From the viewpoint of money received for effort expended, the percentage equalizing grant does precisely that.

In philosophy, then, the plan is designed to make subsidiarity meaningful to all districts. The state pays a share of the locally decided budget; the state doesn't stipulate that a certain level of education should cost so much and that it will support the district only thus far. True, the state must determine relative wealth and, therefore, continue to establish the criteria for task units. But once this relation of relative wealth is established, all districts are engaged in a fair competitive battle for educational excellence; local enthusiasm alone will set the local tax rate, fixing the determining factor.

Basic Mechanics and Implications

The arithmetic of the percentage equalizing grant can be simple. Remember as one principle that what is sought is some way in which all districts can have the same dollars to spend per task unit when they tax at the same rate. It is helpful to think first of state aid as received by a locality according to the ratio of its wealth to that of some other "key" district in the

166 | THE APPARATUS OF PRIVILEGE

state, and for that purpose to use the richest district. Assume
that a poor district has an assessed valuation of $10,000 per
pupil in ADA (note again that some kind of task unit must be
retained to measure wealth); assume that the richest district
has a valuation of $100,000 per pupil in ADA. The ratio of
local wealth to the "key" (in this case the richest) district is
thus 1 to 10; and under the percentage equalizing system the
state will pay 90 percent of the local budget (that is, the
poorer district needs the 90 percent aid to function on a par
with the key district). A simple formula determines this percentage or aid ratio by deriving the state's contribution:

$$\text{state aid ratio} = 1 - \frac{\text{local wealth}}{\text{key district wealth}}$$

or

$$\text{aid ratio} = 1 - \text{wealth ratio}$$

which for our example is: $1 - \dfrac{10,000}{100,000} = 90\%$ aid ratio. A
formula for state dollar aid is also easily fashioned:

$$\text{dollar aid} = \frac{(\text{aid ratio})\,(\text{local share raised})}{1 - (\text{aid ratio})}$$

This is the same as aid ratio times local budget. Therefore, in
our example, if the locality taxes at a rate of 1 percent it will
produce $100 and the state will pay $900:

$$\text{dollar aid} = \frac{.9(\$100)}{1 - .9} = \$900.$$

Hence, through the two shares, the total local budget will
be funded in the amount of $1,000 per pupil in ADA. In the
same example, a 1 percent tax in the rich district will produce
$1,000 locally. But since its aid ratio is 0 (the formula is $1 -
1/1 = 0$), this means no state aid, and it, too, has $1,000 per
pupil in ADA to spend. In sum, the same local effort generates
the same dollar offering regardless of local wealth.

So far we see that this formula equalizes the districts *up* to the key district. With all districts supported at this wealth level, poorer districts are free to opt for as good an offering as that of their richer neighbors but will have to tax at the same effort as their neighbors to get it; if they tax higher than the rich they will have a better offering. Or will they? What if the key district used is not, as it is in our example, the richest district? Then, to be equalized only up to the key district is insufficient — those who are richer can still take advantage of wealth. Therefore: in order to achieve full equalization, either (1) the key district must be the richest one or (2) the rich districts must be equalized *down* to the key district. Such downward equalizing is the essence of the Utah "basic program."

Downward Equalizing: A Hypothetical with the Average District as Key

We now assume a percentage equalizing program in which the district of average wealth is selected as the "key" district. To a legislator such an approach may well appear the most direct and satisfactory way to adjust for wealth. Equalizing to the key district renders the wealth of all districts equal to the average; and to treat all districts as average has the effect of spreading *local* wealth evenly around the state. A wealthier district as the key in effect adds an additional increment of *state* wealth to the total. Why this is so becomes clearer when the program is observed operating at various key levels.

Using the average district as key, the following example demonstrates the operation of the aid formula. First, recall the basic formula, aid ratio = 1 — wealth ratio. Next, assume that the average district in the state has $20,000 assessed valuation per pupil. District X has $30,000; district Y has $15,000; district Z is exactly average. The "wealth ratios" for the districts are 1.5, .75, and 1.0 respectively, yielding from the basic formula aid ratio's of —.5, .25, and 0. Z would receive no aid and

Y would get the state to pay 25 percent of its budget, but what of X? What the —.5 means, of course, is that X should *pay into the state* (probably to the school aid fund) 50 percent of its local budget; it must be equalized down if the object is to eliminate advantage based upon wealth. Thus, if each wants to spend $400 per pupil, all will have to tax at 2 percent. Z will raise $400 per pupil itself; Y will get 25 percent from the state ($100) and will raise $300 itself from the 2-percent rate. X will have to pay the state $200; it raises $600 locally at 2 percent and, less the $200, has $400 per pupil left.

Selection of the Key District

Two things are clear. First, a given level of effort by any district will yield, in a given year, a fixed return. Second, that point to which districts are equalized (up and down) will have a determining effect on the program. If, in the above example, X ($30,000/ADA) were the key district, then 2 percent by each district would yield $600 per ADA pupil instead of $400. When the legislature decides what district to equalize up to (assuming it is willing to force the rich to pay in excess collections if it does not equalize up to the richest), it effectively equates given levels of effort with given levels of offering. Furthermore, as noted, when it equalizes to above the average district, in effect the state adds its wealth to the artificially averaged local wealth and thereby allows a given local effort to generate more dollars. In fact, the key district is a tool by which the state can strongly influence how much money is to come (1) from traditionally "state" resources (such as a state sales or income tax); (2) from redistribution of excess property tax revenues collected locally by the rich districts and paid into the state fund; and (3) from local revenues to be retained and spent locally.

From a planning viewpoint, it might be best for the state policy-maker to use the average district as the key district and then, secondarily, to think about an amount (percent) of aid which the state should give additionally to all districts. Such a two-step approach is conceptually simple: first, in what is the purely redistributive part of the formula, the system is merely reshuffling local district collections from those above the average to those below; this takes care of equalizing. Second, by giving something extra to each district (for example, a percent of the budget or a flat amount) the state commits a supplemental share of its own wealth to each district, thereby relieving local tax burdens and encouraging spending. But besides being simple, the two-step process is also useful from a planning perspective because it neatly segregates two major policy objectives: the legislator may think first in terms of districts being made uniform in wealth and then in terms of all these now-uniform entities receiving an amount of state aid which will best serve some legislative end. What percentage of the school offering *should* be provided by the state for the average district is, of course, problematical, and numerous considerations affect this decision. One is the relative invisibility of state taxes compared to the local portion — especially where redistribution of excess local collections is involved. Once we have adjusted the wealth of all the districts up or down to the average, equalization ceases to be a purpose of subventions. Rather, the state's aid, if any, to the average district involves quite different considerations, such as what local effort can be predicted and what range of offerings the state hopes generally to create.

Illustrating the Two-Step Viewpoint: Aid to the Key District

Building in state aid to the key district complicates the formula somewhat; assuming the key district is the average, the "state aid ratio" (R) for any district can be calculated:

R = 1 − ([wealth ratio] times [1 − percent aid to average district])

Assuming that the state decides to provide 50 percent of the funds for running the program of the average district, calculation of the percentage of state aid for any district becomes:

$$R = 1 - ([\text{wealth ratio}] \text{ times } [1 - .5])$$

Again each district will set the effort it desires, and the state will subsidize it to the extent of the R factor. The formula for dollars of state aid remains the same as when no aid was given the key district. We will call this amount of state aid dollars D. The formula is:

$$D = \frac{(R)(\$ \text{ raised locally})}{1 - R}$$

Under the original example of X, Y, and Z districts, with respective wealths of $30,000, $15,000 and $20,000 per pupil, and again assuming the state average valuation at $20,000, the plan would work as follows. The aid ratios, R, for districts X, Y, and Z are .25, .625, and .50 respectively. If each district taxes at 1 percent, then: (1) Z will generate $200 locally per pupil and the state share in dollars, D, will be $200; Z will have $400 per pupil to spend; (2) X will generate $300 locally per pupil and the state share in dollars will be $100; X will have $400 per pupil; (3) Y will generate $150 per pupil locally, and the state share in dollars will be $250. All three will thus have the same $400 available based upon the same effort. Since the state will provide 50-percent aid for the average district (instead of no percentage as in the simple, one-step, "equalize up and down to the average district" scheme), not one of the three is rich enough to have to pay money into the state. Similarly, note that it takes a 1-percent instead of a 2-percent local effort to achieve the $400 per unit offering.

It should be made clear that, when the state says it will pay 50 percent of the average district's budget, and the average wealth is known to be $20,000 per pupil, it is at the same time saying 1 percent equals $400 per-pupil spending power, 2 percent $800, and so on. By increasing the percent of the average district's budget that it will support, the state ipso facto raises the offering that an equivalent local tax will produce. In general, changing the state share changes the offering-effort relation.

From the viewpoint of tying dollars available for a district to spend to the rate it is willing to tax itself locally, this variable equalizing plan will work well. A glance tells that if, in the above example, any of the three districts were to double the local tax to 2 percent of assessed valuation it would ultimately have $800 per pupil to spend; similarly, if a district taxed at only .5 percent it would have but $200 per pupil. Always these dollar totals would be independent of local wealth.

All the same, like the simple plan giving no state aid to average or richer districts, the problem of "excess wealth" can appear at some point even when there is 50-percent state aid to the average district. To understand this, assume that there is a fourth district, W, with assessed valuation of $50,000 per pupil. Putting its wealth ratio into the formula that calculates the state aid percentage, the problem becomes evident. When the state percentage share for the average district is 50 percent, any "wealth ratio" larger than 2 produces a value for R which is negative. (As concluded earlier, when the aid to the average district is 0, then any richer than average district — one with a wealth ratio > 1 — has a negative R value.) This condition demands that such districts pay some of the money they raise locally to the state for redistribution to other districts; and of course they will receive no state aid.[3] In this particular case, the R value for district W is −.25. In terms of the dollar formula, and assuming that district W taxes at 1 percent, the amount raised locally would be $500 and the D value minus $100. Thus,

3. This, also discussed in the next chapter, is where Benson has yet to make a commitment to reform. Thus far he has said that the negative numbers should be ignored (treated as zero). See Burkhead, *Public School Finance*, pp. 215–235, representing materials contributed by Benson. The consequences of such a decision are most undesirable.

district W would have to pay that $100 into the state (25 percent of its budget of $400) to end up with the same $400 to spend.

Reconsider the basic example but assume an increase in the state participation level from 50 to 75 percent for the average district. (In other words, when the average district raises $200 per pupil locally the state will contribute $600, creating an $800 offering in which $600 represents 75 percent.) Under such an arrangement district W will receive a positive R value of .375. Therefore, by taxing it 1 percent and raising $500 per pupil locally, it will get a D value of $300 and a total of $800, like the other districts.

Under this 75-percent "aid to the average district" plan, there will be no need to require payment into the state fund even from the wealthiest district so long as the wealthiest is no more than four times as wealthy as the average district (in our example, with a maximum R value of 4 and a maximum assessed valuation of $80,000). From these illustrations it is clear that raising the state share to 75 percent of the average district under the assumed facts is the same as (1) making a $40,000 district the key district and paying 50 percent of the key district's budget, or (2) making $80,000 the key district and equalizing all up or down to that level — which would mean no aid to the $80,000 district. Yet, again, for planning purposes, the aid program is more easily understood when the average district is used as the key.

The Percentage Equalizing Systems Proposed

The equalization plan outlined above can achieve its results only if the state will either (1) support every district to the wealth of the richest or (2) have the richer districts pay into the state fund to adjust their wealth downward when the formula requires. Theorists who have developed the percentage equalizing system of state aid have proposed equalization based approximately upon the average district in the state as the "key." But in their practical application they have scrapped the elemental principle of redistribution that could have made it work.

Charles S. Benson has contributed more toward the understanding and eventual reform of existing systems than perhaps any man, certainly any living man. Naturally such a statement is the prelude to criticism of Benson, albeit reluctant and also trivial in relation to his total work. The criticisms are two, the first the less important.

In a book entitled *The Cheerful Prospect*,[4] Benson proposes that the states adopt a percentage equalizing system of distribution of state aid to education based upon the district of average wealth. The method of calculation, though slightly different from that we have examined, is simple and elegant. First, the average assessed valuation of all the districts in the state is computed and divided by the total population of the state, yielding, of course, the average per-capita valuation in the state. Each district's population is multiplied by this figure to derive a hypothetical wealth level based on the average district. Then, the actual valuation of the district is subtracted from the hypothetical figure to derive, wherever the former is smaller than the latter, a "resource" deficit — the measure by which a given district falls below the district of average wealth in the state. The rate at which these districts with deficits are already taxing their own wealth is then applied to the deficit to derive the amount of state aid. Under this formula, each district is supported as a district of average wealth and is rewarded with the same revenue for the same tax rate as the average district.[5]

4. Benson, *Cheerful Prospect* (1965), pp. 90–98.
5. Benson calls the grant a "resource equalizer." The purpose of using this kind of grant is to allow all places of average and below-average wealth to provide themselves with services under a "proportionate structure" of local tax rates; *ibid.*, p. 90.

A peculiarity of Benson's formula is unexplained and is the first object of our criticism. The task unit used to measure wealth is the district's *population*, not its school population. Long ago, Cubberley demonstrated the inadequacy of using population as a task unit; and Benson is well aware of the problem. He proposes that an additional "needs grant" be applied to each school district to adjust for this discrepancy and for others that require a nicer measure. A given number of dollars would be added to a district with an above-average number of students and a given amount subtracted from a below-average district. There seems to be no good reason for choosing population as a task unit and, therefore, no reason for the extra step in the calculation, except for supposed didactic advantages of treating apart from the simple population measurement the more complicated issues raised by such devices as the "weighted pupil." But pupils in average daily attendance or classroom units would seem the simplest of all task units to grasp.

Except for this anomaly, Benson's plan at first blush appears to represent what the percentage equalizing theory, as explained above, would require in an implementing plan based upon no aid to the average district. However, an example will help explain our second objection and demonstrate that Benson's approach to the standard of the average district really is at dramatic variance with the ideal. Assume three districts, one with a valuation of $100,000 per capita, one at $50,000, and one at $10,000, with $50,000 the average per-capita valuation in the state. Also assume that each district taxes at a rate of 1 percent locally. Under Benson's formulation, only districts with below-average wealth receive state aid: for the poorest district the calculation is $50,000 minus $10,000 equals $40,000 (the resource deficit). 1 percent times $40,000 equals $400, which, added to the purely local tax (1 percent times $10,000 equals $100), results in $500 total revenue for the poor district. This is identical to the yield of the 1-percent local tax in the $50,000, or average, district, so that equalization has been attained for those two districts.

In the $100,000 district, however, there is no deficit, and the 1-percent tax yields $1,000 — twice the yield of the other two for the same tax rate. The flaw is obvious: *the plan exempts the rich districts from having to pay into the state.* Moreover, by refusing to recognize the negative numbers that inevitably appear in a complete formula, Benson loses the only rationale for choosing the average district as the key, that is, that it makes planning choices clearer. Benson seems to overlook the point. He is concerned rather with criticism from another quarter when he offers this assurance to the rich districts: "Richer authorities receive no money under the resource-equalizer grant, but as we shall see below, this does not represent a hardship." [6] This is a misleading understatement. In fact, the richer districts are left in a preferred position.[7]

Again we point out that, if one is to avoid demanding the payment of "local" money into the state, the state must equalize up to the richest district, and, what is the same, if the state equalizes to the average district the plan is not honest percentage equalizing unless it accepts the obvious requirements of the negative numbers. There may be excellent political reasons for promoting equalization up to but not down to the average district (at least at first, in order to soften the blow on legislatures). But as more than a temporary measure the choice by Benson is quite opaque considering the basic objectives he expresses in *The Cheerful Prospect.* Calling strongly for equality of educational opportunity, he promises that his proposals will be "shocking," but insists that the "inequalities of provi-

6. *Ibid.,* p. 91.

7. In a sense it is because the richer districts get no money that the below-average districts get *less* money under the percentage equalizing grant; using the richest district as the key, every district (but one — the richest) receives aid and all districts are equalized; under Benson's proposal half do not receive any aid, and that half have an advantage over the half that do receive aid.

sion which are included in our educational development" are more shocking. We concede the need of a shock, but we are unable to discover it in these proposals.

Benson forswears the reduction of our excellent schools to mediocrity as a means of achieving equality in the statement:

> I am certainly not against excellence in any lawful human activity; and I shall not suggest that our great public secondary institutions, such as are found in New Trier Township, Illinois; Newton, Massachusetts; Scarsdale, New York; Clayton, Missouri; and Beverly Hills, California, be "levelled down" to the common standard. Rather, I submit that insofar as these schools have characteristics that are exceptional, they should serve students who are especially qualified to benefit from superior academic instruction, which is to say that they should draw students from a broad geographic area under a process of selective admissions.[8]

This reference to interdistrict attendance is not elaborated in the detailed proposals that follow it. Without changes in attendance criteria,[9] it is precisely such light house schools as Benson names which are likely to be found only in the very richest districts in the state and, therefore, are able to preserve their natural advantage under Benson's equalizing proposals. Benson has described the desire to improve slum schools by compensatory education as a "Peace Corps attitude toward our fellow citizens" better replaced by "such controls of educational expenditure that our economically favored districts can no longer claim the privilege of commanding an undue proportion of educational resources for the exclusive benefit of their resident pupils."[10] However, he proposes a system of state aid that

8. Benson, *Cheerful Prospect*, p. 2.

9. It might be noted that, in fact, any system of equalizing state aid can be seen as an alternative to alterations in the geographic criteria of attendance.

10. Benson, *Cheerful Prospect*, p. 3.

would in effect raise the slum schools to an average level but leave the richer districts in a position of unaffected privilege. Is this really an advance over the foundation plan? As a tactic in a thirty-year legislative war, it may be; as a relevant current answer, it is not.

Paul R. Mort, a pioneer and primary developer of the minimum foundation program, recommended a plan ("Mort II") to the New Yok State Legislature in the 1960's embodying the percentage equalizing grant as a means of equalizing, not merely operational expenditures, but every expenditure that can be incurred in running a school.[11] Mort's arithmetic is slightly different from Benson's, for he uses the more sophisticated approach outlined earlier starting with the average district as the key and building in a state share to that district. Local ability and state average ability are computed, not by means of valuation per capita as Benson suggested, but by the more traditional valuation per weighted pupil (pupils in ADA with cost variations figured in). Local ability is divided by state average ability, yielding the wealth ratio (for example, $10,000/$50,000 or 1/5). This ratio is subtracted from 1 to derive the state share, or aid ratio (1 minus 1/5 equals 4/5).

Mort at that point recommends (his reason is to take some tax pressure off local property) that the state share of educational expenditures should be 42.5 percent for the average district. To achieve this result, 57.5 percent (the complementary fraction of 42.5) is multiplied by the ratio of local to average ability and the result subtracted from 1:

$$1 \text{ minus} \left[\frac{\text{local ability}}{\text{average ability}} \right] .575 \text{ equals state share}$$

11. Mort, "Unification" in Benson, *Perspectives*, pp. 341–343. Not only does Mort propose that debt services be computed in the local share, but he recommends extra subvention to absolve the debts of districts with unusually heavy debts, to the extent of 75% of any debt service that could not be paid by a 2-mill tax; *ibid.*, pp. 342–343.

This is our familiar formula: R equals 1 minus [wealth ratio times (1 minus state share to key district)].

Thus, in a district of average wealth (wealth ratio equals 1), the state share, the aid ratio R, is 42.5 percent — this is equalizing up to a district wealthier than the average. When 57.5 percent is used as a multiplier, all districts up to the district with 175 percent of the wealth of the average district are given equalizing aid, because that is the point at which the aid ratio R becomes 0 as shown here:

$$175 \text{ percent of } \$50,000 \text{ is } \$87,500$$
$$\text{and}$$
$$1 \text{ minus} \left[\frac{87,500}{50,000} \right] .575 \text{ equals } 0$$

To that extent, Mort's proposal is more equalizing than Benson's. But Mort, too, only equalizes up to the district with wealth 175 percent of the average and does not equalize down: that is, he, too, rejects the negative numbers generated by the formula for districts wealthier than 175 percent of average. This, of course, is a limitation contrary to the ideal of this form of grant.

But things get even more depressing. Mort further recommends that in no case shall the state share of local expenditures drop below 25 percent. From the analysis in Chapter 3 one should be wary that this will help only the rich: it is like the Type 2 combination plan, only worse. The first consequence of this "refinement" is, in effect, to drop the level up to which districts are equalized. The district 132 percent as rich as the average would receive the same aid either under the formula or under the guaranteed 25 percent of its budget. Using round figures, 132 percent of $50,000 is $66,000 and

$$1 \text{ minus} \left[\frac{66,000}{50,000} \right] .575 \text{ equals } .25$$

Thus, districts from the 132-percent markup which under the formula should be receiving progressively less state aid than 25 percent, with the guarantee will all receive 25 percent; districts above the 175-percent mark, which should be receiving no aid, also receive 25 percent of their budgets from the state. By introducing this minimum support, the district up to which others are equalized is the one 132 percent as rich as the average instead of the one 175 percent as rich, increasing the number of districts that occupy financially privileged positions. The 25-percent guarantee is dramatically anti-equalizing: it helps the rich only.

Additionally, the 25-percent limitation has what is perhaps an even more serious defect, making it doubly anti-equalizing. In Chapter 1 the effect of flat grants based on a revenue task unit was discussed using the example of Cubberley's teacher-employed task unit. Such grants are anti-equalizing because richer districts have more power to raise money locally than poor districts with the same tax rate and, therefore, can qualify more easily for state aid. Mort's flat 25-percent aid criterion is a classic example of such a revenue distribution because it is based directly on local expenditure levels.

If two districts of unequal wealth are taxing at the same rate, the 25 percent feature increases the resulting dollar disparity because the richer district gets more aid. Assume two districts with wealth of $100,000 and $50,000 per pupil, both taxing at 1 percent; further assume that, as before, the state average assessed valuation per pupil is $50,000 and that the state has adopted the full Mort proposal outlined thus far. The poorer (average) district has an aid ratio of 42.5 percent; hence the 25-percent minimum has no impact. This district is able to spend $870 per pupil, raising $500 per pupil locally (1 percent of $50,000) and getting $370 from the state (42.5 percent of $870). The richer district should have an aid ratio of −15 percent, but, because of the minimum guarantee, +25 percent is used in its place. It is able to spend $1,333 per pupil, raising $1,000 per pupil locally (1 percent of $100,000) and getting $333 from the state (25 percent of $1,333). Without the 25-percent guarantee it would have no aid; using the negative numbers it would have $870 to spend (calculated as follows: negative 15 percent of an $870 budget equals $130 paid to state, and $1,000 raised minus $130 equals $870), as the average district does.

Figures 5-1 and 5-2 help illustrate the impact of the refusal to

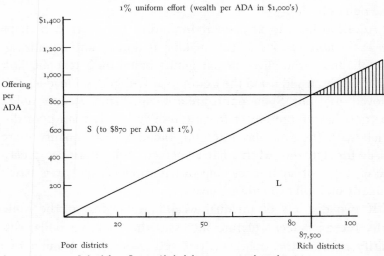

1% uniform effort (wealth per ADA in $1,000's)

S (to $870 per ADA at 1%)

L

L, local share; S, state aid; shaded area, amount to be paid to state
when negative numbers used

FIGURE 5-1

use negative numbers and to employ the 25-percent guarantee, given the factual assumptions we have been using. Figure 5-1 illustrates the offering range for a spectrum of district wealths; the shaded area indicates districts in whose favor the system discriminates if negative numbers are not used. (Recall that this assumes a 1-percent effort by all districts and $50,000 per ADA as the average district. Note how the shaded area begins at $87,-

ooo per ADA in wealth [approximately], or 175 percent of the average district, as noted earlier.)

Figure 5-2 illustrates the impact of the 25-percent guaran-

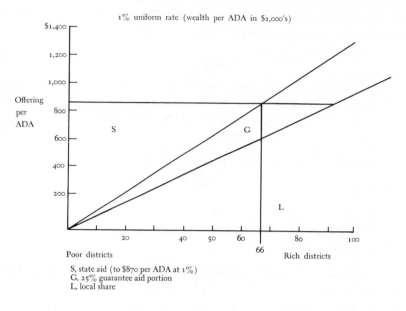

1% uniform rate (wealth per ADA in $1,000's)

Offering per ADA

S, state aid (to $870 per ADA at 1%)
G, 25% guarantee aid portion
L, local share

Poor districts

Rich districts

FIGURE 5-2

tee. Note that the point at which districts take advantage of wealth now begins with the districts 132 percent of the average ($66,000). The widening of the area marked G illustrates clearly that the guarantee is equivalent to a revenue unit form of aid, hence doubly anti-equalizing.

There are yet other limitations of the percentage equalizing grant proposed in various quarters which can and do by themselves destroy its effectiveness as an instrument of equalization. Suppose, for one example, that the state adopts a percentage equalizing grant based on the richest district but places a dollar maximum on the gross expenditure level (local budget) toward which the state will contribute. The effect of using such a dollar maximum in conjunction with the percentage equalizing grant is to construct a minimum foundation program using different arithmetic. The mechanical difference is that, rather than applying a constant percentage to varying degrees of wealth, the wealth itself is converted to varying percentages. Table 17 helps visualize the described effect.

Table 17

State aid (dollars) under two plans to produce foundation level in key district: (1) foundation program of $500 with 1% participation rate; (2) percentage equalizing program with $500 produced in key district

Program	$50,000 AV/PP district[a]	$30,000 AV/PP district	$10,000 AV/PP district
(1) Foundation program	$500 − $500 = $0	$500 − $300 = $200	$500 − $100 = $400
(2) Percentage equalizing	0 × $500 = $0	2/5 × $500 = $200	4/5 × $500 = $400

[a] Richest and key district.

Of course, if the participation rate is lowered or raised, or if the maximum levels differ, results of the two plans will vary. There is an obvious danger, then, in use of the percentage equalizing grant with a maximum dollar level. It is quite possible that what is merely routine revision of the foundation level will be heralded as a revolution in state aid simply because it is formulated in percentage equalizing terms. This would be another case of misbranding.

THE SCHIZOPHRENIC NEW YORK REFORMS

In 1962, New York, on recommendation of the Joint Legislative Committee on School Finance (Diefendorf Committee), purported to embrace the basic principles of the percentage equalizing grant plan.[12] In doing so it abandoned the founda-

12. See N.Y. CONSOL. LAWS ANN. § 3602 (McKinney Supp. 1967).

tion program approach which had existed in New York since the 1920's.

Consider the words of John W. Polley, director of the Division of Educational Finance, explaining why in theory the new New York plan — called the "shared-cost" program — is better than the old Strayer-Haig/Mort-modified scheme: "[A] foundation program is based on state participation in an acceptable *minimum* educational program; while the local district is left free to spend any amount it wishes to finance on its own in excess of the foundation program. The 'shared cost' program, on the other hand, permits each district to develop the best educational program that it is capable of; the state then shares in the cost of this program on an equalized basis." [13]

In reality, the New York formula is little more than the Mort II proposal described in the last section. First the aid ratio (R value) is calculated:

$$R \text{ equals } 1 \text{ minus } \left[\frac{\text{AV/weighted ADA child in district}}{\text{AV/weighted ADA child in state}} \right] .51$$

It should be clear that this formula means the state would be expected to support the average district at the level of 49 percent of its total spending: 51 equals (1 minus .49). The reason for the 49-percent level is not perfectly clear; recall that Mort himself suggested 42.5 percent. It is certain, though, that the expectation of continued local financing exceeding 50 percent in above-average districts had some political importance. Moreover, by the year 1960–61 the amount of state aid as part of the total New York spending pattern under the foundation program already had reached 42.7 per cent. Amounts for the years following have been:[14]

13. University of State of New York, State Education Department, Bureau of Educational Finance Research, *Studies of Public School Support 1966 Series: Vital Issues in Public School Finance* (Albany, 1967), p. 10.

14. University of State of New York, State Education Department, Bureau of Educational Finance Research, *State Aid to New York School District, 1965–66* (Albany, 1967), p. 2.

1961–62	41.8 percent
1962–63	44.4
1963–64	43.6
1964–65	42.6
1965–66	44.9
1966–67	46.2 (estimate)

A formula commitment of 49 percent is in line with the kind of level to which New York districts had been accustomed.[15]

New York, as could be expected, did not go all the way with the variable equalizing program.[16] In the first place, it set a limit of 90 percent on the state matching share: thus, districts having particularly low wealth will not be fully equalized. This seems to have been done from fear that poor districts which had to put up less than 10 percent of the funds would abuse the program and give disproportionate commitments to education so as to gain too many dollars from the state. If such a brake (or maximum) is needed, a limit on taxing power to affect all districts would be more appropriate.[17] New York has adopted this kind of uniform limiting and, perhaps, desirable feature by its requirement of minimum levels of educational offering: that is, a district must tax at least eleven mills before it can fully participate in the "shared-cost" plan.

In contrast to these plausible sophistications within the percentage equalizing plan, New York has added other limitations

15. Although the formula is designed to give 49% aid to the average district, it will be understood shortly that it does not contemplate 49% of the average of all school budgets in the state be supported by state funds. This is because of the unfair advantages the plan has reserved for richer districts. Thus, an operating level of state aid in the lower 40% range is as expected. Perhaps one could say that, given the design of the plan, a 49% aid to the average district was needed to produce a state share near the 42.8% which had been provided under the old foundation plan.

16. See generally N.Y. Consol. Laws Ann. §§ 3602–3609 (McKinney Supp. 1967).

17. It might parenthetically be noted that New York's task unit part of the formula is adjusted for additional items, for the purpose of taking into account other kinds of differences among school districts. For example, there is a small district and a dense population adjustment.

that very nearly emasculate it. First, a ceiling has been imposed in terms of dollars on the amount of the local budget to be subsidized. Thus a district is equalized only up to some given support level, above which any spending will have to come wholly from the district itself. The ceiling on cost sharing (state and local combined) was $500 in 1962 and was raised to $600 in 1965–66 and $660 in 1966–67.[18] In 1961–62 the median expenditure among all districts was $500. Given New York spending habits, this kind of limit is ludicrous and incoherent in a scheme of true shared-cost equalizing. Polley nicely understates the case: "Based upon practical considerations in 1962 the Diefendorf Committee recommended that the state impose a ceiling on the expenditures which would be aided. Since then the concept of the ceiling has been apparently misunderstood. . . ." He is quite aware of the fact that this shared-cost approach with a dollar ceiling is very dangerous, as it can easily "revert back to a foundation program instead." He reports that in 1965–66, for example, "when the ceiling was $600 practically all districts were spending above this level" and warns that if the ceiling is not raised significantly to keep up with rising spending patterns it will "undermine" the new plan.[19]

James V. Vetro, associate in the Division of Educational Finance, candidly concedes that, when adopted "for those districts already spending more than $500 [the then ceiling], the new program simply substituted a new foundation level of $500 for the previous foundation level." This is easily understood: because districts can tax higher than the level of tax necessary to achieve a product of $500 per pupil (or $660 per pupil today), the shared-cost plan is just like the foundation plan. "Since the state does not share beyond the ceiling, the additional amount is borne entirely by the local district. In

18. Much of the New York analysis is based upon data contained in *Vital Issues*.

19. *Ibid.*, pp. 10–11.

the districts of greater taxable wealth this is no particular problem, but in the districts of lesser taxable wealth the tax rate rises very steeply. In the districts with low taxable wealth per child, it would require a prohibitively high tax rate to support a program which the wealthier districts do with relatively little effort." [20] This concise statement, equally applicable to foundation programs, demonstrates that New York has not really moved away from a plan designed to favor wealth.

Second and equally important under the New York plan, as might well be expected in view of Mort's proposal, there is the other limit which is inconsistent with equalizing: there can be no negative aid ratio. We well know that this means very wealthy districts, because their aid coefficient cannot become negative, are not forced to pay into the state part of the dollars they raised in excess of the support level at a given level of effort. This of course allows rich districts to take advantage of wealth. As noted earlier, one way to change some of this would be to raise the 49-percent state share, if the solution of having negative coefficients were unacceptable. This in effect would mean bringing the poor further up so that they could begin to match the rich.

A third anti-equalizing factor is that, under the percentage equalizing plan, each district is guaranteed state aid of $238 per pupil (under the 1966–67 $660 ceiling program).[21] This is somewhat like the guaranteed percentage grant part of the Mort scheme. In effect, this is a flat grant minimum received by all districts regardless of wealth. It is obvious from our earlier analysis that this guarantee benefits the rich only: the poorer districts would get the support under the equalizing program, anyway (assuming they tax at least at the minimum rate). Thus

20. *State Aid*, p. 17.
21. Actually, districts are guaranteed a minimum of $264 per weighted ADA for current expenditures and capital expenditures. NEW YORK CONSOL. LAWS ANN. § 3602(9) (McKinney Supp. 1967).

the rich, who would not receive aid if only equalizing aid were allowed, are seemingly given a bonus for being rich. Although it may be politically impregnable, it is obviously unfair.

Following is a comparison of New York statewide median operating expenditures, arithmetic mean operating expenditures, and operating expenditures ceiling for state aid over six years.

Year	Median	Mean	Ceiling on State Participation
1962–63	$537	$590	$500
1963–64	563	621	500
1964–65	593	669	500
1965–66	635	716	600
1966–67	680 (estimate)	760 (est.)	660
1967–68	725 (est.)	800 (est.)	660

This makes obvious the inability or unwillingness of New York to do anything significant with the percentage equalizing program. Unless the ceiling is above that of the district with the highest expenditure there will not be full equalizing. And, at least until the ceiling is well above the median, a condition of equalization cannot even be approached. In reality, the very idea of a dollar ceiling defeats the philosophy of the whole plan. A limit on taxing is much more palatable. In any case, the absence of negative aid ratios makes the plan scarcely an improvement over the old scheme. It has fallen into the pitfall of Mort II and Benson when it fails to carry through its avowed philosophy that the wealth of the entire state should be available equally to the districts regardless of where the wealth happens to be.

The New York State Education Department has analyzed the impact of wealth on the realities of school finance under the new state aid plan:

. . . the wealthiest districts continue to have the highest total expenditures per pupil and the poorest districts the lowest total expenditures per pupil. . . . This relationship is also true for operating expenditures per pupil. . . . If one examines the amount of aid per pupil paid to districts in 1965–66 at each wealth level, it is clear that the school aid formula has a strong equalization character. But, if one examines the operating expenses per pupil for the same year, it also stands out that despite the equalizing effect of state aid, expenditures per pupil are still very closely correlated with taxable wealth. It also appears evident that the poorest districts tend to be limited to the ceiling in which the state will share . . . and that only the wealthy districts can offer a program involving much more money than this.[22]

TRAGEDY IN A TEAPOT: RHODE ISLAND'S PERCENTAGE EQUALIZATION

Rhode Island has adopted a form of the plan which at first glance is in principle designed more nearly to achieve equalization of wealth than any other in the nation: it has accepted the shared-cost idea on an open-ended basis as the major format of state aid to local school districts.[23] Nevertheless, Rhode Island's overall plan has two major flaws which make it impossible for the variable equalizing formula to achieve its purpose.

Although the Rhode Island formula is a complicated jumble of interim statistics and unnecessary calculations apparently included to explain the rationale behind it, when all the duplicate terms are canceled it works out to the familiar formula for the

22. State Aid, p. 29. For district by district data in New York, see N.Y. State Education Bureau of Statistical Services, Annual Educational Summary 1963–64 (Albany, 1965).

23. RHODE ISLAND GEN. LAWS tit. 16, ch. 7 (Supp. 1967). "Open-ended" means that there is no dollar limitation upon the amount of matching funds provided by the state as there is in New York with the latter's $660 per pupil ceiling.

state aid ratio (R) we have seen before based upon aid to the district which is used as the key:[24]

$$R \text{ equals } 1 \text{ minus } \frac{(AV/\text{weighted pupil ADM in district})}{(AV/\text{weighted pupil ADM in state})} \cdot 7875$$

or

$$R \text{ equals } 1 \text{ minus (wealth ratio times } [1 - .2125])$$

What this means, of course, is that the state will be expected to pay for 21.25 percent of the average district's expenditures. Again, however, there are no negative numbers allowed. That defect plus the fact that the share to the average district is so low immediately raises a warning flag about actual operation of the scheme. These, indeed, are the major drawbacks of the plan; for whenever the wealth of a district is 127 percent of the average district (that is, the poorer is 78.75 percent of the richer), the richer district will generate locally more dollars at any given level of effort than will be available to any of the poorer districts at that level of effort with both state and local funds. And of course it can be expected that many districts will be wealthier than 127 percent of the average district.

A short example demonstrates the problem. Assume the state average assessed valuation at $10,000 per pupil in ADM. District A with $10,000 AV has an aid ratio of .2125 from the formula; thus, if its budget is $100 per pupil, the state will contribute $21.25. District B with $5,000 AV has an aid ratio of .61625; if its budget is $100 per pupil, the state will pay $61.625. It should be noted that to raise the local share — the remaining $78.75 — district A would have to tax at .07875; similarly, district B would have to tax at the same .07875 rate to raise its remaining $39.375 local share. However, if district C has an assessed valuation of $15,000, it has an aid ratio of −.18125. Because Rhode Island does not permit negative coefficients,

24. RHODE ISLAND GEN. LAWS tit. 16, ch. 7, § 20 (Supp. 1967). For an explanation, see Rhode Island Division Local and Metropolitan Government, Municipal Memo vol. III, no. 11, Mar. 30, 1967, pp. 3–4.

though district C will get no aid it does not have to pay "excess" to the state. If it taxes at the same .07875 rate it will generate locally $118.125 per pupil. It is clear that with Rhode Island's state share commitment so small, it will not achieve any meaningful equalization — even though the open-ended theory has been adopted — until rich districts are required to pay "local" funds to the state. If this is objectionable, the state share should be increased.

Rhode Island has a second provision that is truly incredible in view of the low percentage of state aid promised by the formula to the average district: the state will pay at least 30 per cent of every district's costs, regardless of the true aid ratio.[25] The minimum "aid ratio" is set at .30 in Rhode Island by law instead of either the assumed .00 employed in our example above or the real negative ratios which should be used if equalization is intended. This means that for all those districts with true aid ratios of .30 and less, wealth once again counts as a big factor in offering. Furthermore, among those districts the wealthier can raise more total money through a given local effort than can the less wealthy (so as to raise total expenditures), and the state will always pick up 30 percent of the total cost. This part of the plan becomes the doubly anti-equalizing contrivance of the Mort II proposal we described earlier. First, the poor get money through the equalizing plan anyway, so the 30 percent means nothing to them and becomes a subsidy for the rich; second, since this is a revenue unit form of aid, the rich are stimulated to further participation. So it is that the plan pays most to those who can already raise most. Because the state participation level for the average district is just over 21 percent by the main formula, it can be expected that well over half the state's school children will fall under the special 30-per-

25. Rhode Island Special Commission to Study the Entire Field of Education, *The Rhode Island State School Aid Program, A Report To The Legislature* (R.I. State Legislature, 1967).

cent rule. To be eligible for more than the 30 percent aid a district must have wealth less than 88 percent of the average districts.[26]

The combination of these factors — the low state aid share to the average district and the 30-percent guarantee — is an enormous hurdle to full equalization of wealth among Rhode Island school districts. It is therefore no surprise that the special commission which has recently completed examination of school financing under the formula has recommended lowering the .7875 figure to .65,[27] which would mean that the state would be expected to pick up 35 percent of the budget of the average district. The commission candidly reported that for the 1967–68 school year, 20 of the state's 39 districts would be operating at the automatic 30 percent level although their true aid ratio was lower than that. Under the suggested formula, 13 districts would still operate at the 30 percent level. Again, this means that for those districts not only is the formula not equalizing, but its very open-endedness allows them to exploit their wealth to an increasing degree. The irony of the Rhode Island picture is that the open-endedness which was heralded as a powerful equalizing characteristic has become a device by which the rich can enlarge their margin of advantage over the poor with an assist from the state.

Between 1959–60 and 1964–65, the amount of statewide aid per pupil in Rhode Island nearly doubled (1959–60 was the last year under the old state aid plan). Yet, the commission found that under the operation of the new program, the poorer districts have received only a slightly larger share of the additional state aid than the richer ones; the richest 13 (as measured by equalized weighted assessed valuation) received increased state

26. From our prior example it should be noted that, with wealth of 50% of the average district, 61% state aid is provided.

27. See *Rhode Island State School Aid*, p. i. It is of interest that Benson was one of the two special consultants to the commission.

aid in the amounts of 191 percent of 1959–60 levels, whereas the figure for the 13 poorest was 207 percent.

Some disturbing by-products of the financing method were found. First, districts with declining wealth per pupil received increased state aid of only 176 percent. This might mean that districts with falling wealth are less willing to commit as much of their income to schools as others are even though they may be the ones who need education the most. But what really accounts for this is that the 30-percent minimum guarantee is effectively doing as much for the rich as the equalizing aspect of the plan is doing for the poor. Second, the 13 communities with the highest median family income enjoy the most accelerated rate of the increase in the share of state aid they receive. Again, this seems to be happening because of the 30 percent rule.

The commission's consultants also found some interesting facts about stimulus created by the open-ended program. There has not been a rush by the poor districts to take advantage of the open-ended approach to the detriment of other noneducational local services. Rather, adoption of what is, in this respect, the modern approach to financing has been met with the uniformity of local taxing behavior which characterized the older state aid program. It can be concluded that the theoretical expectation of local variation in innovation and incentive, which is the advertised basis for tying the plan to effort, has yet to mean much in practice. Nevertheless, this is hardly an experience to be generalized and applied to a plan that is without the unfair limitations characteristic of the Rhode Island approach.

Tables 18, 19, and 20 examine relations among 39 Rhode Island districts,[28] evaluated in terms of what a fully equalizing

28. The raw data from which the Rhode Island analysis was made can be found in Supervisor of Statistical Services, *1965–66 Statistical Tables* (Rhode Island State Department of Education, 1966); Division of Local and Metropolitan Government, Department of Administration, *Annual State Report on Local Government Finances and Tax Equalization* (State of Rhode Island and Providence Plantations, 1966).

Table 18

Rhode Island: matrix of numbers of districts by effort and offering

| | | Effort | | | |
		T-1[a]	T-2	T-3[b]	Total districts
Offering	T-1[a]	4	5	3	12[c]
	T-2	6	5	3	14
	T-3[b]	3	3	7	13
	Total districts	13	13	13	

[a] High.
[b] Low.
[c] Districts with identical offerings made even thirds impossible.

Table 19

Rhode Island: matrix of numbers of districts by wealth and effort

| | | Wealth | | | |
		T-1[a]	T-2	T-3[b]	Total districts
Effort	T-1[a]	2	3	8	13
	T-2	2	7	4	13
	T-3[b]	9	3	1	13
	Total districts	13	13	13	

[a] High.
[b] Low.

Table 20

Rhode Island: matrix of numbers of districts by wealth and offering

| | | Wealth | | | |
		T-1[a]	T-2	T-3[b]	Total districts
Offering	T-1[a]	5	5	2	12
	T-2	4	4	6	14
	T-3[b]	4	4	5	13
	Total districts	13	13	13	

[a] High.
[b] Low.

formula should produce. They dramatically affirm some of the disappointments felt by the commission. Under a complete variable equalizing plan, there should be a strong relation between effort and offering. The whole philosophy of the plan is to allow districts of varying wealths which are making similar effort to yield the same total dollars. Table 18 shows the Rhode Island relations for 1964–65. (Because of identical offering at the dividing line, a division into even thirds was not made.) Although there is some tendency for effort and offering to be related, the relationship is anything but dramatic, which strongly suggests that the Rhode Island modifications have reduced the effectiveness of the formula in achieving equalization.

Under a completely equalizing plan, wealth and effort should be unrelated. Table 19 shows the relation for Rhode Island. Quite clearly, wealth and effort are strongly *inversely* related, just as they are in foundation plan states. Beyond question Rhode Island has failed to adjust effectively for wealth. To counter any assertion that Table 19 indicates that the poor have taken advantage of the plan much more than the rich and therefore have much better schools, consider Table 20 comparing wealth and offering. Wealth and offering still tend to be related in Rhode Island, despite the much larger effort made by poor districts. Nevertheless, the Rhode Island plan appears to be equalizing at least to the extent that it has reduced the usually strong relation between wealth and offering to a mere tendency.

Under its present limitations, the Rhode Island plan, for all its promise, is a complex mechanism of little consequence. The proposed change in the formula that would enlarge the state share can be of some small assistance in reaching the goal of equalization; but, if the state is unwilling to go all the way and base the aid formula on the richest district, the happier alternative is to recognize the effect of negative numbers which would render the system a fair one while preserving local choice. This would at the same time, of course, terminate the 30-percent state aid minimum guarantee.

Maine and Wisconsin have also adopted percentage equalizing approaches; Maine, however, directly imposes a dollar ceiling in the cost sharing that the state will bear. Thus, as in New York, the new theory results in little more than a new foundation level. In fact, Maine's state aid program expressly guarantees only a minimum of educational offering to Maine pupils. The state supports the local budget in varying percentages which are inversely related to district wealth. Thus districts with assessed valuations of $3,000 per pupil receive 66 percent state aid, and districts with $12,500 and more assessed valuation per pupil receive 18 percent aid. There are 18 classes of wealth and percentages of state support from one end of the spectrum to the other. It should be noted that Maine also supports school construction in the same percentage equalizing fashion; however, this support is granted only up to a low fixed ceiling. Budget desires above that amount, something which can be expected to occur as a general rule rather than as an exception, must be paid for fully from local funds.[29]

Wisconsin achieves the same result as New York and Maine through a different approach. Recall that the percentage equalizing plan which uses the average district as the key in effect treats all districts as if they had at least the wealth of the average district. Similarly, setting a formula giving 49 percent aid to the average district effectively guarantees wealth to an amount above that of the average district. Rather than focusing upon the average district, Wisconsin by statute has established an amount of wealth that is to be guaranteed to the school districts. It is the Benson formulation; the amount varies with the kind of district involved. First, districts are either "basic" or, if they meet some higher standards, "integrated." The state aid

29. MAINE REV. STATS. ANN. tit. 20, §§3721, 3723, 3457, 3722 (1964).

plan tries to stimulate such higher standards, as we shall see, by guaranteeing greater wealth for the integrated districts. The guaranteed valuation is set as follows: basic elementary school districts equal $24,500; basic high school districts equal $55,000; integrated elementary school districts $30,000; integrated union high school districts $76,000; integrated combined (high school and elementary) districts $39,000.[30]

Note at this point that, to the extent that districts in fact have higher assessed valuations than these, which some do, the plan suffers from the same evil as every other percentage equalizing plan that equalizes up to but not down to the key district. It can already be seen, therefore, that the richest districts will be able to maintain their advantage of wealth.

Moreover, in Wisconsin the guaranteed valuation is (for "integrated" districts), operative only up to 17 mills in effort.[31] At tax rates higher than that, the support for the plan must come completely from local funds. At a tax rate of 17 mills the support in Wisconsin of integrated districts, for example, becomes a foundation plan of the following attributes:

Integrated—elementary	$ 501.50
Integrated—high school	1,275.00
Integrated—combined	646.00

At least these tend to be fairly substantial support levels. Yet in principle, while this state has shifted to a *local budget* approach, it has not been willing to support (inversely to wealth) budgets as great as the districts may desire. To that extent, districts with budgets in excess of the support ceiling will perpetuate the same wealth advantage pattern which the rich enjoy under the most elementary of Strayer-Haig foundation plans. Wisconsin also has an anti-equalizing minimum flat grant which

30. WISC. STATS. ANN. §§121.02, 121.07(7) (West 1968 Special Pamphlet).

31. *Ibid.*, §§ 121.07–121.13.

all districts can receive (varying in amount with the kind of district) if they are too rich to qualify for equalizing aid.

Reflection on the philosophy and concrete proposals of Cubberley, Strayer-Haig-Mort I and Benson-Mort II makes it clear that the theory of state aid to education in the twentieth century has become progressively more egalitarian. The progression in theory from flat grants to the foundation program to percentage equalizing grants has been stimulated wholly by a desire for increased financial equality between school districts. Unfortunately, there has been an equally consistent history of successful emasculation of these theories, of last-minute legislative modification or inexplicable compromise by the theorists themselves that has very nearly destroyed the effectiveness of the recommended reform. Thus the foundation program, meant as an offering by the state of the full cost of a certain legislatively determined, but fair, level of education, became a gesture of legislative generosity, expedience, and caprice unrelated to the cost of education. Similarly, the percentage equalizing grant, which would produce complete equality if based on the richest district or if employing negative numbers, has been modified to a point where it is little more equalizing than the foundation program, and often less so. The pressures for full equality of educational opportunity have always been strong; the governments of the states have long been urged to fulfill their commitment to public education. But the pressure has always been diverted by deft and frustrating political compromise. Probably nothing more can be expected in the absence of judicial intervention.

Part II · An Apparatus for Justice

Concentrated power is not rendered harmless by the good intentions of those who created it.

Friedman, *Captalism and Freedom*

6 · Power Equalizing

All power is delightful and absolute power is absolutely delightful.

George Santayana

CHAPTER 5 STRONGLY ENDORSED the principle of the percentage equalizing grant while rejecting its concrete implementations. Of course, it was our chosen standard of justice that gave rise to this enthusiasm. Starting from this inner core, we shall now attempt to construct a fuller and more flexible system of our own.

For us, the great merit of the percentage equalizing grant was its use of shares of the local budget rather than unit costs as the criterion for distribution of aid. This feature would equalize educational wealth at every level of effort and spending. We quarreled with concrete implementations, therefore, because the aid did not in fact operate at all levels of effort and it was not equalizing. The mechanical test for a just system is implied in these criticisms: for a system of local public school finance to be free of wealth determinants it must be *fully equalizing* of the power to raise educational dollars.

There are two basic normative implications of the requirement of full equalization. First, any right of subunits of the state to be relatively wealthy for educational purposes is denied. The total financial resources of the state should be equally available to all public school children. Ultimate responsibility for public schools is placed squarely with the state. Second, on the other hand, the units should be free, through the taxing mechanism, to choose to share various amounts of the state's wealth (by deciding how hard they are willing to tax themselves). And, of course, a great variety of state educational policies, other than favoring the possessors of wealth, may affect the extent of sharing.

A system of aid which has these characteristics we call *power equalizing* in preference to the term "percentage equalizing." The latter system is only one way to power equalize; the label percentage equalizing does not adequately describe all systems which have the required characteristics. A power equalizing system of state aid is one that leaves subunits free to select levels of spending for education while giving each unit equal power to do so. It is this term which we adopt as our own.[1]

Subsidiarity for All

It can readily be seen that a power equalizing system operates by making dollars per pupil a function of effort alone. In this way the dilemma of choosing between subsidiarity and equality is eliminated, because by equality we mean equality of power. Under the foundation plan, these values are largely inverse functions of each other. Under power equalizing, since the education budget is locally determined and the state merely pays a proportion of that budget inverse to local wealth, subsidiarity and equalization coexist. Power equalizing is a commitment by the state to the principle that the relationship between effort and offering of every district will be the same irrespective of wealth and that the district is to determine the effort (within appropriate limits if the state so desires). Through power equalizing subsidiarity for the first time would become meaningful to all districts, not just the wealthy ones. Like the present sys-

1. Benson's term "resource equalizer" carries the sense of "power equalizing." We prefer the latter, because it conveys more directly the notion of equality without sameness, and perhaps because of the current political idiom. See C. S. Benson, *The Cheerful Prospect: A Statement on the Future of Public Education* (Boston, 1961), pp. 90–93, 96, 98.

tem, power equalizing contemplates that districts will value education differently and, therefore, that the offerings throughout the state will differ. Local incentive is stressed to the exclusion of the incompatible value of statewide equality of offering. However, because incentive is stripped of differential wealth obstacles, it is hoped that the distribution of high and low expenditure districts will become random as regards wealth.

It seems permissible for a child to receive a better or worse offering in one district than in another. In fact, power equalizing cultivates the freedom of parents to live in areas (which they can otherwise afford) having the kind of commitment to education which they prefer. Without local fiscal control this is impossible. Statewide uniformity would mean that all children would receive the same compromise level of education and, consequently, that the only freedom of choice for parents would be freedom to leave the state. Further, for those parents, a centralized system terminates the opportunity and responsibility of working at the local level; an important political option is simply gone. All this is not to say that states may not reasonably decide to de-emphasize local choice; we do not oppose uniformity as unfair, but merely as unwise, largely because we prefer to stimulate local incentive. That is why we contrive to preserve subsidiarity.

The distribution of political power probably makes the straightforward legislative adoption of a true power equalizing policy (or any other equality system) impossible at present. But for our purposes we shall assume otherwise, recalling that it remains to examine the potential role of the judiciary in stimulating legislative action. What follows, then, is a brief outline of (1) what the theoretical base or value orientation of an ideal power equalizing system should be and how the mechanics should be established and (2) what variations can be tolerated within the system and what their purposes and impacts would be.

POWER EQUALIZING: THE MECHANICS

Percentage equalizing operates as noted earlier, through some equivalent of this formula:

$$\text{aid ratio equals 1 minus} \frac{\text{local ability}}{\text{key district ability}}$$

In order to see why it does not describe all power equalizing systems, notice two characteristics of the formula: (1) The school budget which results from a given effort is fixed. Depending on what the key district is, all other districts will be "as rich as" that district so that a twenty-mill tax in any district will produce exactly the same spendable dollars per pupil. (2) The formula also assumes, however, without really saying so, that the state share for any individual district will be the same at every level of spending and effort. That is, the state share of the budget is constant regardless of the size of the budget.

The first characteristic is almost the very definition of power equalizing, but the second is a theoretically unnecessary limitation. There is no reason that the state share could not vary with different efforts, so long as at any specific effort all subunits are fully equalized. Perhaps this is clearest if it is first understood that a more flexible and straightforward means of enacting the principle exists. The state may simply establish a table that matches specific local educational efforts with specific dollar offerings in the following form:

Effort (E)		Offering (O)
A	equals	W
B	equals	X
C	equals	Y
D	equals	Z

All possible variations of the power equalizing principle can be expressed in this way, for the table says everything necessary. If offering is solely a function of effort, it is obviously not a function of wealth; the percentage equalizing formulas which have been proposed assumed that, if effort C were twice effort A, then Y must be twice W — but this need not be so as long as all districts taxing at A end up with W and all those at C with Y whether Y be twice, thrice, or fifty dollars more than W or, indeed, whatever the relation. The net effect of power equalizing may be stated conceptually as O equals (f) E, although with the infinite variety of E and O relations permitted by the table specification may be pointlessly difficult.

In order to rationally fill in the table (or construct the E-O relation), the state must decide at least (1) the units in which the relation is measured (per pupil or per classroom unit, for example) and (2) the nature of the functional relation (what amount of E yields O). For example, (1) offering might be measured in dollars per weighted ADA pupil and (2) effort — expressed as a percent of local ability — and offering might be related linearly so that every one percent of effort is worth in offering what it would yield if made against $40,000 in wealth. As an equation it would be:

O per weighted ADA pupil equals $40,000 E

Much easier to follow, however, would be a table that might look like this:

E	O
1 percent	$ 400 per weighted ADA pupil
1½	600
2	800
2½	1,000
3	1,200

Note that O means total spendable income regardless of what is raised by the local tax at the specific effort. It is this "rule" of the table that is responsible for the equalizing effect, for it commits the state to give aid in exactly the amount that local resources are insufficient, or to take away locally generated funds when there is an excess.

It so happens that this particular table could have been derived directly from the simple percentage equalizing formula because in the table the state share for any district is exactly the same for any level of effort. The key district would be a district of $40,000 assessed valuation per weighted ADA pupil; because it is a district in which a 2-percent tax produces $800 per weighted ADA pupil, under percentage equalizing the $800 offering would be available to all districts taxing at 2 percent. This correspondence under percentage equalizing occurs if the table (or the equation) is set up, as in this example, in a simple linear way. But suppose the table looked like this:

E (percent)	O (dollars)
1.0	400
1.5	900
2.0	1600
2.5	2500
3.0	3600

Here the state's share for every level of effort is not the same. The table was constructed by relating effort and offering exponentially (O equals $40,000 E^2); hence, for equal increases in the local tax rate, increasingly higher spendable income results. This means, of course, that the state share becomes increasingly greater as well (for all districts), since the amount actually raised locally by the various taxes has not changed from the first table. As such manipulations increase in complexity and irregularity, expressing what is still a simple table as an O-E formula might become unworkable. Sophistications in policy choices permitted by the tabular approach will have made a nightmare of trying to build such flexibility into percentage equalizing.

The Table at Work: Basic Implications

The extreme simplicity of a power equalizing table, the bare statement of the O-E relationship, may disguise some of the fundamental effects, of which two are reviewed below, of changing numbers in the two columns.

1. *State and Local Share (Percent).* If the table decrees that a 2 percent entitles a district to $1,200 per pupil when the tax actually produces that $1,200 only in the richest 10 percent of the districts, the state has committed itself to making up the difference in many districts and in other words, to a substantial aid program. The exact ratio of state to local contributions would depend both on the degree to which wealth is unevenly distributed and the degree to which poorer (aided more) or richer (aided less) districts are taxing higher. On the other hand, if the average district produces the $1,200, the table would demand no state aid at all (assuming effort to be random as to wealth) except in the sense that some "local" money raised by all districts above the average would be turned in and redistributed to districts below (the concept is something like that of the Utah plan). The exponential table discussed above, it should be understood, would tend to increase the state share, other things being equal, because it treats the local tax as though it were higher than it really is.

2. *Total Size of Education Budget and State Liability in Dollars.* Having a table of possible expenditures obviously means that what the total expenditure for education will be cannot be predicted until the districts exercise their options (which can be done and reported in time for the state to respond, of course). It also means that the liability of the state cannot be predicted even though the state-to-local ratio at various rates and for districts of all wealths is implied by the relations in the table. But these are matters of great importance.

Maximum expenditure and maximum state liability could be predicted if there were an upper limit upon the effort rate and it were assumed that every district would tax at that rate. A realistic prediction of district behavior is more difficult. All that can practically be done is to indicate the kinds of systemic factors that would lead to increased or decreased local taxing and, still assuming effort to be random as to wealth, the consequent changes in state and local spending. For example, to the extent that the state commits itself to providing more of the dollars, it would probably stimulate greater total spending, at least partly because state taxes are thought to be less visible than local taxes. So long as an unsatisfied demand for increased spending exists, the availability of a new revenue source would attract immediate use. This point is really not different for power equalizing than for any system. It says merely that for some time the carrot of increased state presence is likely to yield higher spending rather than burden-shifting in the form of tax relief.

Further, under a power equalizing system there is in a sense a penalty for low taxes paid by any individual district desiring relatively lower school spending. As one district cannot control the actions of another, its high effort must be paid for in part by state taxes collected to some extent from districts of lower effort. If two similar districts seek subsidization from without, each must keep up in the effort race. This "penalty," of course, occurs in any system of subsidy based upon matching grants affected by local decision-making. This factor also may tend to increase expenditures generally.

What would actually happen under a new power equalizing system probably would depend most on the exact levels of support chosen compared to those previously in effect. Suppose a high level is chosen, one under which nearly all districts will be able to maintain their current expenditures at the same tax rate and most will be able to gain immediate substantial increases in offering. Under this hypothesis the average local tax rate in the state is not likely to change much. Few poorer districts would reduce rates; rather, most would delight in the new state funds flowing in. Under this assumption almost all of the newly available state support would be used for spending rather than tax relief (ironically, local tax relief would be cheaper for the state because it means lower taxes, and lower taxes mean, under power equalizing, lower expenditures for the *state* to support). State expenditures would be closely predictable because the few districts most likely to raise their rates would be those rich districts eligible for little state aid, desiring to retain their relative advantage. Hence, by applying the present average local tax rate to the statewide total of local property wealth and subtracting that amount from what the total offering cost would be, based upon the per-pupil spending fixed by the table for the current average tax rate, a good indication of the state's total obligation can be calculated.

What individual districts of various sorts are likely to do under power equalizing will be examined more generally in Chapter 7.

Permissible Variations to Achieve State Legislative Goals

The state may not be willing to permit both the total size of the school budget and the state contribution to be completely dependent on local enthusiasm. It may wish to preserve subsidiarity, but only within upper and/or lower taxing limits, so as to force the achievement of some overriding state goals. Since power equalizing emphasizes effort as *the* subject of local decision-making, it is the effort factor that is most likely to be adjusted when limitations are considered. For example, although the hypothetical charts of E and O values were meant only to illustrate the relation, they could represent the entire permissible spectrum of effort (that is, effort could be confined to a tax between one and three percent). There are several reasons why the state might choose to confine power equalizing in these ways.

Minimum Offering Demanded. The state might wish to require that all districts provide some minimum educational offering, thereby confining subsidiarity on the lower end. The local political process would be denied the option of valuing education less than the statutory minimum; and the children would be guarded to the extent of the minimum against a selfish or capricious political majority in their districts. A lower limit on spending is consistent with the basic principle of power equalizing, for it does not involve any problem of wealth advantage. In fact, fear of a destructive reaction among the wealthy might be the stimulant. In some districts private schools could appear more attractive than either payment of part of the local tax dollar into the state or payment of much higher state taxes. Thus, to guarantee some minimum of education for those who live in such districts and use the public schools, the state could impose a spending floor.

Other fears might be related to the behavior of districts with specific demographic profiles. Perhaps this is protection of families with children from those without; perhaps it is a paternalistic protection of those who are ignorant from their own ignorance. At any rate, the bottom level should not be so high that it makes local decision-making trivial and ineffective (unless that is the state's policy). Rather, it should represent merely a sound educational base. The most esthetic form of the limit would be a minimum local tax rate requiring all districts to exercise their power (E) to some limited extent. Of course a minimum spending level (O) is mathematically equivalent.

Maximum Offering Allowed. The state might also wish to confine subsidiarity on the upper end, for a variety of reasons: (1) Resources are scarce, and other expenditures, private and public, compete with educational ones. (2) Districts receiving very large proportions of their school budgets from the state may be thought to be hyperstimulated in the direction of school expenditures and so cheat themselves on other municipal services or other private purchases. Such "distortion" of the overall budgets of local governments can be controlled by an educational spending maximum.[2] (3) Districts with large proportions of their budget supplied by the state may be thought to lack fiscal responsibility — the drive to spend wisely and economically.[3] There must in theory be a point at which dollars begin to have diminishing educational returns and further expenditures are frivolous.

Many of these considerations reflect good management and fiscal responsibility; nevertheless, spending limits should be cautiously imposed. If there is inflation, an increase in costs, a desire among districts to excel by sacrifice for education, or a general upgrading of educational goals, the state risks losing one of the advantages of subsidiarity.[4] Of course, the proper way to put a ceiling on offering is to do it for all districts — to set a maximum on effort by the table.

Freezing the Effort Rate. Overambitious use of *both* minimum and maximum rates can eliminate subsidiarity altogether. At the point of their convergence, all local option is eliminated in favor of uniform rates and offerings throughout the state. This is certainly congruent with equal opportunity as we have

2. "The attractiveness of matching grants for education may be so great that other local services are put under severe financial distress," Benson, *Economics,* p. 245. However, Benson also observes that, as most of the poorest districts are already taxing at a high rate, the danger of distortion is greatly exaggerated.

3. As Benson points out (*ibid.,* pp. 230–232), all that is really necessary for the existence of fiscal responsibility is that the district (1) feels the burden of demanding more; (2) feels the relief of any efficiency. We assume that these values are fulfilled for the poor district as well as the rich; under power equalizing each must sacrifice the same proportion of its total wealth. There seems to be something magic about getting large shares from the state, however, because even Benson maintains that if more than 75% of the funds issue from the state, compensating central budgetary controls are required. This is admittedly a guess on his part; we guess the opposite, preferring to raise a presumption of equal responsibility from equal effort. The state could avoid the dangers of both irresponsibility and recapture by eliminating extreme cases of district poverty and wealth through selective redistricting.

4. See P. R. Mort, "Unification of Fiscal Policy in New York," in C. S. Benson, ed., *Perspectives on the Economics of Education* (Boston, 1963), pp. 340–341.

defined it, for wealth does not affect offering; for those who prefer equal offering it represents perfection. We regard the loss of subsidiarity as crucial, however, and, in any case, the elaborate power equalizing structure is rather pointless if the effort rate is frozen, or practically so. A centralized fiscal system is equivalent and more efficient.

Horizontal Definitions. Full power equalizing may generate opposing positions, one expansive and one restrictive, with regard to the definition of what is "education." Wealthy districts could retain their edge to the extent that legitimate educational costs are excluded; capital costs are an obvious example. Poor districts, on the other hand, might be tempted to piggyback noneducational municipal building or services on the shared cost program; a public stadium is a typical borderline example. The state will have to set uniform answers for the recurrent question: is this education or not? [5]

MEASURING WEALTH AND EFFORT

If effort is to be the sole basis for variety in level of offering, some accurate way of measuring it is required even though perfection in the method is concededly impossible. In the hierarchy of errata, the arbitrary error is less pernicious than a systematic error that cheats poor districts and subsidizes rich or, perhaps, vice versa.

A simple example will explain the first problem of measurement. Under power equalizing, all districts will be told by the legislature that if they tax some designated item at a certain

5. In addition to setting standards, the state will also be required to review local budgets to determine compliance. In some cases accounting reforms are mandatory, as in New York, where Mort recommended that all municipalities maintain separate accounts for educational and other services. The existing practice of commingling funds made determination of the local budget size impossible; *ibid.*, pp. 34–39.

percent they can spend a certain number of dollars. If poor districts tax lower than that percentage rate because their voters do not care as much about education as those in other districts, under the rules of power equalizing they deserve less and get less: the system is working properly. But if they tax lower because the set rate is a greater burden on them than it is on rich districts, their children will be expected to continue to suffer unfairly, if less so than under existing systems. Some attention must therefore be paid to the details of the tax selected, as the object of local decision-making.

The problems of potential mismeasurement of effort are more practical than theoretical, and they seem to be at least threefold. First is the problem of *incidence*, second the *proportion of local source to total local wealth*, third *marginal utility*. All three, having been discussed in other contexts, are reviewed here as a package because of their interconnected and direct impact on effort; the focus will be not so much on how they can lead the state to make arbitrary errors as upon systematic errors that cut specifically against certain classes of districts.

The problem regarding *incidence* is that a district may be able to pass on the tax it levies to outsiders, both distorting our perception of local wealth and disrupting the relation between tax levy and effort. Suppose that, in implementing power equalizing, a state were to select a tax on all property (tangible and intangible) as the measure of effort, only to discover that in some districts when a 2-percent tax was levied the effective incidence of the tax in the district was only 1 percent, with the other 1 percent of the burden passed outside. This would mean in turn that other districts trying with their own voted effort would also have to bear the 1 percent, so that another district which had voted 1 percent might end up effectively bearing 2 percent. Since it is the economic impact of the tax which counts in determining who is making the effort, if a district can pass on the economic impact, then mere *payment* of the tax in the district means little.

For another example, an excise tax on a manufacturer is often said to be passed on to the consumer. Even though the full tax may seem to be openly passed on, however (that is, the invoice states selling price plus tax), it in fact may not be fully passed on if the market cross-elasticities among products taxed and those not taxed are such that the basic price before taxes (selling price) of the taxed product is forced down.[6] Obviously, the question of true incidence of a specific tax is a very difficult one,[7] although economists have become adept at stating theoretically what kind of tax incidence is shifted and what kind is borne by the taxpayer.

If the problem of shifting is too severe, the tax becomes completely irrational as a basis for awarding money to school districts. The district is supposed to be exercising reasoned choice, and cannot do so if a chosen effort may be transmuted into an unexpected burden or bonus after all similar decisions by districts around the state are analyzed. Yet, if shifting incidence is a fact, then some districts will be making an effort different from that which appears and power equalizing will at best be somewhat arbitrary. For the state, the lesson of incidence is clear: for purposes of power equalizing education,

6. "At present, within a given industry, companies pay different tax rates, depending on the location of a particular plant. This results in unfair competition among industries in the state"; J. A. Thomas, *School Finance and Educational Opportunity in Michigan* (Lansing, 1968), p. 327.

7. Some economists hold the opinion that property taxes are not generally shifted forward in the form of rents but are capitalized in the guise of the willingness of purchasers to invest in rental property. Explanation: the rent market is thought to be governed by influences completely independent of the cost of investing in rental property. Dick Netzer, *The Economics of the Property Tax* (Washington, D.C., 1966), p. 33. This may be only superficially contradicted by the average tenant's experience of property tax rationalization for rent increases. At some point the market will no longer bear such increases and the landlord must absorb the tax.

it should select as the measure of local effort a tax which can with some confidence be predicted to have its incidence upon the voters, so that when they levy a given rate they will feel it and feel it all.

Intelligible incidence is what makes the taxation of realty coherent (putting aside for the moment any question of unfairness in a property tax levied only on realty). We are assuming that tenants feel the primary incidence of the tax on landlords. If this were not so, location of the owners (landlords) would be the locus of the burden, probably rewarding highly tenanted districts with better schools than they deserve.

An example of a systematic error that cheats poor districts is difficult to find when the focus is on incidence alone; in theory, it would be a tax levied and paid in rich districts but felt in poor ones. To be sure that our perspective is clear, the evil of this should be specified. By feeling the incidence of another district's levy, the poor district may be unwilling to set its tax rate as high as it might otherwise. Thus the children will continue to receive a lower-quality education, when the effective burden their district bears entitles them to more. Or, even if the poor districts did not feel constrained to tax lower, they will have the same offering with a higher effort — meaning that their children deserve more.

Perhaps a tax on residents who are members of trade and professional associations and unions as the measure of district effort is an example of a levy which rich districts can shift onto the poor ones. Businessmen belonging to trade associations and doctors, lawyers, and others who belong to professional associations could perhaps pass on the incidence of the tax in the price of goods or fees. Some of the burden surely would be felt by consumers and clients in poorer school districts than those in which the taxpayers live. However, workers who belong to unions may not be able to pass on their tax to anyone (query their ability to include it in their wage contract).

To the extent that union members live in poorer districts and association members do not, the tax in its overall incidence hurts poorer districts to the benefit of the richer ones because he who is "trying" really is not.

The second problem involves the proportion of the local source to total local wealth. Here it is easier to find examples of invidious errors. A tax on something in which poor districts have a greater proportion of their total wealth invested will, at the same rate, burden them more than rich ones. Such a tax, at least when applicable to people, is defined as regressive. Although the simplest case of regressivity is one where the tax rates on the poor are greater than those on the rich, having a relatively larger base subject to the same tax rate is effectively the same thing. We have earlier mentioned the problem of a tax on realty as one that can invidiously harm the poor districts. That is, real property may represent a higher proportion of total local wealth in poor districts than in rich districts.[8] Setting an example on an individual rather than a district basis, imagine a 2-percent tax on realty assuming that tenants bear the burden

8. Conclusions on the degree, if not the fact, of regressivity vary. Netzer concludes that the tax is somewhat regressive compared to current family income, without weighing the further regressivity of taxes on business property; the latter becomes a general consumption tax through forward shifting (ibid., p. 40). The tax is markedly regressive in the lower income groups ($3,000 a year and below); ibid., p. 41. Jesse Burkhead concludes that the real property tax is regressive by income class, even without weighing the further effect of the deductibility of real estate taxes from income for federal tax purposes; State and Local Taxes for Public Education (Syracuse, 1963), pp. 28–29. The authorities all differ on the question of whether assessments are regressive independent of regressivity of the tax.

Note the Michigan data given in Appendix F, Table 5. It is surely true that the tax is markedly regressive compared to current income for certain classes of taxpayers, e.g., retired homeowners living on pensions or social security. Advisory Commission on Intergovernmental Relations, Fiscal Balance in the American Federal System (Washington, D.C., 1967), I, 22. But this example is probably not germane in the context of public school finance. In any case, the direct problem here is not the wealth of individuals but of the district, and that point is hard to resolve.

of realty tax. Realty might represent 25 percent of the poor man's wealth; we will assume that to be the proportion of his wage (income) that goes for shelter, and we will also assume income to be a good measure of wealth. For the rich man, however, this may mean a 2-percent tax on only 10 percent of his wealth (possibly measured by comparing his mortgage payments to his income or his real property to his accumulated property). This means that, while they appear to make the same effort, these hypothetical poor and rich men would be making effective efforts of .5 percent and .2 percent respectively — or, put another way, the poor man is trying two and a half times as hard.

As another example, take as the measure of local effort a school tax levied on ducks bagged by residents while hunting in the district. This tax would be felt quite differently in actual burden among districts because the value of ducks shot (the local source) is sure to be a varying proportion of local wealth from district to district. That is, a tax of 10 percent of the value of the game bagged might be five times as great a true percent of wealth in district A (where it might represent 10 percent of .1 percent of wealth) as compared with district B, where duck hunting is unpopular (there it might be 10 percent of .02 percent of wealth). There is justification for choosing a whimsical example. First, it illustrates this class of problem — local source as a proportion of wealth — in which there is no clear-cut regressivity or progressivity to the tax. In other words, it will result in errors in measuring effort, but it will not systematically injure or help poor districts or rich ones by undervaluing or overvaluing their effort (at least so far as one can tell without detailed analysis). The inaccuracy of the local source as a constant proportion of total wealth will vary, rather, with such elements as the location of ducks and the interest of the residents in hunting.

Secondly, the duck tax will have strong differential impact

on families *within* the district. It will be a burden on only some of the voters. The measure of district effort cannot be a good measure if it does not include the behavior of a great number of people in the district. It is unlike a tax on property or income because it is not something that (1) people will tend to want regardless of whether it is taxed (people may be driven to give up duck hunting) or that (2) most voters realize they personally must pay for when they vote for it, thus choosing education instead of money. In the duck tax, improper considerations will enter the decision-making process, and power equalizing would be diverted from expressing a policy in the field of education alone.

Under present systems, industrial and commercial property generates problems both of proportionality and incidence. In Chapter 3 industrial and commercial property was discussed from the standpoint of isolating the party injured by existing systems when some of the wealth of districts is of this "artificial" sort (for example, owned by nonresidents). Under power equalizing, whether or not the wealth is artificial in that sense does not matter, for the more money a district raises from the local tax (regardless of whether the wealth is artificial or natural), the less state aid it becomes entitled to at that local tax rate.

In fact, the incidence and proportion problem associated with commercial and industrial property is substantially altered by power equalizing. Assuming the local tax to be on realty generally, as now, it is important to note that residents cannot tax nonresidential property without taxing their own. In a sense, then, shifting the burden of such taxes out of a certain district does not help that district directly; but assuming there is some shifting (to consumers? stockholders?), other districts could be *hurt* in some unmeasurable way because they feel extra incidence from taxes used for school fund-raising elsewhere. The district receives an indirect advantage.

There are at least two additional problems with such property. In the first place, it seems to account for many of the freakishly wealthy districts in most states. Such districts make it very hard to establish a rational aid system, requiring under power equalizing, for example, either an enormously high state share and total budget or the politically unpopular provision for payment of locally generated moneys into the state.[9] Secondly, while the classic form of "fiscal mercantilism" (attraction of revenue, repulsion of cost) may not apply under power equalizing,[10] a more subtle form may exist. Either deliberately low taxes, even at the cost of bad schools, can be levied as part of the "bargain" with industry,[11] or, worse, there is even a possibility that artificially low assessments of industrial and commercial property can become part of the bargain.[12] Both situations have the effect of protecting this part of the state's wealth from its fair share of supporting public schools. The second course is particularly pernicious and effective, for under it industrial and commercial wealth is protected but school expenditures need not decline (with the low valuation the tax

9. Of course, these hard choices can be avoided by redistricting to eliminate extremes of wealth.

10. Presently, both the suburb and the industrial enclave may practice fiscal mercantilism. Both attract resources (industry, high stable property values) and repel costs (people who would live where industry locates; people who would live on smaller lots and in apartments); Burkhead, State and Local Taxes, p. 43. In our terms this practice is a deliberate attempt to become "public service rich" — to have better services for a lower tax rate — and therefore to hoard resources locally and prevent the spreading of governmental costs.

11. However, one cause of growing homogeneity in tax rates in metropolitan areas may be the twilight of the high-resource/low-tax community in favor of the high-resource/high-tax community; Netzer, Economics, p. 133, citing Burkhead.

12. For example, if a district has industrial property worth $20,000 and assessed at $10,000, a 20-mill tax will produce $200 rather than $400. Since under power equalizing a 20-mill tax will imply the same amount of spendable income in either case, more state source money results. Note that the residents themselves do pay their fair share so long as their own property is not underassessed.

rate can be "normal" but it means lower local revenues and higher state aid).

The problem of *marginal utility* has been mentioned before and will be discussed again in this chapter at some length in connection with municipal overburden. It can be expressed simply thus: it is a greater sacrifice for some people than for others to devote two percent of their income to education.[13] The marginal utility problem is exclusively a problem of the poor because it is their limited income and fixed needs that make any proportion of wealth put toward education more difficult to surrender. This factor has, deliberately, not been accounted for in our power equalizing formula, for the marginal utility factor is extrinsic to the school financing system: it is the spillover effect of the relative difficulty in financing everything else. Hence, on the notion that an equal effort must in principle produce an equal offering, we have gauged equal effort only by equal tax rate. For marginal utility to be considered directly we would have to adjust the O equals (f)E mechanics for each district based upon its wealth and thus create a more complex new calculus for the power equalizing model. We do not undertake to suggest the form for any such a calculus; nor do we insist upon such a refinement as a necessary component of a rational system. However, we can appreciate that legislatures would want to adjust in some pragmatic fashion for this factor. It may be possible to achieve such adjustment indirectly.

First, the tax object can be selected so that the local tax is effectively progressive. It falls harder on the rich because their tax base for the local source is a greater proportion of their wealth, for example as in the case of a tax on securities. This burden on the rich may offset the marginal utility burden on

13. Marginal utility is believed to be an operative though unquantifiable influence on tax behavior; Burkhead, *State and Local Taxes*, p. 3.

the poor. Second, a tax could be selected that would allow districts suffering from the marginal utility problem to shift the tax burden to the other districts. In sum, because the marginal utility effect makes a tax which is otherwise proportional really regressive, ways to end the evil of the regressive tax are either to allow some of its incidence to be shifted or to start with a progressive one. Neither of these solutions may be very satisfying, however, because of their imprecision and their encouragement of bizarre selection of one factor as a supposed adjustment of another — especially in view of the radical superiority of the third alternative presented by the state's share in the support of the system. If the tax supporting that share has a progressive effect because of rates, source, or both, the effects of marginal utility could be substantially ameliorated. What the district suffers in marginal burdening of the local source it may in part make up in the progressive element embedded in the state portion. The progressive income tax is a traditional response to the marginal utilities problem and seems to us the most promising area in which to seek a rough but pragmatic solution.

The importance of the marginal utility factor should not be overemphasized. Suppose a system has been adopted which takes into account the factors of incidence and proportionality. As observed above, it should be possible to alleviate both problems. Once this is accomplished, it could be fair to regard the marginal utility problem as having less substantial implications for education because of another aspect of power equalizing. To the extent that public education is the only local function which is power equalized, it should represent an area of particularly strong incentive for the poor. Every dollar raised locally for education will bring in a number of state aid dollars for poor districts. The dramatic and novel aspects of this "bonus," and the new opportunity for advancement through education that it represents, may more than offset the effect of marginal utilities upon the willingness of the poor to compete with the rich in the battle of education investment. To the extent that this happens, the school offering in poor districts will cease to feel the otherwise probable impact of the marginal pressure facing local voters to purchase items other than education. Once again, because our focus is on the education of children, this is an adequate, if imperfect, solution. It may mean some small neglect of spending on other items in poor districts in the arena of public and/or private consumption; but this is not of crucial concern, at least so long as the net effect upon the poor — and, specifically, upon education — is beneficial.

To be sure, this factor may mean realistically that the poor districts are actually making greater effort than the rich when they have the same tax rate and that, thus, they deserve to be able to provide better offerings. We think the state can adjust in a general way for this; and yet, this may be one of the areas where principle must yield to pragmatism if power equalizing is to be more than an academic exercise.

Evaluation of the Measurement Problem

In sum, we suggest only rationality, not absolute precision, in the measure of effort. The state must be given a wide choice among tax programs with which to exact and measure local effort. It must be charged with the duty of selecting and administering programs which reasonably indicate relative effort and, particularly, it must if possible avoid one that systematically hurts the poor districts.

As a practical matter, either a local property tax or a local income tax is the most likely candidate. Each represents a levy upon what most would accept as the best practical measures of the otherwise abstract concept of wealth. Because it represents the status quo, the property tax would hold the inside track. Perhaps with industrial and commercial property excluded, this would be a fair system, though the equality of administration is problematical. Personal income may well be the more reliable as a measure of wealth and, thus, in turn, of effort. It also seems to have its incidence on the taxpayer and can be controlled for regressiveness and progressiveness. All in all, it is the best choice.

The state might, of course, choose some special tax, such as a sales tax on gasoline. But this would be a bad choice, for it is a most unreliable guide, primarily because the voter can buy the product elsewhere; voting to tax gasoline sold in your district may have no correlation with the effort people in your district actually make through their purchases. The same is true of a tax on liquor sales; the product is easily purchased out of the district. Moreover, these two examples, particularly the latter, suffer from the "duck hunter" tax problem in which considerations other than education motivate the electorate.

If a district general sales tax is used, the problem appears again that people can and do travel elsewhere to make purchases. This could (1) make all taxes (effort) the same and/or (2) make the taxes low everywhere as competition for business wins out over competition for education — with a disastrous impact on schools. These examples illustrate vividly that where there is a geographically oriented concept of benefit there must be a coincident geographic plan for burden.

A use tax instead of a sales tax is surely better, to the extent that its base does not move around as purchases do; it is tied to a district and will be felt by those who vote it. But unless there is self-reporting, as with income tax, the collection problem is intolerable. Use tax is normally collected by the merchant making a sale; but for our purposes he would have to charge different rates to different purchasers based upon the rules in their districts. Shifting to self-reporting payment is unlikely to yield any advantage over the income tax. The use tax may well be regressive, although with elimination of food from the base it is perhaps proportional. It tends to measure consumption instead of income; and the poor, in an economic sense, have a greater propensity to consume (rather than save) than do the rich.

While income tax may be the best reasoned choice, it is not the only one. It must be remembered always that the problem treated here is not a taxpayer's complaint: it is a complaint by children about education. What we seek to eliminate is the poor-district/poor-schools syndrome. If the various states can end it with a variety of effort measures, so much the better. Flexibility is an additional value we respect. It is strongly implied in the policy of subsidiarity that power equalizing works so hard to protect.

The State Share: Does the Source Matter?

Because the problem of equating effort and offering may be affected somewhat by the state's choice of tax used to raise state aid under a power equalizing system, this choice should be examined briefly. It has already been suggested that the problem of marginal utility may find its solution here. The system must function so that poor districts do not vote a lower local effort because they are poor, but only because they are less interested in education; a progressive state income tax would seem the most felicitous device for this purpose. But the state's choice surely is legitimately wider than this.

Some state taxes would seem rather unfair, for example, a head tax. The state might tax parents on the basis of number of their children in school. Or, it might tax adults or families (not on the number of children) on a simple count basis. (We put aside here any separate legal problem with these taxes.) The first type is the most outrageous, particularly if state aid is large, because it amounts to tuition. It is counter to the principle won in the 1800's that education is beneficial to the whole community, so that taxes for it should be borne by the whole community. In economic terms it is extremely regressive; rich and poor families of the same size would pay the same tax. Poor districts might well be coerced into a lower local effort rate so that the state would not have to tax them so high in order to generate what in large part will be their own aid money. Such a tax scheme is calculated to harm children of poor districts under the guise of an equality approach of power equalizing. The head tax on adults or families suffers from the same evil. It, too, is so highly regressive that it would most likely force poor districts once again to drop from the competition in education.

Warning should be given of another impermissible scheme, which would simply eliminate the state share. Our complaint has been that the children of poor districts receive lower-quality offerings because of the wealth of their districts. Why would it not be a proper response for the state to set a uniform offering for all districts and then tax each district at a rate that raises enough money locally to support the offering? Of course this is not power equalizing, but it would superficially eliminate the poor-district/poor-offering problem. What kind of principle can be invoked to prohibit this kind of device, which brings about equality for children by mercilessly scalping parents and neighbors in poor areas on their behalf? The most convincing response (and we begin to sound like lawyers) is that the state may not select districts as classes which, without choice, are to be subject to different tax rates for the same purpose unless there is a rational basis for such a system. But the only rational basis for having dissimilar efforts at the district level is to permit districts to be able to achieve variations in offerings. Under this device offerings would be uniform and the differential treatment would thus be detached from any valid purpose.

In sum, the state taxing policy is an important consideration. Any political solution that does not discriminate against the poor will probably be tolerable, though a strongly progressive system would be best.

Three Further Measurement Issues

This catalogue of problems is hardly exhaustive of the obstacles, man-made and natural, in the way of a true measure of effort in a power equalizing system. We offer three examples of more minor difficulties: accuracy of assessment of local wealth, comparability in method of measuring effort, and basic fairness in choice of task units.

Assessment Problems. Despite efforts of state equalization boards, the nation abounds with the problems of (1) accuracy and (2) uniformity of assessment. (1) means the problem of consistency among assessors: it is important that property in one district of the same market value as property in another in fact be assessed at the same value. (2) means the problem of consistency among kinds of property: whether residential property, public utility property, vacant land and so on are assessed at the same uniform percentage of market value.

Obviously, satisfactory measurement of wealth can be rendered hopeless by loose assessment. If a district is assessed at ten percent above value it loses ten percent in spendable school dollars. A district cheating on the low side gets a handsome bonus relative to true wealth. Under systems where there was little state aid, or where local effort did not affect the amount of aid, interdistrict valuation differences were unimportant. But under power equalizing, local communities would do well to look at the problem anew and insist on fair and equalized assessment procedures — across the whole state rather than merely the county.

Comparability. Comparability in the measure of effort means that all local revenue raised for the same thing from district to district must be counted as part of the total effort. It would completely defeat the basic purpose, for example, if only certain districts were to pay for portions of current expenses out of an "educational tax" and some special tax but were to count only the educational tax as effort for purposes of power equalizing.

Selecting Task Units. Under power equalizing, the subject of task units is every bit as complicated and interesting as it was when Ellwood Cubberley wrote sixty years ago. The power equalizing table easily establishes "dollars per pupil" in offering at a given tax rate, as we know; but it is not easy to decide what a pupil is in the first place,[14] and, in the second place, the measure has been increasingly weighted by the states for varying cost factors. These "costs" in turn may be costs of doing the same thing in different districts or doing different things because of different "needs" (the latter would probably represent a performance-related education policy, such as extra dollars spent on bright children). In any case, the point here is the same as that for assessment and measure of effort. If "real" costs are not reflected in the measure, the table's offering of "five hundred dollars per pupil" will not equalize the true cost of education, or else it will operate discriminatorily from one place to another.

Under power equalizing, a district's effort is important because of the dollars per task unit ultimately made available to it. If task units are weighted — for example, a rural child counted as 1.15 students — the task unit operates in effect as a multiplier. Such weighting will provide districts with fifteen percent more total dollars at every level of effort.

An interesting dilemma arises if adjustments are adopted by the state on the basis of such perceptions of variation in the number of task units represented by other than the mere number of pupils. If the state gives a certain weighting for low

14. Do we tally students by per-pupil enrollment, average attendance, or aggregate attendance? See the discussion of Cubberley's search for a task unit reflective of true costs in Appendix B.

density, for example, it will in part be motivated by supposedly higher transportation costs. The question becomes whether or not the state will or should then insist that the district attempt to accommodate state judgment of greater task by spending the extra money for the specific purpose that was the basis of the award. A more obvious example is that of the blind child: if the state awards one task unit for the typical pupil and three for the blind pupil, is the district then bound to spend three times as much on its blind students? To the degree that it is so bound, subsidiarity and its emphasis on local decision-making are eroded. Moreover, since all that power equalizing requires is a local budget and a local effort deserving of that budget, it surely does not imply an intrinsic need for state strings. It would be proper, we feel, for the state to award the extra task units and leave to the fairmindedness and intelligence of the local officials (and the Constitution) the allocation of the funds to specific uses. This surely would be most desirable. The state would still have some control for flagrant cases, for it retains the power to approve the local budget; this is necessary if only to be sure that districts are not spending the money on air pollution or civil defense instead of education.[15] The approach is flexible and seems to maximize the opportunity for enlightened local administration.

There is another related problem regarding the adjustment of task units. If the state awards additional task units because of transportation needs, for example, is it proper that those needs should be filled with a different amount of money depending upon the level of effort the district makes? The way in which this problem arises can be seen in a district with 100 task units, given 10 more units for transportation; when it makes an effort entitling it to $500 per task unit, one might say

15. This kind of problem arises especially when the school authority is a mere administrative body, rather than a separate taxing body. See Mort, "Unification," in Benson, *Perspectives*, pp. 348–349.

that it will receive $5,000 because of transportation considera-
tions and $50,000 for the rest of education. When it makes an
effort entitling it to $800 per unit, one can argue that it will get
not only $80,000 for education generally but $8,000 because of
transportation considerations. Transportation has the appearance of a fixed cost. Will the district escort the children to
school in chauffeur-driven Cadillacs? To make such a dollar
result sensible, the principle must be accepted that, with either
the $55,000 or the $88,000 available, there is no real state intention that any particular amount go for transportation. In
short, this is not an award made under the philosophy of a
specific grant for a specific purpose; it is simply a guess by the
state, stemming perhaps originally from a notion of what
kind of extra burden transportation may be, and is no more
than an effort to make districts comparable at what experience
has shown to be the average level of offering.[16] In other words,
the task unit adjustments in many cases involve policies to
award extra dollars because of extra costs; but, of course, extra
costs under power equalizing are only there when the district
makes an appropriate effort. Thus, calculation of the amount
of the adjustment might originally be based on what an average district offering would involve when the district faced
such extra cost problems. However, since there will be little
state control over what is spent for education even by that
average district, there should be no worry that an increasing
amount is received by districts with such task adjustments so
long as they have increasing effort.

Because of this problem, one would expect that under power

16. According to one authority, the process of estimating transportation
costs is so general that it conceals a compensation for rural poverty and lack
of commitment to education, if not outright rural legislative muscle at the
state level; A. J. Burke, "The Density Correction in the New York State
School Aid Formula," in National School Finance Conference, Committee on
Educational Finance, ed., Long Range Planning in School Finance (Washington, D.C., 1963), p. 135.

equalizing the state will adjust for task problems sparingly and only where the problem perceived is clearly differential in its impact among districts. For example, if all districts have a roughly similar proportion of blind pupils, there is no reason to adjust task units on their account; the same goes for high school pupils versus elementary pupils if their proportions are relatively constant throughout the state. If all districts will be adjusted approximately similarly, it serves no purpose to adjust at all. This means that the task unit adjustment may be a gross sort of thing, and one is tempted to say that a simple unadjusted head count would be adequate. Remembering the problems that are unique to certain districts, however, unfairness would be risked with a complete failure to adjust for task. Perhaps the alternative of computing a "variable flat grant" based upon the actual costs of various services is the best overall solution. The grant would be flat in the sense that it would not change according to wealth or effort, but would be variable across districts depending on differential costs.

A final note will illustrate how, occasionally, nonfinancial devices can eliminate differentials in task. The problems of lack of economies of scale from underpopulation, for example, can be solved by stimulating merger of districts;[17] although this does sacrifice rock-bottom subsidiarity, it must be noted that the current reason for refusing to merge (we are richer than you and you will dilute our schools if we merge) no longer exists under power equalizing.

How should we feel about having the burden of financing the state share thrust upon those in districts with little interest in public education, who elect to tax low? The higher other districts tax, the more the former will pay, despite their lack

17. In areas of fragmented local government the reduction in wealth disparities can be remarkable. In California, wealth ratios between all units (not only school districts) as high as 7,000 to 1 could be reduced to no higher than 22 to 1 by political consolidation. Burkhead, *State and Local Taxes*, p. 45.

of interest. The state tax, of course, will be imposed upon units other than districts. Thus, the impact on people in a district of low effort may not be uniform. Further, the state may provide the state share through a tax on industrial and commercial property, the impact of which on people in low-effort districts is at worst unclear and is probably random. Who would pay how much for whom is at this state of history radically incalculable. But, by definition, the taxable population of the low-effort district will help support a higher level of public education for others than they provide for themselves.

But low-effort sufferers are like taxpayers who have no children. They, too, pay more when bigger efforts are voted by others, and their own behavior matters little. This, in the end, must be seen to go to the heart of equality in public education; all pay, so that all children have a fair chance. Note, after all, that such a burden falls as well on the low-trying poor districts which forfeit the chance to get money and whose residents still pay taxes for the state share. In sum, if the poor districts do not compete in effort they, just like the rich, must still support those who do, even if their contribution is meager in absolute quantity. They are given a chance to keep up. If they rise to it, the accompanying burden of state taxes is lighter. If they do not, they carry the dual burden of poor schools and high state taxes.

This is a simple form of incentive program. If on that basis it is unfair, all incentive programs would have to be similarly condemned. Of course, the impact on taxpayers may be uneven; but concern must always focus upon the *education of children*. Regarded simply as a taxpayer issue, such unevenness is probably more frequent than its opposite: the complaint is intelligible but unconvincing. If anything, such potential unevenness will spur high effort and thus generally good schools — an effect we do not consider pernicious. There seems to be really only one qualification. One of the advantages of local choice in spending is that an efficient community is rewarded by as good a school for less money, a better one for the same, and so on. Power equalizing, being a system of local finance, permits this saving in the form of lower local taxes; but inefficient communities can export some of the cost in the form of state taxes (just as some of the efficiency saves state taxes). Actually, power equalizing is not special in this regard because any state aid at all raises the same problem; and a centralized system spreads the inefficiency to a far greater degree.

MUNICIPAL OVERBURDEN:
A SECOND LOOK AT MARGINAL UTILITY

The purpose of the power equalizing system we have recommended is to free public school finance from the influence of "wealth" variations, but only in the sense used so far — namely, from variations in "education wealth" or wealth per school task unit. Equal "school power" thus has meant the ability to spend an equal amount for education for an equal amount of tax effort levied against the local source. Earlier in this chapter, while considering factors that can influence the choice of tax devices to be employed in a power equalizing system, we focused on the school money-raising part of the economy alone. Now we will consider a rather broader view of the problem, based upon an economic phenomenon thought by many to affect school spending adversely; it is a factor for which some authorities have suggested adjustments in state school aid, the differential burden of *nonschool municipal* services, or so-called "municipal overburden."

To the extent that municipal overburden is an "education problem," it is so because the nonschool taxes paid in a district affect ability to pay school taxes. It is a problem which exists even after the power equalizing effort-offering relation has been established for the school financing system, because municipal overburden is a factor outside that system. Power equalizing might fix $200 per pupil as the added spending power gained for a 1-percent tax increase for all districts in the state but, if that tax increment must be added to an already existing municipal levy of 3 percent for all purposes in one district versus only 1 percent in another, the tax rates will not be equally easy to increase.[18] This may be due to a de facto ceiling on tax rates regardless of the benefits received because a 3-percent municipal effort has left the one district with less remaining wealth against which school needs can draw.

But before overburden is treated narrowly as an education problem it should be examined in a more general way. Authorities often identify the differential cost of necessary public services as the cause of an unequal municipal services tax rate. Since high costs of this nature are thought to be characteristic of larger cities[19] the problem has been denominated "municipal

18. "Rising costs of municipal government and of city school systems in the wake of population changes occurring in metropolitan areas have increased awareness of the fact that public schools and city governments draw upon the same tax base. Resistance to increases in school tax rates may reflect a conviction among voters that the total property tax rate is too high." E. L. Lindman, "School Support and Municipal Government Costs," in Committee on Educational Finance, Long Range Planning, p. 129. Some who are interested in school financing (rather than city government financing) have begun to conceptualize school wealth as a matter of total community wealth — assessed valuation per municipal task unit. See P. R. Mort, "Unique Problems of Financing Education in Big Cities," in Committee on Educational Finance, ed., Financing the Changing School Program (Washington, D.C., 1962), p. 71: "A study of New Mexico made in the fall of 1961 by James Slezak shows that the differences in impact of municipal government, even in that state, are sufficient to shake our confidence in our long-time assumption that we could rest with wealth per unit of educational need as a measure of ability to support education."

19. The most readily available comparisons are between cities and the remainder of the SMSA of which they are a part. "The 37 largest central cities had a noneducational (municipal) outlay of $232 per capita in 1965 — $100 greater than their suburban counterparts"; Advisory Commission, Fiscal Balance, p. 6. According to Netzer, while cities generally have a higher effective tax rate (revenue divided by wealth per capita) than do suburbs, their school taxes tend to be lower (Netzer, Economics, p. 122). It is important to realize

overburden," although it is by no means a uniquely urban phenomenon.[20] The higher costs are thought of as (1) the higher cost of buying the "same" municipal service in different areas (for example, the cost of hiring one policeman)[21] and (2) the cost of extra services required by particular areas, especially cities (fighting a high crime rate, extra service for commuters and visitors).[22] But cost burden differences are not all of the problem.

In simple theoretical terms, what could be done to eliminate the municipal overburden problem? First, as indicated, it would be necessary to deal with variation in the costs of municipal government. Perhaps a gross index of the cost of municipal services could be developed which would be applied to

---

that, assuming we use expenditure as a measure of cost, we are taking it on faith that those extra dollars of cost are going into other needed or costlier, rather than simply better, services in the city.

20. The three-layer overlay of federal, state, and local taxing systems makes it impossible to construct taxes on an "ability to pay" principle; Burkhead, *State and Local Taxes*, p. 7. Fragmentation of government results in fiscal inadequacies of taxing units which often are awkwardly compensated for by further fragmentation, a process culminating in a haphazard distribution of costs and benefits (*ibid.*, pp. 12–13). Note once again the effect of urban provincialism. If a municipal overburden correction is adopted it must apply to all districts, and the central cities are by no means the only overburdened communities. "School districts where the municipal costs were most eccentric include not only the great cities in New York State but also individual villages — usually, but not always, suburbs"; Mort, "Unique Problems," in Committee on Educational Finance, *Financing the Changing School Program*, p. 12.

21. "Recent investigations have disclosed that as the size of the city increases governmental costs per capita do not decline. In fact, the program needs of large cities . . . would probably reveal higher per capita government costs for a given level of service if service needs could be measured accurately"; Burkhead, *State and Local Taxes*, pp. 14–15.

22. On the concentration of high-cost citizens in the city, see Netzer, *Economics*, p. 116; Burkhead, *State and Local Taxes*, p. 14; the cited portion of Advisory Commission, *Fiscal Balance*, in n. 19, above. The factor of providing services for noncity residents has so far defied measurement, but there is a general consensus among students of local government that the cities operate at a disadvantage; Burkhead, *State and Local Taxes*, p. 13. Until 1952, the cities recouped their service losses, but with a declining share of commerce came a "balance of payments deficit"; Netzer, *Economics*, p. 117.

every dollar spent by a municipality to determine whether one dollar's spending returns a dollar's service. It would also be necessary to average the cost of special tasks done by cities (or others) that are considered proper to distribute. The point, in any case, would be to develop a measure of relative per-capita burden. It would measure both kinds of cost problems in task units. But adjusting for these task variations alone would not seem to be enough, for one must also be concerned about the different abilities of districts to cope with their overburden: two cities with equally heavy municipal tasks are not in the same boat if one is richer than the other.

If municipal costs were spread fairly so that municipal government cost the same "price" per citizen everywhere, the price still would be in dollars and, thus, differentially available according to variations in the richness or poverty of areas served by the different municipal governments. In short, it should be obvious that the example of a three-percent versus a one-percent noneducational (municipal) tax rate can arise as easily from differences in ability as from differences in task.[23] As with schools, then, it would be desirable to create a composite measuring tool — "municipal wealth" — to amalgamate both ability and burden factors: dollars (some kind of assessed valuation, for example) per municipal task unit (the relatively more burdened, of course, having more task units). Then, how would variation in municipal wealth be adjusted? Clearly the only way to eliminate variation would be either to power equalize or to centralize the support of all municipal services. Or, perhaps some services could be centralized and some power equalized. Thus, in certain other municipal services as in schools, offering would be a function solely of effort.

---

23. The reality is that increased burden probably goes along with declining ability, for while cities vary greatly in wealth per capita, they generally are falling behind the rest of the metropolitan area in which they are located; Advisory Commission, *Fiscal Balance*, p. 6.

The impact of so adjusting for municipal overburden as herein discussed is important and twofold: (1) in the field of municipal (noneducational) finance the quality of local governmental services would no longer be a function of variation in local wealth (either ability or burden caused), and (2) since poor school districts would no longer be spending different proportions of their wealth for municipal services (except, where permitted, through voluntary election of better services), any pernicious effect of municipal spending on school spending would disappear. In simple terms, by eliminating municipal overburden as a general problem it is eliminated as an "education problem" in the operation of power equalizing. Also, the obverse is clear: to the extent that municipal overburden is not adjusted for, it can continue to have an impact upon school tax rate and thus distort an equitably operating power equalizing system.[24]

To review briefly: school districts with low "municipal wealth" (relatively high costs and/or relatively low ability to pay) may well be forced to tax at high rates for quality municipal services. With such a high local tax effort, it will be harder for them to tax at high rates for schools than for a rich "municipal wealth" district. Hence, either they will fall behind in school offering under power equalizing, or they will keep up only by what may appear a greater sacrifice. If we neutralize "municipal wealth" variation among school districts, by power equalizing municipal government financing, for example, we eliminate this distorting impact of variation in "municipal wealth."

If this analysis appears to make overburden a version of the marginal utility problem it is only because that is precisely what

24. Actually trying to measure the impact of thousands of partially overlapping taxing bodies on school-district residents would be a gargantuan task. In 1962, there were over 16,000 local governments with taxing powers in standard metropolitan statistical areas. The largest areas, also among the most fragmented (New York, Chicago, Philadelphia, Los Angeles), sport several hundred local units apiece; Netzer, *Economics*, p. 124.

it is: indeed, this is one of our main points. There may be special normative reasons for distinguishing municipal spending from other spending, but the effects themselves are indistinguishable. Buying a Chevrolet or building a redwood ranchhouse also cost different amounts of money in different places and bear more heavily on poor than rich. In fact, all private spending, like municipal overburden, can affect school tax rates. Both private and public wants are factors outside the school financing system which impinge on its operation. This means that one way to remove the impact of all marginal utilities on school spending would be to power equalize everything. But that would amount to a hundred-percent tax on wealth with the government thereafter repaying or crediting everyone an equal amount. Goods and services — including education, municipal government, and Chevrolets — could then be purchased as easily (or with equal difficulty) by all individuals.

In short, to eliminate the marginal utilities problem from school spending would be to eliminate wealth differences altogether. We are not prepared to scrap free enterprise; one of the driving principles behind our initial demand for equal educational opportunity is the fair operation of the free-enterprise system. Just as we accept most wealth differentials, we do not insist upon either power equalizing or centralization of municipal government financing. We said earlier that each of these approaches is one way of eliminating the impact on school tax effort of variations in wealth generally and "municipal wealth" specifically; but such radical attacks upon the cause in order to eliminate but one effect would be ludicrously disproportionate to the evil. Our concern is school finance reform, not all municipal finance or private wealth redistribution generally; we can live with the causes and be satisfied with solutions that attempt to compensate for their effects upon schools alone.[25]

25. "But compared with financing education, the financing of municipal government on a State-local partnership is still a new field. Accordingly, until

A pragmatic adjustment for the effects of overburden upon school taxing choices is possible through the use of devices of approximation noted in the earlier discussions of marginal utility and similar factors. It is necessary to ameliorate overburden only to the extent that it, under power equalizing, induces the poor, selectively, to have poorer schools. Assuming that municipal overburden does have at least some of this selective impact on school tax rate, and assuming it is desired that it be neutralized, what devices would be effective? The most direct method would be to give credit to those districts with relatively higher municipal overburden — that credit in the form of artificially higher school tax rates than nominally they have chosen, entitling them to better school offerings based upon the effort-offering table. And the easiest way to measure the higher overburden would be to look at municipal tax rates (nonschool), although this would be somewhat hazardous: based upon such a measure, the adjustment could stimulate higher municipal tax rates in place of school rates because of free escalation of the latter when the district increases the former. To the extent that this happens, the school financing plan will in effect power equalize municipal financing. This may call for adjustments or the adoption of a different measure of the overburden.[26] Another problem is that this measure is akin to using the revenue unit which we have discussed previously. Districts without the overburden problem (muncipal financing wealthy) could elect to turn more things over to municipal government — thereby exercising a high tax rate and becoming municipal financing poor — in order to be rewarded with greater school funds.

The limited purpose of this one example of adjustment

---

such time as the municipal house can be put in order it seems essential that the differential impact of municipal government, wherever it becomes disturbingly excessive, shall be taken into account in computing the ability of school districts" (Mort, "Unification," in Benson, *Perspectives*, p. 346; italics added).

26. Another possibility is a comparison among districts of what proportion local taxes are of personal income.

should be clear. Financing ability for other wants is not intended to be affected by such devices, at least directly; rather, the purpose is to make the distribution of high and low school tax rates effectively random among districts with respect to wealth. Yet, can that guide be any more than a very crude measure? We think not. It would have to operate as some kind of clumsy compensation system for the inherent temptations of the poor and in such amount as could be expected to induce the desired behavior.

Superficially, this is the kind of approach taken in existing formulas, which locate areas of plausible overburden through some index such as population density or proportion of school to nonschool revenues and manipulate state school aid formulas so that overburdened districts get extra aid — usually more aid the greater the overburden (school wealth is usually artificially diminished in relation to the overburden).[27] The design of

27. Take, e.g., Mort's recommendation for New York. Except for 14 cities and districts, which were to be governed by a table, the following formula was to be used to compute a VRR (a valuation reduction ratio), where VRR is greater than zero:

$$\text{VRR equals } \frac{\text{Noneducational revenue per student outside of cities of 125,000 or more and continguous counties}}{\underset{\text{the line}}{\text{Same as above}} \quad \text{plus} \quad \underset{\text{in the state}}{\overset{\text{average expenditure}}{\text{for education}}}} \text{ minus } .332$$

(Mort, "Unification," in Benson, *Perspectives*, pp. 345–346.) The reader is free to puzzle over possible effects of this formula; at any rate, the rough character of the whole arrangement is apparent. Still, the bonus could be substantial: New York City's tabular VRR would change the state's share of the school budget under the percentage equalizing formula from 46% to 67%.

For a more puzzling adjustment, consider this (Pa is percent of total state public school enrollment in the district, Pn is percent of total state population in the district):

$$\frac{2 \text{ Pa}}{\text{Pn plus Pa}}$$

Lindman, "School Support," in Committee on Educational Finance, *Long Range Planning*, p. 129). Is this aid to districts with large parochial school

such devices is based upon existing levels of school spending in cities: how much they have already been willing to sacrifice for high-cost municipal services, given their abilities. Thus, despite complicated implementation, they are not very sophisticated. Behavioral response to the adjustment is given little consideration. There is no attempt to actually calculate costs of government or to make lists of included and excluded services; these are only approximated. Moreover, it is peculiar that these formulas, if one examines the adjustments carefully, only purport to adjust for differential costs (task) and ignore the problem of differential ability to bear them. Perhaps this is because other devices, like the progressive income tax, are either operating or are advocated; such devices are geared directly to the "abilities" aspect of the problem in a more general way. On the other hand, the concentration upon task alone may be a deliberate attempt to get more school money to those districts with relatively greater municipal tasks without present concern over the fact that, as among those burdened districts, some need the money more than others.[28]

What, in the end, can be concluded about the desirability of overburden corrections? First, if they are "effect-compensation" oriented, it must be admitted that they will not very accurately measure how much overburden there is or clearly eliminate the problem; it is possible that they may, in fact, overeliminate it. By their own terms, the best they attempt to do is to locate where part of the problem is and to stimulate and/or reward the districts involved enough to put them back in the race for

enrollments? We would be amazed if it were deliberately so intended; but consider the suggestion of Burke, "The Density Correction," *ibid.*, pp. 136–137, that lower educational rate in the cities is a product of lower commitment to education because of, inter alia, the resistance of parents sending their children to parochial schools to higher taxes.

28. Perhaps the proposers of the adjustments want aid to cities, but believe cities to have high municipal ability along with high burden, so that wealth adjustment would not achieve their political objectives.

schools. Second, while government and private expenditures are readily distinguishable, to do something about even the full spectrum of municipal overburden problems is merely to do something about a portion of the general problem of marginal utilities; in an important sense this makes municipal overburden not only outside of the school finance arena, but external to the reform that is the subject of this book. In short, we feel no more strongly about municipal overburden than we did, generally, about marginal utility.

This last point is most important. We have referred to wealth throughout as assessed valuation per pupil. Perhaps the limitations of this definition have not been obvious, though on its face it is narrower than traditional economic definitions of "wealth." Assessed valuation per pupil is a somewhat specialized concept permitting calculation of that percent of local resources represented by any level of educational services. Plainly, it is not addressed to the differences in ability to pay for other goods the cost of which, as we have seen, may affect school spending. Our focus on only one kind of cost reflects a judgment that the state as educator is directly implicated in one kind and less so in others. If the education dollar itself exacts a heavier school tax, that is so as a consequence of the very method of financing education and, hence, is uniquely offensive in its partiality. Other spending may affect school spending, but only from outside the system. The difference perhaps is more meaningful to lawyers than economists; but inasmuch as we must later analyze the problem in legal terms, such a qualification is by no means a defect.

Municipal overburden correction is something like task unit adjustment for particular kinds of pupils: it is important to think about but not essential to act upon, at least until we have a proper power equalizing system the operation of which can be evaluated. Both variation in personal wealth generally and the uneven distribution of municipal costs specifically may have a whole range of effects on school spending under power equalizing, some selectively hurting the poor by forcing them to choose poorer schools, some not. Hence it may be desirable to eliminate or at least temper some of their influences. But we decline to endorse this as a crucial initial step. Simple power equalizing meets the minimum standard of a democratic society.

Note that the municipal-overburden/marginal-utilities problem would not disappear in a centralized system of school finance. No doubt, a centralized system of public education financed by a tax proportional on income would be considered "fair" in most quarters; but even under such a system, because of marginal utilities, the poor would be hurt more than the rich by their proportional contribution for education. School children could only be injured equally, however, because of the statewide nature of the spending program. This persepective further illustrates two points: (1) As "wealth" problems remain under centralization they are clearly external to the school system; similarly, under power equalizing we need be concerned only with the effects upon district behavior.[29] (2) Ours is a concern for children, not for taxpayers, even though a "fair" taxing system is in some respects important to the achievement of our purpose.

29. See Mort, "Unique Problems," in Committee on Educational Finance, *Financing the Changing School Program,* p. 12; and John Polley, *Variations in Impact of Municipal Government on Ability to Support Schools,* Staff Study no. 3 (Albany, 1961), quoted by Mort ("Unique Problems," in Committee on Educational Finance, *Financing the Changing School Program,* p. 71), who opines: "The development in school finance of adequate measures of need and ability has led to equitable treatment of school needs. The unlikely development of a unit of need at the municipal level means that dealing with the effects on the schools of municipal needs then becomes imperative."

7 · Broader Implications of Fiscal Equity

. . . *think of sullen vicissitudes, but beat not thy brains*
to foreknow them. Be armed against such obscurities rather
by submission than fore-knowledge.

Browne, Religio Medici

THE PRACTICAL FUTURE OF PUBLIC education, even under a fair system of distribution, is a matter of agonizing concern to critics and defenders of the present system alike. Change is unsettling to all those, liberal and otherwise, who have enjoyed decent public education for themselves or have fought their way to a suburban district refuge for their children's sake. What would fiscal equity do to the general quality of public (and private) education, how will it affect the disadvantaged child, and in particular, what is the realistic prediction of the political and practical future for power equalizing? Our own fancies in these areas are largely untechnical, largely unsupported, and romantic in varying degrees.

COMPENSATORY EDUCATION

Neither power equalizing nor related systems of fiscal equity, centralization, for example, would resolve the problems facing public education; their only necessary consequence is the removal intrastate of preference for rich districts. These reforms do not guarantee any special support for needy groups or individuals. Still, they are unquestionably a step forward: we cannot have compensation until we have equality.

The last remark appears elementary, but it is understood almost nowhere so far as we are able to tell. Certainly the combatants in the debate over the priority of compensation and integration have not understood it.[1] The concept of compensatory education has been left ambiguous at best.[2] In the argot of today's experts, any new spending of state or federal educational resources on some class of social victims is "compensatory." Such a notion is worse than useless. It distracts from the reality that "compensation," so-called, is typically a minuscule addition to an inadequate base. After the addition is counted in, the education remains second rate compared to that in wealthy (or often even average) districts in the same state. We find it difficult to perceive how dollars can be compensatory even before they are equal. If a systematically undernourished child has received a thousand calories a day and his neighbor two thousand, will the hungry child be "compensated" for his mistreatment and his general debility by another hundred calories?

We trust the point is clear. Compensation makes no sense either linguistically or educationally unless it means receiving *better* than those who have benefitted by the discrimination or those whose need is less. Keeping children consistently behind their peers in quality of education can be considered compensatory only if we wish to abandon intelligible discourse. Compensation means preference or it is meaningless.

Preference as a definition of compensation needs further refinement. For our limited purposes it will be sufficient to recognize two general types, restitutionary and nonrestitutionary compensation. By the former we mean redress for relative dis-

1. The most spirited logomachy appeared in Joseph Alsop, "No More Nonsense About Ghetto Education," *New Republic*, 157:18–22 (July 22, 1967), and Robert Schwartz, "Fake Panaceas for Ghetto Education," *New Republic*, 157:16–19 (Sept. 23, 1967). See also Ivor Kraft, "Retreat to Separate but Equal," *The Nation*, 205:552–555 (Nov. 27, 1967).

2. See A. H. Passow, ed., *Education in Depressed Areas* (New York, 1963); James Coleman, "Equal Educational Opportunity," *Harvard Educational Review*, 38:7 (Winter, 1968).

abilities of the child arising from unlawful state-created inequalities. When that child and all like him are made whole
(insofar as possible), the injustice ceases, and with it ceases one
rationale for compensation. Of course, if the disability is permanent the restitution may need to be permanent, at least insofar as it can be effective to benefit the victim.

Nonrestitutionary compensation, on the other hand, need
not imply a historic discrimination. Its focus is upon existing
objective needs. The child is blind, retarded, disadvantaged, or
gifted (in one view of "need"). No matter how fair the system,
there will always be such children, whose characteristics call for
special treatment costing extra money.

This primitive taxonomy suffices here because our interest in
compensatory education is ancillary to our concern about power
equalizing. There are three introductory points to be made
about the relation of fiscal equity to compensatory education.
The first is already plain. While there may be isolated compensatory programs, there is no system of compensatory education in existence; furthermore, there can be none until an underlying system of financial equity such as power equalizing is
a reality.

The second point is principally analytical in character but is
important nonetheless. It has to do with the verbal interchange-
ability of the ideas of equality and compensation under certain
conditions. Perhaps this is too abstract. Suppose a given state
chooses to adopt the most primitive system of equality, equal
dollars per student throughout the state. In such a distribution
of resources the rhetorics of equality and preference (compensation) can be manipulated to confound the analytical distinction of the two.[3] That is, it can be said that such a system of

3. John Kaplan, "Equal Justice in an Unequal World: Equality for the
Negro — The Problem of Special Treatment," *Northwestern University Law
Review*, 61:363, 365 (1966).

formal equality is in fact unequal because it treats different things as if they were the same; true equality in this view requires recognition of the special needs of children. Likewise, a system that awards preferences can be analyzed as giving no preferences if we merely view the beneficiaries as in need of special treatment so that they can be equal in some other sense such as performance on tests.

Commentators who take this approach should not suppose that they are dealing in intelligible propositions. Any two things — at least, any two children — are bound to be different in an inexhaustible number of ways. When it is complained that schools are treating "different needs" in the same way, selection is implied: selection of those differences that the particular reformer judges to be salient. His concentration upon any one of the vast range of possible "needs" tends to represent a policy or value judgment of his own; it is not only remote from any objective standard, but is vulnerable on the ground that no judgment of inequality is possible without an antecedent and intelligible standard of equality. The reformer's response to such a critique often is the creation of pseudo-standards of a high level of abstraction, as when he complains that one student has been permitted to "develop his potential" more than another. Coupled with an arbitrary measure such as a standard achievement test, the adoption of such nostrums as the basis for public policy could make enormous if unpredictable differences in educational spending patterns. Consider the potential fiscal consequences of the following standards, each sometimes heard as an ideal of public education.

> All schools should produce the same average performance (aid to underachieving schools) (or debilitation of superior schools?)
>
> All children should be stimulated to the same proportion of their capacity (aid to gifted children) (or no aid to anyone?)

All children should reach the same or minimum performance level (aid to slow children) (or less aid to superior children?)

The list of "standards" could be extended; but the point is sufficiently clear: "treating different things differently" means treating differently things that one believes *ought* to be treated differently — and this is not a clear principle, however sensible the substantive judgments of the expert may be in the given case.

Why this detour into confusion? We are troubled by a strain of Cartesian certitude informing much of the debate on compensatory education; the impression is created that the needs of children, like the properties of three-dimensional space, can be logically exhausted. Of course, there is nothing wrong with aspirations for new goals and a changing sense of justice; but there is something bizarre and misleading about arguing such matters in laboratory jackets under a cloak of anatomical precision.

A power equalizing system, like any other, can be adjusted to satisfy the rhetoric either of equality or of compensation. Each can be made to fit neatly into the equal power model by adjusting the task units. Once we admit the propriety of weighting pupils differently as representing different tasks, we can make the most compensatory system look like simple equality. All task units are equal, but some children — perhaps like Orwell's animals — are more task units than others. They may be blind, badly housed, poor, gifted, or fat, live far from school or show promise for Department of Defense research.

At what point in defining special tasks have we passed from power equalizing to compensation to politics? Though we do not know, so long as the reader is sensible of the ambiguity we are content. There is no need for precision until the point at which we begin to worry over the constitutional imperatives of public education. Nevertheless, there is one line of division between equality and compensation that must be kept plain for present purposes. We said earlier that no compensatory education can exist until equality is achieved — that compensation is preference; if we permit equality and compensation to become confounded, that point is meaningless. To put it another way, compensation has ceased to exist as a useful idea. It is necessary to specify once more that equality, as it is meant in that earlier proposition and as we mean it now, does not take differing needs into account. For us, equality would be satisfied by a raw equality in dollars or even by mere district power equalizing that uses pupils as fungible task units; all that is required is the removal of wealth determinants of quality. As for compensation, we might rephrase our view to say that we don't know if compensation begins with such reforms as effective power equalizing or equal dollars, but we know it can begin no earlier.

The third point in respect to the relation of fiscal equity to compensatory education is not merely analytical. We believe that fiscal equity is a necessary first step to making the whole question of compensation intelligible. Effects of compensation on the disadvantaged of all races and classes can never be clarified until we have at least reached the point of removing wealth determinants of quality. A coherent fiscal system unaffected by local wealth variations is a primary criterion for drawing comparisons. Only with a firm grasp of the dollar aspect of education will meaningful investigation into the importance of peer group influence become possible. Only after fiscal equity is achieved can we embark upon the turbulent waters of de facto segregation, whether by race or social class, and feel confidence in judging its educational consequences. This is not a canard of reaction; if change comes, it will come through judicial prompting and it will come in this generation. We are not talking about the year 2000. Nor are we suggesting that decisions on priorities be suspended or programs postponed. The point is, simply, that fiscal rationality may contribute more to understanding the nature of our problem than any single reform.

The Substance of the Equalizing and Compensatory Programs

Moving from systems of inequality to systems of fiscal equity and of compensation will raise many different questions of how to equalize and for what to equalize, how to compensate and for what to compensate. Our brief comments here will be upon the three areas of plant, teacher personnel, and special student needs. Although the focus of this book's inquiry has been toward current expenditures, it has been obvious throughout that the overall solution to the present discrimination would have to deal with the building problem. As observed earlier, once the charade of state subvention plans for current expenditure is exposed the unfairness in plant financing appears a fortiori. Power equalizing can easily account for differences in construction abilities of districts by making each district equally able to build schools, as well as to pay teachers. The fact that this form of school cost is typically paid for by bonds which are then repaid by taxes represents no problem.

There is one significant difference, however, between capital and current expenditures. More lead time is required for districts to put the new dollars into building than into the stream of current expenditures; the visible consequences of discrimination represented by inadequate plant will take time to erase, and poor districts would face special and continuing problems even after the changeover. Compensation for past shortages would be helpful, but for children who enter school in the near future a quality lag seems inevitable. Fortunately, physical plant does not seem to be nearly so important a factor in education as current spending. As a counsel of perfection, perhaps districts could be awarded temporary additional task units on the basis of inadequate physical plant until they are able to catch up, assuming they are willing to make the necessary power equalized effort to do so. This would mean extra current funds which attempt to roughly compensate (equalize?) for the building quality. Inasmuch as schools can be built in fairly short order and because there will always be the problem of some districts having newer buildings and facilities than others, adjustment in this way might not be feasible or necessary. Perhaps less durable "plant" would be a better expenditure for some of the catch-up moneys; among these would be books for libraries, equipment for laboratories or for extracurricular activity, and the like.

If a school is equalized (compensated for?) as to plant, its other qualities continue to affect its hope for real improvement. Most people close to the public school system seem to feel that teachers are the key to healthy change. So long as there is teacher choice, districts with a poor reputation will find it relatively more difficult to compete for new employees, let alone to lure talented people now on other teaching staffs. Continuing with personnel currently employed and adding those they can attract will still most likely leave them with a disadvantage based at least in part upon their heritage. In this area, again, the temporary awarding of additional task units to formerly deprived districts on either an equalizing or compensatory rationale would give them the dollars to be more than competitive with other districts that elect to make the same effort as theirs. This might help; and, to the extent that experienced teachers cannot be brought in, the money could be used to provide smaller class units for new recruits so as to make the opportunity seem more inviting to the more capable of them, and to make education more effective for the children.

Still, the problem of recruiting personnel may not disappear even if past inequalities are accounted for. For the same salary teachers may simply have a natural preference for teaching elsewhere than in poor districts, which could be caused in part by residence patterns (teachers may not generally live in poor districts and may prefer to work closer to home). It could be caused by off-the-job attractions of the community, such as cultural advantages usually offered only by certain areas; or by teachers' desire to teach children with greater abilities, who, after five preschool years of relative advantage, tend to be those of wealthier areas; or it may be that white teachers dislike teaching black students either from prejudice or feelings of their own incompetence. Many of these factors, it is easily seen, can cut against poor districts and will not disappear even when those districts are as wealthy as others for education purposes. Perhaps a more permanent policy of compensatory aid is needed; yet, conceptually, this can be viewed as merely another case in which one district faces a larger task than another because of its very nature. On the other hand, as observed in the Introduction, the administrative solution to teacher placement may be as effective in some cases as more money, suggesting once again a large area of discretion in defining educational task.

Obviously, one of the concerns of task unit adjustment is the child himself. If educators have learned nothing else in the last fifteen years, they have at least become aware of the burden carried by the deprived child in a competitive technological society. We still cherish the hope that education can alter this iron law and feel justified in making adjustments that recognize the problem. Additional task units can be awarded to districts with such educational needs even if their exact number is largely a guess. In part, these would be justified as "temporary" adjustments to compensate (restitution) for past inequities. In part, they would represent the counterweight to existing home and personal deficiencies and thus enjoy a more lasting basis for adjustment. These deficiencies are to be seen as a handicap, arising from no fault of the child, but which can be overcome or ameliorated by education.

It is arguable that at some point this process transcends both equalizing and compensatory education and becomes an effort to approach performance equality. While that goal seems to us whimsical (see Introduction), it is not a bad spirit in which to approach the educational problems of the disadvantaged. In the end, adjustment for inequalities involves more interrelated problems than we care to consider. All we need stress is that a power equalizing system is not only compatible with such adjustments, but provides the basis upon which such remedies can begin.

THE FEDERAL ROLE

The need for compensatory programs adds another powerful and positive reason for structuring the state-federal relation by beginning with state reforms. It is our concern that, under current state practices, federal programs are — or will become — in fact anticompensatory. This seemingly weird perspective is a natural extension of our position that compensation means preference. So long as the poor remain *relatively* deprived in education, there is no compensation.[4] If the education of the rich remains systematically better than that of the poor, you can call the handouts to the poor whatever you like, but the system remains fundamentally designed to keep the poor in their place (their relative place — what else matters?). But this gruesome prospect is precisely the logic of federal aid. The bestowal of federal largesse upon poor districts may raise their level of spending above the existing state average; here and there, a spectacular burst of dollars may produce an outstanding program for a cadre of lucky children. The total effect (except for educational research) is to relieve the pressure upon the states to meet their own obligations. To the extent that federal

4. Federal programs may be anticompensatory even in the most literal sense, however. There is some evidence that amount of federal assistance is positively correlated with local wealth. See, e.g., Appendix F, Tables 6–7.

money supports poor districts, the state is free to spend its resources upon the rich. It does so now and will continue to do so, abetted as it is by federal band-aids. For the conscience and the self-interest of rich districts there is no happier invention than federal grants for education of the poor.

Should we conclude that the problem is too little federal aid? It is surely arguable that, at some point, the quantum of federal assistance would finally make the aid compensatory in fact, that is, would give the best education to those who need it most. But what a millenium we are from that, and what a price in lost subsidiarity we would pay for it, and how many children would suffer in the meantime! The answer, to us, is neither in more nor in less federal aid. We suggest that there simply can be no rational answer to the question of the level of federal contribution until there is fiscal equity in the state. So long as the state is free to leave the poor to their own devices, it will be impossible to predict intelligently what quantum of federal aid would be necessary to bring the poor up to fiscal equality so that compensation could even begin. We concede an element of arbitrariness in this; it suggests that fiscal equity at a $300 per pupil level in Mississippi is the equivalent of fiscal equity at $900 in New York. Even if the logic were sound, which it isn't, this would be absurd. It is clear that differential federal contribution will be necessary from state to state.

Those whose imaginations exceed their political sense may perceive here an interesting potential application of the power equalizing principle at the federal level, based upon an analogy of the state-federal relation to the district-state relation. This is not the easiest comparison to negotiate, but, once the federal government is seen as a state with fifty districts, the rest flows rather naturally. If Congress were to preempt the field of public education finance, it could without difficulty power equalize the states. A national effort-offering table could be prescribed from which the state legislatures would select. The effort, which would be made by the state as a whole and measured against its total wealth, would determine its permitted expenditure per pupil. Each state would determine for its own intrastate purposes whether it wished a centralized state dispensation or a power equalized distict system. The latter would create some complications, since the total state effort which would fix the federal contribution could not be known until all the districts in a state had made their choices. However, the necessary refinements to permit power equalizing on both state and federal levels would not seem unduly cumbersome when weighed against the state's substantial interest in retaining local (district) choice. Federal legislation could easily provide a framework within which the states would retain that option. The result would be an extraordinary maximizing of subsidiarity. *All* levels of government would be functioning in a fashion emphasizing at once both national community and local variety. There would be only one conceivable step beyond: a speculative form of fiscal equity that we call family power equalizing.

FAMILY POWER EQUALIZING

In introducing this refinement it is first useful to distinguish three very general functions of all organization for formal education. Two broad categories easily identified in any system of education are fiscal (deciding how much money is to be provided and then providing it) and administrative (running the program). The fiscal aspect, however, must be treated as two distinct functions whenever *fiscal control*, control over how much is to be provided, is to any degree separated from *fiscal responsibility*, responsibility for the providing. Consider, for example, a state system in which subunits are free to choose among various levels of educational offering but the state is responsible for providing all the money required by each subunit's choice. This would represent a complete separation of fiscal control and fiscal responsibility. By contrast, in a completely centralized system, fiscal control *and* responsibility are-in the hands of the state; in a system of total local finance, they would both be on the shoulders of the district.

Analytically, then, we can divide fiscal responsibility, fiscal control, and administration. It is apparent that these crucial functions, powers, and duties can be retained or distributed, completely or partially, by the state in infinite combination with subunits of widely differing types. The kinds of societal units historically employed to share these various functions are the state, the district, the family, and private enterprise (in the form of private schools).

Our concern with the impact of variations in wealth on public education puts our primary focus upon fiscal responsibility. The wrong in the existing scheme for providing public education is that the state has imposed major fiscal responsibility upon the district. It is thus the relative wealth of a child's district that principally counts today in determining the quality of educational offering he receives.

Fiscal responsibility as a family obligation is the hallmark of the traditional private school system. Clearly, if the state were to impose fiscal responsibility for public education upon the family, great variations in personal wealth would accentuate the existing discrimination and push the plight of the poor to the extreme. In a very real sense, the crucial advance in making education a public function was shifting fiscal responsibility to units with far less variety than families in ability to pay.

Yet it is because precisely the same inequity of wealth variation exists today as a result of district differences that we insist that the ultimate fiscal obligation be treated as a state one. This is the sense of our assertion that in our democracy the fungible young are all simply the children of the sovereign. If the metaphor offends, let us say merely that children have equal claims upon the sovereign; for purposes of public education, it is only upon the pocketbook of the broadest unit in society that involuntary new members (children) ultimately should be dependent. The "ultimately" is important; it suggests that responsibility can be shared as long as the state is the final guarantor — as it is in a power equalizing system.

Treating the state as the final locus of fiscal responsibility in public education is, of course, the pillar of power equalizing, the theory of which is less concerned with a specific locus for either of the two other kinds of functions, fiscal control and administration; for those we concede a wide range of possible combinations. Thus, while the state must hold the residual fiscal responsibility, it need *not* have any control. Indeed, we have argued at great length for keeping important aspects of fiscal control out of the hands of the state. Nevertheless, in a system of power equalizing, simply turning over fiscal control to a subunit is not the end of the matter. Irresponsible exercise of that control by the districts must be avoided; it is for that reason that each district is required to make a sacrifice for education based upon its own wealth and the degree of fiscal responsibility it imposes upon the state. The subunit must pay a price for the control it is granted in terms of its own fiscal responsibility but in proportion to its wealth. Purely private education, like power equalizing, leaves control with the subunit — in that case the family — but, of course, it also leaves the family ultimate fiscal responsibility.

With regard to administrative control there is, of course, a wide range of choices for assigning responsibility; this is true either in public education or in private or mixed systems. In "private" education today the state takes some role when it imposes requirements and limitations on nonpublic schools and when it joins with them in specific cooperative programs. The main administrative burden remains in private hands. The administration of "public" education, on the other hand, is divided largely between purely governmental institutions, the state and the district, with the district at front-line duty. Nevertheless, it should be noted that, even here, families and individuals, through Parent Teacher Associations and other such programs, may be responsible for part of the administrative burden of the public schools. Just as with fiscal responsibility and control, a sharing of responsibility for administration among differing public and private units is possible in public education.

Fiscal control can be placed directly in the hands of the family, in the manner in which we have previously conceived it in the district. In other words, subsidiarity can be maximized insofar as it remains consistent with the elimination of wealth determinants of equality. In order to prevent wealth discrimination, ultimate state financial responsibility of course would be maintained; the shift from district to family decision-making regarding effort, therefore, would mean that each family now would have the same financial backing as any other for purposes of public education. We call this notion family power equalizing.

What might its theoretical advantages be? Presumably, a maximization of the fit between services desired and services supplied could be achieved. A parent could put his child in a school with just the level of offering the parent felt appropriate and for which he was willing to make the effort required. Moreover, parents might alter their attitudes without changing their residences, as their feelings could be translated into action immediately (send the child to a new school); whereas the district must move, over time, from one kind of program to another (alter the existing school). In short, it makes the consumer king: the parents are free to shop — perhaps limited to one choice a year, unless they move — among a great variety of possible choices. Thus, by making the crucial decision a much more personal one, the family is freed from the attitudes of neighbors uninterested in public education who exert voting pressure when issues are decided on the district level. Market decisions are substituted for political action.

At about this time the reader may begin to glance at the footnotes looking for Milton Friedman or Senator Barry Goldwater. The instinct is sound;[5] in an incongruous fashion, the family power model is beginning to resemble classical, or at least neoclassical, liberalism. Professor Friedman would have the state divide the total public education pie into equal slices.[6] Each child would receive a chit redeemable in so many dollars of education at schools public or private. The child would have freedom of choice, and the market would determine which suppliers survive. That private education units be given parity of treatment in the state plan for distribution is acceptable to us. In good classical fashion the system seems to emphasize subsidiarity, and our conservative antennae are receptive to the message. Indeed, the problem with the scheme is not that it is conservative, but that it is not conservative enough. Its subsidiarity

5. See Milton Friedman, *Capitalism and Freedom* (Chicago, 1962), p. 200.

Is it an accident that so many of the governmental reforms of recent decades have gone awry, that the bright hopes have turned to ashes? Is it simply because the programs are faulty in detail?

I believe the answer is clearly in the negative. The central defect of these measures is that they seek through government to force people to act against their own immediate interests in order to promote a supposedly general interest. They seek to resolve what is supposedly a conflict of interest or a difference in view about interests, not by establishing a framework that will eliminate the conflict, or by persuading people to have different interests, but by forcing people to act against their own interests. They substitute the values of outsiders for the values of participants.

6. Two virtually identical discussions were examined: Milton Friedman, *Capitalism*, pp. 85–107, and "The Role of Government in Education," in C. S. Benson, ed., *Perspectives on the Economics of Education* (Boston, 1963) pp. 132–142. In recent years the Friedman proposal has received attention from serious scholars. Theodore Sizer would modify it to give grants to children based in amount upon educational need: T. Sizer and Phillip Whitten, "A Proposal for a Poor Children's Bill of Rights," *Psychology Today*, 2:3 (August, 1968). See also H. M. Levin, "The Failure of the Public Schools and the Free Market Remedy," *Urban Review*, 2:7:32–37 (June, 1968).

is superficial — to provide freedom of choice it is not enough to pass out equal dollars for education; the parent must be given some choice in amount of state support he can attract. Consider this analysis carefully: if the chits are all of the same value and parents are permitted to supplement them with personal funds, the old Cubberley flat grant program upon which wealth discrimination thrives is merely recreated in a new form. Rich families would add to the granted sum and attend rich schools purifying the present role of public education as a system for perpetuation of class. Stripped of the blurring mediation of the school district, the correspondence between personal poverty and school poverty would become perfect. On the other hand, if the equal state grants cannot be supplemented by the family, all schools accepting the state chits will have the same amount per pupil, and the plan will strongly encourage the sameness that is equally destructive of subsidiarity.

The power equalizing principle could be superimposed on the Friedman model to bring that model into true harmony with the high classical rhetoric of its author. The freedom quotient of family power equalizing is considerably higher than Friedman's flat grant proposal. We have not mentioned freedom as a determining value to this point because we have been dealing principally with large collectivities — districts and states. It is apparent, however, that subsidiarity and freedom at the family level are nearly coextensive. The unit "family" is but one step removed from the unit "person" where the values freedom and subsidiarity merge. Whether the Friedman school would welcome power equalizing as a support for family and personal freedom we cannot say. What we can say is that power equalizing does suggest a way — perhaps the only way — in which the family grant system could be purged of most of its antipoor characteristics while retaining the values of freedom and subsidiarity.

How might family power equalizing be managed as a practical matter? We must put aside the many knotty issues that would arise in the initial creation of what is, in effect, an entirely new framework for public education; if the system showed sufficient promise, these could be worked out.[7] We concentrate instead on the functioning of a hypothetical family power equalizing system already in operation. A possible skeleton for such a plan, replete with assumptions, follows. State-determined levels and kinds of offering would be made known in advance, and parents would at some point commit themselves to a specific level. Those who provide educational services would adjust so that, to the extent possible, there are places available at each level of quality to meet the demand. Since the location of schools would be based upon demand, transportation problems would exist but should be manageable[8] (additional subvention for this purpose would be appropriate where insufficient demand leaves children without a local choice). A parent would be taxed at a given, preset rate based upon the quality level he selects for his child. The state would also tax generally to provide the additional resources to pay for the system on a wealth equalized basis.

One can envision some problems with providing schools to accommodate the variety of demands. Clearly, many institutions would be needed, at each level of offering. Transportation problems would of course determine some deployment of resources. In cities, for example, educational parks might com-

7. Friedman maintains that the transition would be "gradual and easy"; he gives two reasons: (1) There would be no waste of capital because, as is true in the decentralization of other activities, existing premises could be sold to private enterprise. (2) The already existing system of local school administration would encourage experimentation on a small scale. (*Capitalism*, p. 97.)

8. Friedman asserts that such factors, once the basis of the natural monopoly condition in education, do not obtain today in urban areas because of "improvements in transportation and increasing concentration of the population" (*ibid.*, p. 93). We are sympathetic to the ideal, but a brief reference to the current turmoil over bussing in metropolitan areas should suffice to raise some doubts.

prise each level of offering. If certain schools were in higher demand than others, even though they were of the same level of offering (many reasons for this can be imagined), assignment could be made on the basis of first come, first served, or by lot, or on the basis of past attendance (perhaps, once a child was admitted to a school, he would have the right to stay so long as his parents continued to select that level of offering for him). One can appreciate various considerations which might dictate one or the other combination of these suggested criteria.

Who would provide the schools, that is, perform the administrative functions? There are three possibilities, which could exist alone or in combination. First, of course, a state agency might run the entire system. In that event the educational administration could be partly decentralized, but from the top the state would direct the building program, the designation of the quality level of any particular school, the collection and payment of moneys, and so on. But in addition to and, theoretically, in place of the public schools, two other types could exist. One would be private schools willing to accept the state grant as the total tuition charge (we will call them "public-private" schools); they could be profit or nonprofit institutions. This is a way of getting private enterprise into the administrative function but within the family power equalizing system. The other would be private schools which would not participate in the state financing system; they would get no state grants. These we will call simply "private," for they would be identical to the private schools of today.

Except for those choosing purely private schools, parents would make known their intentions after shopping among those public and public-private schools of the quality (dollar) level of offering they wished. Educational entrepreneurs and the state would provide schools at the desired levels and shift the level of that which they offer in response to the demands of the marketplace. The hope would be that, by having both types of administration (public and private), individual school responses to demand would be more accurate and more sensitive than state bureaucratic judgments unaided by a competitive market. Besides, in theory, the incentive for profit in the public-private schools would bring costs down and improve innovation and efficiency.[9] Nonprofit institutions would also be expected to multiply.

In the selection of students, public-private schools would not be allowed to discriminate on the basis of any attribute of the applicant forbidden as a criterion to the state (race or social class or the like). Control over the makeup of their student body by all schools accepting money would have to be limited largely to the natural consequences of having a particular dollar level and particular courses, teachers, facilities, past students attracted — rather than to the result of selection of specific individuals by the school. Otherwise, there would be too great a fear that schools would become elitist; the policy of the marketplace for this purpose must allow the seller no such control over the identity of his buyer. Money should be the criterion of admission. The testing of applicants could be permitted but only for counseling purposes, not for screening. Given sufficient notice that a certain program is offered, it might be fairest to let the pupils (families) have full freedom of choice, knowing the risk they face that the pace might be, for example, too fast or too slow.

Religious schools would pose an interesting problem. If they

9. Friedman argues that expenditures on teacher salaries would actually recede because the market principle would reward only good teachers while retaining hangers-on at a mere minimum level (ibid., pp. 95–56). He reckons without unions and state-defined professional organizations. He maintains further that the ability to "tailor" a school to particular needs would result in more education for the money, in the sense that parents could select a school which does more of what they consider important and less of what they consider "frills" (ibid., p. 94). Even in theory this is true only to the extent that there are enough schools to embody all the manifold permutations; furthermore, it leaves out of account the limitations on curriculum which emanate from the state and from professional educators.

agreed to open their doors to any who applied, would they be permitted to become public-private schools under a family power equalizing program? The initial issue would be that of establishment of religion under the First Amendment. If this hurdle were cleared, as seems possible — the aid is to the student, and the recent decision in Board of Education v. Allen[10] is promising — would it be objectionable that only a certain kind of student (Muslim, Catholic, Jewish) would be likely to seek admission? [11]

Obviously there are disadvantages to the family power proposal. Administrative problems clearly exist whether the system is purely public, purely private, or mixed. It may even be that inefficiencies or added costs would produce worse educational offerings for the same cost than we now have.[12] However, the mechanism by which the family would choose the level of offering for the child is relatively simplified; it would merely choose the desired level of educational offering and make the tax effort required by the system. Suppose, however, that a family has more than one child: will it have to make this effort for each? The answer is no, for this would offend the basic principle that wealth — relative wealth — should not determine quality, tend-

10. 392 U.S. 236 (1968). The holding of this case is that provision by the state of textbooks for parochial students does not violate the establishment clause of the First Amendment because the benefit is to the child rather than to the religious organization operating the school. It is a holding which, in one version or another, suggests far wider application. See Jesse Choper, "The Establishment Clause and Aid to Parochial Schools," *California Law Review*, 56:260, 283–288 (1968).

11. Friedman ignores the "technical" First Amendment problem, merely arguing that restriction of payments to schools on the basis of what is taught is hardly consonant with developing values of "freedom of thought and belief" in a pluralistic society (Friedman, *Capitalism*, p. 90).

12. Friedman is skeptical: "Supposed difficulty of administration is a standard defense of the status quo against any proposed change; in this particular case, it is an even weaker defense than usual because existing arrangements must master not only the major problems raised by the proposed arrangements but also the additional problems raised by the administration of schools as a governmental function" (*ibid.*, p. 93).

ing to punish those children whose usable wealth is diminished by having brothers and sisters. The power equalizing formula can easily account for this complication; the family is to make an effort of a percent of its wealth, and its wealth should be measured as ability per task unit, just as with district power equalizing. Accepting this approach opens more room for adjustment. The family might even exercise a different effort for each child and send each to a different kind of school. For example, if the gross ability of the family were $50,000 and it had five children, its wealth would be $10,000 per child. If a 2-percent effort entitled it to an $800 education and a 3-percent effort a $1,200 education, it could make varying efforts against each $10,000 segment on behalf of the individual children. Moreover, since it is ability per task unit to which we refer, the state may designate some children as representing more task units than others if they fit certain criteria. Thus, the same adjustments are possible as under district power equalizing.

But such a system would mean that the "local effort" will come only from families with children in public-private or public schools. Other taxpayers will make no local effort, although they will, of course, have to contribute to the state share through general state taxes. This is in contrast to practice today, for the local effort comes from the entire district and thus from many kinds of taxpayers. From the viewpoint of the family using it, therefore, the system may require a somewhat greater effort than district power equalizing, while the families without public school children would be making less effort. This is because the lower amount of income produced from family effort than from district effort would necessitate greater state taxes; clearly, under family equalizing this hurts those who must pay both taxes as compared with those who in such a plan must pay but once. Of course it is possible to conceive of a statewide tax with heavier incidence upon those without children enrolled in the family power equalizing system.

In any event, parents with school children might consider an enlarged burden fair. First of all, once the state begins to support the poor through state-level subvention, they can have good public education as easily as the rich, and a large part of the rationale for taxing nonparticipants locally disappears. Why should we continue to insist that nonparents and private school families support neighboring families through both systems of taxation? The idea of general community support for education is to help the relatively poor and to compensate for the general benefits that all receive from education; the power equalizing state-aid share is sufficient for that purpose. It is not clear that families with public school children as a group deserve additional support. The parents of children in private schools would bear less of the burden of double payment under family power equalizing than they do today. Of course, they would have to pay the full tuition for private schools unaided by state support, but they would not have to contribute local effort to a district to help the children of others attend public or public-private schools. This is the converse — almost the quid pro quo — of freeing families through power equalizing from the voting power of those of their neighbors who are uninterested in the welfare of the public schools in their district. Those not interested are likely to be those who use private schools instead; thus, for surrendering their political power against local school tax increases, these reluctant taxpayers are rid of the portion of their tax contribution levied at the local level.

There are surely other problems that we have ignored. One is the larger impact of marginal utilities when dealing with the family unit instead of with the large collections of wealth represented by districts. Probably adjustments in the tax rates would be necessary to make the relative family efforts at least bearable and practical for the purpose in mind, even if they were not rendered "equal" in the sense suggested by the full logic of marginal utilities. However, given only such pragmatic adjustments, it might not be sensible to require true "poverty" families to "sacrifice" for public education; their admission to the system might be administered upon some other basis. Finally, family power equalizing as a general idea simply may not be very attractive to many persons because of their social values. It is, however, a coherent system and has been outlined here to demonstrate that power equalizing necessarily implies no more than residual state financial responsibility. The decision concerning effort (fiscal control) might workably be kept by the state or delegated to districts, families, or some other subunit of society.

POWER EQUALIZING AND COMMUNITY SCHOOLS

The current commotion over decentralization of school systems is a complex phenomenon on which we essay no firm conclusion except that it bids fair to be part of the educational scene for the foreseeable future.[13] In many respects the new rhetoric cheers us, for it seems to represent a groping toward an optimal unit — one large enough to contain diversity and dialogue but still small enough to vaguely resemble the extended family. There are inconsistencies and absurdities; but in a general way the proponents are, as we are, expressing simple dissat-

13. The basic document is Reconnection for Learning ("Bundy Report"), New York City Mayor's Advisory Panel on Decentralization of the New York City Schools, 1967, which details the proposal for experimental subdistricts in New York City. For background, see David Rogers, 110 Livingston Street: Politics and Bureaucracy in the New York City School System (New York, 1968). The story of the many crises provoked by the implementation of the Bundy Report is told by Martin Mayer, The Teachers' Strike: New York, 1968 (New York, 1969). Comment in the journals has been prolific: see, e.g., Martin Mayer, "The Full and Sometimes Very Surprising Story of Ocean Hill, the Teachers' Union and the Teachers' Strike of 1968," New York Times Magazine (Feb. 2, 1969); Jason Epstein, "The Brooklyn Dodgers," New York Review of Books (Oct. 10, 1968), and "Martin Mayer's Ocean Hill," New York Review of Books (Mar. 13, 1969). For a general consideration of the political, educational, and economic issues, see Henry M. Levin, ed., The Community School Controversy (Washington, D.C., 1969).

isfaction with the remoteness of systems so large that in no realistic sense can they constitute a "community."

We are not convinced that a mere geographical unity is sufficient to create community; but we are confident that, whatever sound instincts motivate decentralization of administration, they risk frustration unless the movement is accompanied by both the decentralization of fiscal control and the power equalizing of the new and all other districts. The New York experiment has not been a happy one so far, and that unhappiness has clustered about the relation between the community and the multiplicity of educational decision-makers at several levels above it. Their control over the subunit is not concerned exclusively with money, but the crucial decisions of such overseers frequently must, and in the 1968 crisis did, in one way or another, involve the distribution of economic power.

Power equalizing is available to transmute Ocean Hill-Brownsville or any subordinate unit into an independent cluster of power; once this is seen clearly, the multilevel structure of the Bundy experiment is difficult to justify.[14] Unless the state is simply unwilling to accord to such a community the same trust it reposes in Scarsdale, it is difficult to understand why it should be subject to the intervening jurisdiction of the city. There is obviously no necessary subordinate fiscal relation to the city, and the maintenance of such a relation helps defeat the very purposes for which independence presumably was justified. This is not an argument for exemption of the decentralized unit from the state rules of administration, academic freedom, and general fair play. It is only a suggestion that it may be hypocrisy to deny the independent district that power which alone can confirm its independence. If the state is serious about decentralization, it can be managed.

14. The Bundy Report (*Reconnection for Learning*) describes at great length the division of authority it proposed.

The Shape of the Future under Power Equalizing

The legislature which turns to the challenge of fiscal equality — freely or at the inspiration of the court — will enjoy many options. A rich assortment of systems is likely to mushroom. If a family choice system is unlikely, power equalizing systems based upon existing school districts are a real possibility. Our reading of the future of public education under such systems and our guess at some of their other social consequences assume only a political consensus supporting the retention of school districts and the equalization of their power in a given state. Nothing will be assumed for the moment about the level of spending permitted the districts, a matter of great importance to which we turn first.

What factors affect the dollar range of offering that the state will permit a district to choose? Clearly, the state cannot set up the power equalizing relationship out of the blue; it must have some landmarks. It might start with a plan which simply redistributes locally raised taxes and matches the current average offering in the state with the current average effort. It should be evident by now, given unchanged district effort, that this would result in a drastic lowering of the offering in many of the presently high-offering rich districts while dramatically raising that of many poor districts. It might result not merely in a leveling, but, in many places, in an inversion of the current offering pattern; at least, this is so to the extent that poor districts are presently taxing higher.

But surely the state should not expect such behavior. Assuming rationality in district response, the likely consequence of power equalizing is a change in the current pattern of effort; but the nature of that change will depend in turn upon the detail of the plan adopted. If the state gears the program to a simple redistribution up and down to the current average offering and effort, it must be willing to jeopardize the present light house schools. The poor districts may reduce effort, and the rich districts may prove unwilling to bear the cost when the cards are not stacked in their favor. Light house education — like the Taj Mahal — may be the frail flower of freak concentrations of wealth. But the gamble would not really be large. Such model schools are more than monuments, and their crucial role in generating status for their graduates will prompt some districts, whether rich or poor, to make the greater effort such institutions require.

The state might want to protect and encourage these institutions; it could conclude that the fine schools of surburbia should be able to maintain their quality at their current tax effort. Of course, at a comparable effort all districts would then be able to achieve that dollar offering, and this would mean a greater overall commitment from society. The costs of such a plan would be relevant to the state's decision concerning its adoption.

Consider Ohio as an example.[15] Of the city districts, Shaker Heights had the best dollar offering in 1965–66: $806.93 per pupil in ADM for current expenditures. The weighted mean for all Ohio districts in that year was $439.19. Suppose the state decides that Shaker Heights should be able to keep its quality education at the same local effort it is now making; assuming that all other districts were to make this same effort (it would be more than some are now making, less than others), expenditures would increase by $367.74 per pupil in ADM. These extra dollars would have to be provided by the state as a whole. Since Ohio has more than two and a half million children in public schools (using the figures from 1965–66), the increased cost would be slightly under $830 million. The Ohio investment in public education for current expenditures in 1965–66 totaled somewhat over $990 million.

15. See discussion pp. 73–80 above.

Thus, we are talking about more than an 80-percent increase in spending for public education in Ohio. The pattern could be similar in other states, although perhaps not so dramatic since Ohio is one of the states with the greatest range of offerings at present. The increased national expenditure might approximate $15 to $20 billion. Of course, the notion that all districts, including rural ones, will want light house schools is simply, if not demonstrably false. Many — perhaps most — poor districts will decide to take part of the benefit in tax relief. Nevertheless, a substantial increase in state expenditure is conceivable. A decision by the state to preserve the light house schools for the rich districts and to make them available to the poor districts would require no revolution in society's attitude toward education. The poor districts already have given earnest of their general interest in quality education by their high tax rates; the rich have done so by their high expenditures. The only attitude to be reformed is one about proper distribution of resources, and this will be changed, if at all, by the courts; only thereafter will the dollar level of the consensus for educational spending be tested.

Whether spending would increase is also a function of what the state can "afford" compared to its present commitment. What can be afforded is a slippery concept, but it is probably relevant that the share of gross national product spent on the whole field of education has not changed since the nineteenth century. It is probable and important that the lack of competition enjoyed by rich districts has affected our national investment; once you see you are going to win, it doesn't matter if the score is five or fifty to one. Power equalizing could well stimulate the rich districts to fight for the position they formerly enjoyed as privilege. Competition for the first time would become a significant determinant of quality, and, in the contest for excellence the districts could well bid up the overall commitment of society to public education. Contrast a centralized plan in which universal, unthreatened, and changeless mediocrity guarantees security and equality at the cost of anesthesia.

Of course the standard caveat concerning inflation should be inserted here. Would an increase in total dollars mean merely an increase in cost of educational goods and services? — would all those districts in Ohio which are making an effort equal to that of Shaker Heights be able to buy the same things for their money that Shaker Heights does today? Much depends upon whether higher teacher salaries will eat up all the higher spending. Whether today's teachers deserve a general raise is, of course, beside the point. If real improvement in teacher quality is sought, higher pay may well be necessary to attract additional competent people into the profession; yet, for such changes in salary to be translated into performance takes a long time. In the short run, it is possible that more dollars will be buying the same product (and teachers' salaries often comprise seventy percent or more of all current expenditures). But at least *all* districts would be doing the buying. Perhaps we should accept this, as the price of justice. If, as now, the same teachers get less pay but the services of the best of them can be purchased by the richer school districts, that is hardly a lesser evil.

Some Political Concerns

The prospects for a power equalizing system incorporating a significant range of taxing choices for the districts depend not alone or even chiefly upon the rationality of legislators. Political power and alliances will shape the program. The distribution of that power will differ from state to state and district to district; yet, some common elements and a patterned overall response are to be expected. The chief political bugbear invoked to oppose reform (power equalizing and all other wealth-free systems) is the potential defection of the nonpoor to private education; we will consider briefly the meaning and likelihood of such behavior. First, however, observe that much nervous speculation about the behavior of the rich flies in the face of experience. Even those rich for whom the costs of private education are relatively insignificant have, for the most part, chosen public education. This phenomenon is somewhat regional (the South and New England are exceptions), but it strongly suggests that many motivations in this area of life are not accounted for simply by market considerations.

The departure of a child for private school is itself a purely neutral fact. The goal of public education is availability, not use. If all the nonpoor were to bail out of public schools because — other things equal — they preferred private education, none could object to this personal choice so long as public schools that are competitive (with each other and with private education) are left behind. The danger from defection is in its second-order effects upon the general support for public education: that is, widespread defection, for whatever reason, may imperil the political base for good public education. Are we then involved in a dilemma? If public education (when fairly distributed) becomes "too good," will it lose its own support by its high cost? Is fair public education self-limiting in quality? Since fair distribution of public education has never existed, any answer is risky, for the imponderables are legion; but perhaps we can suggest a part of the answer by asking who is likely to turn to private education under what circumstances and in so doing cast the weight of their votes against high support levels for public education?

Such issues will obviously be relevant in some respects to all new kinds of systems. Here, however, we will assume that the state has already decided to use some form of power equalizing. Such a two-level system opens the whole range of political issues that would be raised by a centralized finance structure, plus some special features of its own. Because of the duality of such a system the questions must be divided. First, as with any system, it must be asked what the political behavior will be of whom at the *state* level on the issues of the permitted range of local tax and the size of the state share? Second, assuming that a strong operating system of power equalizing is created by the legislature, what will be the pattern of political behavior in the *districts* in determining local tax rates?

Statewide Political Support. The bulk of families that fall into the middle ranges of wealth in America are unlikely candidates for purely private education. They are nearly certain to continue to support substantial public education as they have in the past for reasons of habit, political morality, and self-interest. That they will simply abandon the very poor is improbable, and they are themselves sufficiently impecunious that private schools would seem to them unrealistic or, at least, a burden; all their experience, instincts, and probably self-interest, tend to public education. Their support, plus the support of the very poor out of sheer necessity, makes the substantial erosion of present average levels of public education difficult to imagine. Given this much, an important consequence follows. If there is in fact an irreducible consensus for substantial public education, this spending should itself in turn stimulate even more spending. Families slightly richer than the middle groups (families who might opt for private education if the burden of public education were nominal) will very likely desire and support a level of expenditure permitting the really good education to which most of them have become accustomed. The middle and upper classes by and large have no choice but to pay for a substantial public system; but if they have to pay for it most of them will use it; and if they use it, they will seek to and be able to muster support for a system better than mediocre. For less than the cost of two mediocre systems, public and private, they can have one good system.

The tendency to accelerate spending in any fair system

(compared to existing systems) might well become magnified by the unique flexibility in power equalizing. That is, given power equalizing as the state choice, those middle class voters whose support is crucial will be seeking, when lobbying at the state level, not a fixed rate for the whole state but, rather, a range of rates which will permit them a local tax choice suited to their own aspirations. It may well be that they will imagine — rightly or wrongly — that their own educational aspirations exceed those of the poor (those perceived as living elsewhere). They well may conclude that *permitting* a high local rate in a power equalizing system will be significantly less costly than would be *requiring* the same rate statewide in a centralized system. For these and perhaps other reasons it should not be politically difficult to establish maximum rates of expenditure well above the present average. Perhaps this is obvious; after all, the very logic of the percentage equalizing system suggests the opportunity for districts to sacrifice more (and less) than the average for education. Indeed, if no districts in fact choose rates lower than the maximum, the rate system by definition is improperly adjusted. If this is seen as true, nonpoor voting groups could be co-opted for a high rate system by their conviction that the potential cost of such a system statewide will exceed substantially the cost in fact.

Of course, this predicted phenomenon of accelerating support will be limited; above a certain point, each higher level of spending will create added political resistance even while it forces more families into public education. But if, as we have argued, the resistance to higher rates will never amount to a consensus against public education itself, there is reason, at least in a power equalized system, to predict a substantial increase of permitted rates over their existing average levels. To answer our original question, a fair system of public education is, to be sure, self-limiting in quality; but the statewide level of that limitation is likely to be reasonably high and, in a power equalizing system, should be even higher.

District Political Support. Here we assume that an operating and substantial power equalizing system has been created by the legislature. The behavior of the nonpoor within their own districts under such a system may prove less predictable than their behavior statewide, simply because of the wide variation in socioeconomic characteristics of districts within any and all states. Power equalizing removes differences in district wealth; but because it does not affect individual wealth, differential behavior from district to district is highly probable. We do not consider such variation in itself pernicious; it is the very purpose of the system to give a choice to the local electorate. Nonetheless, it will be important, if only for planning purposes, to speculate about the configuration of local majorities.

We are most concerned with the behavior of nonpoor groups who can afford and would consider using private schools. The question is, under what circumstances could they and would they force the local tax to the minimum permitted level? Our best guess is that the political influence of this kind of group will be quite different depending, oddly enough, upon the wealth of the district as a whole. This is true, first, because although private-school families inhabit poor districts in substantial numbers, they are rarely, if ever, a majority of the population. Second, poor districts under power equalizing will for the first time be able to improve their public education to the point where it becomes competitive with good private schools and becomes so at a tax rate equal to that under the old system. Thus, in poor districts, the general movement of the nonpoor will be *out of private and into public* schools; indeed, if such families formerly were able to choose private education, they should now be willing to support a significantly higher tax level for public education. Such nonpoor families in poor districts should be counted among those who would give political support at the level of state politics to a generous overall power equalizing system. It is to their personal advantage to do so.

What will the behavior of rich districts be? Let us assume some correspondence between individual wealth and the wealth of the district; will it not be in the interest of those who can afford private education to gang up on the poor of the district and deny them good public education? The answer is probably yes, but this only suggests that the same majority which creates the state system should ensure provisions discouraging such behavior. The primary insurance for that purpose is a fair required minimum rate. This device has the twofold effect of securing the minority poor of the district against gross discrimination while providing the middle class with an economic incentive to choose public schools for themselves and, thus, to vote for a rate above the minimum in order to ensure their quality. Another device is one discussed more fully in Chapter 6; the offering-effort relation may be shaped by the state so that the funds generated from the local source are always less than the amount the district will be permitted to spend. This means that the state has equalized up to above the richest district; an implementation of this might be to have the local source valued at 50 percent of its worth. This would reduce much of the incentive to withdraw.

An alternative question is whether rich districts will systematically choose higher rates than poor under a power equalizing system. That is, will they continue to have better education because they are willing to make greater sacrifices? Arguably they may do so for two reasons: the socioeconomic characteristics of a district count in its ability to translate attitude about education, whatever that may be, into results at the ballot box; and the socioeconomic characteristics of a district condition its attitude toward education.

Regarding the first reason, it may be that those who run the school system and will push for excellence are more easily identified with by people in rich districts than in poor. These leaders tend to be educated and successful like their rich constituents. Or it may be that rich districts generate more talented community leaders who participate in and promote school matters; or that there are more low-level school program campaign workers who can afford the time to canvas for better education. Further, rich districts may tend to have a fairly homogeneous and cohesive population, whereas poor ones tend to be atomized and hence less effective vehicles for political decision-making.

As for the second point, rich districts on the whole simply may prove to be more interested in education and more willing to make the effort for it, perhaps because parents in such districts are more concerned about the future of their children, or because their own experience with education makes its value clearer. Or, perhaps excellence in all things is a matter of community pride. Possibly, the people in poor districts feel that the amount of social mobility that becomes available to their children through education is worth only the lesser commitment they make to it; the young in their community should be prepared to move up only a rung or two in the class ladder, because this is all that most can realistically expect or even desire.

We do not suggest that any of these notions necessarily make sense or would determine the behavior of poor districts. They are, in fact, inconsistent with what we know of effort patterns in poor districts as a whole today. They are purely hypothetical and are stated to pose the difficult question of whether or not something should be done if the poor districts, after being given the chance to compete with the rich in the form of a power equalizing plan, somehow do not. We think it unnecessary for society as a direct matter to decide for the poor districts what is best for them. Nevertheless, there may be subtle and important ways of illuminating for the poor the available options and of encouraging local organization to support greater effort in education. This would be an appropriate role even for a government social agency.

We would hope and expect, however, that at least some poor districts will be taxing high so that poor families of like mind could live there and see their wishes reflected. The mounting of successful education enterprise by the poor could provide the kinds of success stories of which we stand in need.

On balance there is every reason to hope that rich-poor patterns will simply disappear from public education: that rich districts will not systematically stay ahead. Education is a commodity the poor should covet as an exit from the cycle of poverty. Even under discriminatory conditions, poor districts have striven harder than the rich to support public schools. Once they are able to get their money's worth, they may buy education before anything else. In any case it is plain that the political process will be crucial. The mass of the people whose interests will be at stake will have the onus to exert political force for a fair level of education at both state and district level.

Lateral Consequences of Power Equalizing: Impact on Private Schools, Residential Patterns, and Other Governmental Services

Private Schools. The impact of a power equalizing approach to school finance on certain other institutions can be predicted. For private schools there is considerable uncertainty: if we are wrong, and public education is poorly supported, private schools may be in for a boom in attendance. If, on the other hand, a healthy district power equalizing plan is adopted, the future of private schools might well be bleak.

Consider first the implications of power equalizing for the nonreligious private schools. A strong power equalizing plan means an increase in investment in public education statewide. Patrons of private schools will have increased obligations for public education, regardless of their personal desires. They may be less willing to abandon the public system, as well as less able. Second, if the competitive race among districts becomes heated, private schools will face increased costs if they are to offer comparable quality, and this will force them to extract even higher tuition.

For the religious private schools, the same problem appears in aggravated form. Indeed, to the extent that religious education is a value widely held by members of the middle and lower middle classes, a plan of tax relief for parents electing to send their children to private institutions would probably be a condition of their continuance. Membership rolls of religious schools are likely to be made up of pupils from families with less wealth on the average than those families who support the nonreligious private schools. Any increase in tuition costs, along with continued and even increased taxes for public schools, could be the beginning of the end for already tottering parochial systems. These private schools are the ones which will be hardest hit in the competitive battle, and many will have to dramatically increase costs if they are to maintain a comparable offering. Particularly when religious schools compete in the poor areas will pressure be intensified by the rise in public school quality. Of course, none of this speculation takes into account the possibility of a system of family power equalizing, which would probably produce an explosive growth in quantity and quality of all kinds of public-private education.

Housing Patterns. At the moment, residential housing patterns seem to be affected by the quality of government services offered in the community, and schools in particular appear to be an identifiable factor in selection of a place to live. In the folklore of suburban migration, the quality of suburban schools is a prominent rationale for desertion of the city. No doubt there is more than a little truth in this, even if it is impossible to quantify.[16]

As regards schools, under the present plan of financing it pays to move to the richest district one can afford. This is a great financial stimulus for the rich to live together in closed communities. But since the attraction of moving to where schools are better and taxes are lower will be blunted by power equalizing, people may be more willing to stay in locations which they find convenient and in which they have put down roots. This could cut down on social class isolation. Besides, if it proves true, it may mean the narrowing of the wealth differentials which now obtain in the various communities; this, in turn, would create a more evenly distributed support for other municipal services than exists today. But too much must not be made of this point; many other strong factors are operating to influence family location which are independent of the often articulated desire for better schools. Also note that these predicted effects might be expected as well under a centralized system of financing.

Other Governmental Services. Power equalizing in education potentially represents quite a variety of impacts on other governmental services. At one extreme, it is possible that the principle of equal effort means equal dollars would eventually be carried over into all phases of local government services. This would mean that poor areas would get the chance at equal quality facilities in a multitude of areas.

At another extreme, the increase in investment in education which power equalizing can bring might come at the expense of other governmental services. This effect would tend to be more prominent in poor districts; central cities face the problem because of the special weight of municipal overburden. The neglect of police and fire protection seems unlikely, but

16. Rogers, *110 Livingston Street,* p. 38.

education may drain off funds from recreation, community planning, pollution control, and so on. Ultimately, the impact of such neglect would be felt outside the particular community, illustrating perhaps that much of what we now attempt on a local basis needs broader treatment, not because centralization is better administratively, but, again, because localism in the sense of pure local finance is simply unequal to the task.

Part III · The Cutting Edge

. . . there was something to be done about it, and . . .
waiting for the great civilization of the future to arrive was
not enough. . . . Destiny, like the God of the Jews, gives no
unconditional promises.

Wells, Experiment in Autobiography

8 · In Quest of the Judicial Role

Walter, be wise, avoid the wild and new,
The constitution is the game for you.
Chesterton, The Revolutionary, or Lines to a Statesman

THE READER WHO HAS SURVIVED PASSAGE through the jungle of educational economics is prepared to consider the cutting edge of the hypothesis: the social tools that make change conceivable. Reform in educational policy will not be an automatic response to manifest injustice, as seventy years of frustration demonstrates. But how to kill the old system? Or, better — for those admiring local option — how to take the first step toward infusing old structures with the minima of equality? The remainder of this book suggests the process by which the reform of educational finance can begin. The key figure in the drama will be the judiciary and, most prominently, the Supreme Court of the United States in its role as final arbiter of the nature and limits of state power under the Constitution.

BEWARE OF THE BULL

Because we will be so much concerned with judicial role, it is important to sensitize the nonlawyer to problems that arise whenever the power of the court is invoked to settle issues of the magnitude of the school question. It may be too much to hope that the later discussions of precedent will be lucid to all readers; but at least we may convince the layman that all is not beer and skittles simply because a reasonably persuasive technical argument can be presented on equal protection grounds. Although almost any alleged mistreatment by government of a class of persons can be analyzed plausibly in equal protection terms, few cases move the courts to action. Before reaching the technical questions, however, there are larger — or at least other — questions and dangers arising from peculiarities and limits of the judicial function that cannot be ignored, even if our discussion must be truncated and tentative. The school finance problem resembles more a disarranged china shop than a condemned building. The appropriate remedy may be something other than the unconsidered release of an egalitarian judicial bull.

The function of judicial review is one now familiar to Americans, at least in its more spectacular aspects. It is popularized in the weekly news magazines and analyzed by television commentators. Billboards inform us which of the justices deserve impeachment. The court occasionally has been a storm center since 1801; commentators since de Tocqueville have observed that all important social isues in America eventually become judicial issues.[1] But until our time the court had not become the constant object of those forms of public attention which are associated with the political process. Furthermore, it is probable that, historically, the public impression of the court has been one of general conservatism. Twenty years ago Chesterton's sarcastic advice to the Tory politician to stick to the Constitution would have appeared to most Americans a motif of reaction and one quite appropriate to the court. To stick to the Constitution meant to stick indeed: that document was flaunted to still the waters, not to ruffle them.[2] Such a picture of the court is, simply, dead; where the Constitution is

1. Alexis de Tocqueville, *Democracy in America*, rev. ed. (New York, 1965), p. 280.
2. In 1944, Dennis Brogan still found it possible to wonder "how the American nation ever got going and kept going if the job of finding authority for action was as arduous in the early days as it is made to seem today"; Brogan, *The American Character* (New York, 1944), p. 125.

the game today, the wild and new is often the public's expectation, and the court is perceived as the very architect of novelty.

The reasons for the change in public attitude are complex, but they surely are related to changes in the court itself. Its increasing willingness — indeed, its occasional eagerness — to engage itself in the process of fundamental social change has given to partisans and public alike the sense of a third force to be reckoned with when public stakes are high. The Supreme Court took no side on United States participation in Viet Nam, but it was inevitable that it would be asked.[3] For many of the uninitiated, the impression of the court seems to be one of undifferentiated power to be harnessed at random by whichever partisan can gain the ear of an evanescent majority of five for the purpose of slaying whatever dragon may seem the particular torment of the season. That this image is absurd and that we exaggerate its public acceptance is almost irrelevant. Our point is merely the inevitability that the school finance issue would be offered to the Supreme Court for resolution. Recently it has been,[4] and it will be again.[5]

3. Mora v. McNamara, 387 F.2d 862 (D.C. Cir., 1967), cert. denied 389 U.S. 934 (1967). See also United States v. Holmes, 387 F.2d 781 (7th Cir. 1967) cert. denied, 391 U.S. 936 (1968); United States v. Hart, 382 F.2d 1020 (3rd Cir. 1967) cert. denied, 391 U.S. 956 (1968).

4. McInnis v. Shapiro, 293 F. Supp. 327 (N.D. Ill. 1968), aff'd mem. sub nom., McInnis v. Ogilvie, 394 U.S. 322 (1969), Mr. Justice Douglas dissenting without opinion.

5. A number of cases are now at varying stages in trial and appellate courts. Serrano v. Priest, General Civil No. 938254 (Super. Ct., Los Angeles County, Calif., complaint dismissed Jan. 8, 1969); Burruss v. Wilkerson, General Civil No. 68-C-13-H (U.S.D.C. W.D. Va., complaint dismissed May 27, 1969); Board of Education v. Michigan, General Civil No. 103342 (Cir. Ct., Wayne County, Mich., filed Feb. 2, 1968); Rodrigues v. San Antonio Independent School District, General Civil No. 68-175-SA (U.S.D.C. W.D. Tex., filed July 30, 1968); Silva v. Atascadero Unified School District, General Civil No. 595954 (Super. Ct., San Francisco County, Calif., filed Sept. 26, 1968); Guerra v. Smith, General Civil No. A-690CA-9 (U.S.D.C. W.D. Tex., filed Jan. 28, 1969).

The attacks have and will continue to come by way of the equal protection clause. Approaches of two general sorts are available in equal protection cases. First, the court can be asked simply to declare the existing legislation invalid as an irrational classification;[6] second, it can be urged to elevate the conflict to the level of one involving a "fundamental" interest or "invidious discrimination," thereby requiring development of a separate and additional standard by which to test the validity of state action.[7] Our preference for the latter approach will become clear later, and we will offer our own standard by which to judge the financing plans of the states. Before we reach that point, however, it would be well to inquire in a rather general way into the qualities that should inform whatever judicial strategy is adopted for resolving the issue for or against the state. To say that the United States Supreme Court will have the opportunity to face the school finance issue[8] is not to demonstrate that it should do so or that it can effectively dispose of it. Much of the lengthy discussion that follows will suggest that judicial review in this instance can take many forms, some of them clearly destructive. Whether the court should act[9] and how depends largely upon three fundamental and interrelated aspects of judicial review: standards, preemption, and enforceability.

The standards problem is essentially one of achieving intelligibility. If the present state financing systems are condemned, it is not enough simply to declare them invalid. If the court hopes to generate the consensus necessary to mean-

6. See pp. 316–337 below.

7. See pp. 338–393 below.

8. There is no question that the court has jurisdiction of the subject matter. McInnis v. Shapiro, 293 F. Supp. at 329–330.

9. Technically, the court has no choice if the suit arises under its appellate jurisdiction. But even then the court, by disposing of the appeal summarily, may diminish — or at least becloud — its practical significance while giving a technical disposition on the merits. See n. 41 below and accompanying text.

ingful change it must identify with reasonable clarity the locus and nature of the constitutional defect. Society cannot or will not respond to canons incapable of communication. The reapportionment field provides an example of a problem of standards solved by the court: the need for an intelligible measure of equal protection drove the court to a one-man, one-vote principle that, whatever its other defects, has qualities of intelligibility unmatched by any of the tests competing for adoption.[10] In other areas the court has been less successful in articulating standards. The state action and obscenity concepts have plagued and continued to plague the court because of their inherent inscrutability.[11] Where substantive rights depend upon Delphic distinctions the court stands endlessly on flypaper, unable to clear more than one foot at a time. Unless the court can find an effable essence, its judgments tend to be ad hoc and unpredictable, qualities which in the school finance case will evoke nothing but criticism of the court and evasion by the legislatures.

Within the term preemption are included two consequences of judicial invalidation of state legislation that are distinct but related and that pose questions about the prudence of judicial intervention in this instance. One is the antidemocratic effect of the court's sapping of the legislative power of the states; the other is the court's excessive narrowing of alternatives available to a state legislature.[12]

The antimajoritarian criticism, whatever its merits, is an objection that tends to dissipate to the extent that the in-

10. Gray v. Sanders, 372 U.S. 368 (1963).

11. For copious illustration of these two troublemakers at work and for references to scholarly comment thereon, see W. B. Lockhart, Yale Kamisar, and Jesse Choper, Constitutional Law, Cases-Comments-Questions (St. Paul, 1967), pp. 1276–1325, 1047–1115.

12. See generally Alexander Bickel, The Least Dangerous Branch (Indianapolis, 1962).

dividual seeking protection is of a class effectively unrepresented in the political process.[13] But if cases of de facto disenfranchisement escape the objection that judicial review is antidemocratic, the school finance problem appears to be a classic instance. What better example of political impotence than a class of persons by definition unqualified to vote? Of course, one might take the view that, functionally, parents qualify as political surrogates for their children. Even if this is accepted, however, the political debility of the parents is equally certain for another reason. We have shown that the injury under existing systems is visited principally upon those living in districts with wealth below the average of the state. It is improbable that parents in these districts ever could rally sufficient political muscle from other districts to overthrow a system which is perceived as advantageous to all the richer districts and which is effectively indifferent to the interests of districts near the average in wealth — districts whose political support would be required for change.[14] Further, the testimony of

13. An example is the class of the criminally accused, one notably deficient in political potency. We are not likely soon to see the formation of a powerful National Criminal Defendant's League. See the remarks of former Senator Kenneth Keating, reprinted in *Harvard Legal Aid Bureau, Annual Report 1965–66* (Cambridge, February, 1965), pp. 18–20. See generally Jesse Choper, "On the Warren Court and Judicial Review," *Catholic University Law Review*, 17:20 (1967). The special role of the Supreme Court as a rescuer of unrepresented victims of state action probably is traceable to the insight and influence of Chief Justice Harlan Fiske Stone; N. T. Dowling, "The Methods of Mr. Justice Stone in Constitutional Cases," *Columbia Law Review*, 41:1160, 1171–1181 (1941). The first beneficiaries of the approach, ironically, were interstate businesses that were the objects of xenophobic state action (South Carolina State Highway Department v. Barnwell Bros., 303 U.S. 177 [1938]; see also the recent decision in WHYY, Inc., v. Borough of Glassboro, 393 U.S. 117 [1968]). The first appearance of this rationale as a source of protection for civil liberties was in Stone's dissent in the earliest flag salute case, Minersville School District v. Gobitis, 310 U.S. 586 (1940).

14. The situation resembles that described by Chief Justice Stone in United States v. Carolene Products, 304 U.S. 144, 153 (1938) — one of "discrete and insular minorities [whose] special condition . . . tends seriously to curtail the operation of those political processes ordinarily to be relied upon to protect

seventy years of frustration of legislative reform strongly confirms the futility of political commotion at the state level, where to invoke the democratic process is to ask privileged society to surrender the advantage that as much as any other is the keystone of its privilege.[15] Change, if it is to come (an event by no means fated) is not likely to commence with political puissance. Before the democratic process can assemble a new consensus for the compromise we propose or for any other solution, the principle of rich district-poor district must perish. Only the court can liberate the legislature for the consideration of alternatives.

The second problem of preemption is that of excessive limitation by the court of legislative alternatives. How far should the court specify forms of legislation that do satisfy the Constitution? Some partisans in school finance cases urge prescription in detail of the very form and structure of school finance for the states. That hope is probably vain; if not, it is merely horrifying. Perhaps the worst service the court could render would be the enunciation of a principle that would leave the state no flexibility in its choice of financial structure for education. For example, requiring equality of expenditures per pupil statewide might be a catchy device for terminating the existing injustices; it might also be an effective way to terminate public education. There is certainly no question that such a solution could pretermit forever the possibility of legislative reexamination of a host of alternatives to the rejected order of

minorities, and which may call for a correspondingly more searching judicial inquiry." Since the Colorado reapportionment case, the importance of showing a practical disenfranchisement is unclear (Lucas v. Forty-fourth General Assembly, 377 U.S. 713 [1964]); however, we doubt that we have overemphasized its persuasive value.

15. There is one limitation upon our confidence about the relative lack of representation for the poor school district. The same state legislator occasionally represents a balance of rich and poor districts. He may enjoy, as a consequence, a greater degree of independence than we have assumed. It is possible to argue that, if large numbers of legislators represented such balanced constituencies, the problems would diminish.

things. There is great virtue in the court's confining itself whenever possible to minimal proscriptions in the interest of legislative flexibility. Our proposed constitutional standard satisfies this criterion.

Ultimately the Court must rely upon other branches of government for enforcement of its orders. The last fifteen years have demonstrated how difficult it can be to realize in practice the implications of a judicial ruling on a fundamental social question that is not supported by reasonable consensus in the state. If there is doubt of this, the current statistics on school desegregation in the South should quickly dispel it.[16] The Supreme Court will be sensitive to the enforceability question, both when it decides whether or not to condemn the existing finance system and when it chooses the form that condemnation is to take. The latter is intimately related to the search for an intelligible standard, the absence of which has done much to frustrate successful desegregation.

In summary, the best service the court can perform is fourfold: (1) break the logjam of the status quo and thus free the state from a politically immovable system; (2) give the state wide latitude in its re-examination of the finance problem; (3) speak with clarity in a standard capable of intelligent interpretation; (4) remain keenly sensitive to the likely legislative and popular responses to the various forms its decisions and orders might take. We happily endorse the monition of Phillip Kurland: "Let's place the responsibility where it belongs. Let's permit the state an opportunity to experiment with different answers to these difficult problems and free them to undertake the experiment." [17]

16. U.S. Commission on Civil Rights, *Racial Isolation in the Public Schools* (Washington, D.C., 1967), II (appendixes), 2–4.

17. Phillip Kurland, "Equal Educational Opportunity: The Limits of Constitutional Jurisprudence Undefined," *University of Chicago Law Review*, 35: 583, 600 (1968).

EQUALITY AND THE COURT

Eventually our constitutional position must be tested against the limiting conditions of judicial effectiveness. First, however, the question of substance should be addressed in a similarly general fashion. Assuming that the judiciary can be an effective agent of change, how does it go about deciding what change to effect? Specifically, in an equal protection problem of the kind we face, what kind of value framework can be descried within which judicial deliberation can proceed? At the beginning of the book we promised to avoid overambitious excursions into the philosophy of equality, and we intend to honor that commitment. Nevertheless, in dealing with the legal question of equal protection it would be impossible to clarify the role of the court without placing it in broader context. Indeed, doing so may even assist us in simplifying the discussion.

Nowhere does the Constitution mention equality; the Fourteenth Amendment speaks only of equal protection. This is hard to remember as a practical fact at a time when the Supreme Court speaks on occasion as if equality itself were a basis of constitutional right,[18] but the word is simply absent from

---

18. In Gray v. Sanders, 372 U.S. 368, 381 (1963), the majority opinion explicitly reaches outside the Constitution, invoking "the conception of political equality from the Declaration of Independence, to Lincoln's Gettysburg Address. . . ." Elsewhere the court merely assumes the propriety of such exotic sources, as in Harper v. Virginia Board of Elections, 383 U.S. 663, 669 (1966), where it allows with enthusiasm that "we have never been confined to historic notions of equality. . . ." On occasion the court has shown a positive allergy to the language of the amendment itself. In Douglas v. California, 372 U.S. 353, 358 (1963), it speaks of "that equality demanded by the Fourteenth Amendment," but never of equal protection. The references to equality in this fashion are usually found in opinions by Justice Douglas, but they have generated no explicit reservations from the majorities for which he speaks. At least one quondam member of those majorities would seem to approve further expansion of the search for egalitarian sources. Former Justice Goldberg, while still on the court, published a lecture virtually amalgamating the values of equality and liberty. "[T]he framers did not find it necessary to mention equality. They naturally assumed it was encompassed within the concept of liberty";

the full and familiar language of the relevant part of the amendment: "No State shall . . . deny to any person within its jurisdiction the equal protection of the laws." If equality denotes an inherent attribute of mankind, as the court sometimes seems to imply, the relevance of this human equality to the legal question of equal protection is not obvious. The amendment's sole object is a certain kind of *protection* for persons, not their equality. Note that even if the equality sometimes spoken of by the court were an attribute of "persons," this would add nothing to the amendment. Persons enjoy its guarantee of protection irrespective of their equality.

Perhaps the only sensible way to view the use of the term equality by the court is to see it as a nontechnical shorthand description, not of an attribute of men, but of a state of affairs in which there exists equal protection for persons, themselves equal or unequal. That is, when there is equal protection, there is equality, and vice versa; since the terms are synonymous, the use of equality adds nothing to the court's perspective or to its grasp.

However, this does not seem a realistic description of the court's behavior. In fact, the court gives every appearance of regarding human equality as a value to be considered in judicial decision-making. The critics are perfectly correct, and it is hard to see how it could be otherwise. The reason is native to the notion of equal protection of the laws. There is but one way to give that expression a clear meaning, and that way is absurd: that is, equal protection could be said to exist when all persons in whatever class defined by legislation are treated similarly. The question thus could be reduced to one of evenhanded enforcement of law however barbaric its content. The elimination

Arthur Goldberg, "Equality and Governmental Action," *New York University Law Review*, 39:205, 207 (1964). For a general development of the theme, see Archibald Cox, "Constitutional Adjudication and the Promotion of Human Rights" (foreword to "The Supreme Court 1965 Term"), *Harvard Law Review*, 80:91 (1966).

of all red-haired infants would not offend, so long as no favoritism was shown within that class. It is only when one entertains doubts about the propriety of such a classification in the first place that a spectrum of broader and vaguer issues of human differences and similarities is revealed. Of course, this is what inevitably has happened. Even in its earliest applications the clause was stretched beyond discriminatory enforcement to invalidate arbitrary legislative classification,[19] and who would wish it otherwise? The history of the amendment alone would require such an expansive view for use against racial discriminations.[20] Some would prefer that substantive injustices of other kinds be checked judicially by invocation of constitutional guarantees other than equal protection,[21] but it is now too late to take such a stance as a practical persuasion of future judicial action. The court is engaged in giving value content to the equal protection clause, and the only relevant question is how to contain and direct the process so as to keep it intelligible, predictable, and moderate. Once the court began to review the propriety of legislative classifications, the sources of judgment easily expanded to include such rich ores as the multiform concepts of human equality. If equality is not relevant, it is difficult to imagine what is.

What can it mean to say that the court has embarked upon the protection of human equality? Surely this is not an absolutist notion that each and every man is indistinguishable before the law. Taken literally, this would spell the end of law that, after all, is itself a way of creating classes—that is, drawing distinctions between men (Welsh is a thief, Berg is a conscien-

19. Strauder v. West Virginia, 100 U.S. 303 (1880).

20. See generally Alexander Bickel, "The Original Understanding and the Segregation Decision," *Harvard Law Review*, 69:1 (1955); L. H. Pollack, "Racial Discrimination and Judicial Integrity: A Reply to Professor Wechsler," *University of Pennsylvania Law Review*, 108:1 (1959).

21. Phillip Kurland, "Equal in Origin and Equal in Title to the Legislative and Executive Branches of the Government" (foreword to "The Supreme Court 1963 Term"), *Harvard Law Review*, 78:143 (1964).

tious objector, Call is a bona fide purchaser; Bowles and Heaslip are none of these). Absolute equality is absolute lawlessness. It is no accident that Marx associated both with the withering of the state.

But if we mean equality to be limited, who can tell us the metes and bounds? We will not pause to examine the literature on the nature of equality. Suffice it to say that it is plentiful and chaotic.[22] Our object is the practical and limited one of generating specific educational reforms through judicial decree. Perhaps this could be effected by the factual showing we have already made plus the more or less traditional legal analysis to come. But we have confidence that whatever preliminary clarification of concept is possible will operate to the benefit of our practical proposals; before we examine judicial expression and behavior on the subject, therefore, we offer abstractions of our own about formal equality. It should appear that these notions ultimately are related to and limited by the judicial process. If nothing else, this effort may make more explicit the general kind of intellection and judgment we think the Supreme Court or any court should exercise when it uses equality as a standard.

Equality is a relation, not a thing; it is neither form in the Platonic idiom nor is it a quality of any existent thing considered by itself. For an equality to "exist," two entities are necessary; it is not truly an aspect of either entity to which it relates except insofar as it is a property of both. When this is clear,

22. S. A. Lakoff, *Equality in Political Philosophy* (Cambridge: Harvard University Press, 1964). For two interesting collections of disparate perspectives, see J. R. Pennock and J. W. Chapman, eds., *Equality: Nomos IX* (New York: Atherton Press, 1967), and Sir Isaiah Berlin and Richard Wolheim, "Equality," in *Proceedings of the Aristotelian Society*, London, NS, 56 (1956). The subject can be viewed ontologically as a branch of the enduring controversy over universals in philosophy and mathematics; for an overview of the general problem of individuals and classes from a nominalist perspective, see I. M. Bochenski, Alonzo Church, and Nelson Goodman, *The Problem of Universals* (Notre Dame, 1956).

there is no harm in describing one thing as equal to another. All this applies also to *inequality*, which, from this point of view, differs from equality only in being infinitely variable. Equality is the unique instance; in this it resembles an equation for which there is a single correct answer but an infinity of wrong ones. Of course, this absolute must be immediately defused. For practical purposes — and especially for constitutional purposes — varying degrees of sameness must be accepted as the equivalent of equality.

Two other criteria should be imposed before characterizing any relationship as equality or inequality for present purposes. The first seems implied in the very idea of a relation: that is, we speak of equality or its absence only when the entities described are mutually influential — if Adam had been created in Asia and Eve in Africa, at least on the natural plane there could have been no equality or inequality. To be meaningful the idea probably requires reciprocal awareness, and it certainly requires some interaction such as competition or affection. This aspect is relevant in determining the proper limits to ethical claims of equality among men of different nations and cultures or even of different governmental divisions of a state. Its relevance to a putative equality of school children is plain.

The second criterion can be introduced by asking whether this equality can be posited of any entities except man. The issue may appear purely theoretical, but its explication may help clarify the general character of what we mean by equality, for it permits us to dispose of false analogies from the world of nonconscious beings. There are, of course, in the world of the imagination, logical identities that can properly claim the relationship; they constitute the world of pure mathematics and logic without existential link to the world of men or indeed of any material substance. These equalities inhabit a realm to which the concept justice is irrelevant and they are not germane to our present concern. But it is common to extend the egalitarian idiom into descriptions of the animal, vegetable, and mineral kingdoms; we wish to make it clear that this is often mere metaphor and can mislead. When in literature or common speech animals are related to each other as equals or unequals, this is ordinarily so only through observation of them by humankind and through attribution to them by man's mind of an anthropomorphic scale of values. Like Orwell, one may purport to judge a certain pig superior to another in temper or physique, but the measuring rod is either human utility (this pig is fatter) or an attribution of pseudo-humanity to the pig (this pig has a sweeter disposition). When the human observer is removed from the picture such statements seem foolish. And this is the important point; they seem so, we submit, because the notion of equality is ethical in content. To speak of equalities among pigs is to speak of nothing, for as far as we can tell pigs are not free and cannot behave in an ethical fashion or, for that matter, an unethical one. They are . . . well, they are pigs, and that's the end of it. Any porcine ethic can be imposed only by remote analogy to human aspirations of behavior, beauty, and utility. And so it must be for the rest of creation save man. Man carries the burden of determining identities and differences among his own kind because he alone is free to fashion for and of himself an identity which can deserve recognition or blame. In recognizing these human identities and differences and deciding which are significant man's moral life is centered. Equality theory is not merely concerned with the ethical; in large measure it forms the very substance of ethics.[23]

But nothing has been offered yet to indicate how it should be determined which personal qualities and which degrees of similarity are to be regarded as significant. Equality typically has been conceived as a dyadic relationship, man versus man,

23. The general ethical analysis of equality nearest our own seems to be that of John Rawls; see, e.g., "Distributive Justice: Some Addenda," *Natural Law Forum*, 13:51 (1969).

with theoretical concentration upon man's nature and the common elements thereof. With some oversimplification it can be said that, from Cicero through the Founding Fathers to contemporary philosophy, the central concentration has been upon substantive questions of sameness and difference. This is proper, necessary, and first in importance; but it obscures a crucial aspect of equality that might be called its triangular character. An ethical issue of equality between one person and another cannot be understood clearly while remaining at the same level as the two. When one claims equality with the other, he invokes explicitly or by implication an extrinsic standard by warrant of which the relation he claims is to be legitimated. The claimant must appeal to some measure or measurer other than himself, which may be custom, authority, reason, or revelation. In a juridical setting the measure takes the form of a judge — a man, but that judge in turn must be a receptacle and censor of the multitude of conflicting values which in specific cases clamor for expression and which assert their appeal in ethical terms for either the common treatment or the differentiation of men. Equality is now seen as a relationship of A and B to C, with C representing and filtering a congeries of influences radiating from custom, philosophy, precedent, and prejudice — in other words, all influences on the decision-maker — until the trail of influences eludes us in complexity. What preserves at least apparent simplicity in the model is the identifiable role of C and the intelligibility of his judgment. It may be objected that the effort here is to turn equality into a mere lawyer's mechanism sans content, a kind of Hohfeldian contraption useful for settling disputed claims but bearing little freight of humanity and begging all substantive issues.[24] That was precisely the intention. What has been presented is formal equality almost without

24. The reference is to W. N. Hohfeld, whose taxonomy of legal interests has influenced generations of precision-seeking law professors (*Fundamental Legal Concepts as Applied in Judicial Reasoning, and Other Legal Essays* [New Haven, 1923]).

flesh and blood, except, of course, for our insistence that equality is ethical in content.

Indeed, if one looks closely he may conclude that equality is simply a legal relation like any other (ownership, liability) between persons. A court (C) must characterize every interaction of persons (A and B) brought to litigation as having or not having legal significance. The only difference that equality poses as a problem in legal relations is its relative ubiquity; its existence is in fact assumed in most legal relations in the common law. For example, A is as entitled to due care from B as is B from A and is so entitled upon an assumption of fundamental sameness. This assumption becomes a problem, however, when the state specifies one and not the other as the locus of special burdens or benefits. There is that enduring something which causes us to ask the state to make its case for distinguishing two humans, if it is to treat them differently; the state may make that case in a thousand ways and it may be assisted in this by presumptions galore, but make it it must.

All this is useful primarily to state rather plainly the responsibility of the Supreme Court. Obviously the court is (by coincidence) "C" in our model, and the issue is cast in constitutional terms. The court must decide in the future, as it has in the past, which likenesses and differences among men it will validate as a basis for which government action. The opinions of the court may or may not be cast exclusively in terms of the constitutional rubric of equal protection. By habit or necessity, the justifications for or the objections to legal classifications can be found in notions about the order of primacy among competing values, some distinctly egalitarian, others not; but what endures in every issue of equality in public action is a sensitivity to the ethical claims of similarity among men.

All this may leave an impression that, in constitutional litigation of equal protection issues, any result is possible and that state legislatures are at the mercy of the court. Formally this may be so, and the perception that it is so may have something to do with the historic reluctance of the court to venture far-down the path of equality. Almost any argument can be cast in equal protection form, since nearly all legislation draws distinctions among classes of persons. Holmes observed that equal protection ". . . is the usual last resort of constitutional arguments." [25] However, the practical constraints on the court are significant, and they are bolstered by the powerful claims of judicial self-restraint, the system of precedent, and the political decisions embodied in the Constitution and statutes. From whichever perspective one views the egalitarian revolution of the Warren court, it cannot be seen simply as the obituary of judicial restraint. The court still takes a great deal of convincing, and recent changes in personnel increase the risks of prediction.

Within the framework just described, that convincing must be done in terms of the minimum ethical demands of children to be treated in some practical sense with substantial equality in education by the state. Which of the countless individual attributes of children can be tolerated as the basis for differential bestowal of benefits and burdens becomes potentially a question for the court. But it is a question that can and should enter the judicial arena only in a very particularized fashion and not simply in terms of some general abstract educational justice for children. The question properly may be reduced to the form, does such and such a statute with such and such an effect satisfy the minimum demands of the Constitution? The question can be further particularized for school finance cases by asking, simply, whether the state may continue to bestow preference in education by wealth. The answer that we will propose and defend is implied in the simple principle with which we began,

25. Buck v. Bell, 274 U.S. 200, 208 (1927). The general failure of the countless equal protection attacks upon state economic legislation is documented in R. J. Harris, *The Quest for Equality: The Constitution, Congress, and the Supreme Court* (Baton Rouge, 1960).

that *the quality of public education may not be a function of wealth other than the total wealth of the state.*

This principle will be titled Proposition 1, both to eliminate the need for endless repetition and as a recognition that other forms of discrimination in public education have arisen before and may continue to arise once variations in wealth are eliminated as determinants of quality. Occasionally it will be referred to as the no-wealth principle, and systems that satisfy the principle will be described as wealth-free. No properly elegant labels seemed sufficiently precise. The rest of this book will examine the principle (continuing to assume that dollar expenditures per pupil constitute a reasonable measure of quality in education[26]) in an effort to answer two general questions: Does Proposition 1 fit the criteria we have set for judicial action? Is it defensible as a substantive principle of equal protection?

Proposition 1 as a Constitutional Standard: A Preliminary Evaluation

So far, the litigation and literature on the school finance issue have produced a number of proposed formulations of a Fourteenth Amendment duty of the state to treat education as a "fundamental right." To call these proposals exotic is scarcely to do justice to the uninhibited imagination of their authors. The proffered formulas range in their ambitions from a hum-

26. We are not suggesting that a demonstration of specific differences other than in terms of money between districts is either improper or irrelevant; it is merely distracting and unnecessary.

The Supreme Court had its own modest experience in comparing educational quality in the "separate but equal" cases leading up to Brown v. Board of Education, 347 U.S. 483 (1954). See, e.g., Missouri ex. rel. Gaines v. Canada, 305 U.S. 337 (1938); McLaurin v. Oklahoma State Regents, 339 U.S. 637 (1950). Cf. Hobson v. Hansen, 269 F. Supp. 401 (D.D.C. 1967); In Re Skipwith, 180 N.Y.S.2d 852 (1958). These cases presented such gross disparities that any test would have sufficed for the result, including cost. The court is unlikely to wish to repeat the experience in the subtler jungles of nonracial discrimination.

drum "one kid-one buck" levelism[27] to the vaulting ecstasies of a duty to spend for each child what is needed to equalize everyone's achievement.[28] Consider, for example, the complaint recently before the Supreme Court in McInnis v. Ogilvie (hereafter referred to as McInnis);[29] the plaintiffs argued denial of equal protection in the following respects.

27. This expression does not appear in the literature; it is contemporary argot for the kind of minimal outcome tolerable to some reformers.

28. This brief sampler gives some sense of the debate so far:

(1) "The Act . . . is . . . repugnant to the equal protection clause . . . in the following respects . . . The Act . . . fails to take into account . . . the added costs incurred in providing substantially equal educational opportunity to those children . . . who . . . lack the preschool background and extracurricular educational experiences enjoyed by most of the children"; Complaint in Board of Education v. Michigan, General Civil No. 103342 (Cir. Ct., Wayne County, Mich., filed Feb. 2, 1968).

(2) "Equality of educational opportunity exists when a child's educational opportunity does not depend upon either his parents' economic circumstances or his location within the state"; A. E. Wise, Rich Schools, Poor Schools: The Promise of Equal Educational Opportunity (Chicago, 1968). Wise offers and analyzes 9 possible definitions of the concept; unfortunately, he neglects Proposition 1 (ibid., pp. 143–163).

(3) "The state owes a vastly greater responsibility to all of its schoolchildren than it presently accepts. It is constitutionally obliged, not merely to open its doors to all comers, but to provide effective equality to all. A reconsideration of effective equality in the light of recent and extensive educational research studies, such as the Coleman Report, suggests that the state's obligation to provide an equal educational opportunity is satisfied only if each child, no matter what his social background, has an equal chance for an equal educational outcome, regardless of disparities in cost or effort that the state is obliged to make in order to overcome such differences . . . the pertinent question for the court is whether everyone has an equal share of the goods, measured according to need"; David Kirp, "The Constitutional Dimensions of Equal Educational Opportunity," Harvard Education Review, 38: 635, 636, 642 (1968). Kirp elsewhere criticizes Wise's standards as "so imprecise as to provide no guidance to a court anxious to fashion a rule that is feasible to administer and likely to have beneficial educational consequences"; Kirp, review of Wise, Rich Schools, Poor Schools, Yale Law Review 78: 908, 915 (1969).

(4) "Geographical considerations should be eliminated as a basis for pupil assignment where the result is a loss of equality measured either in terms of money or total educational program"; R. B. McKay, "Defining the Limits," in C. Daly, ed., The Quality of Inequality: Suburban and Urban Public Schools (Chicago, 1968), p. 77.

29. McInnis v. Shapiro, 293 F. Supp. 327 (N.D. Ill., 1968) aff'd mem. sub. nom., McInnis v. Ogilvie, 394 U.S. 322 (1969).

(a) . . . *classifications* upon which students will receive the benefits of a certain level of per pupil educational expenditures are not related to the educational needs of these students and are therefore arbitrary, capricious and unreasonable;

(b) . . . the method of financing public education fails to consider . . . (ii) the added costs necessary to educate those children from culturally and economically deprived areas (iii) the variety of educational needs of the several public school districts of the state of Illinois . . .

(c) . . . the method of financing public education fails to provide to each child an equal opportunity for an education. . . .

In this baroque company Proposition 1 is a country cousin; nevertheless, it may have its charms for a court with a lingering fondness for judicial restraint and a hope to be understood by its clientele.

Modesty, Flexibility, Simplicity

Proposition 1 embodies the indispensable political quality of flexibility. Within its expansive boundaries there is ample room for the harmonization of equality and subsidiarity through a power equalizing system — that is, if the legislature prefers it that way. In fact, adoption of this standard would validate most of the existing structure, including the use of school districts as a locus of decision concerning the quality of education. If, on the other hand, the legislature wishes to emphasize equality in the sense of uniformity, that choice may be given expression in a wholly centralized system and subsidiarity may be permitted to disappear. Majoritarian politics, far from being stultified by the court, necessarily would be invoked. The political processes of each state would give expression to the interests at stake disposing them over a broad spectrum of alternatives.

Nothing, indeed, is foreclosed except the linking of quality and wealth. The state, if it wishes, may choose centralization; it may experiment boldly with family power equalizing; it may leave the districts intact; or it may abolish public education altogether. Some states may wish to rationalize spending according to need and/or promise. Others may employ one system at one level, another at others. We can imagine full equality for spending or a power equalized model from kindergarten to third grade with expenditure according to need or promise thereafter (or vice versa). The one predictable aspect of the future structure under this proposal is its unpredictability. Freed of the historic domination by balkanized affluence, each of the fifty legislatures would be at liberty to adjust its educational system to a new equilibrium determined by the perceived conditions and interests of the states. Proposition 1 is a liberating, not a pre-emptive principle.

Proposition 1 also satisfies the criterion of simplicity, at least in its application to existing systems. As demonstrated in Part I, a mere examination of public records regarding assessed valuation, tax rates, and sources and amounts of district revenue — indeed, a sophisticated examination of the statutes alone — ordinarily is sufficient to reveal whether the state permits offering to vary by assessed wealth of its districts.

In short, Proposition 1 appears tempered to the needs of the situation and to the demands of the judicial role. It does not grandly insist that children be treated differently because of their biological, cultural, or intellectual differences. It does not even require that they be treated uniformly because of their essential sameness. It insists only that they be treated fairly in the choice of economic mechanisms by which their public education is supported. We are content with a constitutional meaning for equality of opportunity that can be understood and then can be applied to the grosser objective aberrations of the existing systems, those springing from state-created wealth determinants of quality.

The Supreme Court seems likely to share this modesty and to prefer, at least for the time being, to leave the finer distinctions between children to be drawn by legislatures and administrators. Nothing disturbed the three-judge court in *McInnis*, the first of the school finance decisions, so much as the employment by the plaintiffs of a "needs" standard. The court went so far as to hold that:

> Even if the Fourteenth Amendment required that expenditures be made only on the basis of pupils' educational needs, this controversy would be nonjusticiable . . . [T]here are no "discoverable and manageable standards" by which a court can determine when the Constitution is satisfied and when it is violated.
>
> The only possible standard is the rigid assumption that each pupil must receive the same dollar expenditure. . . .[30]

The gross error represented by the last sentence is probably traceable to the court's overreaction to the plaintiffs' emphasis upon a "needs" criterion. The court simply never grasped the opportunity for simplicity, clarity, and flexibility.

The same approach by counsel produced almost precisely the same reaction from the three-judge panel in Burruss v. Wilkerson in the Western District of Virginia: "the plaintiffs seek to obtain allocations of State funds among the cities and counties so that the pupils in each of them will enjoy the same educational opportunities. This is certainly a worthy aim, commendable beyond measure. However, the courts have neither the knowledge, nor the means, nor the power to tailor the public moneys to fit the varying needs of these students throughout the State." [31] This apprehensiveness of the district judges underscores the practicality of a modest and simple standard.

30. 293 F. Supp. at 335. The quote within the quote is from Reynolds v. Sims, 377 U.S. 533, 557 (1964).
31. See n. 5 above.

Limitation of the objective in Proposition 1 represents not only a value choice but a constitutional battle plan. By the no-wealth principle we disengage ourselves from the bootless argument for a Fourteenth Amendment obligation to treat disadvantaged children differently, that is, according to some occult perception of the personal characteristics of each. That such an argument is unlikely to succeed is small comfort if its effect is to debase other and intelligible standards for reform. It may be that constitutional arguments for preference according to personal need will eventually succeed, but we neither expect such a result nor support it.

A Potential Complexity or Two

We assert, then, that Proposition 1 is an intelligible and feasible standard; indeed, once it is understood its application to existing systems is sheer simplicity. Concededly, however, purely hypothetical systems can be posed in which the application of the principle becomes at least relatively more complex, even if it remains judicially manageable. Some such subtleties are now obscured by the larger wealth discriminations we have described; they would become visible only after a state had either centralized fiscal control or equalized the tax bases of its districts. Once either had been accomplished, we might begin to worry about differences in the cost of offering the same educational services from district to district. The added costs of student transportation in certain areas or the common variations in price for the same services or goods are obvious examples. Perhaps an adjustment for such objective school-cost differences could be required by the principle that wealth shall not determine quality, necessitating only minor refinement of our original educational task units to account for them.[32] Such

32. The same is true for provable claims of overassessment of the property of one's own district and underassessment of the property of other districts.

factors represent extra costs of furnishing to the child of one district the same objective school experience available for less elsewhere. They increase the task assigned to the district and are closely analogous to an increase in student population — a factor which clearly would entitle the district to increased funds. Because they are objective and measurable, such adjustments could well be judicially required; however, there would be no reason to push this refinement to the point of requiring by the Constitution what would be purely an intuitive and indeterminate dollar adjustment for the cultural disadvantage of students.[33] We are concerned to reach through the Constitution only those measurable economic disadvantages for students that the state itself has created in its employment of particular administrative and financing mechanisms for education. The line between the hard and objective costs of purchasable educational goods and services on the one hand and the purely hypothetical costs of producing a particular academic result on the other can be and is kept reasonably clear by Proposition 1.

The problems of variation in school costs should not be confused with those economic differences associated with marginal utilities. It was shown in Chapter 6 that, even in a power equalized district system, both personal wealth and uneven distribution of nonschool costs may continue to affect spending on education because of the marginal utilities effect. For example, a city district with a high proportion of poor people may be relatively less able to levy even a "power equalized" tax for schools because fixed costs (perhaps relatively high fixed costs) have already been paid out of relatively limited means. It was

33. The state, of course, would be *permitted* to adjust for cultural disadvantages as a matter of legislative judgment. Perhaps one can imagine even a duty to compensate for the state-inflicted injuries of children who have in the past been victims of the systematic violation of Proposition 1; the problem is to specify the victim and the quantum of injury — is he every child in every district below the richest? Are dollars the measure? Is the tax rate in the child's district relevant? Retroactive application of the principle is not likely, nor does it seem wise.

emphasized that this municipal overburden is merely a special case of the more general marginal utilities problem.

Whether the effect of municipal overburden or of marginal utilities generally on educational spending should be considered by the court is an issue with possible vitality, but whether it should be considered under Proposition 1 is by definition not an issue at all. When Proposition 1 refers to wealth, it denotes merely the per task unit value of the tax source selected, ordinarily assessed valuation per pupil. This limited definition is a measured response to the evil in the system; it is by deliberate and specific employment of variations in this kind of wealth that the state has decreed unequal schools for poor districts. The objection to the present dispensation expressed in Proposition 1 is simply that the very system legislated by the state for the raising of money for public education is itself designed to create differences in school quality; it need not and does not follow that there is a constitutional objection to every human condition, or even every act of the state, with a similar effect. An area may be "city poor" (because of high costs, low wealth, or both) and the condition may affect school spending, but the cause of this relative poverty is by definition outside the system of public school finance.

The legislature is free to adjust as it sees fit for the influences of marginal utility. We have encouraged it to do so in an effort to offset in a practical way the effects of such factors upon the taxing behavior of the districts. It is not the sort of adjustment that can be made properly by mandate of the judges; there is no need for it to be made under Proposition 1.

A FALSE START: THE McInnis CASE

The decision in McInnis deserves notice as the first case on the question to receive appellate adjudication — in this instance, at least formally, by the Supreme Court itself. McInnis was the second complaint in point of time. The original action was filed in the state court of Michigan in February, 1968, by the school board of the city of Detroit and by individual public school children of the district.[34] Following the Detroit complaint similar litigation was soon begun in other states.[35] In mid-April, poverty lawyers representing individual clients in Chicago and suburban districts launched *McInnis* before a three-judge federal court in the Northern District of Illinois.[36] While the Detroit and other cases languished, *McInnis* rose and fell like a flare. Before the year was out the complaint had been dismissed on the merits at the district level; propelled by the eccentricities of federal appellate practice, a direct appeal was before the Supreme Court by the following February;[37] in March, 1969, the decision was affirmed per curiam without opinion.[38] In eleven months *McInnis* had blazed, sputtered, and died. With it perished the naive hope for a quick, cheap revolution in education by the invocation of the federal judiciary.

But whether long-range significance should be attached to this case is doubtful. It does not seem likely to become another Plessy v. Ferguson.[39] Probably merely a temporary setback, it was the predictable consequence of an effort to force the court to precipitous and decisive action upon a novel and complex issue for which neither it nor the parties were ready. As suggested above, the plaintiffs' virtual absence of intelligible theory

34. Board of Education v. Michigan, General Civil No. 103342 (Cir. Ct., Wayne County, Mich., filed Feb. 2, 1968).

35. See cases cited, nn. 4 and 5 above.

36. In suits in federal courts to restrain the enforcement of state statutes, on ground of unconstitutionality, a 3-judge court is required; 28 U.S.C. § 2281 (1964).

37. From the decision of the 3-judge court, a direct appeal lies as of right to the United States Supreme Court; 28 U.S.C. § 1253 (1964).

38. *Sub nom.* McInnis v. Ogilvie, 394 U.S. 322 (1969), Mr. Justice Douglas dissenting.

39. 163 U.S. 537 (1896). This is the decision establishing the "separate but equal" doctrine which so long permitted the state to enforce racial segregation.

left the district court bewildered.[40] Given the pace and character of the litigation, confusion may have been inevitable; but that same confusion probably foreordained the summary disposition of the appeal. The Supreme Court could not have been eager to consider an issue of this magnitude on such a record. Concededly, its per curiam affirmance is formally a decision on the merits,[41] but this need not imply the court's permanent withdrawal from the field. It is probably most significant as an admonition to the protagonists to clarify the judicial options before again invoking the court's aid.

In our judgment the court does well to wait for clarification. As we have suggested, thus far the constitutional debate inside and outside the courts has featured utopian reforms on the one hand pitted against utter immobility on the other. The latter school of thought has seen clearly the considerable risks represented in this issue; the former has seen the substantial opportunity.[42] Neither has yet perceived the moderate course

40. So bewildered that the district court held the issue as presented nonjusticiable; 293 F. Supp. at 335.

41. The Supreme Court's jurisdiction is not discretionary in appeal cases; 28 U.S.C. § 1253 (1964). Technically, any decision affirming a decision that was rendered below on the merits is itself a decision on the merits. R. L. Stern and Eugene Gressman, *Supreme Court Practice: Jurisdiction, Procedure, Arguing and Briefing Techniques, Forms, Statutes, Rules for Practice in the Supreme Court of the United States*, 3rd ed. (Washington, D.C.: Bureau of National Affairs, 1962), pp. 195–196. However, where the disposition is summary and without opinion, the practical meaning of such action by the court is inscrutable. "It has often been observed that the dismissal of an appeal, technically an adjudication on the merits, is in practice often the substantial equivalent of a denial of certiorari." David Currie, "The Three-Judge District Court in Constitutional Litigation," *University of Chicago Law Review*, 32:1, 14 n.74 (1964). The *McInnis* decision was affirmed, not dismissed, but there is probably no significance in this distinction. It is the historic practice of the Supreme Court, in direct appeals from federal courts, to affirm rather than to dismiss the appeal — an order reserved for appeals from state courts. Stern and Gressman observe that "only history would seem to justify this distinction"; *Supreme Court Practice*, p. 195.

42. See Phillip Kurland, "Equal Educational Opportunity." The *McInnis* opinion cites the article favorably in two places (293 F. Supp. at 334, 336). Kurland finds much of the Supreme Court's recent work "awful" and antici-

for court and legislature represented in Proposition 1. It is reasonable to hope that the Supreme Court will be receptive to well-planned litigation based upon intelligible and workable standards.

It is even arguable that, for our purpose, the affirmance of *McInnis* has no significance whatsoever; the holding of the three-judge district court may be so limited as to constitute no threat to litigation based upon Proposition 1. The opinion in the district court repeatedly emphasizes that the plaintiffs relied upon a "needs" rationale. After determining that it had jurisdiction of the subject matter, the court summarized the holding on the merits as follows: ". . . we further conclude that no cause of action is stated for two principal reasons: (1) the Fourteenth Amendment does not require that public school expenditures be made only on the basis of pupils' educational needs, and (2) the lack of judicially manageable standards. . . ."

Elsewhere, it is true, the district court clearly suggests its general approval of the Illinois statutes;[43] but it is fair to argue that the court in its holding rejected only the right asserted by the plaintiffs, the right to expenditure by individual need. As the opinion pointedly observed, "students are not deprived of their civil rights under 28 U.S.C. § 1343 because *the asserted guarantee* does not exist under the Constitution . . ." (emphasis supplied).[44]

The affirmance of *McInnis* by the Supreme Court (under its new title, McInnis v. Ogilvie) unquestionably will have some

pates more of the same in the finance cases. Compare Daly, *Quality of Inequality.* Most of the reform-bent conferees recorded in this book seemed preoccupied exclusively with urban eschatology in various forms. Both sides in the argument conceived the problem to be essentially a city-suburban struggle, as the title of the book from the conference suggests. In fact, this mis-states the issue badly, for the problem is endemic. The title of the book by Arthur Wise is also misleading; the relevant collectivities here are school districts, not schools.

43. *McInnis,* at 332–334.
44. *Ibid.,* at 335.

chilling effect upon potential judicial support in the lower courts, whatever theory is employed by plaintiffs;[45] but there was little hope of victory below the Supreme Court level anyway.[46] We believe that, as before *McInnis*, the reality of hope for positive action from the Supreme Court remains largely a function of the development of a satisfactory rationale. The first skirmish is over, but the war has merely begun.

45. Although the recent decision in Burruss v. Wilkerson, General Civil No. 68-C-13-H (U.S.D.C. W.D.Va., complaint dismissed May 27, 1969) appears to rely for support only on the district court decision in *McInnis*.

46. With the possible exception of Serrano v. Priest (n. 5 above), when and if it reaches the California Supreme Court.

9 · A Formalistic Rationale for the School Finance Cases

Thus, in sum, we may conclude, if there is no one, there is nothing at all.

To this we may add the conclusion. It seems that, whether there is or is not a one, both that one and the others alike are and are not, and appear and do not appear to be, all manner of things in all manner of ways, with respect to themselves and to one another.

Most true.

Plato, Parmenides

EQUAL PROTECTION THEORY IS PROTEAN and no attempt will be made here to survey all possible forms of argument. Indeed, to some extent the detailed factual approach taken in this book should diminish dependence upon technical argument. If we have been successful in exposing the anatomy of the financing systems, we already have delivered an argument more persuasive than any possible rendering of precedent and analogy however adroit.[1] In some crabbed and narrow sense Phillip Kurland's suggestion that the legal argument is "easy" is quite true.[2] But much remains to be done in the way of legal analysis. The court must be assured that there are substantial elements of continuity in the new pattern of law. Further, it must have some confidence that it can effectively implement the change it seeks.

In considering forms in which the Supreme Court historically has cast the issues of equal protection, it is tempting to divide the hundreds of cases along the lines chosen by Robert McKay in his treatise *Reapportionment*.[3] McKay simply sep-

1. See H. W. Bikle, "Judicial Determination of Questions of Fact Affecting the Constitutional Validity of Legislative Action," *Harvard Law Review*, 38:6 (1924).
2. Phillip Kurland, "Equal Educational Opportunity: The Limits of Constitutional Jurisprudence Undefined," University of Chicago Law Review, 35:583, 584 (1968).
3. R. B. McKay, *Reapportionment: The Law and Politics of Equal Representation* (New York, 1965), pp. 169–180. For a more encyclopedic approach

arates the cases on the basis of their subject matter into those few involving "Basic Civil Rights of Man" on the one hand and the remaining bulk of equal protection cases on the other. He styles this dichotomy "The Two Faces of Equal Protection." In the "non-basic rights" cases the test of the validity of a classification is its reasonableness, and the state has the benefit of a strong presumption of constitutionality; in the "basic rights" cases either all classification is forbidden or it is subject to rigorous examination by the courts. Of course this facile judicial lobotomy begs the hard questions about what is "basic," but as a description of what the court is doing today it is fairly serviceable; for McKay's limited purpose it was quite adequate. The difficulty with it for our purposes is its incapacity to produce any specific rules. We are promoting an articulated proposition about the relation between education and wealth. All that the "two faces" can do for us is suggest that, if this is a "basic rights" issue, the present structure is more likely to tumble. It cannot suggest the form of argument by which the tree can be made to fall in the proper direction. That there are risks here is evident.

For example, on an equal protection rationale the court recently struck down a New York procedure for committing former convicts to mental hospitals. Baxstrom v. Herold [4] would certainly fall into the "basic rights" class on any view of its substance. The opinion, however, adopted a wholly traditional theory: the court found that there was a misclassification in light of the state's purpose and held that a convict finishing his term is entitled to procedural protection similar to that accorded nonconvicts on the issue of commitment for mental illness. The opinion passed no judgment upon the inherent adequacy of the process by which the petitioner had been com-

---

to the older cases, see R. J. Harris, *The Quest for Equality: The Constitution, Congress, and the Supreme Court* (Baton Rouge, 1960).

4. 383 U.S. 107 (1966).

mitted. This seemingly left it open for New York — at least as far as the equal protection clause is concerned — to reduce the protection provided in standard civil commitments to the level of that procedure for convicts which the court had just invalidated, and thereby to effect both the reincarnation of that very procedure and the debasement of the civil process. The tree will have fallen on the woodsman.

The point to be learned is that, while the "basic rights" may be subject to identification and special treatment, they may be protected under a variety of theories; which theory is employed can make a difference either in the result of the particular case or in the rule it announces. We therefore cannot safely rely upon a division of cases solely on the basis of substance of the right involved, though it is scarcely an element we can afford to ignore.

The most useful division of the court's equal protection work is this. *First,* in many or most cases the court has emphasized formal equality and formal discrimination. It has done so more frequently, to be sure, in the nonbasic cases involving taxation and regulation of business; but it has also done so in certain "basic rights" cases such as Baxstrom v. Herold, Skinner v. Oklahoma (compulsory sterilization),[5] and even the recent poll tax case.[6]

Second, the court occasionally has gone straight to the subject matter of the discrimination. This approach is limited thus far to cases within a few special areas involving voting and political association, travel, race, indigence, and the criminal process; where it has been employed, it has rather consistently invalidated the classification at stake. In effect, the court has carved out an inner circle of cases for close and unfriendly scrutiny of legislative propriety. The population of cases in this metaphorical circle is slightly smaller than McKay's basic

5. 316 U.S. 535 (1942).
6. Harper v. Virginia Board of Elections, 383 U.S. 663 (1966).

rights category, for it does not include cases from that category which, like *Baxstrom*, were decided solely under one of the formalistic methods.[7] In other words the "inner circle" is defined by its method, but its very method is the evaluation of substance. The cases populating the inner circle will be considered in Chapters 10 and 11.

Finally, before considering the "formal" approach to equal protection, the often fuzzy boundary between equal protection and its cousin, due process, should be mentioned. There is no need to elaborate the various lines of differentiation except to say that due process in general concerns the fundamental fairness and rationality of the state's treatment of an individual, while equal protection concerns itself with distinctions in the treatment of classes of persons by the state. If a state abolishes trial by jury, a question is posed about due process;[8] if it does so only for civil cases involving less than ten thousand dollars, an equal protection issue is presented. If the state requires the criminal defendant to have a transcript of an appeal but he must pay for it himself, the two issues may be difficult to distinguish, as they were for the Supreme Court in *Griffin v. Illinois*.[9] Is such a case merely an issue of unfairness in itself, or is it also a question of a distinction between classes, rich and poor? We will find the opinions in *Griffin* to be properly enigmatic on the question. Our problem is easier to pigeonhole. There is little doubt that the school finance question is to be treated as one of equal protection. The issue is classification, even if the question of just what the classes are is somewhat puzzling.[10]

7. Many of the decisions in the "formal" mode also stress the fundamental character of the right involved. The *Skinner* and poll tax cases both are examples of this. Indeed, the distinction in method has a slightly factitious appearance if we look only at the "basic rights" cases, where the methods usually are employed in tandem. Nevertheless, the distinction can be important, and we will elaborate its potentially special significance for the school finance cases.

8. Duncan v. Louisiana, 391 U.S. 145 (1968).

9. 351 U.S. 12 (1956).

10. The victimized class may be viewed as the children of the poorer dis-

The Classical Approach to Equal Protection

In the great bulk of the court's equal protection opinions involving economic regulation[11] and, occasionally, in a "basic rights" case like Baxstrom v. Herold, the analysis is cast in terms of rationality of the relation of legislative purpose to the means chosen by the legislature for realization of that purpose. The thought is variously expressed, but first we may put it that the court requires the legislative means chosen to bear a reasonable relation to the evil that the state seeks to eliminate or diminish — or to the good it seeks to achieve. We will style this form of analysis variously as the "ends/means," "purpose/means," or merely "classical" approach.

The style is congenial to lawyers. It has a veneer of judicial restraint, conceding the legislature apparent freedom to select any purpose whatsoever; and the professed standard for judgment is disinterested rationality in the highest tradition of the neutralist style. Further, under this approach the lawyer's role in the process of judgment is one of exposing inconsistencies between purposes and means, a task for which he regards himself as exquisitely equipped, especially when called to the repair of concepts drafted by laymen.

Before proceeding, we should clarify the somewhat specialized sense in which we use the term "means." The reference is not to concrete machinery of enforcement such as policemen or school buildings. A legislative, or administrative, means is a *classification of persons* upon whom the law will operate. It is the legislative use of selected facts as a way of distinguishing one group of humans from another for an end the legislature

---

tricts, but certainly the state legislatures did not talk in these terms. One of the issues will be to what extent a formal classification (e.g., geographical districts formally equal) may be penetrated in quest of the practical effect of the system upon a de facto class of persons.

11. See, e.g., Railway Express Agency v. New York, 336 U.S. 106 (1949) — regulation of advertising on commercial vehicles.

has in mind. The chosen facts may be ownership of something (cows, pistols, houses); personal qualities (race, age, acuity of vision); acts (possession of burglar tools); location, profession, wealth, sex, size, intelligence, or police record. Each of these separates its human referents as a group from everyone else — an effect which serves some legislative purpose, or must if it is to survive scrutiny.

Joseph Tussman and Jacobus tenBroek pointed out in 1949 that application of the classical approach involves comparisons of what are in fact two classifications: "[We] are really dealing with the relation of two classes to each other. The first class consists of all individuals possessing the defining Trait; the second class consist [sic] of all individual [sic] possessing, or rather, tainted by, the Mischief at which the law aims. The former is the legislative classification; the latter is the class of those similarly situated with respect to the purpose of the law." [12] Note that Trait corresponds to legislative "means" and Mischief to legislative "end."

The question of equal protection becomes one of the reasonableness of the relation to one another of these two classes. There are five possible logical relations (Traits are T and Mischief M):[13]

1. All T's are M's and all M's are T's
2. No T's are M's
3. All T's are M's, but some M's are not T's
4. All M's are T's, but some T's are not M's
5. Some T's are M's, some T's are not M's, and some M's are not T's

Case 2 would of course be pure unreason and invalid — that is, occurrence of the trait is never an occasion of the mischief. Case 1 represents perfect congruence and validity, that is, oc-

12. Joseph Tussman and Jacobus tenBroek, "The Equal Protection of the Laws," *California Law Review*, 37:341, 347 (1949).

13. *Ibid*. This scheme is drawn nearly verbatim from the Tussman and tenBroek article.

currence of the trait is *always* an occasion of the mischief and *exhausts* all occasions of mischief. The other cases present problems of underinclusion (3), overinclusion (4), and both (5). Underinclusion might be exemplified by the regulation of milk farmers in counties over fifty thousand in population in order to reduce tuberculosis. Overinclusion might be seen in a regulation forbidding pets in order to reduce psittacosis. Both might be involved in a regulation of the sales of all implements with longer than six-inch blades in order to reduce crimes of violence. Some such implements are never so used; some implements so used are not included in the regulation.

In none of these problem cases does invalidity follow automatically. Rather, other considerations, such as the difficulty or ease of administering a broader or narrower regulation, would be taken into account. In the milk regulation example the fact that tuberculosis is spread by other media and that it thrives and wanes irrespective of county size may be relevant but hardly decisive. The creation of unintended side effects may also become crucial. Indeed, if the use of T and M and other abstractions suggests a picture of legal geometry, consideration of a few specific cases will dispel the illusion that the classical approach can be captured in a formula.

A favorite example of the classical style is Railway Express Agency v. New York.[14] The city of New York by a traffic regulation had barred from its streets all vehicles carrying advertising on their sides except those used to advertise the business of their owners. Railway Express, like many another transportation company, commonly rented advertising space on the exterior of its trucks to other businesses; this was now forbidden, with very substantial economic effect. The apparent purpose of the regulation was to reduce dangerous distractions to pedestrians and to other drivers. REA protested that the exemption for self-advertising was a denial of equal protection to REA:

14. 336 U.S. 106 (1949).

324 THE CUTTING EDGE

considering the purpose of the regulation, there could be no rational justification for picking on one and not the other. Thus, said REA, the regulation had no reasonable relation to the traffic problem.

The Supreme Court made short work of the case in a unanimous judgment upholding the regulation. The court's opinion accorded enormous deference to city authorities on the question of difference between the two kinds of advertising in their relation to the danger: "The local authorities may well have concluded that those who advertise their own wares on their trucks do not present the same traffic problem in view of the nature or extent of the advertising which they use. It would take a degree of omniscience which we lack to say that this is not the case. If that judgment is correct, the advertising displays that are exempt have less incidence on traffic than those of appellants." [15]

Note that the court would be content with the ordinance even if merely the *extent* of the forbidden advertising differed; the limit, if any, of that justifiable difference in extent is unexplored. Would a bare majority of the forbidden type be sufficient? If the balance altered, would the ordinance then lose its validity? Note also that the court manifests little or no interest in the actual differences between the two types of advertising in either their nature or extent, but is concerned only with what the local authorities might have concluded about such matters. The language leaves room for empirical demonstrations of the lack of relation of means to purpose, but not much room.

The opinion in *Railway Express* further discouraged equal protection attacks with the following observation: ". . . the fact that New York City sees fit to eliminate from traffic this kind of distraction but does not touch what may be even greater ones in a different category, such as the vivid displays on Times Square, is immaterial. It is no requirement of equal protection

15. *Ibid.*, at 110.

that all evils of the same genus be eliminated or none at all." [16] If this passage is intelligible it is only because one is willing to assume that the court perceived a standard for determining which differences amount to differences of "kind," "category," and "genus" — a standard which it failed to disclose. One can guess that the court means no more than that the state may attack particular evils one step at a time; but what is a step?

In 1957 the court used the classical approach to strike down an economic regulation — a rare application of the clause in recent times and one accomplished in a manner contrasting strongly with the *Railway Express* case. Morey v. Doud [17] involved an Illinois statute regulating currency exchanges but excepting by name from such regulation the American Express Company. The purpose of the statute was ". . . to protect the public when dealing with currency exchanges." The court gave its standard endorsement to the ends/means formula saying that ". . . a statutory discrimination must be based on differences that are reasonably related to the purpose of the Act in which it is found." In this instance it viewed the relationship as "remote," whatever that means, despite a demonstration by the state that American Express is a unique "worldwide enterprise of unquestioned solvency and high financial standing" and despite the court's concession that exception by name is not by itself forbidden. It was somehow the conjunction of the two, that is, (1) the alleged remoteness of the discrimination to the purpose and (2) the "creation of a closed class" by naming its object, that apparently was too much for the court to abide.

A example of ends/means analysis in the setting of a civil rights case is Harper v. Virginia State Board of Elections,[18] the 1966 poll tax case. Here the class of special legislative "traits"

16. *Ibid.*
17. 354 U.S. 457 (1957). See also WHYY, Inc., v. Borough of Glassboro, 393 U.S. 117 (1968).
18. 383 U.S. 663 (1966).

that disqualified an otherwise eligible voter was nonpayment of the tax. At least, that was the superficial trait. The majority of the court through Justice Douglas saw it as the subtle de facto classification of voters by affluence. How the legislative "purpose" was perceived is not entirely clear, but the court did refer to the widespread failure "to participate intelligently in the electoral process"; this was probably intended as a description of the evil aimed at by the legislature. Although the court's approach was a medley of ideas — some inconsistent with the ends/means approach — it stated decisively that "voter qualifications have no relation to wealth nor to paying or not paying this or any other tax."

There are many other examples of the classical approach to be found in every corner and context of equal protection.[19] We are interested only in providing enough examples to demonstrate some genuine difficulties in this approach in general as well as in specific application to the school finance issue.

THE TROUBLE WITH THE CLASSICAL APPROACH

Of our six objections to the classical approach, the first concerns its incapacity either to explain or predict judicial actions. The three cases described above present a curious pattern in this respect. Of the three legislative "traits" involved, those that seem most intimately connected with legislative purpose are the ones found invalid. To suppose, as does the *Harper* opinion, that affluence has nothing to do with "intelligent participation in the electoral process" cannot be taken seriously. The problem is clearly the opposite: affluence has far too much to do with intelligent participation. It is not treasonous to observe that those who pay taxes in general, and rich men in particular, form a class of better educated, better equipped political animals. That is precisely the trouble — it is not the lack of rela-

19. See generally Harris, *Quest for Equality.*

tion, but rather the super-relation between politics and wealth that offends ill-defined democratic values.

The same is true of the Illinois currency exchange case, but in a milder degree. That American Express was "in a class by itself" among the private entrepreneurs in this business is a simple fact. This logically should have supported the state; the relation of statutory class to the danger is patent. Perhaps what aroused the court's antipathy was not that there was no reason for the exception, but that the state was simply too blatant in naming it. Distinctions based upon total assets or some other sterile criterion which de facto would have included only American Express might have succeeded. Such a device at least would have palliated that vague sense of outrage humans experience when the famous and mighty are selected for preference without at least perfunctory test of their qualifications. There is something offensive about bestowing explicit privilege, even on the deserving, and it is especially irksome to those who would like to compete on equal terms for the perquisites of privilege. But, if this sense of injustice was decisive in Morey v. Doud, it surely was not a part of an intelligible ends/means approach, nor was it even consistent with such a rationale.

The New York traffic regulation falls the other way. Any suggestion of a relation between the class of self-advertisers and the class of traffic dangers from advertising on vehicles is nearly, if not actually, ludicrous. There may be other bases for the classification of course. It might be, as Alexander Bickel has suggested, simply a policy to favor owner-operated vehicles.[20] As such, is not the classification defensible as a means reasonably related to that purpose of discrimination in favor of such owners? Clearly yes, and if the congruence of ends and means is the only criterion of equal protection, that should be the end of the matter. This is true also of racial classifications, many

20. Alexander Bickel, The Least Dangerous Branch (Indianapolis, 1962), p. 225.

of which represent a closer connection of means and purpose than did the New York regulations. If the legislative aim is white supremacy, segregation is a means well designed to effect it. The answer may be that certain purposes are simply not permitted the legislature, and that is quite so; our immediate question, however, is not how to slay each injustice but how to make sense out of equal protection. The classical approach to equal protection does not explain well the cases we have examined, primarily because we have the impression that the court changes the rules without notice and smuggles in values other than those permitted by the theory. Although the rationale is cloaked in apparent disinterest, its neutrality barely survives the first step of its application. When the going is rough on an issue of classification upon which a majority of the court has strong feelings, its tolerance for disparity between means and ends is necessarily a product of a rather personal judgment. How will that judgment be rendered except by individual estimates of the importance of the interests at stake, the state's administrative convenience, and perhaps other values to which each justice must assign relative importance in an arbitrary and personal manner? Perhaps the classical approach acts as a governor upon the degree of over and under-inclusion, but its power to explain judicial behavior is extremely low and, as a basis for dialogue with state legislatures, it utterly fails. If intelligibility is an important criterion of judicial action, the classical test is a questionable technique.

The *second* objection to the classical theory is its dependence upon a legislative purpose that is seldom plain. Now and then a clear statutory preamble is available to the court; but where it is not, the search for purpose can become mere ascription by the court of those legislative objectives which seem to assist a judgment already reached upon other grounds. This approach can be employed quite easily to upset the legislative classifications in school finance structures. Conversely, it can be used to validate the same legislation. Any ambiguous purpose can be construed by the court so as to conform to the adopted means classification. It was no trick for the court in the *Railway Express* case to view the city's purpose as limited to the supposed special hazards posed only by vehicles advertising for hire.[21]

Third, the classical approach loses all meaning as a coherent system for analysis of legislation in those instances where the legislature is clearly aware of the effects of legislation but leaves it unchanged. The most obvious cases of this kind involve four characteristics: legislation that (1) is of long standing, (2) is not in desuetude, (3) is frequently re-examined (especially where appropriations are necessary), and (4) produces a constant effect. Where such a constellation exists, almost perfect congruity obtains between purpose and classification, for the legislature constantly views and approves the effects of its work. Put another way, in the case of long-standing legislation, the only sensible test of legislative purpose is the empirical one: what the statute does in fact it is intended to do. Any application of the classical approach to such legislation seems either hopeless or disingenuous; the antagonist of the statute must depend rather upon some variation of the "fundamental rights" approach. The legislation must be attacked in terms of the validity of the purpose itself or in terms of its effects, not upon the fit of means to purpose.

The financial structures of public education represent the classic example of a mature legislative system, long endured

21. The 3-judge court in McInnis v. Shapiro was less nimble. It actually described the Illinois system as "designed to allow individual localities to determine their own tax burden according to the importance which they place upon public schools"; 293 F. Supp. 327, 333 (N.D. Ill. 1968). If this description of purpose were accurate, surely the chosen statutory mechanism would be invalid, for its true effect is nearly the opposite of that described by the court. Where wealth of districts varies the tax burden is, almost by definition, unrelated to the importance accorded public schools — unless what the court had in mind was an inverse relation.

and thus approved. The legislature clearly is getting what it wants. To seek out a legislative purpose such as "providing equality of opportunity" or "maximizing potential" or "rationalizing expenditures" is fruitless. The legislature intends the three effects it is achieving: (1) basic education for all, (2) better education for children living in rich districts, (3) higher sacrifice for poor districts, limited only to the extent that equalization is provided.

It is possible to eschew this empirical view of purpose in long-standing legislation, but only at a cost.[22] One can select among the various effects of any statute and argue that this or that effect is the *only* purpose the legislature has had over the years — that other effects were merely uninvited consequences. For example, in the school problem, it could be said that the legislature's sole purpose is a basic minimum of education for all; the legislation is achieving this, ergo the system is valid. Never mind the other hurtful consequences of the system — they are merely the inscrutable product of blind economic forces for which the state cannot be held responsible. Aside from its adoption of a purely subjective view of legislative intent, such a rationale has the weakness of excusing the legislature even in cases where the very "unintended" effects that the state concededly deplores could be avoided at the same time the legislature is achieving completely its claimed purpose.[23] At that point the judicial method becomes itself sufficiently arbitrary that the court forfeits all justification for judging the rationality of any system whatever.

Fourth, the invalidation of legislation merely as irrational can constitute the most trivial of judicial outcomes. Absent the

22. Obviously this objection diminishes where major structural revisions, however wrongheaded, have recently been effected, as in New York; see Chapter 5 above.

23. This weakness is not without constitutional relevance, as noted in our discussion of the cases involving "less onerous alternatives" (see Chapter 11 below).

silent insinuation of a substantive standard into its deliberations, the court must view the evil as purely formal in character. In theory it would even permit legislative repair by a mere restatement of purpose to fit the observable effects.[24] We have urged the wisdom of preserving wide legislative discretion, but it is not inconsistent to hope that the court at least would require the legislature to come to grips with the problem of educational finance on the substantive level.

Of course, no legislature is politically free to be candid about such a purpose. No state will re-enact its system with an avowal of preference for rich districts. What is more likely is the obfuscation of the problem by the creation of a new structure for public education replete with new offices, new labels, and a complicated new formula destined to produce the old discriminations — and all this without any statement of legislative purpose whatsoever. For example, if the Illinois system falls as an unconstitutional mismatch of means and ends, the legislature could well adopt the New York or Rhode Island scheme[25] without risk of injury to rich districts; and there would be little point in the legislature stating its purpose for this new scheme. The total effect of such a reprise would be to present the court with a new system to analyze in its purposes and its mechanisms. Observe, as the years between such decisions pass, that the plaintiffs in these cases will not be prisoners freed when the old statute falls; they will be children who will continue to be cheated until the old statute is replaced with a fair system. And they are growing older.

So long as the court does not deal with the substance — so long as it avoids stating a rule — it must stand ready to deal with the individual structures of each of the fifty states; there

24. See Comment, "Rational Classification Problems in Financing State and Local Governments," Yale Law Journal, 76:1206, 1212 (1968).

25. The 3 state systems mentioned are discussed in Chapters 4 and 5 above.

will be no generality in the decision that a particular state financing program is an irrational classification. There are significant formal, and even practical, differences between state systems. The mere demise of the Illinois statutes will not reform Rhode Island.

Fifth, it is not even clear why legislative purpose matters at all under the equal protection clause. What is it in the notion of equal protection that calls purpose into question in this fashion? Perhaps the answer is that some meaning must be given to the clause, that no other interpretation of the formula makes any better sense of the words than this, and that the ends/means test is in itself a desirable limitation upon legislative power. So viewed, the classical approach is no less a tour de force than the forbidding of "invidious" classifications under the same clause. Neither approach is more than dimly implied, if it is implied at all, in the words "equal protection." It may be argued that the words must be given meaning, and that the rationality test is as good as any, but this is an inadequate rationale for anyone troubled by such open-ended invitations to judicial review. It is here that the "conservative" critics owe the court some credit in terms of their own proclaimed standards of judicial behavior. Once they concede the radical unintelligibility of equal protection, they should be grateful for any judicial limitations however factitious. It is mere irony that such limits can be forged only in those very acts of power for which the court is upbraided. The only real benchmarks in equal protection theory are the "basic right" decisions for which the court is most criticized. It is the candid intrusion by the court into specialized substantive areas that permits the articulation of such intelligible boundaries as one can discover; outside of such demarcations all is darkness. To say that enforced separation by race is impermissible may be a bold thing. It is also a very limited act, considering the bullying and erratic judicial interference one can imagine under an activist court addicted to an inscrutable ends/means rationale. Camus was correct: "The only real formalism is silence."

A *sixth* and final objection to the classical approach lies in the special awkwardness of its application to state spending programs such as education, health, or public aid. Prior cases have asked why it is that X is regulated and Y is not; the *Railway Express* case and Morey v. Doud are examples. In the spending cases the question will not be one merely of inclusion, but the harder question of more or less. *All* children receive a free public education; they *all* are compelled to attend. On that formal level of mere inclusion no equal protection problem is evident. The mirror begins to darken only when we commence to weigh the state's differential treatment of individuals realistically in a quantified comparison. This limitation of the means/ends approach is closely related to what may be a general, if vague, distinction between the examples, on the one hand, of programs of spending designed primarily to provide goods and services to persons in need of them and, on the other, of criminal or regulatory statutes imposing undesired restrictions.[26] The distinction can be simplified as one between benefits bestowed upon and burdens imposed upon classes of persons. Regulatory and punitive (burden) classifications can more readily be specific in their purposes, whether these be eradication of tuberculosis, prevention of theft, or the raising of a billion dollars. Contrast these with the purposes of education, which are constantly debated by philosophers. The problem for which education is the corrective is the very humanity of the beneficiaries of the legislation. The evil is unfulfilled potential; in a sense, the evil is evil. Such a benefit classification in relation to its purposes can therefore be seen as underinclusive insofar as all men need done for them what education is supposed to do; on the other hand, it can be viewed as overinclusive insofar as

26. For a parallel suggestion, see Flemming v. Nestor, 363 U.S. 603, 611 (1960).

some of the beneficiaries (the rich) do not need the state's aid to accomplish the end. But, even more fundamentally, since the central issue is one of *more* or *less*, the very notion of inclusion may be largely irrelevant.

Considering all these objections we may be deluding ourselves by undertaking seriously a classic purpose/means approach to the school finance problem. Nevertheless, we can now briefly outline such an argument.

An Argument in Classical Form

Although the classical approach in this case could take a multitude of forms, the structure of the argument could be simple indeed once the court characterizes the legislative purpose. Counsel for the child might describe that purpose as the provision of equal opportunity in public education for development of the potential of every child who comes to the state to be formally educated. While such a purpose is nonexistent, it is the kind of fantasy that is difficult for the state to repudiate explicitly without thereby admitting the gross reality of the system. In some states there is egalitarian language in the state constitution itself.[27] Instead, the state may concede the purpose but concentrate upon the identification of competing values and "practicalities" which frustrate its full achievement.

Let us assume that the purpose of "equality of educational opportunity" is agreed to inform the system, or that the court so holds. One crucial "trait" or class chosen as the legislative means to that objective is the school district. This creature of the state is the delegate of the power and duty to provide the educational opportunity.[28] In the districts' power to educate

27. "A general and uniform system . . . equally open to all. IND. CONST. art. 8, §1.

28. We have not thought it necessary to elaborate the state action concept. The issue is trivial in this case, as the structure attacked is avowedly public.

they are formally equal; in practical fact they are grossly unequal in that power. It can thus be said that a uniform purpose has been rendered incapable of achievement by its delegation to a class of agents which is in reality no class at all in relation to the function assigned to it. The means are radically inappropriate to the legislative purpose, with the inevitable consequence of significant injury to those in whom resides the right to a rational relation of means and ends — namely, the children who are its intended beneficiaries.

At that point a prima facie case of invalidity would be established. The state's response would be cast in terms of judicial tolerance for legislative imperfection; "some play must be allowed for the joints of the machine," and "the law does all that is needed when it does all that it can." Further, as the *Railway Express* case put it, "it is no requirement of equal protection that all evils of the same genus be eradicated or none at all." [29] We would expect the state to emphasize the administrative conveniences of the existing system, and its historical acceptance. The state's hope to experiment with light house schools is a plausible makeweight; no doubt the existing system can be viewed as a grand experiment involving a variety of quality levels. The political impossibility of equality can also be trotted out, though its invocation by the state may backfire in that it bolsters the case for judicial intervention.[30]

Of course, one can identify important elements in the context which are non-public. The disparity in district wealth is the most obvious; this, it would be said by the state, is the "cause" of the problem, the state system being perfectly uniform and egalitarian — and quite irrelevant to the injury. The court has shown no disposition to take such argument seriously. Its bent has been rather to expand than to contract the state action concept; Reitman v. Mulkey, 387 U.S. 369 (1967). The wisdom of this erosion of the nonpublic sanctuary is not our question, of course; we merely observe that the school finance case requires no extension of doctrine.

29. 336 U.S. at 110.

30. See Chapter 8 above. See also Tussman and tenBroek, "Equal Protection of the Laws," pp. 349–350. Most of these considerations were offered as justification by the district court in *McInnis* under the mistaken assumption

The principal response to this otherwise plausible display is simply that all these educational and administrative considerations offered as justification for inequalities could be satisfied under a number of alternative systems which would not frustrate the general purpose to provide equal opportunity. In other words, the state has neglected "less onerous alternatives" [31] which would permit light house and experimental education and a wide variety of financing mechanisms based upon local or even individual choice; we have already suggested some of them.

There is no predicting how the court would come out under such an argument from the classical rationale. Bickel has called the approach a "mirage" [32] and that it is. It may be a mirage that occasionally produces springs of pure water; but the problem is not that mirages are never effective, rather, it is that they are not to be trusted or even understood. Candor and predictability are not the only constitutional values, but they are values, and they are peculiarly weighty in those cases where the court can expect sophisticated legislative responses to its mandate. The purpose/means approach is available to the court but is unlikely to be used unless a majority wishes to finesse the real problem, which is that of discrimination by wealth.[33] The invalidation of state systems by a rationale of this purely formal character would invite legislative hypocrisy; it would not necessarily evoke (since it would not seek) legisla-

---

that any relief to the plaintiffs would jeopardize local control and experimentation; 293 F. Supp. at 333–334.

31. For a fuller exposition of this concept see Chapter 11 below.

32. Bickel, *Least Dangerous Branch*, p. 221.

33. However, if the sympathies of Justices Black, Harlan, and Stewart are to be aroused, this is likely to be the only rationale for invalidation which is consistent with their approaches to equal protection. See, for example, their dissents in Harper v. Virginia, 383 U.S. 663, 670, 680 (1966), and Kramer v. Union Free School District No. 15, 395 U.S. 621 (1969). Even if the court voids the existing systems, it will not be surprising if no majority opinion is possible, at least in the first cases.

tive reform on the level of substance. Ultimately the court would have to deal with the substance. There may be reasons for waiting, but there are millions of reasons for not waiting — and they are children.

10 · Viewing the Substance: The Inner Circle of Equal Protection

The extent to which one can distinguish a just "license" from a mere botch or failure of unity depends on the extent to which one has grasped the real and inward significance of the work as a whole.

C. S. Lewis, Miracles

THE BEST HOPE FOR PROPOSITION 1 lies in the demonstrated willingness of the Supreme Court to carve out from among the
populous herd of equal protection issues seeking its attention
an inner circle of cases to be given special scrutiny on substantive grounds. Such a process of differentiation and ordering
among equalities is at least as old as Strauder v. West Virginia,[1]
and race cases still stand in the bull's-eye of the inner circle as
the archetype of special or "invidious" discrimination.[2] Hovering about this racial nucleus like electrons in an atomic model
are specimens of discrimination ranging from dilution of the
franchise[3] to discrimination by wealth.[4] The decisions are relatively few in number, and the rules they establish are fewer yet.
Within this area the court has not been content merely to review adjustment of the legislature's purpose to the means
chosen for its effectuation. Instead, it has sat in candid judgment upon the very purpose and, more often, upon the objective effects of legislation.[5] Here in the inner sanctum of equal

1. 100 U.S. 303 (1880) — statutory exclusion of Negroes from juries.
2. The term was first used in Yick Wo v. Hopkins, 118 U.S. 356, 367
(1886).
3. Reynolds v. Sims, 377 U.S. 533 (1964).
4. Griffin v. Illinois, 351 U.S. 12 (1956).
5. See, e.g., Douglas v. California, 372 U.S. 353, 357 (1963): "The present
case . . . shows that the discrimination is not between 'possibly good and
obviously bad cases,' but between cases where the rich man can require the
court to listen to argument of counsel . . . but a poor man cannot." A number

protection we see how the Fourteenth Amendment "may embody a particular value in addition to rationality." [6] The sculptor of transcendent values, of course, is the court.

If the present population of the inner circle is small, there will be other candidates for admission. Discrimination in prosecution,[7] bail,[8] sentencing,[9] and intradistrict municipal services[10] are the current possibilities. They may or may not mark the outermost perimeter, at least for our generation; no obvious theoretical limits to the elasticity of the circle have yet developed. One of the challenges to the court and its acolytes is the

---

of recent articles consider the scope and method of the "new equal protection," either generally or in the context of a specific problem: Comment, "Developments in the Law — Equal Protection," *Harvard Law Review*, 82:1065 (1969); L. G. Sager, "Tight Little Islands: Exclusionary Zoning, Equal Protection, and the Indigent," *Stanford Law Review*, 21:767 (1969); H. D. Krause, "Legitimate and Illegitimate Offspring of *Levy v. Louisiana* — First Decisions on Equal Protection and Paternity," *University of Chicago Law Review*, 36:338 (1969).

6. Harper v. Virginia, 383 U.S. 663, 682 n.3 (1966), Mr. Justice Harlan dissenting.

; 7. See Note, "The Right to Nondiscriminatory Enforcement of State Penal Laws," *Columbia Law Review*, 61:1103 (1961).

8. See generally Caleb Foote, "The Coming Constitutional Crisis in Bail," *University of Pennsylvania Law Review*, 113:959 (1965).

9. Here there are two general questions, the first of validity of the alternative sentence — fine or jail — as imposed upon the indigent; see generally Note, "The Equal Protection Clause and Imprisonment of the Indigent for Nonpayment of Fines," *Michigan Law Review*, 64: 938 (1966). The second issue is that of simple disparity of severity in indistinguishable cases. This question seems considerably more difficult to handle because of the need for wide discretion. It has received broad attention as a policy matter but little or none as an equal protection problem. See Note, "Appellate Review of Primary Sentencing Decisions: A Connecticut Case Study," *Yale Law Journal*, 69:1453 (1960).

10. L. G. Ratner, "Inter-Neighborhood Denials of Equal Protection in the Provision of Municipal Services," *Harvard Civil Rights — Civil Liberties Law Review*, 4:1 (1968); Ralph Abascal, "Municipal Services and Equal Protection: Variations on a Theme by Griffin v. Illinois," *Hastings Law Review*, 20:1367 (1969). The protagonists will no doubt be relying upon the fine recent work of C. S. Benson and P. B. Lund, *Neighborhood Distribution of Local Public Services* (Berkeley, 1969).

fashioning of criteria for selection of the insiders and outsiders. That task exceeds our purpose; we are content to show that financial discrimination in education is easily digestible within the more obvious lines already drawn by the court. Of course, in doing so we cannot help but suggest some perspective of our own on the problem of boundaries, if there are any, of the concept of special cases: on the problem, that is, of what makes them special. We will also express our relative confidence that development of this approach to equal protection poses no unmanageable hazard to proper judicial administration.

One might at first suppose that the sole common characteristic of these special cases is their substantive importance and that sheer magnitude explains their power to evoke reactions of anguish from critics.[11] The Supreme Court has used the equal protection clause to undergird several of the most significant judgments in its history. This very determination to engage significant issues is itself one of the reasons to expect the court's serious attention to educational finance.

But magnitude of outcome is hardly the sole criterion for the court's special handling of a case, nor is it a necessary one. The provision of a transcript to an indigent appellant in Griffin v. Illinois[12] did not amount to a procedural earthquake, and one may even view Harper v. Virginia[13] as relatively trivial. Snuffing the life of the moribund poll tax was little more than euthanasia. Something in addition to the proportions of the discrimination must be operating. Mr. Justice Black worries that the fundamental criterion of judicial action here is the personal dislike of five judges for the state policy at issue. He sees and fears a return to "the 'natural law due process formula' under which courts make the Constitution mean what they think it

11. Phillip Kurland, "Equal in Origin and Equal in Title to the Legislative and Executive Branches of the Government" (foreword to "The Supreme Court 1963 Term"), Harvard Law Review, 78:143 (1964).
12. 351 U.S. 12 (1956).
13. 383 U.S. 663 (1966).

should at a given time"[14] — a form of activism once indulged with unhappy consequence under the due process clause. Justice Black does not cry in the wilderness; the chorus of dissent is formidable and is closely identified with the "neutrality" school of constitutional jurisprudence.[15] A persistent theme of the critics is the alleged particularism of the court's approach in these special cases in the equal protection field.

QUALIFYING FOR THE INNER CIRCLE: FACT AND INTEREST CONSIDERATIONS

To show what the court is doing and to view the neutralist criticism in perspective, a simple classification of the two distinct types of factors operative in these cases is helpful. First, as in any equal protection case, the court is concerned with the *classifying fact*,[16] inevitably a fact attributable in one way or another to an individual — some personal characteristic. This need not be a fact intended by the legislature as the defining characteristic of the class; it may be merely a de facto classification, as was the fact of relative wealth in the criminal procedure and poll tax cases.[17] The facts which have played a role in these special cases until now are race (and the related qualities of alienage and national origin), relative wealth, and — arguably — residence. Second, unlike the classical approach, which focuses upon legislative purpose, the cases in the inner circle tend to fasten upon certain *interests* to whose enjoyment the factual classification is relevant. The special interests so far

14. *Ibid.*, at 675, Mr. Justice Black dissenting.
15. Herbert Wechsler, "Toward Neutral Principles of Constitutional Law," *Harvard Law Review*, 73:1 (1959); Kurland, "Equal in Origin."
16. Justice Harlan's analysis is helpful here. See Shapiro v. Thompson, 394 U.S. 618, 655 (1969), dissenting opinion.
17. Griffin v. Illinois, 351 U.S. 12 (1956); Harper v. Virginia, 383 U.S. 663 (1966).

identifiable in the decisions are voting, travel, and fair criminal procedure.[18]

The court's special attention to the classifying facts of race and wealth is not equivalent to either favor or disfavor for the state's policy. That a fact is disfavored as a basis for one legislative classification does not mean necessarily that it will be disfavored as the basis for another. Whether it will be favored, disfavored, or ignored depends in varying degrees upon the interest the classification affects and how it affects it. To classify by wealth for voting purposes is now forbidden;[19] to classify by wealth for progressive taxation is, to say the least, approved. To classify by race with respect to the marriage interest is forbidden;[20] to do so to promote school integration may well be valid.[21] Thus the relative potency of the fact-interest combination in its effect upon legislation may be rather different depending upon which fact is used and which interest is at stake.

But to say this is not to say that the process is utterly amorphous. Most lines of decision are rather clear: for example, racial classifications are clearly disapproved where used to segregate, no matter how trivial the interest at stake.[22] Indeed, this is so plain that race cases must be largely ignored in evaluating which interests will be preferred. The very presence of a racial classification overwhelms whatever influence otherwise might have been manifested by the particular interest at stake; thus

18. See Justice Harlan's analysis in Shapiro v. Thompson, 394 U.S. 618, 655 (1969), dissenting opinion. The interest in procreation should perhaps be added, but the judicial method in the relevant decision is ambiguous; Skinner v. Oklahoma, 316 U.S. 535 (1942).

19. Harper v. Virginia, 383 U.S. 663 (1966).

20. Loving v. Virginia, 388 U.S. 1 (1967).

21. See John Kaplan, "Equal Justice in an Unequal World: Equality for the Negro — The Problem of Special Treatment," Northwestern University Law Review, 61:363 (1966).

22. Perhaps this should be qualified where the competing interest is prison security. See Lee v. Washington, 390 U.S. 333 (1968).

race cases offer little about a special constitutional status for
the interest in education.

Conversely, the court's quite different handling of the classifying fact of relative wealth clearly implies the importance of
the interests that so far have received special protection. In
those decisions involving relative wealth as the classifying fact,
except where that fact has been combined with either the
voting interest or the interest in fair criminal process it has
shown no capacity to move the court. This limitation recently
was challenged without success in Williams v. Shaffer:[23] a
Georgia tenant put at issue the right of the landlord to use a
summary eviction statute which, in order to leave the tenant
in possession and obtain a trial, required the tenant to "tender
a bond with good security." The security required was an
amount twice the rent for six months, and the tenant was indigent. As a consequence the tenant received no hearing and
was summarily evicted. Over the dissents of three justices the
United States Supreme Court denied certiorari. Justice Douglas' dissent complained specifically of the limitation of the line
of "poverty" cases to the criminal process.[24] Conceding the
hazardous nature of all inferences drawn from denials of certiorari, the message of Williams may be one of reaffirmation
by the court of the special status of the interest in fair criminal
procedure.[25]

The same is true of the voting interest, which, when combined with the fact of relative wealth, voided the poll tax. In
fact, unlike the interest in fair criminal procedure, the voting
interest has shown its independence of any combination with
wealth classifications. In the reapportionment cases and succeeding decisions it has demonstrated an unaided capacity to

23. 385 U.S. 1037 (1967).
24. Ibid., at 1039–1040.
25. The outrageous character of the Georgia procedure reinforces this view.
See Note, "Poverty and Equal Access to the Courts: The Constitutionality of
Summary Dispossess in Georgia," Stanford Law Review, 20:766 (1968).

invalidate the use of such common classifying facts as military status, place of residence, and property ownership.[26] The interest in interstate travel is ambiguous in this respect. Its one appearance in an equal protection context provided the occasion for invalidating periods of residency as criteria for public aid to indigents.[27] Whether the invidiousness of the burden upon travel was attributable in any degree to the presence of the poverty element is difficult to say; the discrimination was against, but also among indigents.

The number of classifying facts other than race and wealth that could be accorded special status is potentially infinite. Classification by redheadedness, Irishness, party, and accent each would be just as suspect, just as invidious as race or wealth, if but one assumption is permitted. Merely let such a fact become a common basis for classification for purposes of bestowing benefits or imposing burdens, and the court will begin, bit by bit, to draw the victims into the warmth of the inner circle. In First Amendment cases a similar process is sometimes described as the creation of "preferred freedoms."[28] In equal protection cases it would be more accurate to label it the identification of preferred persons — preferred in the inverted sense of receiving special attention from the court in order to maintain their very equality. For equal protection purposes the characterization of the person affected often may prove more important than the specification of the right.

This potential for growth in the ranks of the special classifying facts is true also of the special interests. Indeed, we shall at

26. Carrington v. Rash, 380 U.S. 89 (1965) — military status; Reynolds v. Sims, 377 U.S. 533 (1964) — residence; Kramer v. Union Free School District No. 15, 395 U.S. 621 (1969) — property ownership. The right of political association appears similarly independent; Williams v. Rhodes, 393 U.S. 23 (1968).

27. Shapiro v. Thompson, 394 U.S. 618 (1969).

28. L. B. Franz, "The First Amendment in the Balance," *Yale Law Journal*, 71:1424 (1962); R. B. McKay, "The Preference for Freedom," *New York University Law Review*, 34:1182 (1959).

several points examine the credentials of the interest in public education as a candidate for such treatment,[29] at least when that interest is conjoined with the two classifying facts of relative wealth of the district and tender age of the victims. Perhaps it is obvious by now that all governmental services are potential aspirants for "special" protection. This risk of overkill we deal with somewhat later.

THE NEUTRALITY QUESTION

Most civilized critics of the court would concede the propriety of applying the equal protection clause in a forceful fashion to racial classifications because of the special historical purpose of the Fourteenth Amendment. But the continued extension of judicial protection to other victims of discrimination leaves many critics upset. Such an approach, they say, imperils the fundamental aim of a reasoned judgment rendered according to neutral principles.[30]

The idea of "neutral" principles is not free from ambiguity. Obviously, there is something in it of the categorical imperative. The articulated rule of a case is supposed to be good for other cases like it; otherwise it is not a rule (principle) at all, but a whim. Such a dichotomy may or may not be valid for judicial systems outside our own culture, but within the context of western emphasis on "rationality" it is intelligible and important. Thus, the concept of neutrality has a great deal to do with the element of generality in rule-making; indeed, the

29. For a brief and insightful assessment of education as a candidate for special treatment, see Comment, "Developments in the Law," p. 1129.

30. Professor Herbert Wechsler is properly credited with stimulating the renaissance in neutralism with his confessions of doubt over the decision in Brown v. Board of Education and some of its per curiam progeny. See H. Wechsler, "Toward Neutral Principles." For a supersophisticated review of the various protagonists, see J. G. Deutsch, "Neutrality, Legitimacy, and the Supreme Court: Some Intersections between Law and Political Science," *Stanford Law Review*, 20:169 (1968).

two may be identical. If so, however, this tells us little. We have almost no idea what level of generality is implied. If we can find principles that will be applicable to large numbers of cases — principles that will explain and predict — presumably we will be entitled to call such principles neutral. But what this really means is merely that some generality is better than none and that, generally speaking, more is better than less. So long as neutrality does not suggest absolutism in the delineation of rules, but only a constant care for reasonable comprehensiveness of principle, we have no quarrel; such a view is cousin to our own insistence upon intelligibility of standards. But there is one polarized sense of neutrality, suggested by Phillip Kurland for application to equal protection issues, which we find unacceptable:

> [T]he proposition is that there are certain factors that a state is precluded from taking into consideration in establishing classes. Mr. Justice Jackson called these "neutral facts" and thereby, unknowingly, damned the standard to Purgatory or worse. Concurring in *Edwards* v. *California* he said: "The mere state of being without funds is a neutral fact — constitutionally an irrelevance, like race, creed, or color." Mr. Justice Harlan I, in his dissent in *Plessy* v. *Ferguson*, thought that color was a neutral fact and could not form the basis for imposing a burden or failing to grant a benefit. "Our Constitution, he said, is colorblind." It has been suggested that religion is a neutral fact on the basis of which the state may not classify either to grant or deny benefits or to impose or relieve from burdens. . . .[31]

Neutrality in this sense is not merely generality; it is supergenerality or, more precisely, universality. Those factors to which it attaches become constitutional irrelevancies; no action or classification can be predicated of race or religion, or maybe

31. Kurland, "Equal in Origin," pp. 146–147.

wealth. Such an approach, says Kurland, "is meaningful, definite, and usually ignored." [32] He is certainly correct about all three, but the last is most significant. There is not now, has never been, and in all probability never will be any fact that for any and all constitutional purposes will be irrelevant. For this we are not sorry. Race is as close to neutrality as any factor is likely to get, but who expects the court to prohibit prudent efforts by the state to reduce de facto racial segregation? That, however, is precisely what neutrality in the Kurland sense would forbid, for race would be an irrelevance. Lest the tidbit that Kurland quotes from Justice Jackson confuse anyone, we should recall that the "irrelevant" state of being without funds is in reality one of the most relevant considerations imaginable — that is, unless Kurland is willing to argue the invalidity of graduated state income taxes, not to mention state welfare codes.

One of the apparent ironies of the neutralists is their reputation for general judicial conservatism, a quality that the court would hardly manifest if it embarked seriously upon the development of neutralities in the nature of the "irrelevancies" noted.[33] Of course, as Kurland recognizes, what Justice Jackson had in mind was keeping wealth constitutionally irrelevant only for cases in which its use by the legislature would burden the poor. That is, it is a sometime neutral fact, or maybe a generally general rule, or, shall we say, a limited universal — which leaves us about where we came in.

This does not suggest that such "limited universals" are not useful; quite the opposite is true. Practically all workable rules

32. *Ibid.*, p.146.
33. We should observe, however, that (for Professor Kurland at least) the only neutral principle justified in the equal protection field seems to be that of race. It may follow, for him, that this is the only subject matter of equal protection. So defined, neutrality would be credible if, for our part, undesirable. Indeed, we should add this view to our catalogue of approaches to equal protection. It occasionally finds adumbration in Supreme Court opinions, though always in dissent: see, e.g., Justice Harlan's dissent in the poll tax case, 383 U.S. at 682, n. 3.

of human conduct, certainly all workable rules of law, are of this limited generality. With respect to equal protection, as with most terrestrial experience, the yearning for true universals is the shortest road to disappointment. If judicial neutralism is to be more than utopian, it must be ready to make some concessions to the court's need for principles whose level of generality is sufficiently modest that the rules are compatible with the reality of a world full of anomalies and surprises. Perhaps Louis Jaffe strikes at about the right level when he speaks of "intermediate premises." [34] At least, that is roughly the level at which we aim; for us the approach of neutrality in the polarized sense of universal principles would obviously be insupportable. Proposition 1 could be an "intermediate premise"; it is not a universal. To make it such would require its recasting in the form of the Jacksonian dictum that the state of a man's pocket is simply irrelevant to *any* legitimate state concern. Justice Jackson didn't intend this, and neither do we.

We do not think the court has ordinarily been insensitive to the need for neutrality. If its work in the inner circle of equal protection occasionally lacks appropriate generality or includes too many per curiam reversals, we do not believe the disease is endemic. Herbert Wechsler to the contrary notwithstanding,[35] the now clear rule that de jure racial segregation is forbidden strikes us as pitched at an appropriate level of generality, particularly when the available alternative rules are considered. And whatever the other objections to the rule of one man one vote, it scarcely qualifies as a judicial sport; a whole nation was able to respond to its sweeping and clear command. Such decisions may be striking, novel, or wrong; but this, in itself, does not impeach the generality of the rules they have established.

34. L. L. Jaffe, "Was Brandeis an Activist? The Search for Intermediate Premises," *Harvard Law Review*, 80:986 (1967).
35. See Wechsler, "Toward Neutral Principles."

Whatever the merits of the neutralist criticism of the court's method in these equal protection decisions, we question its relevance. The court is so well committed to the maintenance of a vigil over selected discriminations that the only real question for the practical critic is how to assist the intelligent shaping of the process by which the selection is made and the rules articulated. Even if the level of predictability were zero, which it surely is not, the legal and allied professions could serve best by maintaining dialogue with the court on the question of which discriminations deserve eradication and what manner of rule will serve this end with the least injury to other values. Further, the identification of "invidious" discriminations is a process at least as predictable as the results of the "classical" approach whose dizzy pace of contradiction was described in Chapter 9. If predictability is a high value, it is hard to appreciate the critics' longing for the good old days of equal protection.

Proposition 1 and the Constitution: The Place and Race Cases

In justifying a special constitutional status for the educational interest, arguments of the most simplistic order, but with a superficial appeal, can be assembled from race, voting, and wealth cases.[36] These cases, though suggestive, are by them-

36. See, e.g., A. E. Wise, *Rich Schools, Poor Schools: The Promise of Equal Educational Opportunity* (Chicago, 1968), p. 167, with these "three tentative arguments":

1. Discrimination in education on account of race is unconstitutional. Discrimination in criminal proceedings on account of poverty is unconstitutional. Therefore, discrimination in education on account of poverty is unconstitutional.

2. Discrimination in education on account of race is unconstitutional. Discrimination in legislative apportionment on account of geography is unconstitutional. Therefore, discrimination in education on account of geography is unconstitutional.

3. Discrimination in education on account of race is unconstitutional.

selves an inadequate base for invalidating school finance structures.

The reapportionment cases established the invalidity of a pied public policy when it results in weighting votes by residence; they are an arsenal of dicta suggesting vaguely that discrimination by geography is constitutionally suspect.[37] Consider their easy application to discrimination in school finance: if a man's address ought not to determine the weight of his vote, should it not also be impermissible that his address dilute the quality of public education available to him? Indeed the case is a fortiori; no one is compelled to vote, but the child is compelled to attend school. Further, in a free society education is intrinsically as important as voting, we would say — and later we will say it seriously — and geographical discrimination is thus, on all grounds, at least as invidious as malapportionment of the franchise. As arguments go, this one is hard to out-simplify; but despite this important virtue, it is rather clearly wrong.

First, the reapportionment cases held nothing which is inconsistent with the use of geographical classification by the state either for administration of elections or anything else. Indeed, the whole point of the cases is that such devices be

Discrimination in voting on account of poverty is unconstitutional. Therefore, discrimination in education on account of poverty is unconstitutional.

For a similar "simple" argument see Phillip Kurland, "Equal Education Opportunity: The Limits of Constitutional Jurisprudence Undefined," *University of Chicago Law Review*, 35:583, 584–589 (1968); Kurland's argument is, we think, intended as a reductio ad absurdum. At least, as he has stated it (citing Wise), the rationale is, if not absurd, grossly unbalanced. This is partly because it fails to perceive the possibility of a feasible standard, but even more because it is not anchored in an understanding of the nature of school financing. It is, like the Wise rationale, a form of free-floating logic pulled together from scattered wisps of Supreme Court dicta and showing little organic connection to the facts. Unfortunately, this form of argumentation seems to have been offered to the 3-judge court in McInnis v. Shapiro, 293 F. Supp. 327 (N.D. Ill. 1968). The court made short work of it.

37. See, e.g., Reynolds v. Sims, 377 U.S. 533, 567, 580 (1964); WMCA v. Lomenzo, 377 U.S. 633, 652, 653 (1964).

used but used properly. Elections at large were not a policy goal of the Supreme Court; they were merely consistent with the one point the court had in mind, a point which turned out to be utterly simple — one man, one vote. But there were and are a multitude of geographical districting techniques consistent with that holding. As a curative, the old districts could have been retained and the representation adjusted to equalize the weighting. It was not geography that bothered the court; it was the fact of differential weighting, a state of affairs which would have been no less invidious if voters were grouped, not by geography, but alphabetically or according to height. No matter what the classifying fact, if votes are weighted the system is void. The cases do not suggest that the use of geography as a factual classification in itself gives any cause whatsoever for unusual judicial scrutiny, although the mere presence of the voting interest does.[38]

Geography is ordinarily a perfectly rational basis upon which to administer the provision of state benefits or the imposition of state burdens, and it is sometimes the only possible basis. Examples are legion. The location of the state capital must be relatively inconvenient to politicians representing large numbers of a state's citizens, just as a state university must be relatively inconvenient to a majority of its students. But even burdens and benefits that could be geographically uniform, but are not, ordinarily are subject to no special scrutiny simply because of that territorial difference. The judicial disfavor that does appear in cases involving territoriality is related rather to the interest at stake and the classifying fact or facts other than territoriality; this is confirmed by Harold Horowitz and Diana Neitring, who recently surveyed the decisions:

The relevant cases have involved: (a) the administration of justice; (b) the enforcement of various types of crimi-

38. Carrington v. Rash, 380 U.S. 89 (1965); the classification was military status (the case is discussed more fully in Chapter 11 below).

nal standards; (c) the regulation of economic activities; (d) the demarcation of boundaries of local governmental entities; (e) the closing of public schools; and (f) the apportionment of state legislatures. Considered in that order, the cases move from those in which it has been said that there is practically no conceivable constitutional violation in intrastate territorial differences in law to those in which it has been held that practically any territorial difference constitutes a constitutional violation.[39]

The decisive factor in the (d) and (f) categories of cases was the voting interest; in (e) it was the classifying fact of race. This merely supports our general view that race and voting are a fact and an interest in the "inner circle." Nor is the low position of the criminal justice decisions, categories (a) and (b), inconsistent with our position; none involved an issue of discrimination by wealth of the defendant.

Horowitz and Neitring demonstrate that although state and federal courts have generally upheld legislation providing for local option (for example, regarding the sale of alcoholic beverages[40]), few local option cases seem to have involved the inner circle of interests or classifying facts. When they have, as in Brown v. Board of Education,[41] in which the state provided to its school boards the option of racial segregation, local option has fallen along with the state's power to impose the discrimination upon all of its territory.

Perhaps the clearest manifestation of the Supreme Court's emphasis upon the character of the other classifying facts, and of the interest at stake rather than the mere territoriality of application, comes from the opinion in McGowan v. Mary-

39. Harold Horowitz and Diana Neitring, "Equal Protection Aspects of Inequalities in Public Education and Public Assistance Programs From Place to Place Within a State," *U.C.L.A. Law Review*, 15:787, 788–789 (1968), citing the relevant cases.

40. *Ibid.*, pp. 795–797.

41. 347 U.S. 483 (1954).

land.[42] The Sunday closing laws held valid were imposed upon dealers in some counties and not in others:

> . . . we have held that the Equal Protection Clause relates to equality between persons as such, rather than between areas and that territorial uniformity is not a constitutional prerequisite. With particular reference to the State of Maryland, we have noted that the prescription of different substantive offenses in different counties is generally a matter for legislative discretion. We find no invidious discrimination here. . . .[43]

Summarizing, it might be suggested that geography is not very different from any other noninvidious classifying fact — adulthood, blindness, or the state of being an optometrist or a housewife. As such, it is colorless — or at least it deserves the standard deference accorded any classification. It is not a suspect fact like race, and there is no special branch of constitutional law waiting to be developed for territoriality.

Two final points relating to territoriality: even if we were willing to focus upon *place* as the operative discrimination and assumed that the reapportionment or other cases treated geographical dispensations as suspect, the use of geography for education is functionally a thing apart from its use for regulating the franchise. The difference lies in the fact that the voting interest, unlike the interest in education, is easily regarded as a fungible commodity. Whatever the wisdom of doing so, to equate one man's vote with another's is a very natural and easy thing to do; to equate one man's education with another's requires elaborate rationalizations — witness this book. Any distribution of education requires an offering diversified according to age, grade, and a dozen other factors. Despite this

42. 366 U.S. 420 (1961). See also our discussion of Griffin v. Prince Edward County School Board, 377 U.S. 218 (1964), in Chapter 11 below.
43. 366 U.S. at 427.

variety, it may be possible to establish the basis for an "equality" of education, but its informing principle could not very well be absence of geographical distinctions. The misuse of geographical districting is best viewed as merely a medium of discrimination by wealth.

In addition to its invalidity, the argument from geography is risky. It tends to become an argument for a standard of undifferentiated sameness such as that represented in the reapportionment cases.[44] We believe this to be undesirable as a policy result in education, and its imposition by constitutional fiat would be even more pernicious. Thus, Proposition 1 is structured so as to leave plenty of room for variety from district to district if the state or the district chooses, so long as the criterion of difference is other than wealth.

The residual relevance of the reapportionment cases for our purpose lies principally in two other directions. First, these cases confirm the reality of special categories of equal protection based upon the interest at stake; they give reason to hope that factors in the school finance cases will equal the power of the voting interest to move the court to bestow special protection upon victimized children. Second, and related to this, these cases offer in their elevation of the voting interest a standard of importance against which the significance of the interest in education can be measured.

Race: The Irrelevance of Brown and Its Progeny

There is an understandable tendency to treat the school finance issue as an outrider of the racial problems of public education. The reasons are not hard to find. Money discriminations have become visible largely as a by-product of the prodi-

44. Which is precisely the pit into which Dr. Wise falls with the "definition" attempted in *Rich Schools, Poor Schools*, p. 146: "Equality of educational opportunity exists when a child's educational opportunity does not depend upon either his parents' economic circumstances or his location within the state."

gious effort to expose and eliminate racial discrimination in the schools. Since the 1930's the strategy of civil rights counsel has combined attacks upon segregation with those upon discrimination in quality, including differentials in expenditure.[45] The latter have rarely been successful in any meaningful way[46] and, until 1968, have not been directed to differences between school districts. Until the recent litigation all attacks upon financial discrimination had been based upon an alleged relation between race and underfinancing. Finally, an easy association of poverty with black people is the incessant theme of public utterance. It is not surprising that even the present litigation is understood by many of its close supporters as a racial struggle.

The fact is otherwise. There is no reason to suppose that the system of district-based school finance embodies racial bias. Districts containing the great masses of black children ordinarily also contain great masses of white children.[47] There may

45. See the law and graduate school cases discussed in Chapter 11 below.

46. Part of the problem is the enormous expense of establishing the fact of intradistrict differentials, especially in their relation, if any, to race. This burden has bogged down such litigation as that directed against the Board of Education in Chicago since 1961. A suit known as Webb v. Board has been on and off the docket in the United States District Court for the Northern District of Illinois for over 8 years without trial, principally for this reason. Webb I (General Civil No. 61-C-1569), filed Sept. 18, 1961, was dismissed without prejudice Aug. 29, 1963, by Judge Hoffman; plaintiff's motion to reinstate was denied on Oct. 21, 1963. Webb II (General Civil No. 63-C-1895), a virtually identical complaint, was filed Oct. 23, 1963; it was dismissed without prejudice on Jan. 4, 1965, by Judge Marovitz. Webb III (General Civil No. 65-C-51), again practically the same suit, was filed Jan. 14, 1965; the defendant school board filed an answer on Apr. 5, 1965. On Mar. 5, 1965, defendants served plaintiffs with voluminous interrogatories, which, so far as the record showed in early 1969, have never been answered.

Recently another action was filed in the same court against the Chicago school board, by new plaintiffs objecting to similar and related forms of intradistrict discrimination; Brinkman v. Board (General Civil No. 69-C-246), filed Feb. 6, 1969. Some of the many difficulties are aired in L. G. Ratner, "Inter-Neighborhood Denials of Equal Protection." The kind of factual difficulty characteristic of such litigation will not attend the interdistrict school finance discrimination cases.

47. Of the 119 school districts in the sample of Southern, border, and Northern state described by the U.S. Commission on Civil Rights in 1967, only 4

well be very significant racial/dollar discrimination *within* districts, but that is another problem;[48] to lump it with interdistrict discrimination is totally misleading. No doubt there are poor districts which are basically Negro, but it is clear almost by definition that the vast preponderance of such districts is white. Of course the class injured by the present school financing discrimination may be defined in many ways. For example, it may be seen as the class of children resident in districts having an assessed valuation below the average in the state or even those in all districts below the richest. But the injured class is neither black nor white. If there were no black people in America the inequity in the system would in no way be diminished.

This simple fact suggests the political unwisdom of making the issue a racial one. There will surely be enough upset over the question on social and economic grounds without evoking all the furies of racism. It could well be that some of the very forces that could give the necessary political support to institute a positive legislative response to the court's decree would

---

districts (including the District of Columbia) had a public school population less than one-third white. U.S. Commission on Civil Rights, *Racial Isolation in the Public Schools* (D.C. 1967), II (appendixes), 1–7. This is not to state categorically that the average wealth of disproportionately Negro districts always equals the average wealth statewide; but if a discrepancy either way were shown, its relevance would not be immediately apparent.

If racial discrimination were measured by the percentage of all minority students who reside in districts below the statewide median AVPP, California would manifest inverse discrimination. Fifty-nine percent (683,919) of minority students live in districts above the median AVPP. The percentage is considerably higher for Negroes; Indians and those with Spanish surnames are nearly evenly divided above and below the median. The minority figures were taken from an unpublished survey for the State Department of Education by F. R. Gunsky, "Racial and Ethnic Distribution of Public School Pupils, District Report, October, 1968." The AVPP's are from *California Public Schools Selected Statistics, 1967–68* (Sacramento). Mr. Roger Haines was responsible for the necessary comparisons and calculation of figures from both sources.

48. See Harold Horowitz, "Unseparate but Unequal — The Emerging Fourteenth Amendment Issue in Public School Education," *U.C.L.A. Law Review*, 13:1147 (1966).

be paralyzed or even set in opposition to reform if the affair were falsely cast in racial terms.

The problem's nonracial character also suggests the limited relevance of a long line of equal protection cases stretching from Strauder v. West Virginia[49] in 1880 to the recent decision in Loving v. Virginia[50] that has forbidden discrimination by race. For our purpose the only significance of these decisions, as with the reapportionment cases, lies in their affirmation of the court's separate and special approach to certain combinations of factual classification and interest. Even this element of analogy is attenuated, however, by the Fourteenth Amendment's genetic connections with the racial issue.

Yet another misuse of the racial cases is likely to be promoted in the school finance cases. It is true that many important racial discrimination decisions have dealt with the interest in public education, and the decision in Brown v. Board included an encomium upon education. This dictum can be the basis for an argument that education is to be included with voting and fair criminal procedure as a specially protected interest or even a "right" in itself. Horowitz and Neitring, Wise, and Kurland have suggested that possibility.[51] We will indicate later the form such an argument is likely to take before the Supreme Court; it will be suggested at that point why reliance upon race-education cases for the canonization of education is risky at best. For the moment it is adequate to observe that, though racial discrimination is a clear constitutional benchmark, discrimination against the children of poor districts is not the same thing.

49. 100 U.S. 303 (1880).

50. 388 U.S. 1 (1967).

51. Horowitz and Neitring, "Equal Protection"; Kurland, "Equal Educational Opportunity," pp. 583–584; Wise, *Rich Schools, Poor Schools*, pp. 21–24.

Proposition 1 and the Constitution:
The Relative Wealth Cases

The empirical relationship between wealth of a school district and quality of each child's education is clear and close. Perhaps the best hope in the quest for judicial analogies is in the line of equal protection cases that considers the relevance of relative wealth to the scope of the state's power to treat citizens differently. These cases, which appear to thrust the classifying fact of wealth into the inner circle of equal protection, may be the key to the establishment of Proposition 1.

Unlike racial discrimination, relative wealth has begun only recently to play a role in decision-making, and decisions emphasizing it are few. It is nevertheless widely viewed by commentators as potentially either a cornucopia or a Pandora's box, depending on the observer. Justice Clark spoke fearfully of the "new fetish for indigency," [52] and his colleague Justice Harlan has repeatedly warned that, when the court comes to define the limits of that fetish, it may find itself negotiating a slippery slope.[53]

Developments so far can be outlined briefly. Aside from a lonely concurring opinion of Justice Jackson,[54] indigence had gained no purchase whatsoever on the problems of equal protection until 1956, the year of Griffin v. Illinois.[55] The facts, as the court saw them, were simple: for full, direct, appellate review of his conviction, Illinois required a criminal defendant to furnish a certified bill of exceptions. Practically speaking, this often required him to purchase a transcript of the record. Only in capital cases did the state purchase it for him; all other impoverished defendants thus were denied effective appellate

52. Douglas v. California, 372 U.S. 353, 359 (1963), dissenting opinion.
53. See e.g., the Harlan dissent in each of the major cases to be discussed in this chapter.
54. Edwards v. California, 314 U.S. 160 (1941).
55. 351 U.S. 12 (1956).

review. Griffin based his claim upon invalid wealth discrimination, and he won. The court split five to four on the decision and the majority split four to one on the reasons. Black spoke for the majority four in a brief and Delphic opinion that apparently rested on both due process and equal protection. Frankfurter, by himself, relied plainly upon equal protection. Neither said the state must in all cases supply transcripts to indigents; both affirmed the absence of any duty to permit appeals. However, the discrimination between rich and poor on the facts before the court was for Black's part "invidious" and for Frankfurter's "squalid" in its application to the petitioner's interest in fair criminal proceeding.

Justice Harlan in dissent was careful to observe — as he has done repeatedly in succeeding wealth cases — that the majority was not merely interested in Griffin's plight as a problem of misclassification. A necessary aspect of their concern about his poverty was the character of the interest Griffin had at stake. In this view, said the Harlan opinion, the question was less one of classification than one of fundamental fairness and, arguably, was more nearly a due process case than one of equal protection.[56] His dissent embodies a clear recognition and a condemnation of the bifurcation of method in equal protection cases that we have already described. There is in fact an inner circle, and the Griffin case clearly is within it. Just why the court preferred this method to the exclusive invocation of the due process clause need not concern us here. That it did so and has reaffirmed that preference in similar cases is enough to justify our tracing the subsequent history of the developing line of crime-poverty cases.

In 1958 the court made the result in Griffin retroactive and reaffirmed its intention to employ an equal protection approach to discrimination against "those who cannot afford to pay for

56. See also F. A. Allen, "Griffin v. Illinois: Antecedents and Aftermath," University of Chicago Law Review, 25:151 (1957).

the records of their trials." [57] The following year the rule was extended to invalidate the imposition upon indigents of a twenty-dollar filing fee as a condition precedent to all criminal appeals to the Ohio Supreme Court.[58] In 1961 a similar result was reached with respect to a four-dollar fee for the filing of a state habeas corpus and a three-dollar fee for the appeal in such a case.[59]

As the vestigial fee and transcript problems petered out[60] the court extended the wealth principle to a new area of criminal appellate procedure. In Douglas v. California,[61] it required the appointment of counsel for indigents by the state for the single appeal guaranteed by California law. Indigence did not

57. Eskridge v. Washington State Board of Prison Terms and Paroles, 357 U.S. 214, 216 (1958).

58. Burns v. Ohio, 360 U.S. 252 (1959).

59. Smith v. Bennett, 365 U.S. 708 (1961). This decision also gave evidence of the court's sensitivity to the potential constitutional fecundity of the emerging poverty "rule." The issue arose in Smith because of the accepted and historic identification of habeas corpus as a civil proceeding: was the court now extending the influence of the wealth factor beyond the criminal process? The court denied any advance in that respect:

> We shall not quibble as to whether in this context it be called a civil or criminal action. . . . The availability of a procedure to regain liberty lost through criminal process cannot be made contingent upon a choice of labels. . . . To require the State to docket applications for the post-conviction remedy of habeas corpus by indigent prisoners without the fee payment does not necessarily mean that all habeas corpus or other actions involving civil rights must be on the same footing. Only those involving indigent convicted prisoners are involved here and we pass only upon them (*ibid.*, at 712–713).

The Griffin rule was applied to habeas corpus in Long v. District Court, 385 U.S. 192 (1966).

60. Lane v. Brown, 372 U.S. 477 (1963); Draper v. Washington, 372 U.S. 487 (1963); Long v. District Court of Iowa, 385 U.S. 192 (1966). In 1967 the Court, in a per curiam opinion, applied the principle at the trial level and required the furnishing of the transcript of a preliminary hearing, in order to prevent "differences in access to the instruments needed to vindicate legal rights, when based upon the financial situation of the defendant . . ." Roberts v. La Vallee, 389 U.S. 40, 42 (1967).

61. 372 U.S. 353 (1963). For a later modest extension of the Douglas rationale, see Anders v. California, 386 U.S. 738 (1967).

reappear thereafter as a special ground of equal protection until the 1966 interment of the poll tax in Harper v. Virginia.[62] The state had imposed a poll tax of $1.50 as a condition of suffrage. In a windmilling opinion employing both an ends/means and an invidious discrimination approach, Justice Douglas discovered a de facto discrimination by wealth. Wealth was not only declared constitutionally irrelevant for the purpose of qualifying voters, but, irrespective of its rationality, its use for such classification was invidious because it unfairly burdened an interest which is "a fundamental matter in a free and democratic society."

Strong dissents were delivered by Justice Black and also Justice Harlan, whose opinion was joined by Justice Stewart.[63] The objections went both to substance and method. Justice Harlan argued that wealth discrimination, unlike race, had never become a ground for special scrutiny, and he deplored the abandonment of the traditional ends/means analysis of equal protection issues.[64]

The Harper decision is important if only because it represents the debouchment of the wealth factor from its former cloister within the criminal law. If the classifying fact of wealth can be significant for the voting interest, it may demonstrate further expansibility and became significant for the interest in public education. This potential for diffusion is, of course, precisely the complaint of the critics. We concede — indeed, we insist — that the end of the poverty game is not in sight; but we doubt the boundless elasticity of the concept. Its thirteen-year career since Griffin has yielded extremely modest results. Granting that the mountain is still heaving, there is no reason to expect a judicial monster; but perhaps this depends on how one feels about Proposition 1.

62. 383 U.S. 663 (1966).
63. Ibid., at 670, 680.
64. Ibid., at 683–685.

On the surface, Proposition 1 nicely fits the philosophy of Harper v. Virginia and the criminal appeals decisions. If the principle is that wealth classifications, explicit or de facto, may not determine the state's disposition of fundamental personal interests, and if the ledger of such interests is even slightly pregnant, the argument for Proposition 1 is nearly implicit. The interest in education is important and personal; the present system is grossly discriminatory and victimizes children. Perhaps best of all — and unlike the interest of the criminal accused — once the court liberates the legislative energy through Proposition 1, education may well find itself propelled into basic structural reforms by a new political consensus in the states. But easy transition from Griffin, Douglas, and Harper to Proposition 1 is an illusion. Whatever the rhetoric in these cases, analogies are risky until close scrutiny has been given to differences in both the importance of the interest at stake and the practical prospects for a remedy.

Evaluation of the Wealth-Crime Analogy to the School Case

At least six plausible differences between the wealth-crime cases and the school finance cases can be briefly stated. (1) In the Griffin line of cases (and in Douglas) the court dealt with the sensitive interest in freedom from personal confinement and from all the stigmata of the convicted criminal. This interest is unique in character and, it can be argued, in importance. (2) Focusing the state's power specifically upon one man makes the interest of the criminal defendant appear intensely individualized and personal and gives it greater clarity and poignancy than any other interest that can be imagined, including education. (3) the remedy for the discrimination is simple, clear, and effective: give the appellant a transcript, and a lawyer, or else let him go. (4) The remedy is cheap. (5) The judicial nose under the state's tent is petite and the alarms of federalism correspondingly muted. (6) The Douglas line of cases involves a right (representation) which is in no way *egalitarian* in nature but which merely establishes a *minimum*. That is, there is no suggestion that appellate representation has to meet the standard of hired counsel or any definable standard above the base line of "competence." From Douglas, therefore, the easiest analogy is to a minimal or "foundation" education, which, of course, is precisely what as a practical matter now obtains. An initial evaluation of these six plausible distinctions between the *Griffin-Douglas* lines of decision and the school finance problem follows, although major issues will be re-explored in Chapter 11.

The Differences in the Interests at Stake. The first two points both deal with differences in the nature of the interests at stake and can be considered together. This aspect is important if we hope to show that the interest in education should be given the special status of the "inner circle" of equal protection. In speaking of the relative importance of the affected interests in these two kinds of cases it is useful first to inquire: important to whom, the individual or the state? To what extent is this problem to be viewed as one of doing justice to an individual and to what extent as a question of general policy? The relative emphasis upon one or the other may influence any judgment about whether education can compete successfully for the court's attention, even though it should be conceded that, in its criminal-wealth opinions, the Court itself has not yet clearly distinguished between the interests of the individual and of the public.

With respect to the *public* or *policy* aspect of the interest in education we note first that education not only affects directly a vastly greater number of persons than the criminal law, but it affects them in ways which, to the state, have an enormous and much more varied significance. Aside from reducing the crime rate (the inverse relation is strong), education also supports each and every other value of a democratic society:

participation, communication, and social mobility, to name but a few. Secondly, and still from a policy perspective, the comparison is one of cause on the one hand and effect on the other. In the criminal law the state deals principally with particular social effects; in and through education it influences — indeed, in some measure determines — the incidence and distribution of all social effects, of which crime is only one example. Third, in education the state deals with a classification of citizens which, on the whole or statistically (our present focus) appears more deserving than the class of criminal defendants. By definition the class "children" is incapable of deserving less than the full solicitude of parens patriae; they are innocent even without benefit of presumption. We do not denigrate the policy significance of fair criminal procedure by calling attention to the conviction rate that obtains even under the fairest of systems.[65]

With respect to the relative importance of the *individual interests* in the two cases, that of the criminal defendant appears relatively more significant. The threatened deprivation is immediate, personal, and decisive. In education the state is not focusing simply upon an individual child, but upon a collectivity. The fact of the relative poverty of that collectivity may or may not work an injury to the child; his district may tax higher, or the child may be rich and go to a private school. What the injury in the individual case may be is much less certain and less easily identified than the sudden loss of freedom by imprisonment. On the other hand — in the criminal appeals cases — it was by no means certain that the provision of a transcript to Mr. Griffin and a lawyer to Mr. Douglas would effect any difference in the outcome of their appeals; if certainty is relevant, it may be that in properly planned school finance litigation it

65. Or, we might add, the number of guilty pleas. See President's Commission on Law Enforcement and Administration of Justice, *Task Force Report: The Courts* (Washington, D.C.: U.S. Government Printing Office, 1967), pp. 9–14.

will be possible to pinpoint the plaintiff whose academic profile strongly suggests a causal nexus with the poverty of his school. The latter considerations are only slightly off the point. They do not go to the importance of the interest, but to the likelihood of injury to that interest. Nevertheless, the two are sometimes nearly inseparable, and the court is by no means unconcerned with the practical question of who is being hurt and to what degree, and how its intervention will affect the practical outcome of education.

In one sense, whatever diffuseness characterizes the injury to the child's interest in education makes the school cases more persuasive, for it emphasizes the class character of that interest and, thus, the equal protection aspects of the case. The *Griffin* opinions do not focus upon the class aspect of the petitioner's interest. Indeed, the petitioner is so immediately and personally threatened in the criminal cases that the lawyer's instinct is for due process, and not equal protection, as the essential problem. In that light the court's use of equal protection in *Griffin* not only demonstrates the uncommon vitality of equal protection, even for cases of individual discrimination, but renders the equal protection rationale in the school case all the stronger because of the more obviously class interest at stake.

Comparing Remedies and their Effects upon State Government. The remedy and federalism questions are closely related; what the court orders it must always order against the existing dispensation of the state.

Judicial strictures in the wealth-crime cases and the school finance case vary widely from each other in their implications both for the court and for the state. As we noted, the *Griffin* remedy is utterly simple, clear, and effective. Compared to such judicial child's play, a decree invalidating an entire system of educational finance for failure to comply with Proposition 1 may seem to critics an act of quixotry. That there is some difference between the cases in this respect we concede; but we think its importance is exaggerated and note that the most significant distinction between the cases may actually cut in favor of Proposition 1, for that difference is not the threatening complications of judicial remedy but the promising complications of state response. In other words, the disadvantages of the more difficult remedy are offset by the greater flexibility in response permitted the state. Indeed, that very flexibility will enormously ease the problems of enforceability by encouraging the state to respond.

Available remedies will be elaborated in Chapter 12, but we note here that their essence is the ultimate power of the court to shut down a system of public education that does not comply with Proposition 1 or such other standard as the court chooses to apply. That the court would need to provoke such an Armageddon is unlikely in the extreme; we shall explore some subultimate and much more likely approaches the feasibility of which is, again, supported by the promise of significant political support for quality public education — support which will be liberated from its present state of paralysis by Proposition 1. This potential political puissance for educational equality is in marked contrast to the political impotence of the values in fair criminal procedure. That difference will not be overlooked by the court in assessing probable responses to its decree. Moreover, the ultimate power to close offending school programs becomes rather less a nightmare when set alongside its counterpart in criminal procedure, the power to free all similarly situated convicts.

In any event, these genuine difficulties about what the court effectively can do should not be merged with the separate problem of what the state can do. The state's option after *Griffin* and *Douglas* is really no option at all. The court there has very nearly specified the state's response in criminal appeals: give the transcript, provide the lawyer. In the school cases there is no need for such imposition; the state can remain free to invent, as we have repeatedly indicated. It is this very freedom and the rich variety of appropriate responses to the essentially simple Proposition 1 that produces complexity exactly where complexity is desirable.

Sheer cost is a related and distinguishing feature of these two kinds of cases. The wealth-crime cases were relatively inexpensive for the state to set right. Transcripts and lawyers are not cheap, but compared, for example, to the cost of raising all school districts to the spending level of the highest district, their cost seems trivial. Of course the court will not prescribe any level of spending, and a diminution of educational expenditure is conceivable. Practically, however, legislative responses are very likely to raise the educational ante in substantial amounts, and, whether this happens or not, the court is certain to be accused of meddling indirectly with the level of state spending for education. Our view is that, although this is a plausible distinction from *Griffin/Douglas*, it is not clear that the distinction makes Proposition 1 less attractive, for it helps to drive home the enormous magnitude of existing discriminations. No doubt the court will consider the potential economic fallout from such a decision with extreme care, but, if our general thesis is sound, such extra effort to understand the implications will be all to the good.

The Douglas Case and the Basic Minimum Analogy. We have suggested that the analogy of *Douglas* is hurtful because its guarantee of representation, not equality of representation, appears to correspond to the widespread foundation programs in public education and thus tends to validate existing discriminations. The easiest answer to this is that the question of equality in quality of representation was not raised by the petitioner in *Douglas*. But let us assume for the moment that such a right were claimed and denied (as it would surely be). The denial would prove nothing; the analogy is treacherous to begin with, for we are comparing things which are quite unlike. The hypothetical right to counsel case just posed would compare the quality of state-supplied counsel with privately employed counsel. But Proposition 1 involves only a comparison of state-supplied education with state-supplied education, not with private or the "best" education, whatever that is. Proposition 1 is not a demand that the state supply everyone with the highest quality education available anywhere in the state. It is in fact not in strict terms a demand for equality at all, for it only insists negatively that quality not be made a product of wealth differentials, thus leaving room for inequalities that do not offend any other constitutional principle. If there is a right to counsel case which is analogous, it would be a demand that the quality of appointed counsel from district to district not be a function of local wealth. Such a claim, so far as we know, has not been made.

EVALUATION OF THE WEALTH-VOTING ANALOGY

Harper v. Virginia is bound to play a prominent role in the argument on school finance before the Supreme Court. If a $1.50 poll tax is an invidious discrimination, how can a $150 per-pupil differential in education be tolerated? Yet the case may be too remote an analogy for Proposition 1. As with the wealth-crime cases, the important plausible distinctions principally involve the nature of the interests in voting and education and the feasibility of remedy. Among these distinctions are the following. (1) Harper involves the unique activity in democratic society: voting is arguably more basic even than the interest in fair criminal procedure. (2) The definition of the evil (injury) is simple compared to that in the education cases; the economic imposition upon the franchise is avowed and direct. (3) The remedy is clear, simple, and effective. (4) The remedy is cheap.

In part these objections, especially the second, can be seen as straw men in their relation to Proposition 1, for they are, in some respects, primarily objections to notions of equality of education we have already rejected. We concede that the notion of a Fourteenth Amendment duty to educate according to individual needs is intolerably vague in comparison to the *Harper* standard; but our sole purpose is to compare *Harper* to Proposition 1.

A Comparsion of the Interests at Stake. The voting interest can be analyzed functionally either as of modest importance or as crucial. One's view of its significance is largely a product of the level of analysis chosen. On the level of the individual the voting interest is principally symbolic. Many find it quite unnecessary to vote, even in important elections; the practical effects of casting a ballot upon the objective quality of a voter's life is largely limited to cases where his vote makes or breaks a tie. Of course his self-image and reputation may be involved, but these are not the stuff of which important constitutional rights are made. Judge Learned Hand made the point even more strongly: "My vote is one of the most unimportant acts of my life." [66]

There is an important "related" distinction: whatever the individual's interest in the weight of his vote, that need is never demonstrably greater for any one individual than for another. Poor voters need the vote to gain power, rich to keep it. As

66. Learned Hand, "Democracy: Its Presumptions and Realities," in *The Spirit of Liberty*, 2nd. ed., ed. Irving Dilliard (New York: Alfred A. Knopf, 1953), pp. 90, 93. On (shall we say) the other Hand, we have the following grace note whose harmonization with this view requires a certain breadth of perspective: "When I go to the polls I have a satisfaction in the sense that we are all engaged in a common venture. If you retort that a sheep in the flock may feel something like it, I reply, following St. Francis, 'My brother, the Sheep' "; Learned Hand, *The Bill of Rights* (Cambridge, 1958), p. 74.

Of course, one may view the interest at stake as other than "my vote." That is, it may be defined as the individual's interest in not having the total influence of his district diluted. How much this adds, of course, is problematical. A voter in the minority within his own district is sometimes better off for the dilution.

voters we are fungible. However, individuals have differing needs for the state's aid in supplying education; and, as an observation of fact, where the need for education is likely to be greatest today it is the least available. The poor district is most likely to have the academically necessitous student. In the reapportionment cases there was a uniform need and a skewed distribution of the resource; in the school finance case there is a skewed distribution of need with an inversely skewed distribution of the resource.

But the court has not viewed the voting interest solely from the perspective of injury to the individual voter, nor should it. Realistically, the *Harper* decison and the reapportionment cases are concerned with injury to the interest of collectivities. This conclusion is supported by the court's distinctive emphasis upon the right of political association in a very recent decision unrelated to indigence. William v. Rhodes[67] required the state (Ohio) to cease discrimination against third political parties in giving access and appearance upon the ballot to presidential electors. Individual plaintiffs in all these cases could show substantial injury only to the extent of injury to the collectivity of which they were a part. The point here is this: in comparing the voting (political) and education interests we are comparing (on the voting side) an interest which is essentially a group and societal interest with one (on the education side) of vital concern to the individual, society as a whole, and all intermediate collectivities, including but hardly exhausted by voting groups. In judging the relative importance of voting and education, therefore, we need not be diffident about the comparative *scope* of the educational interest, whatever its comparative weight.

Even from the aspect of a group interest alone, education seems the equal of voting and association in sheer importance to a democratic society. It underlies the whole substance of the political process and is antecedent to voting and political organ-

67. 393 U.S. 23 (1968).

ization in the orders of both time and cause. All political behavior inevitably must reflect the presence or absence and the quality of education. A man's understanding of public issues is a function of those communications which are intelligible to him. The broadening of the franchise which currently is taking place in this country in no way neutralizes this point. The potential entry of millions of Spanish-speaking and Southern black people into the franchise[68] represents no national policy to cheapen the qualifications to vote. Any movement in the direction of universal suffrage is *in spite of*, not because of, the desirability of education for political participation. Such expansion merely renders fair treatment in education all the more crucial.

If society's stake in the preservation of the "voting interest" really is broader than protecting the mechanical act of pulling a lever — and surely the court perceives it so — education must be viewed as a crucial interest. The model of the voting citizen, we trust, is not one of passive absorption and Pavlovian reaction; it is the model of *response* and *participation*, a role for which education is the fundamental preparation. But this is only the beginning, for participation in elections is but one of the many roles society expects of the citizen qua citizen. Perhaps not all these roles require education, but the exceptions are few.

Another point of difference between the voting and education interests that may have great significance in the legal argument cuts in education's favor: the compulsory character of education. To put it argumentatively, voting may be an interest that, because of its importance, approaches the level of a right, but education is considered so significant that the state has bypassed the establishment of the right and rendered education

68. See Archibald Cox, "Constitutional Adjudication and the Promotion of Human Rights" (foreword to "The Supreme Court 1965 Term), *Harvard Law Review*, 80:91, 99–108 (1966).

a duty — a duty imposed in the name of preparing citizens for full participation in modern society. We are tempted to say that, unlike voting, it is such an important right it must be exercised. At any rate, as we shall have occasion to remark below, its compulsory character will not be ignored by the court.

Finally, the prospects for an intelligible standard for defining the constitutional injury in the school case are admittedly less promising than the one-man, one-vote rule or than the *Harper* rule for no tax on voting. Proposition 1 is not so easy of application as these. But perhaps the proper comparison is not with one-man, one-vote or with no tax on voting, but rather with the other and vaguer standard of injury to the voting interest also employed in the *Harper* decision, the violation of which obtains "whenever [the State] makes the affluence of the voter . . . an electoral standard." [69] The wealth/voting rule, as it may properly be called, is not only no more definite than, but bears a striking resemblance to Proposition 1. Paraphrased in school terms the *Harper* language could read: "whenever it makes the affluence of the family or school district an educational standard." Nevertheless, the practical difference in the two tests is considerable, simply because the apparatus of the poll tax to which it was applied was so simple compared to the school finance jungle.

Comparing the Remedies. The remedy for the poll tax was no poll tax — a simple result that the court could easily guarantee through its equity power if the state chose to balk. Implementing Proposition 1 concededly will be more challenging to the court.

With respect to pre-emption of legislative alternatives, what is true of the wealth-crime cases is true here. The *Harper* decision effectively leaves the state even less choice than did *Griffin* or *Douglas*; the state's program is simply annihilated and cannot be saved by broadening the class. Proposition 1, on the

69. 383 U.S. at 666.

other hand, leaves the state all the many choices it had before, minus only one.

Whose Poverty?

There is an additional question about the analogy to indigence cases which we would prefer to treat briefly and separately. We have noted at several points that, in the school finance issue, the poverty involved is always that of the district and only sometimes (though usually) that of the individual. What difference, if any, should this make in our evaluation of precedent involving individuals asserting personal poverty as a relevant constitutional fact? A short answer is that the school finance cases are not necessarily different in this respect. After all, the coincidence of personal and district poverty is probably fairly high; second, it would be easy to select an indigent plaintiff; third, all children should be regarded as poor in any case. These points should be useful and are perhaps true, but it will probably be observed that, though they are helpful to show that poor people are being injured, that injury is not an effect of their own poverty but of the poverty of their district. The poor who live in rich districts are simultaneously preferred.

Another kind of response is more convincing; properly viewed, discrimination by district wealth actually is worse than that in personal poverty cases. In the latter there can be at least a soupçon of responsibility on the part of the individual for his condition: though determined largely by events beyond his control, still, his own qualities are the cause of his poverty. But consider the school finance case. Here, not only is the victim not responsible for the relevant poverty, it is the state itself which has created it (and, worse, has done so deliberately) in the very creation of the district. Indeed, then, there is a difference between the cases, but that very difference reinforces every argument based upon the poverty rationale in *Griffin*, *Douglas*, and *Harper*.

Does Poverty Count?

One can argue that no "poverty" line of cases exists — that *Griffin*, *Douglas*, and *Harper* do not ultimately depend upon poverty at all. In the poverty-crime cases we may say the essence is not poverty, but merely the inability of the accused, for whatever reason, to provide those necessities for a fairly considered appeal that are normally left to his initiative. For example, how different from *Griffin* would be the case of a convicted person who is rich but has become incompetent and thus unable to contract for purchase of a transcript? Could the state deny him the appeal, or would it be constrained constitutionally to provide a guardian to secure his rights? That the answer is easy and the process so familiar should not blind us to the principles at work. It is not the appellant's indigence as such which counts; indigence is but the most common subspecies of all those personal disabilities that might prevent fair consideration of the appeal. This line of thought supports the Harlan position that the *Griffin* problem is one of due process to which the element of poverty is merely incidental. Similarly, it can be said that the poll tax case is concerned with poverty only as one of a great many imaginable burdens upon the voting interest — certain literacy tests, for example[70] — that might be intolerable and, if they were intolerable, would be so because of the unique character of the interest, not of the burden.

The argument seems unconvincing. There is clearly a special, if narrow, niche for judicial scrutiny of discrimination against the poor.[71] Yet, however they may be interpreted, the poverty cases by themselves are insufficient as a base for our position. Much still depends upon one's evaluation of the character and

70. See Lassiter v. Northampton County Board of Elections, 360 U.S. 45 (1959).

71. The Court has recently gone out of its way to recognize the special role of poverty. McDonald v. Board of Election Commissioners of Chicago, 394 U.S. 802, 807 (1969).

importance of the educational interest at stake, and of the ethical claims of the victimized class, as both are weighed against those interests of the state served by present systems.

DEVELOPMENTS IN THE 1968–69 TERM

In its 1968–69 term, the Supreme Court considered several equal protection issues parallel in some respects to the school finance problem. Wealth classifications played only a minor role, but these opinions develop further the distinctive approach to fundamental rights and add to the inner circle the interests in political association and interstate travel. On the whole, the work of the court in this session suggests the likelihood of continued development along lines compatible with eventual elimination of wealth criteria in public education.

In October of 1968 the Court decided Williams v. Rhodes,[72] striking down an Ohio statute creating special obstacles for new political parties seeking a position upon the ballot in presidential elections. Justice Black spoke for the majority. Surprisingly, the opinion was cast largely in the style of the equal protection method which Black himself had rejected in his dissent in Harper v. Virginia.[73] He now emphasized that the interests asserted by the plaintiffs "rank among our most precious freedoms," and that the state carried a special burden of justification "where rights of this kind are at stake. . . ." Specifically, these were the right "of individuals to associate for the advancement of political beliefs, and the right of qualified voters . . . to cast their votes effectively. . . ."[74]

Six months later, in the welfare residency cases[75] the interest in unburdened interstate travel triggered special scrutiny by the

72. 393 U.S. 23 (1968).
73. 383 U.S. at 670.
74. 393 U.S. at 30, 31.
75. Shapiro v. Thompson, 394 U.S. 618 (1969).

court of certain conditions upon eligibility for public assistance. The consolidated appeals in these cases (involving two states and the District of Columbia) challenged the validity of the one-year waiting period for new residents commonly imposed by the states as a qualification for public aid. The majority, per Justice Brennan, held the waiting period to be an invalid burden upon the interest in interstate travel because it discriminated against new residents. Rejecting the more deferential rationality test for evaluating equal protection claims, the court gave close substantive scrutiny to the legislation because of the character of the interest at stake.

It can be argued that, because of their proximate ties to specific provisions of the Constitution, the interests in interstate travel and political association differ from the interests previously included in the inner circle. The right of political association has been established as part of the protection afforded by the First Amendment.[76] The right to travel (interstate and foreign) has been traced variously to the Due Process Clause of the Fifth Amendment, the Interstate Commerce Clause, and the Privileges and Immunities Clauses.[77] In his concurrence in the welfare residency cases this distinction was taken up by Justice Stewart as the sole justification for giving any interest preferential treatment under equal protection. Hence, when the majority's evaluation of the interest in interstate travel caused Justice Harlan to object that his colleagues "pick out particular human activities, characterize them as 'fundamental,' and give them added protection," [78] Justice Stewart denied the charge. "The Court simply recognizes, as it must, an established constitutional right [interstate travel] and

76. NAACP v. Button, 371 U.S. 415 (1963); NAACP v. Alabama, 357 U.S. 449 (1958).

77. The theories and sources are identified and distinguished in the dissenting opinion of Mr. Justice Harlan in Shapiro v. Thompson, 394 U.S. 618, at 666–671 (1969).

78. 394 U.S. at 662.

gives to that right no less protection than the Constitution itself demands. . . ." [79]

Some limitation of this kind upon the source of the interests preferred would be a comfort to those who are uneasy about the expansive tendencies of the inner circle. The chief weaknesses of the Stewart limitation are its low predictive power and its misdescription of the court's work to date. Such a device cannot tell us what interests hereafter may be converted into rights in the Stewart sense; nor can it account for the preferential equal protection treatment accorded the voting interest and the interest in fair criminal procedure both before and after the welfare residency cases. Within two months after the decision in those cases the court again used the inner circle approach to protect both those interests. In Kramer v. Union Free School District Number 15[80] and in Cipriano v. City of Houma[81] it invalidated limitations upon the "fundamental right" to vote in school elections and municipal bond referenda. Mr. Justice Stewart split with the majority in both cases over the method employed — as logically he should. Dissenting in Kramer he declared: "this statute is not one that impinges upon a constitutionally protected right, and that consequently can be justified only by a 'compelling' state interest." [82] The Stewart position, so far at least, is a lonely one, though it did succeed in gaining the concurrence of Justice Black in these two most recent voting cases.[83]

For those inclined, like Justice Stewart, to recognize a limited number of special interests under the equal protection clause,

79. 394 U.S. at 642.
80. 395 U.S. 621 (1969).
81. 395 U.S. 701 (1969).
82. 395 U.S. at 639.
83. Justice Black's stance is increasingly dubious. His opinion in Williams v. Rhodes clearly gives to the voting right the preferential equal protection treatment that he had rejected earlier in Harper v. Virginia and has rejected subsequently in Kramer v. Union Free School District No. 15, 395 U.S. 621, 634 (1969), and in Cipriano v. City of Houma, 395 U.S. 701, 707 (1969).

a number of different potential "stopping points" or progressively inclusive circles could be imagined. The boundary for preferred interests could be narrowed to include only those rights guaranteed specifically by the language of the Constitution, such as freedom of speech. It seems that no member of the court takes this view. A second concentric band would embrace, as well, those rights drawn by inference from specific rights in the manner that the right of association is drawn from speech and assembly. This presumably is the perimeter adopted by Justice Stewart. The right to travel seems comfortable here, and the right of privacy,[84] though the latter might also be assigned to a third band representing rights inferred from the less specific guarantees of the Constitution, such as due process, but still excluding the equal protection clause.[85]

The outermost band will include those rights grounded in the equal protection clause itself. This final group is the only one into which education could be fitted comfortably. The present membership of that group is not clear. Possibly the right to fair criminal procedure should be placed here, though it surely belongs in the previous band as well.[86] The right to equality of power among voters most likely goes here; the equal protection clause has been the source specifically invoked in the voting cases. Because these cases have produced a reasonably secure consensus on the court, it seems fair to say that a majority of the justices is prepared, when necessary, to seek fundamental rights in the equal protection guarantee itself without

84. See Griswold v. Connecticut, 381 U.S. 479 (1965). The court discovered a "zone of privacy created by several fundamental constitutional guarantees." The zone was created by inference from such specific rights as that against unreasonable searches and seizures and such broad formulas as rights retained by the people.

85. "Probably every interest found to be fundamental and therefore protected by the due process clause will also be fundamental under the equal protection clause" (Comment, "Developments in the Law," p. 1130).

86. Griffin v. Illinois, 351 U.S. 12 (1956), and Douglas v. California, 372 U.S. 353 (1963), both invoked due process as well as equal protection.

recourse to other provisions. There is hope, at least, that an asserted interest otherwise unrecognized can evoke special scrutiny if it is merely considered essential to a democratic society. If, like voting, education is "preservative of basic civil and political rights," it stands a chance of being elevated to the same status.

For cases in which it has already been determined that a fundamental right is at stake, the form of the test to be applied to state action has been embellished by the welfare residency decision. Speaking for the majority, Justice Brennan put the standard in the following terms: "Since the classification here touches on the fundamental right of interstate movement, its constitutionality must be judged by the stricter standard of whether it promotes a *compelling* state interest." [87] Oddly enough, the court did not find itself required to apply this standard. In the welfare residency cases the primary interest offered by the states and the District of Columbia as justification for the waiting period was fiscal integrity. The court declared such an interest "valid" but gave it no weight because of the means chosen to protect it. The relevant legislative histories demonstrated that the waiting periods were designed to discourage indigent persons from entering the jurisdiction. This "purpose of inhibiting migration" was declared to be an illegitimate end of government. The respect otherwise due the state's objective of frugality was vitiated by the "invidious" subsidiary purpose to discourage indigents. On the same rationale of illegal purpose the court went further and forbade any classifications designed to discourage even those indigents migrating *solely* to enjoy higher welfare benefits. Likewise, it rejected any policy intended to limit welfare benefits to persons who previously had contributed to the state through taxation.[88]

87. 394 U.S. at 638.
88. In the course of setting the state's frugality to one side as a factor to be

The remaining interests claimed by the state in the welfare residency cases were administrative; the court found them either (1) not proved, (2) capable of satisfaction (or satisfied in fact) in other ways less onerous to the free movement of individuals,[89] or (3) simply irrational as underinclusive.[90] In effect, having prescribed a "compelling interest" test, the court never had to employ it; it never became necessary to strike the balance between individual and state interests, for the court discovered no interests which, under the circumstances, the state could properly assert.

As a consequence, the decision sheds no light upon the kind of state interests that may be thought of as "compelling." In fact, the notion of compulsion is so thoroughly metaphorical in this context that it is difficult to perceive how its use advances the analysis. It should be added that the strong emphasis upon the necessity of the state's showing "compelling interests" is itself a relatively new development. The expression has been used occasionally in both due process and equal protection cases as a counterpart to adjectives such as "fundamental," used to describe the competing interest of the individual.[91] It ap-

weighed, the majority draws an interesting parallel: "A State . . . could not, for example, reduce expenditures for education by barring indigent children from its schools"; 394 U.S. at 633. In other words, such a forbidden classification would provide the court another opportunity to declare irrelevant what otherwise might amount to a compelling interest of the state.

89. The doctrine of the "less onerous alternative" is likely to play an important role in determination of the school finance issue. It is discussed in detail in Chapter 11.

90. "Pennsylvania suggests that the one-year waiting period is justified as a means of encouraging new residents to join the labor force promptly. But this logic would also require a similar waiting period for long-term residents of the State. A state purpose to encourage employment provides no rational basis for imposing a one-year waiting period restriction on new residents only" (394 U.S. at 637–638).

91. Apparently the term first appears in NAACP v. Alabama, 357 U.S. 449, 463 (1958). See also Bates v. Little Rock, 361 U.S. 516, 524 (1960); NAACP v. Button, 371 U.S. 415, 438 (1963); Sherbert v. Verner, 374 U.S. 398, 406 (1963).

peared prominently in Williams v Rhodes;[92] but the opinion in the welfare residency cases is the first to endow the phrase with such independent and seemingly totemic significance. On the basis of this emphasis Justice Harlan was induced in dissent to label the entire method the " 'compelling interest' doctrine." [93] Nonetheless, it is again doubtful that anything was intended by the majority beyond a more candid recognition of the balancing of interests involved in the inner circle approach.

The somewhat factitious vacuum of legitimate state interests served by the waiting period in the welfare residency cases appears to be the basis for another interesting remark by the majority: "in these cases [the States] do not use and have no need to use the one-year requirement for the governmental purpose suggested. Thus, even under traditional equal protection tests a classification of welfare applicants according to whether they have lived in the State for one year would seem irrational and unconstitutional. But, of course the traditional criteria do not apply in these cases." [94]

This concluding remark is hardly so obvious as the court suggests. Several previous cases were decided in whole or part upon an evaluation of "rationality," even where fundamental interests were at stake.[95] Any suggestion that a majority of the court intends to ignore the rationality criterion altogether in such cases is important, for this approach would foreclose the kind of restrained minimalism described in Chapter 9. All cases involving inner circle interests hereafter would turn solely upon an evaluation of the substance of the conflicting interests of state and citizen. Perhaps the court meant to say no more than that it would be *unnecessary* in such cases to rely upon tradi-

92. 393 U.S. at 31, quoting NAACP v. Button, 371 U.S. 415 (1963).
93. 394 U.S. at 658. Ironically, it was Justice Harlan who fathered the term in NAACP v. Alabama, 357 U.S. 449 (1958).
94. 394 U.S. at 638.
95. See, e.g., Harper v. Virginia, 383 U.S. 663 (1966); Carrington v. Rash, 380 U.S. 89 (1965); Skinner v. Oklahoma, 316 U.S. 535 (1942).

tional criteria; even this would have been very significant if it augured a determination to speak to the substance of the discrimination when it would be important to the inducement of meaningful legislative response. However, two later voting cases suggest that the court meant precisely what it said. In McDonald v. Board of Election Commissioners of Chicago,[96] the court carefully determined that neither a "fundamental right" nor a classification "drawn on the basis of wealth or race" was involved before it proceeded to apply the classical analysis of rationality. Again, in Cipriano v. City of Houma,[97] the majority employed the inner circle approach to invalidate the state practice even though it could have gained support for an opinion in the classical mode from Black and Stewart, both of whom concurred on the basis of irrationality of the statute.

The Cipriano case and its companion decision, Kramer v. Union Free School District Number 15,[98] are interesting for additional reasons. In Kramer the court considered the validity of limitation of the franchise in school elections to property owners, lessees, and school parents. The plaintiff was a nonpaying boarder in his parents' home. As in the welfare residency cases, the court thrust upon the state the burden of demonstrating a compelling interest at stake in the limitation. The state argued that its interest was to limit the franchise to those "primarily interested" in the election. Again, as in the welfare residency cases, the court did not reach the question of whether this goal of the state was in fact compelling. Making several delicate judgments about who is truly interested in such elections and who is not, the court found that persons with "distinct and direct interest" were excluded by the statute and others with "remote and indirect interest" were included; thus the state did not "accomplish this purpose with sufficient preci-

96. 394 U.S. 802 (1969).
97. 395 U.S. 701 (1969).
98. 395 U.S. 621 (1969).

sion to justify denying appellant the franchise." The state's interest not only must be compelling, but the legislative instrument must be well calculated to achieve it. This one wasn't, and there was no need to go into the hypothetical question of whether a well-tailored limitation of the franchise would be found to foster some interest that the court might declare compelling. In *Cipriano* the franchise had been limited to property owners in referenda upon municipal bonds that would be paid off by general municipal taxation. The court again engaged in an evaluation of the character and extent of the excluded citizens' interests in voting in such an election: finding that some were "substantially affected and directly interested" to an extent equal to property owners, the conclusion was that the "statute clearly does not meet the 'exacting standard of precision we require of statutes which selectively distribute the franchise.' " [99]

The notion of a "standard of precision" designed to test how neatly the state's purpose has been accomplished is curiously reminiscent of the language of the classic equal protection test. But in the 1969 cases the court denies that it examines only for rationality, and surely that is correct; nor does it merely insist that in seeking its object the state employ alternative means which are less onerous to the individual. Some additional criterion is operating here. The classification must be "tailored" and have an "exacting" fitness for the end as the court determines that fitness. It must reach the object with a technician's elegance. It is void unless "all those excluded are in fact substantially less interested or affected than those the statute includes." The essence of this standard is elusive, but clearly it is not mere rationality. Perhaps it is super-rationality; but, however it be delineated, this willingness to deal with the substantive details of claimed discrimination is significant for the interest in public education.

99. 395 U.S. at 706.

The Role of Wealth in the 1968–69 Decisions

Wealth as an overt basis for classification played almost no role in the court's analysis of equal protection cases in the 1968–69 term. Only in Williams v. Oklahoma City, in which the court affirmed and extended the rule of Griffin v. Illinois, might wealth discrimination be seen as the heart of the matter.[100] The state will now be required to make available to indigent criminal appellants the record of the trial even in convictions for "petty offenses." Insofar as the original Griffin case involved equal protection, this 1969 decision solidifies the position of relative wealth as a classifying fact in the inner circle.

Underlying rich-poor aspects of two other cases in the term deserve attention. The temptation is strong to discover in the welfare residency cases some special role for indigence of the plaintiffs. One could imagine that the interest of public aid recipients in satisfying basic needs might fall within the inner circle of "fundamental rights"; there is in the Brennan opinion a suggestive passage declaring that "the very means to subsist — food, shelter, and other necessities of life" [101] is the matter at stake for the plaintiffs. In his dissent Justice Harlan notes this passage as the possible harbinger of another ill-defined but fundamental interest.[102] The rest of the long majority opinion suggests nothing of the sort, however: its entire weight rests upon the right to travel, not upon an interest in "necessities," however defined.

---

100. 395 U.S. 458 (1969). The case involved a drunken driving conviction carrying a 90-day sentence and a $50 fine. The opinion is per curiam and brief.

The emphasis upon indigence appeared in a pure due process case at the end of the term. Sniadach v. Family Finance Corporation of Bay View, 395 U.S. 337 (1969), struck down procedural inequities in garnishment proceedings with half a dozen references to the special and onerous effect of garnishment upon the poor.

101. 394 U.S. at 627.

102. Ibid., at 661.

Several other passages of the opinion give the impression that the case somehow involved a de facto wealth classification. For example: "the purpose of inhibiting migration by needy persons into the State is constitutionally impermissible." [103] This passage is paraphrased at several other points, and the distinction between old and new indigent residents is declared an "invidious" one. Does this reinforce a wealth rationale? Seemingly not; the opinion emphasizes only the distinction among indigents. It skirts the de facto division between rich and poor potential travelers — the classification most truly significant for the interest in unfettered movement interstate. However, if the court consciously avoided dependence on the wealth factor, it is peculiar that it found it important to damn specifically and repeatedly the state's purpose to burden the exercise of travel rights by indigents. One might predict that analogous waiting periods for nonindigents will prove valid on the rationale that the burden upon the right to travel is not, for such individuals, substantial. After all, if the test is a balancing test, and if the burden upon the cherished interest in interstate travel is relatively less for nonindigents, that difference may be accounted for in the weighing. It is quite possible that relative wealth will be taken into account in those cases where the benefit withheld or the burden imposed is economic in character, as in tuition-free college or eligibility for the bar examination.[104] But this is largely speculation, and until there is further development it does not seem proper to categorize the residency decision as a "wealth" case.

Another reference to wealth in the 1968–69 term is dicta

103. *Ibid.*, at 629.

104. The Court carefully left such questions open in a footnote: "We imply no view of the validity of waiting period or residence requirements determining eligibility to vote, eligibility for tuition-free education, to obtain a license to practice a profession, to hunt or fish, and so forth. Such requirements may promote compelling state interests on the one hand, or, on the other, may not be penalties upon the exercise of the constitutional right of interstate travel"; 394 U.S. at 638 n. 21.

from the opinion in McDonald v. Board of Election Commissioners of Chicago.[105] Prisoners awaiting trial complained of the failure of the state to furnish them absentee ballots. In the course of rejecting the appeals, the court spoke to the general question of the approach appropriate to equal protection issues: "a careful examination on our part is especially warranted where lines are drawn on the basis of wealth. . . . Such an exacting approach is not necessary here . . . [because] the distinctions . . . are not drawn on the basis of wealth. . . ." [106] The language is helpful, of course, but its particular application is not greatly encouraging. The fact is that at least one of the prisoners was in jail at the time only because he could not afford bail; further, he had explicitly raised the wealth discrimination issue. But according to the court there was no classification by wealth because of a failure of proof "that appellants are in fact absolutely prohibited from voting by the State. . . ." [107] It was not certain from the record that the state was unwilling to make other arrangements to permit appellants to vote.

Comparison of Travel and Education Interests

The interest in interstate travel is to be given preferred treatment under the equal protection clause as a consequence of the welfare residency cases. The significance of this to Proposition 1 can be explored here in a brief comparison of the two interests involved.[108] It is arguable, of course, that no comparison between travel and education is proper because interstate travel is a "constitutional right" established independently of the

105. 394 U.S. 802 (1969).
106. Ibid., at 807.
107. Ibid., at 808 n. 7.
108. Further discussion of the right of political association which was given equal protection treatment in Williams v. Rhodes seems unnecessary in the light of the comparison already made (see text accompanying n. 67 above) to the closely related voting interest.

equal protection clause. However, since it is doubtful that the
majority of the court attaches great importance to this distinction, the effort may be worthwhile — a conclusion reinforced by the court's own repeated evaluation of the substance
of the interest at stake in inner circle cases. Travel here will
mean the movement of persons interstate, conforming to its
use in the residence cases; we shall, however, refer occasionally
to judicial treatment of the related interest in foreign travel.

The cases — some very old — that have touched upon the
special importance of the travel interest recognize two general
aspects of that importance: the interest of the nation in maintaining and preserving the federal union and the national economy, and the special significance of interstate travel to the purposes of individual citizens of an open society.[109] The opinion
of the court in Edwards v. California exemplifies the emphasis
upon national unity. The court there based its protection of
travel upon the commerce clause, stressing the incompatibility
of state barriers to immigration with " 'the theory that the
peoples of the several States must sink or swim together, and
that in the long run prosperity and salvation are in union and
not division.' " [110] An important source of that unity is unfettered travel: so long as intercourse among the states is lively, the
nation is bound together by the uniquely adhesive effects of
multiple personal interaction.

So at least runs the argument. To a degree it is convincing,
though it is fair to wonder whether the free movement of mere

109. The principal cases are cited and discussed in the majority opinion in
the welfare residency cases, 394 U.S. 618, 629–631 (1969), and in the Harlan
dissent at 666–671.

110. 314 U.S. 160, 174 (1941), quoting Justice Cardozo for the majority
in Baldwin v. Seelig, 294 U.S. 511, 523 (1935). See also United States v.
Guest, 383 U.S. 745, 757–758 (1966): "The constitutional right to travel
from one state to another . . . occupies a position fundamental to the concept of our Federal Union. . . . [A] right so elementary was conceived from
the beginning to be a necessary concomitant of the stronger Union the Constitution created."

goods and the development of freight transportation has not had a unifying effect exceeding that of the sheer movement and interaction of people. After all, the immediate practical effect of emigration often is not unity but separation; departure of the pioneer creates the need for, as well as the possibility of, unification. But quite apart from this, given the goal of political union and a national common market, barriers to personal travel interstate would simply be incongruous. Further, the national market is a market in ideas as well as goods, and perhaps it is in the transport of ideas that the right to personal travel plays the more important role. So long as the state cannot shield itself from the physical presence of individuals entering from other states, it cannot remain insulated from their intellectual baggage.

In respect to its importance to the federal system, how stands the interest in education when compared to the interest in travel? The initial instinct is to downgrade education's relative importance principally because of the apparent parochialism of much of public education. Education, after all, is primarily a function of state government; indeed, there is no formal interstate aspect whatsoever. Further, the xenophobic habits not only of local school boards but of states and even regions of the country are only too familiar. Education in our society can appear a divisive as well as a unifying force.

There are various responses to this criticism. First, concededly curricular parochialism may be significant; its extent is quite impossible to estimate with confidence. But the one inescapable fact is not education's provincialism, but rather its essential nationalism expressed primarily in its historic role in the unification of our language. No more powerful centripetal force can be imagined than the fact of a common language imposed through public education. But there are other grounds as well for supposing that the mass of public school students are exposed to a curriculum with relatively expansive and national perspectives. One is the national market in textbooks; another is the character of teacher training, which, whatever its faults, is rarely conducted for subcultural or local goals. This is the very burden of considerable current criticism of teacher preparation.

Second, no matter how narrow the social and cultural ethos of a school system, the basic skills necessary even to an absorption of that very ethos are also relevant to performance in a national polity and economy. No public school system has abandoned literacy as an objective; neither, to our knowledge, has any district deliberately imbued its students with a contempt for economic success, irrespective of those schools that may have succeeded inadvertently in doing so. The development of reading and listening skills through public education also makes information and opinion purveyed by the national media — matters that otherwise might remain unintelligible — intellectually accessible to all persons.

Finally, the criticism based upon educational parochialism confounds two objectives of a federal union: one, to be sure, is union, but another is diversity. As a people, we seek and achieve unity; but diversity also enjoys the blessing and protection of the organic law. It is, therefore, cause not for criticism but for satisfaction that the states contribute variously through their schools to the deposit of competing values in the ideological market. Each citizen may reject this or that item in the value spectrum, but the educational systems that foster them can scarcely be faulted judicially for their contribution so long as they play the game within the broad limits permitted by the First Amendment. The only remaining question is whether our public schools really are, in practice, a medium for the transmission of values. Of this we have no doubt; but upon the opposite assumption the criticism based upon parochialism largely evaporates. The fact is that education exerts a mixed influence upon our national life, in part to unify and in part to diversify, and each effect is beneficial and important.

It would be tedious to embark upon a grocery list of the blessings for individuals attributable to travel and then to stack them against a similar list from education. What can be said generally is that interstate travel is beneficial to the individual principally to the extent that it (1) constitutes a means of education and/or (2) serves functions also served by education. It is primarily an instrumental activity, a means to extremely diverse purposes; one rarely travels interstate for the sake of sheer locomotion. When the traveler's objective is simply new experience and the pleasure, knowledge, and self-development such experience makes possible, travel is merely instrumental to education; if our interest is in comparing the two, it would be peculiar to elevate the means above the end in importance. This perspective also emphasizes the special and intimate relation between education and those cherished rights of the mind guaranteed by the First Amendment.

On the other hand, travel often is instrumental to various forms of action, economic, social, political, or personal. Education, too, may be a preparation for action, but it differs from travel in being vicarious and removed from action in time. Whether this should render it less significant is unclear. There is a temptation to view education as unspecific in its objects and on this ground to denigrate its importance; but, at least by comparison to travel, this seems to invert the proper perspective. It is in fact education and not travel that concerns itself with the specific objects of human action; travel is merely a neutral medium. If our interest is in the wellsprings of human action, one can say that the men of all purposes who pursue their affairs interstate owe at least as much to their education as to the indifferent machines that transport their bodies.

The court and individual justices have pointed repeatedly to the importance of travel to those same personal values which are central to education:

> [T]ravel within the country may be necessary for a livelihood. It may be as close to the heart of the individual as the choice of hat he eats, or wears, or reads. . . .[111]

> . . . the right of locomotion . . . according to inclination is an attribute of personal liberty. . . .[112]

> . . . that mobility which is basic to any guarantee of freedom of opportunity . . .[113]

> Freedom of movement, at home and abroad, is important for job and business opportunities — for all the commingling which gregarious man enjoys. . . .
> Like the right of assembly and the right of association, it often makes all other rights meaningful — knowing, studying, arguing, exploring, conversing, observing, and even thinking. . . ." [114]

The substitution of public education for travel in each of these passages would scarcely be noticed. As a value instrumental to personal freedom, economic opportunity, and political and social action, education is easily as important to the individual as the freedom to travel between states. And, when viewed as a value in itself and not as an instrumentality, education is plainly superior in every respect to the rather trivial interest in sheer locomotion across state boundaries.

111. Kent v. Dulles, 357 U.S. 116, 126 (1958).
112. Williams v. Fears, 179 U.S. 270, 274 (1900).
113. Mr. Justice Douglas concurring in Edwards v. California, 314 U.S. 160, 181 (1941).
114. Mr. Justice Douglas concurring in Aptheker v. Rusk, 378 U.S. 500, 519–520 (1964).

The overall import of the 1968–69 cases is unclear, particularly since wealth classifications were so little involved. The most important development is the court's use of equal protection to promote rights defined under other provisions of the Constitution. This may imply an increasing sensitivity to complaints that sound solely in discrimination rather than in any intrinsic injustice in the state's treatment of the individual viewed apart from its treatment of others. Many limitations, even of basic freedoms such as speech, are tolerable so long as they are uniform;[115] and where the matter at issue is a benefit rather than a burden, often the sole complaint is to its differential dispensation.[116] Many such cases will arise in the next decade. If the court remains as open to persuasion as it now appears, this can only be helpful for children complaining of discrimination in education.

115. See the Black opinion, concurring in part, in Cox v. Louisiana, 379 U.S. 536, 581 (1965): "I have no doubt about the general power of Louisiana to bar all picketing on its streets. . . . But by specifically permitting picketing for the publication of labor union views, Louisiana is attempting to pick and choose among the views it is willing to have discussed. . . . [This] amounts, I think, to an invidious discrimination forbidden by the Equal Protection Clause."

116. Lest the discussion become euphoric, we should recall the court's language of only a decade ago: "Particularly when we deal with a withholding of a noncontractual benefit under a social welfare program . . . the Due Process Clause can be thought to interpose a bar only if the statute manifests a patently arbitrary classification, utterly lacking in rational justification"; Flemming v. Nestor, 363 U.S. 603, 611 (1960).

11 · An Argument for Proposition 1

Set it down to thyself, as well to create good precedents as to follow them.

Sir Francis Bacon, Of Great Place

In GATHERING SOME THREADS and sketching an equal protection rationale for Proposition 1, we will by no means exhaust the possibilities of argument;[1] moreover, the sketch will scarcely touch upon the specific weaknesses of particular state systems.[2]

1. For example, the court in *McInnis* cites as relevant cases brought by taxpayers to protest the manner of levy and distribution of state tax funds. These cases are principally concerned with state requirements of "uniformity" of taxation and certainly do not involve the question of a Fourteenth Amendment right of the school child to equality of opportunity in education. Presumably none of their plaintiffs would have had standing to raise such a question. See Miller v. Korns, 107 Ohio St. 287, 140 N.E. 773 (1923); Dean v. Coddington, 81 S.D. 140, 131 N.W.2d 700 (1964); Sawyer v. Gilmore, 109 Me. 169, 83 A. 673 (1912). See also Hess v. Mullaney, 213 F.2d 635 (9th Cir. 1954). For a penetrating equal protection analysis of this area, see Comment, "Rational Classification Problems in Financing State and Local Government," *Yale Law Journal*, 76:1206 (1967).

The plaintiffs in both the Illinois and Detroit suits also have stressed what seems a pointless argument so far as the Fourteenth Amendement is concerned. Each is at pains to show that a "responsibility for education rests with the state" under state law. The assumption seems to be that state constitutions create federally enforceable rights; but see Calder v. Bull, 3 Dall. 386 (1798); Baker v. Carr, 369 U.S. 186 (1962). Wise makes the same error (*Rich Schools, Poor Schools: The Promise of Equal Educational Opportunity* [Chicago, 1968] pp. 93–104).

2. Such vagaries as special limitations on the taxing power of specific districts may require separate analysis. This issue was raised by the complaint in *McInnis*. One especially interesting device is the automatic diminution of state equalizing money to the extent of federal aid. It seems safe to predict that the state responsibility will be assessed separately and not diminished by aid from extrinsic sources that reduces the discrimination; see Shepheard v. Godwin, 280 F. Supp. 869 (E.D. Va. 1968).

As shown in Chapter 9, with some strain the classical or ends/ means rationale is adequate if we are content simply to void existing systems state by state. But if the court wants to encourage the states to embark upon planned reform rather than planned evasion, it may wish to be more explicit in identifying the evil to be avoided — an evil broader than mere formal misclassification. For this purpose the approach that accords special weight to selected classifying facts and "fundamental" interests is more promising. Of course, the two approaches are not mutually exclusive, and we may wish to combine elements of both.[3]

Concededly, Proposition 1 is no logical extension of any existing doctrine, and the argument for it will rely more upon policy than syllogisms. That argument is essentially an accumulation of separate and converging persuasions involving education, federalism, and judicial role. Because the approach is cumulative, it is difficult to suggest the specific point at which the demonstration is sufficient. The package of persuasions includes at least the following, most of which have been adequately covered prior to this chapter:

(1) The factual showing of gross discrimination by wealth.
(2) The practical unavailability of legislative relief.
(3) The fundamental significance of the interest at stake.
(4) Precedent rendering wealth suspect as a classifying fact, at least when used to affect "fundamental interests."
(5) A class of defenseless victims similar in interest and suffering serious injury.
(6) Available practical alternatives which satisfy legitimate state goals without continuing the existing discrimination.
(7) An intelligible and limited standard preserving legislative discretion.

3. The court used both the "invidious" and "classical" approaches in its recent decision striking down discrimination against illegitimate children under the wrongful death statute of Louisiana; Levy v. Louisiana, 391 U.S. 68 (1968).

We have shown that in several respects education compares favorably in importance with those interests that the court already has chosen for special protection; nevertheless, our next step will be to inquire further into whether the court either already has selected or, at least, ought to select education for admission to the inner circle of interests — point (3) — and if it does so whether this implies that other governmental services must be subject to the same constitutional limitation. We will suggest in this chapter, regarding point (5), that this favored interest is held by persons who constitute, in effect, a favored object of judicial protection; and finally — point (6) — we will briefly review available alternative financing systems that are practical and that, without discriminating against the poor, serve all legitimate interests of the state now being served, arguing that the existence of such alternatives is constitutionally relevant.

EDUCATION AS A FAVORED INTEREST: LEGAL POSTURE AND PRECEDENT

Education could constitute a favored interest in at least two quite distinct senses. It could, first, be elevated to the status of a "right." The state would be compelled to tax in its support; the state would no more be free to close its public schools than to close its courts. The thought is both obvious and preposterous. It is obvious insofar as universal public education in our culture is taken as a datum; its abolition is unthinkable (or nearly so). The transition from the familiar to the necessary is painless; there is even a dictum here and there in judicial opinions, plus a flood of popular literature, to support the notion. It is, however, fundamentally preposterous. Being radically unintelligible it is incapable of forming the subject matter of that complex relation to the state we denote by the word "right." To give content to such a relation, the court would have to determine what minimum expenditure for what minimum number of years, and what learning in what time and place, constitute "education." The thought is a judicial nightmare, but, worse, it is an educational nightmare. Because it would have to be couched in terms of minimums, there is no reason to suppose that it would not support all existing or even inferior systems. At any rate, since it deals in absolutes, the minimum would have to be set low enough to permit its effectuation in poor as well as rich states, leaving the richer states unaffected.

As some would prefer,[4] the right may be defined instead by reference to characteristics of the individual child and not by the characteristics of the state system. We might, for example, say that every child has a right to an education suitable to his need or to his potential or something of that sort. This, of course, is saying nothing intelligible until someone has judged for each child, according to a reasonable standard, his need or potential or whatever (which characteristic is chosen makes another enormous difference). Note also that if this individualized "right" is to become a right in fact, it must be a subject of judicial protection. It is beyond imagining either that the court would accept such a responsibility itself or that it would supinely relegate judgment on such a question to bureaucrats whose radical inability to judge need or potential has been itself a ground for judicial interference.[5] We say this even though we recognize that certain children have special needs objectively manifested, such as blindness. Judicial intervention in such cases is quite imaginable but it is least necessary, for they are seldom the cases of relative legislative neglect. It is always arguable that the state should do more for the physically handi-

4. See, e.g., complaint in Board of Education v. Michigan, General Civil No. 103342 (Cir. Ct., Wayne County, Mich., filed Feb. 2, 1968).
5. See Hobson v. Hansen, 269 F. Supp. 401 (D.D.C. 1967).

capped. It is not an argument properly addressed to the judiciary.

Much more could be said, but our purpose is simply to distinguish education as a right from education as a favored interest. By the latter we mean merely that the court ought candidly to give closer scrutiny to legislative classifications affecting education than it does to those involving the run of other interests. This does not mean that the court would be readier to substitute its judgment for the legislature's in education cases as it did in the reapportionment cases with the one-man, one-vote straitjacket. It need imply nothing further than its willingness to say no when education is distributed by wealth. The court should limit its strictures to those cases in which the already suspect fact of wealth and the now to be favored interest in education are linked in a manner which systematically discriminates among children.

Intimations from Nonracial School Cases

The next question is whether the court, as a historical fact, has treated education as a fundamental value. The answer is not very clear. An early suggestion favoring education comes from the Holmes opinion in Interstate Railway Company v. Massachusetts,[6] in which a statute compelled a street railway corporation to transport school children at half fare. Holmes found that the statute went "to the verge of constitutional power" of the state but was spared by the peculiar weight of the subject matter:

> Education is one of the purposes for which what is called the police power may be exercised. . . . Massachusetts always has recognized it as one of the first objects of public care. It does not follow that it would be equally in

6. 207 U.S. 79 (1907).

accord with the conceptions at the base of our constitutional law to confer equal favors upon doctors, or workingmen, or people who could afford to buy 1000-mile tickets. Structural habits count for as much as logic in drawing the line. And, to return to the taking of property, the aspect in which I am considering the case, general taxation to maintain public schools is an appropriation of property to a use in which the taxpayer may have no private interest, and, it may be, against his will. It has been condemned by some theorists on that ground. Yet no one denies its constitutionality. People are accustomed to it and accept it without doubt.[7]

Did Holmes's reference to "first objects," "structural habits," and public acceptance mean that education was different simply because the state had regulated it generally for a long time? How much longer than "doctors or workingmen"? The statute at issue had been passed in 1900. It is risky to make too much of this cryptic passage, particularly when the next decision upholding the education interest finds Holmes dissenting: this is Meyer v. Nebraska,[8] which considered a state statute forbidding the teaching of German in public and private schools to children below the ninth grade. Meyer was convicted of violating this prohibition, and the Supreme Court held his conviction a violation of due process. The theory seems to waver among the teacher's right to teach, the parent's right to educate his child, and the child's right to learn, although only the first was at issue. In any event, all three constitute educational interests and they inspired the court to the following description: "The American people have always regarded education and acquisition of knowledge as matters of supreme importance which should be diligently promoted. . . . Corresponding to the right of control, it is the natural duty of the parent to give his

7. *Ibid.*, at 87.
8. 262 U.S. 390 (1923).

children education suitable to their station in life; and nearly all the States, including Nebraska, enforce this obligation by compulsory laws." [9]

Within a few years the *Meyer* case was cited as controlling in a decision that today plays a prominent role in the debate over aid to private schools. Pierce *v.* Society of Sisters[10] settled the question of the Fourteenth Amendment right to satisfy the statutory duty of compulsory education by attendance at a private school, secular or religious, meeting appropriate state standards. The *Pierce* opinion is lackluster and terse, with little language helpful here; it is the *Meyer*-based result that is significant for our purpose. Without the reference to *Meyer*, the *Pierce* case could be contained within routine substantive due process analysis: education, like property, cannot be monopolized by the state. Apart from the state's legitimate interest in standards and its power to provide schools as a public service, education is, simply, private. But *Meyer* has no place in this syllogism; and its presence alters the whole approach. Education is not simply private; it is *education*, and the state cannot lightly make it in its own image. The individual's interest in education is personal and important, important enough to subdue the arguably rational purpose of the state to democratize its children and thus avoid the divisions of sect and creed.

These cases are old, if vigorous. The court has not dealt with the educational interest directly recently[11] (unless its work in

9. *Ibid.*, at 400.

10. 268 U.S. 510 (1925).

11. But see the recent dictum in Epperson v. Arkansas, 393 U.S. 97 (1968), where the court described the Meyer decision as follows: "The state's purpose in enacting the law was to promote civic cohesiveness by encouraging the learning of English and to combat the "baneful effect" of permitting foreigners to rear and educate their children in the language of the parents' native land. The court recognized these purposes, and it acknowledged the State's power to prescribe the school curriculum, but it held that these were not adequate to support the restriction upon the liberty of teacher and pupil" (393 U.S. at 105). See also the court's panegyric of Pierce and Meyer in Griswold v. Connecticut, 381 U.S. 479 (1965).

the racial segregation field is so viewed), but it is worth noting a few passages from the opinions of Justices Frankfurter and Brennan in establishment of religion cases involving released time and Bible reading. Concurring in McCollum v. Board of Education, Frankfurter described the public school as "the most powerful agency for promoting cohesion among heterogeneous democratic people. . . . The public school is at once the symbol of our democracy and the most persuasive means for promoting our common destiny." [12]

In Abington School District v. Schempp, Mr. Justice Brennan, concurring, noted: "Americans regard the public schools as a most vital civic institution for the preservation of a democratic system of government. It is therefore understandable that the constitutional prohibitions encounter their severest test when they are sought to be applied in the school classroom." [13]

In contrast to the *Meyer* and *Pierce* cases, these last two sources emphasize the *public* versus the *sectarian* aspect of the educational interest in public schools. Justice Brennan called specific attention to this: "It is implicit in the history and character of American public education that the public schools serve a uniquely *public* function. . . ." [14] Whether this emphasis on the "common" or "public" character of public education indicates an egalitarian spirit with dimensions broader than the "religion" cases is, unfortunately, imponderable.

The court, then, has not been indifferent to the special qualities — private and public — of the educational interest. But it is clearly too much to say on this evidence that education is

12. 333 U.S. 203, 231 (1948).
13. 374 U.S. 203, 230 (1963). In the recent "evolution" decision, Epperson v. Arkansas, 393 U.S. 97 (1968), the court added (quoting Shelton v. Tucker, 364 U.S. 479, 487 (1960)): "The vigilant protection of constitutional freedoms is nowhere more vital than in the community of American schools" (393 U.S. at 104).
14. 374 U.S. at 241–242 (emphasis added).

within the "inner circle" of equal protection. The references are oblique, and the issues were not approached as equal protection problems.

Intimations from the Race/Education Cases

Many lawyers consider the segregated education cases a potential prop for the educational interest. Horowitz and Nietring argue that "analysis . . . of interdistrict inequalities in educational opportunity must begin with the Supreme Court's statement in Brown v. Board of Education. . . ." [15] This is the oft-repeated dictum that "education is perhaps the most important function of state and local governments. . . . In these days, it is doubtful that any child may reasonably be expected to succeed in life if he is denied the opportunity of an education. Such an opportunity, where the state has undertaken to provide it, is a right which must be made available to all on equal terms." [16] To make full use of this language the analysis should begin even earlier, with those cases which culminated in the Brown decision. An argument in that historical form is superficially attractive and will surely be made at some point in the litigation ahead. We will set it out in some detail for examination.

The argument for education as a historically favored interest rests on the line of "separate but equal" cases beginning with Plessy v. Ferguson[17] and terminating in Brown. It is necessry in making the argument to extricate education from race, the presence of which has a tendency to obfuscate all other considerations. The issue of financial discrimination between districts, as we have shown, has literally nothing to do with race.

15. Harold Horowitz and Diana Neitring, "Equal Protection Aspects of Inequalities in Public Education and Public Assistance Programs from Place to Place within a State," *U.C.L.A. Law Review*, 15:787, 808 (1968).
16. 347 U.S. 483, 493 (1954).
17. 163 U.S. 537 (1896).

In fact the holding in Brown can be viewed as a decision upon equality of education, not upon racial discrimination as such. The question was simply whether the plaintiffs were being treated equally. In short, the cause of the inequality was race-connected, but the object of judicial concern was the plaintiff's interest in education — hence the reverence for education quoted above. As Judge Wright explained the matter in Hobson v. Hansen: "The crime which Plessy committed was that in applying its standard it concluded that de jure segregated facilities were or could be equal. The Court, ruling in Brown that deliberately segregated schools were inherently unequal, implicitly accepted the separate but equal frame of reference, exploding it from the inside so far as its application to de jure schools was concerned." [18]

In "exploding" de jure segregated education "from the inside," the court is seen to have accepted racial segregation as such; what it could not accept was inequality in education. Actually, this concern for equality of education can then be viewed as one of sixteen years' standing that Brown merely affirmed. It began in 1938 with Missouri ex rel. Gaines v. Canada,[19] involving exclusion of Negroes from the University of Missouri. The court defined the issue as follows: "The question here is not of a duty of the State to supply legal training, or of the quality of the training which it does supply, but of its duty when it provides such training to furnish it to the residents of the State upon the basis of an equality of right." [20] Gaines' exclusion was struck down, and his victory began the series of cases leading up to Brown.[21] These decisions involved admission to formerly white, segregated law and graduate schools that

18. 269 F. Supp. 401, 497, n. 165 (1967).
19. 305 U.S. 337 (1938).
20. Ibid., at 349.
21. Sipuel v. Board of Regents of the University of Oklahoma, 332 U.S. 631 (1948); Sweatt v. Painter, 339 U.S. 629 (1950); McLaurin v. Oklahoma State Regents, 339 U.S. 637 (1950).

were superior in quality to the Negro schools available within the state.

The real question in these cases is how much did race count toward the result which was uniformly favorable to the petitioning student? Another way to put the question would be: If the plaintiffs had been white would the results have been different? It is not quite enough to respond that if the plaintiffs had been white the discrimination would not have occurred in the first place. The discrimination might not have sprung from the same cause, but our factual analysis has made it clear that economic discrimination in education against members of all races is, and has been, an inherent part of the state systems, North and South, nearly since public education began.

Why, then, have injured whites failed to raise the question until 1968? The answer is partly low visibility of the discrimination. The statutes make no explicit requirement of inequality; the system is characterized by formal equality with even an element of compassion for the poor district expressed in the local foundation plan. It takes sophistication to understand that the poor pay more for less, in education as elsewhere. Nor was financial discrimination made obvious, like segregation, by skin color. To the extent that it was perceived as a problem it may also have been accepted as part of the general debility of local financing of services. Further, it is possible that white mobility rendered the system tolerable; the imposition was seen as temporary by those who expected to move up and out. And those whites who would be of the class most likely to appreciate the uses of litigation had the least need for it, since they were most upwardly mobile. It is relevant to observe that those cases that did come up to the court were planned and executed by middle-class Negroes for middle-class Negroes and at the college level, where either literally no alternative Negro segregated facility existed or what existed was absurdly inferior.[22]

22. The private sources were themselves participants in these cases. See also

So runs the argument for the educational interest, which climaxes, of course, with the Brown decision and its special kudos for education. In *Brown* the proponent sees the educational interest joined with the invidious classifying fact of race to compass in one opinion the demise of segregation and the emergence of equality of education.

The argument, though not strictly illogical,[23] is unconvincing. The separate but equal cases preceding *Brown* had nothing to do with education as such. It may be that the Negro plaintiffs wisely chose to attack the system of segregation at the point most important to them. It may be that their judgment of the relative importance of interests and the court's choice of school segregation as the most promising point at which to initiate the prohibition of race as a classifying fact are fair indications of the intrinsic significance of education. Nevertheless, nothing the court said or did prior to the *Brown* opinion suggested that education was special; much of what it did suggested the opposite. Plessy v. Ferguson, the basis of these cases, forbade discrimination elsewhere than in schools. If these cases elevated education, they also elevated the interest in sleeping cars;[24] and a court which elevates every interest elevates none. The court's attention was upon race, not upon the substance of the particular discriminations.

It is true that the quotation from the *Brown* opinion seems stunningly relevant. Taken literally it would be decisive in some

C. E. Vose, *Caucasians Only: The Supreme Court, the NAACP, and the Restrictive Covenant Cases* (Berkeley, 1959), detailing the similar background of litigation involving restrictive covenants.

23. On behalf of the argument for education, the *Brown* case could be viewed as divorced in its rationale from all that preceded and succeeded it. It could be said that it departed from the prior cases in rejecting the possibility of equality in education with desegregation; it is inconsistent with the succeeding cases insofar as it permits racial segregation wherever this does not result in discrimination. Thus, it is a pure expression of the court's special interest in education, emerging like a century flower for its one appearance in our time.

24. McCabe v. Atchison, Topeka, and Santa Fe Railway, 235 U.S. 151 (1914).

sense upon the central question. Education "must be made available to all on equal terms." From the vantage point of 1968, however, it is no longer clear that *Brown* was specially concerned about the interest in education. The decision had scarcely appeared before the "fundamental" character of education became the fundamental character of golf and swimming rights;[25] and all the cases since *Brown*, even those involving education, have shown complete preoccupation with the racial factor.[26] Meanwhile, the court has done nothing further to suggest that education enjoys a constitutional life of its own. In practical effect the hope for an emerging and independent educational interest based upon the words of *Brown* has been a casualty of the all-consuming racial crisis.

Indeed, in Griffin v. Prince Edward County School Board [27] the court came perilously close in dictum to rejecting the *Brown* language about education. It refused to allow a county to close its schools rather than desegregate, but the rationale was race discrimination and the court suggested vaguely that a variety of policies by school districts was not necessarily bad where not based upon race: that is, the state could provide educational opportunity on unequal terms, as long as it was not unequal for racial reasons.[28] Within the racial line of cases the only plausible exception to the court's indifference to education as such appears in its affirmance, without opinion, of the judgment in St. Helena Parish School Board v. Hall,[29] a case involving one

25. The cases involve many other equally trivial interests. See catalog of cases in W. B. Lockhart, Yale Kamisar, and Jesse Choper, *Constitutional Law, Cases-Comments-Questions* (St. Paul, 1967) pp. 1228, 1240.

26. *Ibid.*, at 1230–1235.

27. 377 U.S. 218 (1964).

28. "A State, of course, has a wide discretion in deciding whether laws shall operate statewide or shall operate only in certain counties. . . . But the record in the present case could not be clearer that Prince Edward's public schools were closed and private schools operated in their place with state and county assistance, for one reason, and one reason only" (*ibid.*, at 231).

29. 368 U.S. 515 (1962). The case below was Hall v. St. Helena Parish School Board, 197 F. Supp. 649 (E.D. La. 1961).

segment of Louisiana's rear guard action against school desegregation. School districts were given the option to close, and the defendant did so; the plaintiff sought and obtained an injunction. Judge Skelly Wright's opinion for the three-judge court divided the issues into racial discrimination on the one hand and discrimination "geographically against all students, white and colored," on the other. His rationale for forbidding the "geographic" discrimination was summarized as follows:

> . . . absent a reasonable basis for so classifying a state cannot close the public schools in one area while at the same time, it maintains schools elsewhere with public funds. And, since Louisiana here offers no justification for closure in St. Helena Parish alone, and no "state of facts reasonably may be conceived to justify it," except only the unlawful purpose to avoid the effect of an outstanding judgment of the court requiring desegregation of the public schools there, it seems obvious that the present classification is invidious, and therefore unconstitutional, even under the generous test of the economic discrimination cases." [30]

The opinion in *Hall* is hardly clear on the issue of a special status for education. At one point, Judge Wright attempts a distinction between "private activities" and "governmental benefits," education being among the latter but apparently not among the former. "When the state provides a benefit, it must do so evenhandedly." [31] This would apparently lump education with every other benefit and apply to all the benefits some notion of equality that is yet to be explained. Other parts of

30. 197 F. Supp. at 656. The "economic discrimination cases" referred to by Judge Wright are not the "wealth" cases but are decisions dealing with differential regulation of business, such as McGowan v. Maryland, 366 U.S. 420, 425–428 (1961) and cases cited therein.
31. *Ibid.*, at 659.

the opinion, however, cast doubt on this homogeneity of interests and use the term "invidious," which is typical of the special interest cases but here may connote only the racial aspect of the case. The whole opinion is so concerned with race that it is risky to make too much of it as either a prop for or a threat to the special educational interest. It is even unclear on the "geographical" discrimination point; if discrimination was against all children in the parish it may not have been by race, but it was clearly because *because* of race. Geography was purely and simply a mechanism. Finally, the silent affirmance by the Supreme Court is at best neutral on these points, since it had at least one strong orthodox ground upon which to rely. Later, in the *Prince Edward County* case,[32] the Supreme Court relied upon *Hall* as a racial precedent.

It seems, in candor, that in this line of cases the language of *Brown* in praise of education stands alone; until the court speaks again, its role as authority remains inscrutable for our purposes. Nevertheless, Horowitz and Nietring are right: this is a good place to start, not because those words from *Brown* establish any judicial doctrine about education, but because they are a good description of objective truth. It is not crucial whether the court already has put education on the pedestal it deserves. It is only crucial that education deserve it.

EDUCATION AS A FAVORED INTEREST: POLICY JUSTIFICATIONS

A good deal has been said about the virtues of education in a comparative way in our discussion of voting and poverty cases. Now it is appropriate to consider education on its own. The principal embarrassment in showing education's title to special treatment is one of riches heaped upon riches: no point is more frequently made in the public forum or in our folklore

32. 377 U.S. 218 (1964).

than that of the universal virtues of school. We have already
compared education favorably to the interests in voting, fair
criminal procedure, and travel. It would be ludicrous to add to
the libraries of educational encomia yet another glowing assurance to Everychild that the shortest way to the White
House is through the schoolhouse. In the interest of economy
we incorporate by implied reference all paeans from Plato to
Dr. Conant, our own included. We will be content here to
consider a few qualities of the state's educational activities that
(1) affect in a unique way the tension between the values of
freedom and equality, and (2) distinguish education in character and in significance from other services expected of the state.

An abiding dilemma for our society, as for most, has been the
frequent incompatibility of freedom and equality. We have
trimmed here and patched there in a living compromise, but
always with more or less discomfort. Redefine and obfuscate
as we will, we cannot at the same moment recognize an employer's right to choose his workers and the applicant's right to
receive equal treatment. So we constrain the employer and
declare that the quantum of freedom overall is increased, when
we really mean that equality seemed the more important value
in that particular contest. Fair housing presents the same
antinomy of values; in fact, much of the field of civil liberties
can be analyzed in these terms. The problem is endemic.

Public education may be viewed as an important exception to
the dilemma: here the values of equality and liberty can merge
without subordination, or even diminution, of either. By "liberty" we mean the right and power of the individual to make
decisions with significant economic, political, or social effects.
If we start with the reasonable assumption that education has
a "liberating" effect (increases the practical choices available
to the individual), and assume further that this effect is random with respect to populations of the size with which the

financing of public education deals (districts), it follows that we do not increase that liberating effect by systematically preferring some such groups over others in the distribution of available educational resources; nor do we decrease that liberating effect by eliminating existing preferences. The total quantum of freedom is logically independent of the distribution of available education among such groups.

If we make the further assumption that the liberating effect of public education for any such population of students is also a relative one, which depends upon the state's having done nothing to prevent that group's education being at least equal to the education available to those with whom it must compete (that is, if we adopt a market model of liberty), a somewhat different consequence follows. In a system marked by preference, only those groups preferred by the state will enjoy this liberating effect; and their gain is offset by the relative unfreedom of the disfavored. Only when equality of opportunity for public education exists can freedom for every group be increased through education.

No doubt other, more complex, assumptions about the relation of freedom and education may set the values in apparent conflict. For example, if we assume that children of poor districts cannot benefit from education as much as those of rich (assuming we are agreed what "poor," "rich," and "benefit" mean) we can infer a negative correlation between the values of freedom and equality. But such a result seems to require assumptions about masses of persons that, even if they were empirically demonstrable, would be at least constitutionally questionable as a criterion for the dispensation of state benefits. The most sensible assumption for the present context is the market model relationship, in which public education has its liberating effect for all groups only if it is dispensed without state-engineered inequality. In this competitive model the state can prefer no entity without destroying the liberty of another.

It is certainly proper to wonder whether all this airy concep-
tualizing means anything. It treats freedom as a term subject to
quantification, which is questionable, and it is a far cry from the
kind of practical analysis of discrimination we have attempted
above. We see its limited role in the argument for Proposition
1 as essentially syncretic. The semi-Darwinian market analogy
is addressed to the natural fears of the conservative that the
levelers are at work here sapping the foundations of free enterprise. We would like him to see that there is in fact no graver
threat to the capitalist system than the present cyclical replace-
ment of the "fittest" of one generation by their artificially advantaged offspring. Worse, where that advantage is proffered to
the children of the successful *by the state*, we can be sure that
free enterprise has sold its birthright.[33] Even if that special advantage were not awarded systematically to the successful but
were utterly random in its dispensation, the same would follow.
The state has no business giving differential pushes upon an
arbitrary basis. Thus, to defend the present public-school finance
system on a platform of economic or political freedom is no
less absurd than to describe it as egalitarian. In the name of all

33. Note the comment of one observer rarely suspected of Fabian tendencies:

The difference of natural talents in different men is, in reality, much less
than we are aware of; and the very different genius which appears to distinguish men of different professions, when grown up to maturity, is not
upon many occasions so much the cause, as the effect of the division of
labour. The difference between the most dissimilar characters, between a
philosopher and a common street porter, for example, seems to arise not so
much from nature, as from habit, custom, and education. When they
came into the world, and for the first six or eight years of their existence,
they were, perhaps, very much alike, and neither their parents nor play-
fellows could perceive any remarkable difference. About that age, or soon
after, they come to be employed in very different occupations. The difference of talents comes then to be taken notice of, and widens by degrees,
till at last the vanity of the philosopher is willing to acknowledge scarce
any resemblance (Adam Smith, *An Inquiry into the Nature and Causes of
the Wealth of Nations*, ed. J. E. T. Rogers, 2nd ed. [Oxford, 1880] I, 16–
17). See also F. A. Hayek, *The Constitution of Liberty* (Chicago, 1960)
pp. 91–93.

the values of free enterprise, the existing system of public school finance is a gross scandal. Properly articulated, this can be convincing to the classical liberal and may have something to do with his reaction to the court's decision.

But co-optation of the free enterpriser is only half the battle. His support is dearly bought if the court must forfeit the natural support for Proposition 1 that exists among contemporary liberals. There is, however, little risk of this; although their preference, like our own, will run strongly for *compensatory* education, they will support *equality* as a half loaf of significant dimensions — and recall that we deal here only with constitutionality and only with the judiciary. Compensation is a question we would leave to legislation, and the gulf between liberal and conservative should become apparent only at that point. Thus the emphasis upon the harmony of freedom and equality may be useful in pulling together normally polarized ideologies; there is no reason the court cannot succeed in that aim, so long as it does not concern itself with compensatory education.

Our own point of view may appear incongruous to the extent that we have indicated our support for compensatory education by legislation. Does not such preference by the state for the disadvantaged disturb the proper relation between freedom and equality in education as much as preference for the rich? The state's thumb is merely on the other side of the scale. Those who argue for compensation as a constitutional duty of the state may answer no, that true equality must imply compensation in our society. We have already rejected this constitutional position; indeed, we would consider the propriety even of legislatively determined compensatory programs dependent upon how that compensation is dispensed. If the criterion for compensation is underachievement (or overachievement or some other relevant distinguishing characteristic of the child or his district, other than poverty) we see no more difficulty in extra state assistance than in the case of preference for the blind child. Perhaps there is some loss of freedom in the Darwinian or market sense; if so, we regret it but do not see this as more than a makeweight. To argue that the provision of educational equality is compatible with classical freedom is not to reject every act of the state which is not.

If the criterion of preference is poverty, however, we face potential embarrassment. Can we hold that wealth ought not to determine quality of education and then permit it to do so when it works to the advantage of the poor? The answer is that we do not so hold. Later we will indicate why we would apply the standard "neutrally."

The Problem of Stopping at Education

The argument that the interest in education is crucial and distinctive has a twofold purpose. It seeks first, of course, to justify giving education the kind of special judicial treatment now accorded voting. At the same time, and for many of the same reasons, it seeks to remove education from the herd of interests that may not deserve entry to the inner circle. If the court is to "prefer" all interests, it prefers none; but why stop with education? If the equal protection clause eliminates relative wealth as a determinant of the quality of public education, by what warrant can wealth continue to determine the quality of other public services? If the distinction between education and all other services is merely that of the sheer importance of the service at stake, shall we prefer being educated to being alive? — police, firemen, and sewers protect our most precious possessions, yet the quality of their service, like that of education, is tied securely to the standard of community affluence. In the years ahead the court will be asked repeatedly to remove wealth determinants (and probably other nonegalitarian influences) from all public services. It is possible to imagine such a result.

There is a certain ethical appeal to the broad notion that, at least for government, it is prima facie improper either to assign the same social task to unequal units or to assign tasks of varying difficulty to equal units. As a legislative principle the idea of universal power equalizing, or even universal equality of services, is well within the range of reason; as a judicially generated inference from the Fourteenth Amendment it is almost, but not quite, inconceivable. It is barely possible that the court could move that far by constant incremental expansion of the "egalitarian revolution." The reasons for our opposition to such a cosmic extension of equal protection can be inferred from our previous discussions of judicial restraint, which we will not further elaborate. What is important here is the question of whether the extension represented in Proposition 1 is subject to prudent containment.

The principal safeguard lies in special qualities of the educational interest — qualities that justify, if they do not dictate, unique judicial response. In several respects public education differs from all other services or benefits of the state, and differs not only in importance but in ways that may make it distinctly and uniquely appropriate for Fourteenth Amendment protection. We do not intend to repeat everything we have already said about education's unique significance to the individual and to the political process, though it is all relevant; our concern here will be only with factors that distinguish education from other state benefits not yet in the inner circle but no doubt hovering in the wings.

The first is public education's role in maintaining "free-enterprise democracy" and the economically open society implied by that phrase.[34] No other governmental service can claim such a seminal role in preserving entry to and competition within the market. Man as competitor is first and foremost educated man; we do not expect him — indeed, we do not permit him — to compete until he has been educated. The demands of laissez-

34. See John Dewey, *Democracy and Education* (New York, 1923), pp. 101–102.

faire must be postponed; but once the age of basic education is passed, competition and its fruits make a great deal more sense, at least if free entreprise makes sense. If we encourage people to become rich, we should be slow to prohibit their living together and taking advantage of their wealth by constructing a desired package of municipal services; nor should we confuse the issue by conjuring up visions of rat-bitten slum children suffocating in garbage and adapting to life on inadequately protected streets. We can and perhaps will solve these problems of physical living standards with a minimum level of public services, whether or not the court can intelligibly match the moral imperative for that minimum with a constitutional standard.

The next and most obvious distinguishing quality of education is its compulsory character,[35] a quality it shares with the criminal process. It is, of course, not to be compared on this ground with the criminal process, which, unlike education, few seek voluntarily. Nevertheless, the element of compulsion has its uses in the argument when to the compulsion of attendance is added the compulsion of assignment, first to a particular district and then to a particular school. For the poor this combination of compulsions is confining indeed, at least when compared to the freedom of the more affluent to select among private educations. Nor is it insignificant in this context that the freedom of the affluent is one firmly grounded upon the Fourteenth Amendment itself. Pierce v. Society of Sisters[36] represents perhaps the only example of a constitutional right to substitute private action for a state-imposed duty; but, more than this, the court's special concern for educational freedom

35. Mississippi abolished compulsory attendance in 1956 for reasons unconnected with school finance. See 5 Miss. CODE ANN. §§ 6509–6510 (1942), repealed by Miss. LAWS ch. 288 (1956). It is noteworthy that the absence of compulsion has not diminished the state's obligation to provide equality of education by race.

36. 268 U.S. 510 (1925).

AN ARGUMENT FOR PROPOSITION 1 | 417

in the *Pierce* case easily implies a corresponding concern for the child whose family condition makes the exercise of that freedom impossible. In the ambience of *Pierce*, a child of the poor assigned willy-nilly to an inferior state school takes on the complexion of a prisoner, complete with a minimum sentence of twelve years. It is hard to find an analogy to such durance among the competing public "benefits," and one remains tempted to draw the parallel of the criminal law.

A third feature of education distinguishing it from all other benefits is the universality of its relevance. Not everyone finds it necessary to call upon the fire department or even the police in an entire lifetime. Relatively few are on welfare. But everyone benefits from education;[37] and if formal education were not compulsory, most would seek it anyway, those who did not substituting something in its place. The only service approaching it in universality is medical aid, and even medicine is avoided by some on the grounds of religious conviction.

To an extent that surpasses other benefits, education is also a continuing process, not an episode. In this it even exceeds welfare, which is never continuing by intention of the state and is probably rarely so by intention of the receiver. Education is the only relation with the state that is planned, active, continuing, and universal. Of all the state's benefits, therefore, it represents both the largest opportunity for and the most significant danger to the individual caught in its maternal embrace.

Finally, education is that service through which the state deals with every man *as man*. In this relation the state has made the fateful choice of reaching out to touch the self and personality of its children. Here there is more than the warming, feeding, preserving, and healing of bodies — services appropriate to the lower orders of life. Such actions, laudable as

37. Perhaps the point is overdrawn. Even those who do not "call upon" the police benefit from their services.

they are, are neutral at most with respect to the human personality; they provide a context of security in which man, without undue interference from the elements and hostile humans, may develop in the directions and to the extent that he wishes and is able. But it is public education that enters actively to shape this development in a manner chosen not by the child or his parents, but by the state. When the state educates, it stamps its mold on the personality of the child. Often it does so explicitly; the preambles of legislation are rich with expressions of intention to shape young minds. Always it does so implicitly, by determining which part of the deposit of learning is to be transmitted to the next generation.

We need not fear this aspect of public education in order to appreciate its unique role, but there are thoughtful men who do fear it.[38] For some of them education's inevitable impact on human personality is the basis of an argument, not for equality in, but for abolition of the public school. They would deny the state's right to maintain a *system* of education in the sense of state norms for educational content. There is, of course, a dilemma here — and one uneasily resolved by the *Pierce* decision protecting freedom for those who can afford it. For those who cannot, the state's influence upon personality is inescapable. It is this that, as much as any other factor, makes discrimination in public education distasteful and that distinguishes education from all other public services.

These are distinctions the court cannot fail to see; on the other hand, their persuasive effect is imponderable. The court is not bound by our notions of where to stop expanding the inner circle of equal protection. It is enough for us that the distinctions are there, and that the end of wealth discrimination in

38. Christopher Jencks, "Is the Public School Obsolete?" *The Public Interest*, no. 2 (Winter, 1966), 20; E. G. West, "The Uneasy Case for State Education," *New Individualist Review* 4:38 (1966); Milton Friedman, *Capitalism and Freedom* (Chicago, 1962), pp. 376–395; Hayek, *Constitution of Liberty*, pp. 376–395.

education does not imply its necessary demise for all public services.

The Role of the Victim

It is likely that the argument for Proposition 1, or for equality in any form, will be assisted by the characteristics of that class of persons — children — whose interest in education is the subject matter of the litigation. Children we define operationally as persons younger than the age at which they may leave school under state law. The claims of children for an equality, in some sense, of treatment with other children seem ethically sound. This conclusion is obvious, but the reasons behind it may not be. Aside from age there is little about children to suggest sameness or uniformity for educational purposes, with two exceptions.

First, it is very difficult to predict for most children the upper limits of development, at least during the first years of school. Testing is notoriously fallible, culturally biased, and inclined strongly to measure achievement rather than pure potential.[39] Further, by the time testing becomes plausibly reliable for that purpose, school itself may have had a major impact upon potential; thus there is a sameness among children in the sense of a general substantial uncertainty about their potential role as adults. Being yet indeterminate as a group, children are classless — or, their class is classlessness. Second, there is a certain equality of deserts: no child of tender years is capable of meriting more or less than another, or at least our ethic forbids the recognition of that possibility. This outlook finds a negative form of expression in common law and statute in the blanket

39. See Judge Wright's assault on the system in Hobsen v. Hansen, 269 F. Supp. 401 (D.D.C. 1967). For the very interesting sequelae to this case, see Smuck v. Hobson and Hansen v. Hobson, both decided Jan. 21, 1969, by the U.S. Court of Appeals for the District of Columbia, 408 F.2d 175 (D.C. Cir. 1969).

toleration for crimes and certain torts by persons under seven years of age and the de facto immunity of children for such acts up to the age of ten or twelve.[40] It could be put positively as an equality of innocence. In this respect the equality of adults is always problematical; even social and economic differences among them are plausibly ascribed to their own deserts. Our socioreligious history is full of explanations for the attitude,[41] but, in any event, adults as a class enjoy no presumption of homogeneous virtue and their ethical demand for equality of treatment is accordingly attenuated. The differences among children, on the other hand, cannot be ascribed even vaguely to fault without indulging an attaint of blood uncongenial to our time.

If children are similar in their deserts, they are not similar in their needs. But for purposes of achieving legal equality of opportunity, this very dissimilarity, ironically, is helpful. There is widespread agreement that the current dispensation of resources is generally in inverse proportion to the needs of children. The ethical claims of disadvantaged children thus even exceed the requirements of our rationale. As we have explained, this does not tempt us to satisfy those ethical demands for preference through the medium of the Constitution, but it may help toward convincing the court to move as far as equality in the sense of Proposition 1.

40. Immunity was based upon inability to achieve the mental state necessary for the wrong. The common law of crimes exempted those under 7 absolutely and presumed that children from 7–14 did not possess "the degree of knowledge essential to criminality"; James Stephen, A History of the Criminal Law of England (London: Macmillan, 1883) II, 98. The tort immunity has been narrower because "the state of mind of the actor is an important element" in only a limited number of torts; William Prosser, Law of Torts, 3rd ed. (St. Paul: West, 1964) p. 1025.

41. The classic study is Max Weber, The Protestant Ethic and the Spirit of Capitalism (New York, 1956).

Protection of Children's "Welfare" Rights

A special status for children under the Constitution is a question that has not reached the Supreme Court in anything approaching pure form. However, there are hints here and there that can be briefly explored without any effort to be exhaustive. A number of Supreme Court cases deal with state regulations intended to benefit children by limiting their exercise of those freedoms recognized for adults; but the issue has not been cast in terms of the discriminatory effects of regulation among subclasses of children (*Brown* is a possible exception, but, as we have seen, subsequent cases make it appear much broader in scope). The point of these cases is usually the special breadth of the state's power to legislate for the benefit of children because of their unique needs. Thus, in Prince v. Massachusetts,[42] a statute limiting the freedom of children to sell magazines was applied to a nine-year-old Jehovah's Witness who sold religious tracts on the street in violation of the act. The defense was put solely on grounds of the free exercise of religion clause. The court split five to four. The majority appeared tortured by the choice between private right and the state's parens patriae role, but held for the state:

> Against these sacred private interests, basic in a democracy, stand the interests of society to protect the welfare of children, and the state's assertion of authority to that end, made here in a manner conceded valid if only secular things were involved. The last is no mere corporate concern of official authority. It is the interest of youth itself, and of the whole community, that children be both safeguarded from abuses and given opportunities for growth into free and independent well-developed men and citizens.[43]

42. 321 U.S. 158 (1944).
43. *Ibid.*, at 165.

The same tone is evident in the recent decision upholding limitations upon distribution of literature to minors that were more restrictive than the rules developed for adults in the obscenity cases. In Ginsberg v. New York[44] the court approved the *Prince* decision and specifically confirmed the broader power of the state to regulate the conduct of children. The apparent difficulty with these and other cases of this genre is not that they fail to distinguish children, but that they seem to distinguish them for purposes of limiting rather than increasing their rights under the Constitution. The recent decision In Re Gault,[45] sprucing up the procedures of the juvenile court, seems to confirm this second-class citizenship by making exceptions to it.

Fortunately, this gloomy perspective leaves out of account a crucial distinction. In *Prince*, *Ginsberg*, and *Gault*, there was a sharp conflict between two interests held by the same child. The child's "welfare" interest promoted by the curfew, obscenity, or juvenile delinquency laws clashed directly with either the child's interest in freedom of religion (*Prince*), freedom of communication (*Ginsberg*), or personal liberty (*Gault*). The court in every case was forced willy-nilly to reject one or the other of the interests — either that claimed *by* the child or that claimed *for* the child. If from such a zero-sum game one can draw any conclusion, it might be the ironic one that the cases in which the child's "civil liberty" interest was subordinated to his welfare interest are the ones which most clearly suggest a preferred status for children. It was the welfare interest that truly belonged to the child qua child. His civil liberty interest was no different from that of any adult; it was asserted not as a class interest but as the interest of an individual who happened to be a child. And observe that the interests which failed in *Ginsberg* and *Prince* were the most jealously protected liber-

44. 390 U.S. 629 (1968).
45. 387 U.S. 1 (1967).

ties, the interests in speech and religion. The welfare interest of the child failed to dominate in *Gault*, but it is worth noting that the court emphasized grave doubt about whether the juvenile's surrender of procedural protection under existing systems was in fact compensated by any substantial benefits from coming into the state's custody. As Mr. Justice Fortas put it:

> It is claimed that juveniles obtain benefits from the special procedures applicable to them which more than offset the disadvantages of denial of the substance of normal due process. As we shall discuss, the observance of due process standards, intelligently and not ruthlessly administered, will not compel the states to abandon or displace any of the substantive benefits of the juvenile process. But it is important, we think, that the claimed benefits of the juvenile process should be candidly appraised. Neither sentiment nor folklore should cause us to shut our eyes. . . .[46]

Now the point: if the child's interest in the benefits of state policy is so potent against Fourteenth Amendment rights, as *Prince, Ginsberg*, and even *Gault* suggest, how stands his claim when that welfare interest is itself asserted — not to offset, but as an additional foundation for such a right? The school finance case is not one where the child asserts the liberty of playing truant against the weight of the state educational policy designed to benefit children as a class. It is a case where he asserts a Fourteenth Amendment right to equality with respect to the very benefit (education) the state will force upon him even if he does not wish to enjoy it. He draws strength both from the class welfare interest *and* the civil liberties interest. Being in the peculiar position of withholding from the child what it acknowledges to be for the child's benefit, the state not only cannot rely upon but must counter whatever strength

46. *Ibid.*, at 21.

it would ordinarily have drawn from the child's minority status. The child's claim thus embodies *all* the relevant interests except those of the state's administrative convenience.

If there exists here a special role for childhood, it is tempting to compare it to the role of race under the Fourteenth Amendment. One can imagine the category "child" and the category "Negro" together forming a broader class of "precious people" for equal protection purposes; but the comparison is false, at least for our problem. Discrimination in school finance is not against the class "children," it is within that class. The advantaged children are equally "precious." It is no help to our argument to distinguish children from all other classes, as the equal protection cases occasionally seem to do with the class "Negro." This, however, does not mean that the court's special concern for children will not be helpful. There may be a difference betwen using that concern to distinguish children from adults and using it as we suggest, but the difference is hardly crucial. If the court is as solicitous of children as we believe it to be, this concern is likely to be expressed inside as well as outside the class.

Comparison to the special use of equal protection on behalf of the Negro is questionable for a second reason: it may carry the implication that children should be viewed as another pressure group in a social revolution. That is, in the context of equal protection cases dealing with race, the poor, urban voters, and the like, it is easy to misconstrue reform in school finance simply as a weapon in a class struggle, with loyalties to be recruited according to the lines of cleavage between the jarring sects and segments of society. The divisive social consequences of such a view could be a net loss, even if the court ultimately sees it our way. Success for the constitutional proposal here advanced would surely cost the rich in the short run, but this does not make it essentially a program for redistribution of wealth. It is merely a long overdue effort at redistribution of public education. Its objects and beneficiaries are neither poor children nor rich; urban nor farm; black children nor white. They are children.

Children and the Neutrality of Proposition 1

It is now possible to answer the question of whether the application of Proposition 1 should be "neutral." That is, would it be improper for the state to prefer children of the poor as such? Suppose, for example, a statute directing per-pupil expenditure by district in inverse proportion to the relative wealth of the district. Clearly, such a statute offends Proposition 1 as we have cast it, for quality is made a function of wealth. Should an exception be made where the poor are advantaged? How concerned should we be about symmetry in this respect when a number of other governmental programs of incontestable validity prefer the poor quite explicitly?

The answer is that Proposition 1 probably should operate with neutrality; the hypothetical statute just posed should be subject to the same constitutional restrictions as a preference in public education for the rich. The central reason lies in what we have just said about the class of victims. The state ought not to discriminate among children upon the basis of a characteristic of any persons other than the children themselves; the wealth of his parents, or of some artificial collectivity such as a district, seems to us a questionable basis for denying a child equal access to public education. Perhaps one could argue that the wealth of the child himself would be a proper criterion, but since children are notoriously impecunious, any concession on this ground would be largely theoretical. Their very poverty and dependence is an additional index of that universal democracy of children that we have invoked. We see little reason to punish the penniless children of the rich.

The issue is not one of extreme importance, if only because it is easily avoided.[47] In this country we have found it possible to legislate preference for Negroes by legislating about poverty; if poverty were our immediate target we would, no doubt, find it possible to legislate about that subject by legislating about achievement scores, I.Q.'s, and reading levels. Poverty should not be conceived as the direct object of legislation designed to improve our schools: the object is rather the individual educational needs of children who are not properly distinguishable from each other as rich or poor. It will not overtax our imagination to find ways of meeting those needs without applying an irrelevant means test to parents or districts.

Our posture here may suggest that the federal legislation in aid of education in defined areas of poverty should be held invalid under the unwritten equal protection clause of the Fifth Amendment.[48] The point is arguable. It could be escaped by suggesting that use of the poverty test in those statutes was simply a legislative shorthand for all those other characteristics of children about which Congress is free to legislate; indeed, this is probably the fact.[49] Nevertheless, although it is not the present subject, the superficial inconsistency with Proposition 1 is somewhat unsettling. We would at least prefer that Congress more explicitly invoke the relevant criteria in establishing such programs. On the other hand, there is little doubt that Congress (or the state) could give unrestricted grants to the poor

47. For the converse problem of "compensatory" education of the gifted rich, see Chapter 12 below.

48. See Bolling v. Sharpe, 347 U.S. 497 (1954).

49. We do not wish to become too pure about this. It is clear enough that Congress was in fact interested in "the special educational needs of educationally deprived children," 20 U.S.C. § 241a (Supp. 1968), and that use of the poverty standard could realistically be regarded as merely an instrument to define what are purely educational needs. Actually, the federal standards are sufficiently complex to support any argument; see 20 U.S.C. §§ 241a, 241c (Supp. 1968). Cf. NEW YORK UNCONSOL. LAWS § 3602(2)(b) (McKinney Supp. 1967).

that recipients could spend for education if they chose. At some point our neutrality may verge upon fatuous formalism.

REASONABLE ALTERNATIVES AND THEIR RELEVANCE

There is a principle of constitutional law which runs something like this: in assessing the validity of state action that significantly injures an individual, it is relevant to inquire whether the state's legitimate purposes could have been achieved by an alternative form of action that would have avoided the injury. This would appear to be an elementary principle of personal ethics. Its spirit informs a number of basic principles of the common law, and it played a prominent role in the now moribund field of economic due process.[50] It has recently insinuated itself into the civil liberties field and seems now to bear a name that arose out of its application in antitrust cases: the doctrine of "less onerous" or "less-restrictive alternative." [51] It has appeared in a number of equal protection cases in the last few years.[52]

Application of the principle can be illustrated by the problem of the criminal accused who seeks release on bail. The state has a strong interest in assuring his presence for trial, hence a substantial bail requirement is sensible. Such a system harshly discriminates against the man who cannot make the amount of bail, however; he remains in prison until trial despite all presumptions of innocence.[53] Assuming that other adequate in-

50. See, e.g., Pennsylvania Coal Co. v. Mahon, 260 U.S. 393 (1922).

51. See Harold Horowitz, "Unseparate But Unequal — The Emerging Fourteenth Amendment Issue in Public School Education," *U.C.L.A. Law Review*, 13:1147, 1161 (1966); G. M. Struve, "The Less Restrictive-Alternative Principle and Economic Due Process," *Harvard Law Review*, 80:1463 (1967).

52. Carrington v. Rash, 380 U.S. 89 (1965); Rinaldi v. Yeager, 384 U.S. 305 (1966).

53. See Note, "Discrimination against the Poor and the Fourteenth Amendment," *Harvard Law Review*, 81:435, 446–447 (1968).

centives for his appearance are available, the state may have the duty to use one of them in place of bail. Some such general rule is a valuable item of judicial hardware. It permits the court to protect the interest of the individual without frustrating the state's purpose, if the state is merely willing to adopt the ameliorating alternative.

The Supreme Court has been escalating its use of this concept in the area of fundamental rights. Its description in Shelton v. Tucker,[54] in which a statute requiring schoolteachers to make broad disclosures of their private associations was struck down, is often cited now as the classic form:

> . . . even though the governmental purpose be legitimate and substantial, that purpose cannot be pursued by means that broadly stifle fundamental personal liberties when the end can be more narrowly achieved. The breadth of legislative abridgement must be viewed in the light of less drastic means for achieving the same basic purpose. . . . Mere legislative preferences or beliefs respecting matters of public convenience may well support regulation directed at other personal activities but be insufficient to justify such as diminishes the exercise of rights so vital to the maintenance of democratic institutions.[55]

Note that the degree of the court's willingness to reject the state's interests served by the statute is a function of the fundamental character of the personal right. It is therefore likely that, if the concept of a less onerous alternative is relevant to equal protection problems, it will be limited to the protection of those interests in the "inner circle." In 1965 the device was given clear expression in Carrington v. Rash,[56] involving the voting interest. A Texas statute had excluded military personnel stationed in Texas from the franchise. The state feared "infil-

54. 364 U.S. 479 (1960).
55. Ibid., at 488–489.
56. 380 U.S. 89 (1965).

tration by transients" whose concern for state affairs was often not substantial. The court found such state interest valid, but the statute invalid because the state could with relative ease have distinguished between those servicemen who intended in good faith to stay in Texas and those who didn't. Similarly, the following year in Rinaldi v. Yeager,[57] the court invalidated a classification affecting criminal appellants because there were alternatives available to the state making the classification unnecessary. The technique reached full flower in 1969, most prominently in the welfare residency cases.[58] The majority opinion, after noisy preparation to weigh the right to interstate travel against compelling state interests, deftly avoided doing so. A careful examination by the court of the apparatus of welfare administration demonstrated that the state neither needed to nor did in fact rely upon the period of residency for the purposes it claimed.

There is little doubt that the concept of less onerous alternative will be used with increasing effect in equal protection cases, but our brief encounter here should not leave the impression that the idea is altogether clear or predictable. Later, in the very term of court in which the Shelton case was decided, the court upheld Sunday closing laws imposing significant restric-

---

57. 384 U.S. 305 (1966). New Jersey required indigent appellants who asked for and received free transcripts to pay for them out of prison wages if (1) the appeal was unsuccessful and (2) the sentence involved imprisonment. The court found irrational and "invidious" the financial amnesty for those who were not imprisoned and struck down the reimbursement obligation for those imprisoned. The court added: "[Any] supposed administrative inconvenience would be minimal, since repayment could easily be made a condition of probation or parole, and those punished only by fines could be reached through the ordinary processes of garnishment in the event of default" (ibid., at 310). Rinaldi can be viewed as the one criminal case of the "inner circle" in which the discrimination is not by wealth: it is between subclasses of indigents. One might even stretch a point and call the interest at stake a purely financial one, viewing Rinaldi as the first purely civil, nonracial, nonvoting case in the inner circle. The court, however, clearly viewed it as part of the Griffin line.
58. Shapiro v. Thompson, 394 U.S. 618 (1969).

tions upon Saturday Sabbatarians even though the state could have altered the prohibition so as to leave the choice of day of rest to the individual. Many other states had made an alternative day available to such minorities. In Braunfeld v. Brown[59] the court admitted that "this may well be the wiser solution . . ." but it allowed the state's interests to prevail. Among these interests the court noted the problems of more complicated enforcement and of potential injury to other state policies.

A point worth noting is the distinction between "less" and "least." The doctrine has been described as that of the "least onerous alternative";[60] the use of "least" is misleading, however, for it suggests too much. The court is not engaged in a detailed examination of alternatives in an effort to tell the state how to rewrite the statute: the ameliorating alternatives are merely one of the factors of judgment. The imposition on the person "must be viewed in the light of less drastic means for achieving the same basic purpose." [61] As we see from *Braunfeld* there is no "rule" here other than the soft rule of balancing the interests of the person against those of the state; it is also unclear just how completely the interests of the state must be served by the available alternative. One commentator suggests that, in the field of economic due process, the alternative must be rather precisely applicable.[62] It seems certain that no such precision will be required in the area of fundamental rights, but the fit of the alternative to the problem clearly cannot be too wide of the mark.[63] It is in this perspective that the general

59. 366 U.S. 599 (1961).
60. Horowitz, "Unseparate But Unequal," at 1161.
61. Shelton v. Tucker, 364 U.S. 479 (1960).
62. See Struve, "The Less Restrictive-Alternative Principle," at 1463.
63. In this respect it may be instructive to consider the approach in Kramer v. Union Free School District No. 15, 395 U.S. 621 (1969), which considers the degree of precision with which the state has achieved its purpose. At some point the less onerous alternative concept seems to merge into the old rationality test.

concept of less onerous alternative can be applied to the school finance issue.

ALTERNATIVES FOR FINANCING PUBLIC EDUCATION: PRESERVING STATE INTERESTS

The important state interests served by the existing decentralization of the responsibility for education are (1) subsidiarity in administration of the school system and (2) subsidiarity in decision-making about the level of sacrifice that is appropriate for education in the light of other local needs.

It is abundantly clear that the states' interest in decentralized administration can be served under a wide range of financing systems, some of which we have already identified. The following breakdown includes but twelve examples of financing systems that do not discriminate by wealth and that are compatible with local administration of varying kinds and degrees.

A. Centralized (total state) financing
   Equality of allocation to districts on a per-pupil basis
   (1) District free to allocate to all reasonable uses.
   (2) District compelled to spend on an equality per-pupil basis.
   (3) District compelled to allocate to various categorical uses (compensatory, experimental, and so on).
   Allocation to district on reasonable basis other than per-pupil
   (4) Categorical special aid for the blind, gifted, and disadvantaged.
   (5) Categorical special aid for curricular specializations (science, art, experimentation, for example) to be chosen by the district.
        Direct aid to students
   (6) Either all or some of the state budget for education — implies freedom to spend in private schools.

B. Local financing (partial)

    (7) to (12) All the administrative systems possible under (1) to (6) are possible under local financing; they would, however, require power equalizing to be constitutionally valid if Proposition 1 is accepted.

All twelve systems would be less onerous alternatives insofar as they would remove the effect of poverty upon quality without sacrificing subsidiarity in administration. Indeed, as we have demonstrated, subsidiarity would be augmented by any form of power equalizing.

The Interest in Local Fiscal Control

The state's other principal interest, the interest in retaining a substantial local fiscal control, could be satisfied by a slightly smaller number of alternative programs having the same ameliorating effect upon the interest of the child. All would involve some aspect of power equalizing,[64] either through the district or the family or both. Where the district is involved they would probably not be more difficult to administer and enforce than the existing foundation and flat grant programs they would replace. Use of the family as the equalized unit would involve some additional complications, but it would at the same time diminish those state burdens, including financial responsibilities, connected with the administration of districts.

All of these options, of course, frustrate any interest the state might assert in imposing either a heavier load or inferior education or both upon poorer districts. The history of educational finance would suggest the pursuit of such an interest by the states; to say that it is illegitimate and does not deserve recognition begs the question asked by this book. Whether the

64. The only exception is a program of constant redistricting in order to keep district tax bases equal. This seems sufficiently cumbersome as to exceed the definition of an "alternative."

rationale offered here will carry the court is of course unpredictable, but it is difficult to imagine the court tolerating the existing scandal in education if it is provided with an approach that assures change without preordaining the form that change is to take. Proposition 1 serves these ends.

12 · Conclusion: Tactics and Politics

GOD: You angels keep quiet an' I'll pass another miracle. Dat's
always de trouble wid miracles. When you pass one you
always gotta r'ar back an' pass another.

Connelly, The Green Pastures

LEGAL AND POLITICAL STRATEGIES must be developed to give practical meaning to the theories offered here. Many approaches are possible, and we do not intend to be exhaustive; prediction is difficult and tactics are peculiarly a matter of time and place. Nevertheless, a number of courses deserve particular attention.

Considering that our purpose is to challenge the entire structure of education finance, the most promising places to start are with those states manifesting in significant degree all the inequalities analyzed in Part I. States such as Illinois[1] and California[2] seem ideal, since they have coupled the foundation plan with flat grants in a relation which makes the flat grants often anti-equalizing. In our discussion we will assume that litigation is planned in such a state.

Who Sues Whom for What? The plaintiff must be someone who is being injured by the wealth discrimination built into the system: there are two types to choose from, children and school boards. The child plaintiff (represented by his parent, and himself representative of a class in most cases) should be a public school pupil who (1) resides in a "poor" district which is (2) taxing above the minimum participation rate of the foundation plan. This child's district can be compared in

1. ILL. STAT. ANN. ch. 122, § 18–8(2) (Smith-Hurd Supp. 1967).
2. CAL. EDUC. CODE § 17901 (West Supp. 1967).

435

wealth, effort, and offering to specific districts above the state median in wealth in what is the only factual showing essential to the theory. It would be preferable, of course, if the district were extremely poor and had a tax rate at or near the permitted maximum.

For obvious reasons, the plaintiff child might best be from a poor family, though this is not necessary. If the parent's employment requires his residence in the district that is also a makeweight, emphasizing the "captive" aspects of the situation. As indicated earlier, the child's race is legally quite irrelevant; but, for political purposes, in order to stress this irrelevance, a white plaintiff (or a preponderance of whites in a class action) is probably desirable.[3] In most cases it would also be desirable for the school board of the plaintiff child's district to join as plaintiff, at least where the board is not subordinated to political influence and frequent shifts of view (an important consideration). There could be difficulty concerning the district's standing to attack the legislation under which it is created,[4] but the original presence of the district in the litigation would lend importance to the matter even if it were to be forced out for

3. If the reaction of practicing attorneys who have heard us speak on this subject over the last years is typical, we can expect a rather general rejection of the advice. That sampling of the fraternity, by and large, has stressed to us what it considers the strategic value of "riding the racehorse" in litigation. As developed later in this section, we fear the dampening effect of race upon the development of a consensus to support meaningful legislative change. The racial emphasis would be designed to convince nine men, its de-emphasis to convince all men. We are also confident that discrimination against minorities of an interdistrict character will fail of proof in most states; see our discussion in Chapter 10 above.

4. See Columbus and Greenville Railway Co. v. Miller, 283 U.S. 96 (1931); Braxton County Court v. West Virginia, 208 U.S. 192 (1908). But cf. Board of Education v. Allen, 392 U.S. 236, 241 n.5 (1968). The two older tax cases involved state officials asserting the invalidity of a state action injurious to a unit of government or to the state itself. Would the official's standing be improved or weakened if he purported to act on behalf of persons for whose welfare he was in part responsible under state legislation? Is a school board responsible for representation of those interests of its students arising outside the statutes?

lack of standing. Its involvement would render it doubly important that the tax rate for that district reflect a level of sacrifice well above the state median.

The complex legislation under attack can be put in two categories. First, there are laws creating districts with power to perform the educational task. Second, there are laws tying students to such districts. Given Proposition 1, the objection to the first, the district mechanism, has a double aspect: (1) By empowering districts to tax "local" wealth at a rate above the foundation level [5] the state has preferred rich districts and permitted them to spend more than their share of the state's educational resource; or (2) by limiting the power of districts to the taxation of "local" wealth the state has unfairly injured them unless there is an adequate subvention, which there is not.

The second general category of laws, the assignment rules, fits the inequality to the child. These rules create three kinds of potentially objectionable restraints: (3) children are required to attend school; or (4) their attendance is in general limited to the district of their residence; or (5) if they wish to attend elsewhere (private schools or other districts) they must pay out of their own pockets.

It is the combination and interaction of these five factors that create the total problem; but the system as a whole can be brought under fire employing any one of the five, each different attack stressing a slightly different kind of injury and remedy. The five strategies, stated first in legal and then in simple normative terms, would seek the following ends:

(1) To prevent richer districts from receiving an unfair percentage of the general resource for education (Jones, in the richer district, deserves no more than what I am receiving for the same tax).

5. Or even by permitting rich district spending to exceed the foundation amount at the participation rate.

(2) To obtain a fair amount of money for the plaintiff's education in his own district (I deserve to receive in my district at least what Jones receives for the same tax).

(3) To gain admission for the plaintiff to a district with a fair budget per child (if I cannot have in my district what I deserve, considering our tax rate, I should be permitted to attend Jones' school).

(4) To excuse the child from attendance so long as less than a fair sum is available in his own district (if I cannot receive what I deserve in my district, considering our tax rate, I should not have to go to school).

(5) To obtain a fair sum for the plaintiff to purchase education elsewhere (if I cannot secure what I deserve in my district, considering our tax rate, then I should be given as much money as is spent on Jones to spend on my education elsewhere).

In evaluating the five kinds of confrontations it is crucial to recall the purpose of it all: we do not aim to end or injure public education, compulsory attendance, districts, or even the variations in the number of dollars spent per pupil. We hope simply to free the state from the existing straitjacket of wealth-determined quality and thus force a basic legislative reexamination of the system to the probable benefit of all education. We bank on the commitment of the state to education and thus do not shrink from creating through the courts a choice for the legislature between two systems of equality, one viable, the other intolerable — in the reapportionment cases the plaintiffs did not seek to end elections, hold them at large, or declare state legislation unconstitutional. Of course, the trick is to avoid such ultimate confrontations wherever possible.

In order to evaluate potential lawsuits, we will reorder the five strategies and consider first the assignment-type restraints upon the child. After all five have been viewed separately we will consider their use in combination, as a sixth alternative.

If I Cannot Receive What I Deserve in My District, I Should Not Have to Go to School. Here the constitutional question arises by way of defense to the application of the compulsory attendance law to the child or his parents. The child merely stays away from school and lets the state come after him. The parallel intradistrict case, except for its racial overtones, is In Re Skipwith,[6] a 1958 decision in a trial court in New York. In a child neglect action parents successfully defended by showing that teaching and other services in the child's school were inferior to the other schools of New York City.

The simplicity of the strategy is attractive. There are, however, risks that the state will not prosecute, or that it will moot the matter after the defense is offered. To force the state to meet the issue might require escalation to the level of boycott, possibly jeopardizing the constitutional defense for the organizers and risking political support for the reforms that are the real issue. Nobody, after all, really wants the children out of school. On the other hand, as a test case, this device may produce an alliance of the truant and the authorities rather than a clash. The school board, after all, would also like to increase the district school budget. A single chosen child, absent for one day, could provide the basis for the test in a manner reminiscent of the litigation testing the Connecticut birth control statutes.[7] The court might be concerned about the adequacy of representation for the state's interest,[8] but there is nothing to bar the entry of the state as a proper party.

6. 180 N.Y.S.2d 852 (1958).
7. Griswold v. Connecticut, 381 U.S. 479 (1965).
8. United States v. Johnson, 319 U.S. 302 (1943), expresses the general rule against collusive litigation.

The approach has substantive weaknesses. The court may well regard the relationships between truancy and equality as too attenuated to establish a constitutional defense. There is an incongruity in seeking equality of education by claiming a right to none at all — a weakness that could be expressed judicially in terms of an estoppel or lack of standing, at least when other remedies are available.

The legislature's probable response is also a matter of concern for both the children and the court. The legislature in theory could moot the specific case by abolishing compulsory education, though this is almost inconceivable before judgment and only slightly less after; in any case, it would merely postpone more basic legislative consideration. The constitutional argument does not depend on compulsion, and another lawsuit should produce the desired result. However, the possibility of such temporary legislative frustration shows how the truancy approach is directed at a target which is not the crux of the discrimination. It could thus cloud the issue and sap whatever appeal the case otherwise might have had for the court. The judges will be keenly aware of what a short handle they have on the legislative process in this case in which the only order can be to let the defendant go.

If I Cannot Have What I Deserve in My District I Should Be Able to Go to Another District. Here the child is plaintiff. He seeks free admission to a public school in a neighboring richer district, is refused, and seeks a judicial order requiring admission. By way of answer the defendant school and district set up the present attendance rules; the plaintiff raises the constitutional question in reply.[9] An exhaustion of remedies

9. A similar approach was taken in many of the historic racial segregation cases: see, e.g., Sweatt v. Painter, 339 U.S. 629 (1950); Missouri *ex rel.* Gaines v. Canada, 305 U.S. 337 (1938).

might be an intervening requirement where relief of the sort requested could be sought administratively.[10]

There are obvious pitfalls. If plaintiff attends in his own district in the meantime does he lose standing? If he doesn't is he truant? Will the rich district moot the case by admitting him, thus ending the case and forcing plaintiff to travel long distances to a school he really didn't want to attend? Does this mean that large numbers of plaintiffs will be necessary to discourage mooting? Unlike the truancy test case, this one will not elicit cooperation from the defendant district whose present and ultimate interests both are adverse. Further, there is doubt whether this confrontation involves the proper defendants for the broad purpose of the plaintiff. The rich district may admit the plaintiff under court order, but it has no power to change the whole system by itself. Very likely the district would implead the state and its appropriate officers; but, as we shall see, there may be problems here, too, about the power of such individuals to effect the necessary change.

Would the legislature respond to an adverse judgment by abolishing district attendance lines but retaining fiscal discrimination? This is unlikely, as no coherent result could be obtained except under a statewide plan. Such a plan, of course, in itself would end the discrimination unless the state chose to discriminate directly and explicitly by spending more state resources in rich areas of the state — an unlikely and in any event short-lived expedient. If the legislature does not respond at all, the result could be a ponderous drift toward equality. If numbers of children transferred from poor to rich districts, the districts would tend to draw together in educational wealth. At some point the formerly rich districts would become "sending" schools; worse, since districts are "rich" or "poor" only in

10. Few state systems, however, provide a realistic avenue of relief. See, e.g., the system at issue in McNeese v. Board of Education, 373 U.S. 668 (1963).

relation to each other, a district would be a "sending" district for some districts and a "receiving" district for others. The administration of all this would be unimaginably confusing and involve a multiplicity of litigation. Again, concentration on one element — here geographical assignment — gives the remedy a skewed and absurd appearance and makes it one that a judge would hesitate to use unless he had some confidence in a quick and healthy legislative reprise.

If I Cannot Secure What I Deserve in My District, I Should Be Given as Much Money to Spend on Education Elsewhere as Is Spent Per Pupil in Another District. Here the plaintiff child is suing for what might be thought of loosely as damages or compensation for the taking of property without due process. He says: my district is spending X dollars on me when, in a fair system, I would deserve Y dollars (determining Y is difficult and very important; the easiest method is by comparison to some richer district, Q). The Y dollars awarded by the court would be spent by plaintiff on education in either public or private school.

This has attractions: it does not depend on any false assertion about not wanting to attend school and, if the "damages" can be fixed, it is simple. Its allure fades when we think of the effect of large numbers of children using it. First, when sufficient numbers of children have left a poor district, that district becomes "rich" — indeed, each departure reduces the measure of injury to those remaining. Second, unlike the previous remedy, although there is no problem of making the receiving district poor (since it would receive the child's judicially determined stipend), one wonders where all the schools would come from to serve those who leave one district's schools for those of another or for private schools. Third, would not such a system of relief cause private school children in poor districts to enroll in public school simply for the purpose of qualifying for their stipends and then transferring back to private school? Finally, could the parent supplement the stipend, and if so would the court not be supporting the very wealth discrimination it hoped to end? Could such supplementation be judicially forbidden?

There is also a problem regarding the proper defendant. It is not the child's own district, but who is it — the tax collector for a rich district? He may be collecting too much, but whence arises his duty to pay what he collects to this particular child? [11] Clearly, the defendant — or one of them — must be a statewide body or official. Could he be reached under a state claims act, or is there some hope under the Civil Rights Act of 1871? [12] In what sense is this "damage" if the child is asserting a right to *future* behavior by the state? [13] And even if it can be treated as such, wouldn't its measure be Y minus X, not simply Y? But what good will the mere difference do the child — does he go to school in his own district and hire Y dollars worth of tutoring? Victory in such a suit would have the advantage of driving the legislature into an immediate panic; but it is doubtful that such relief could be won, and it seems a questionable incentive to sensible and measured reform.

I Deserve in My District at Least What Jones Receives in His. The powers and limitations of the districts now swing into focus. The plaintiff (child and/or his district) asserts directly a right to share in the total public educational spending in the state, unaffected by wealth differences in the districts. His demand is for more money for his district; in making it, of

11. If the action were a class action, the measure and distribution of damages would be a forbidding task.

12. 42 U.S.C. § 1983 (1964), which, however, is confined in its reach to offending individuals: Monroe v. Pape, 365 U.S. 167 (1961). Thus any hope to use state tax funds for damages might depend upon a theory of "taking" under the Fourteenth Amendment.

13. Perhaps any child above the first grade could allege the wrong with respect to the preceding year.

course, he compares the district's wealth and effort with that of
richer districts. This approach has the advantage of direct and
complete relevance to the central problem. It keeps the child
going to school and to his own school. Its spirit is one of raising
the level of education, and it is not immediately and necessarily
disruptive of rich districts, though its success will probably
affect most districts eventually.

Suppose the legislature does nothing to arrest the discrimination; how will the court go about effecting the necessary
changes? Can it raise money? The *Prince Edward County* decision recognized the judicial power to "require the Supervisors
to exercise the power that is theirs to levy taxes to raise funds
adequate to reopen, operate, and maintain . . . a public
school system . . . like that operated in other counties in
Virginia. . . ." [14] The state capitulated, and it proved unnecessary to attempt that judicial rope trick; we are left with a
precedent that has never been applied. It is not easy to imagine
just how it could be applied in our case: what level of tax in
what form upon whom for which purpose shall the court decree? If the court were to permit the richest district to continue to spend at current levels, all the districts taxing at the
rate levied in that district would have to be elevated to match
it. The economic consequences of such a change in some states
would be very significant. If the decree were pegged to any
other district but the richest, the court would have to restrain
the spending in all districts richer than the level chosen, and
to that extent it would depress the quality of education. The
judge-levied tax is not a promising prospect for these and many
other reasons.

Note that the existence of an equalization fund is no answer. By definition a foundation plan fund is inadequate to
equalize, and its present allocation is often as near to a fair

14. Griffin v. Prince Edward County School Board, 377 U.S. 218, 233
(1964).

distribution of that exiguous sum as any court could manage. The court might make some headway with the impounding and reallocation of the flat grant fund, but this is no final solution — and what if the legislature abolishes both funds in favor of purely local financing?

In this form of litigation the proper defendant is again difficult to identify. All the relief sought is beyond the power of any agent of the state operating under the existing state law. The real target is the legislature in all these cases but even more directly here. Perhaps the legislature should be named defendant as it was in the *Colorado Assembly* case.[15] The problem is that in reapportionment there was, at least in theory, a *duty* of the legislature to act; here there seems no duty, for public education is concededly not a right. Yet there is at least this right, that public education be either validly structured or abolished.[16] Seemingly the state legislature has a duty to do one or the other which would render it the proper defendant. Even if such a duty exists, however, the inclusion of the legislature as a party is awkward and undesirable unless it is clearly necessary.

District Q Students Deserve No More than What I Have. Instead of using the court to permit the poor district to catch up to the rich districts, the plaintiff can pull the whole system down around his ears by blocking access of the rich to their superadequate tax base. The court would be asked to enjoin the operation of any part of the state system exploiting a wealth advantage over the plaintiff's district. State officials would be enjoined from the distribution of flat grants and equalization for relatively rich districts, and the richer districts would be

15. Lucas v. Forty-fourth General Assembly, 377 U.S. 713 (1964).

16. The thought is reminiscent of the prescription of Brown v. Board of Education, 347 U.S. 483 (1954), which passed no judgment upon the right to an education, but only upon the right to its dispensation without racial segregation.

prevented from spending any more per child than their tax rate would raise in the plaintiff's district. There are clear emotional objections to this dog-in-the-manger approach, but it is vastly more manageable than the others from the judge's point of view. For one thing, it need raise no money. In fact, surpluses would accumulate from unspent state and local funds that could be impounded by the court; these might actually be distributed to poorer districts in a judicially created power equalizing scheme using the average district as key in a purely redistributive manner.[17] (If this worked at all, however, it would soon cease to work if the state and local units stopped collecting the taxes.) Another advantage is its point-blank aim at the rich districts, those politically least sympathetic to equality; at the same time, it would leave schools in poorer districts unaffected except as beneficiaries. Self-interest would require the rich districts to cast about for those judicially acceptable solutions that involve the least surrender of local control. What they probably could not tolerate is inadequate or closed public schools.

There is a possible question of standing. The dog-in-the-manger plaintiff gets no immediate tangible advantage from victory; what he gets is fair competition. The suit resembles that of the businessman who asks that a subsidy be denied his competitors. There is some ancient precedent that the plaintiff in such a case lacks standing.[18]

17. This would seem to offer a more feasible field of operation for the judicial tax-raising suggestion of Griffin v. Prince Edward County School Board, 377 U.S. 218 (1964).

18. See Tennessee Electric Power Co. v. Tennessee Valley Authority, 306 U.S. 118 (1939). The cases are collected and considered in Norwalk CORE v. Norwalk Redevelopment Agency, 395 F.2d 920, 935–936 (1968). The T.V.A. case, however, is at least moribund and probably irrelevant. Allied Stores v. Bowers, 358 U.S. 522 (1959), recognized the standing of a taxpayer to challenge the exemptions of others similarly situated, even though the exemption would not affect the plaintiff's own tax.

An Eclectic Approach. The disadvantages of these action-oriented tactics can be diminished without losing any advantages. What the child really seeks is a fair hearing on the merits of the constitutional issue, plus a declaration of principle, and the broadest possible freedom for the judge to coax and impel the legislature to a relevant response. On the whole, the approach that will most often serve these needs best is an action for a declaratory judgment naming as defendants state and county officials — and perhaps district boards and superintendents — who have the duty and power to collect the tax or spend for public education. Such a forum can produce a judgment upon the constitutionality of the whole package of laws.[19]

Furthermore, having declared the system invalid, no immediate action would be required of the court. It could, as in *Brown*,[20] wait a period to consider the remedy or await legislative reprise; this would be especially appropriate in a case where an intervening legislative session could address the question of

19. 28 U.S.C.A. § 2201 (1964) provides: "In a case of actual controversy . . . any court of the United States . . . may declare the rights . . . of any interested party seeking such declaration, whether or not further relief is or could be sought."

20. 347 U.S. 483 (1954). The Court concluded that:

Because these are class actions, because of the wide applicability of this decision, and because of the great variety of local conditions, the formulation of decrees in these cases presents problems of considerable complexity. On reargument, the consideration of appropriate relief was necessarily subordinated to the primary question — the constitutionality of segregation in public education. We have now announced that such segregation is a denial of the equal protection of the laws. In order that we may have full assistance of the parties in formulating decrees, the cases will be restored to the docket, and the parties are requested to present further argument . . . (347 U.S. at 495).

The court then specified questions concerning the appropriate relief that it wished to have argued. The outcome is reported in the second *Brown* case, 349 U.S. 294, 301 (1955) which adopted the gradualism of "all deliberate speed." For criticism of that approach, see Louis Lusky, "Racial Discrimination and the Federal Law: A Problem in Nullification," *Columbia Law Review*, 63:1163 (1963).

the proper state response. All the political forces could participate in the remodeling of the state scheme while the court retained jurisdiction and awaited local developments. If the state
did not respond in an acceptable fashion, the court could
proceed by stages on motion of individual plaintiffs to excuse
students from the duty of attendance, order admission in other
districts, possibly award money compensation, begin to im-
pound and then to redistribute equalization and flat funds, and
then tie up the money of the richer districts. Before the court
would shut down the entire system, use its contempt power, or
raise taxes, it could even take a leaf from the book of reapportionment by hiring the computer expert who would assist the
court in redrafting school districts to produce a uniform wealth
base for each.[21]

Existing Litigation and the *McInnis* Case

The original action involving the problem under examination
filed in the state courts of Michigan by individual children who
are residents of Detroit and by the Detroit school board [22]
represents questionable strategy. The first difficulty is in the
choice of plaintiff. Not only is Detroit's tax effort mediocre, but
the district is not poor by the test of per-pupil assessed valua-

---

21. J. B. Weaver and S. W. Hess, "A Procedure for Nonpartisan Districting: Development of Computer Techniques," Yale Law Journal, 73:288 (1963).

Even if the court did nothing but pronounce principle, the consequences
ultimately could be significant. One need not be a Jules Verne to imagine a
future Congress addressing itself to the protection of such rights under sec. 5
of the Fourteenth Amendment. Concerning this "vast untapped reservoir"
see Archibald Cox, "Constitutional Adjudication and the Promotion of Human
Rights" (foreword to "The Supreme Court 1965 Term"), Harvard Law
Review, 80:91, 99 (1966). Cf. the use of the analogous Congressional powers to
enforce the Thirteenth Amendment: Jones v. Alfred H. Mayer Co., 392 U.S.
409 (1968).

22. Board of Education v. Michigan, General Civil No. 103342. (Cir. Ct.,
Wayne County, Mich., filed Feb. 2, 1968.)

tion.[23] The plaintiffs have adopted a standard of state responsibility keyed to characteristics of children rather than of the legislative system. That is, the plaintiffs assert that they need more education than the average child and that such need is the constitutional criterion of equality. Our objections to this have been specified.

The Detroit suit also seeks a somewhat peculiar remedy. It first asks that legislation establishing the state equalization fund be declared void and its administration be enjoined; it suggests that the legislature be given time thereafter to reapportion the state contribution and that, if it fails to do so or do so properly, the court undertake the apportioning itself. Presumably, if the legislature no longer appropriates the state contribution, the plaintiffs will be satisfied with local taxation as the support of public education. This strategy may involve a prediction that such a result is impossible because intolerable. The prospect for the suit in its original form is not promising — at least, we hope not.

In the stampede to the courts in 1968, the Detroit complaint was taken as the original model for most of the other suits, including the ill-fated *McInnis* case, which involved plaintiffs from Chicago and several Cook County suburbs.[24] The choice of Chicago residents as plaintiffs was unfortunate, again be-

23. Its 1967 state equalized valuation divided by "resident" membership ($16,244) slightly exceeded the median for Wayne County ($14,622) and for the whole state ($14,526). Neighboring districts in Wayne County range from $5,252 to $383,940. The poorest district levied an education tax rate nearly the highest in the state and nearly half again the Detroit rate. J. W. Anderson, "Poverty Stalks A Neighborhood," *Washington Post*, Dec. 24, 1967, p. 81. Of course the plaintiffs could emphasize that poverty is relative and that the proper comparison is with the richest district.

24. McInnis v. Shapiro, 293 F. Supp. 327 (N.D. Ill. 1968), aff'd mem. sub nom., McInnis v. Ogilvie, 394 U.S. 322 (1969); Burruss v. Wilkerson, General Civil No. 68–C–13–H (W.D. Va., complaint dismissed May 27, 1969); Rodrigues v. San Antonio Independent School District, General Civil No. 68–175–SA (W.D. Tex., filed July 30, 1968).

cause the district is about average in assessed valuation per
pupil.[25] Other plaintiffs from poorer districts were included, but
the litigation had from the beginning the aura of an effort to
achieve compensatory education for the inner city through litigation. This impression was amplified by the emphasis upon
"needs" in the complaint and by the failure to articulate any
clear standard.[26]

The defendants included the governor, state auditor, state
treasurer, and state superintendent of public instruction. The
complaint challenged the whole structure of Illinois school
finance, not just the equalization fund, and sought a declaratory
judgment finding the package as a whole invalid. As remedy
it prayed an injunction against enforcement of the financing
statutes and the submission of a plan by the defendants. The
use of a plan has played an important role in the racial desegregation of schools;[27] the court retains jurisdiction but places the
burden of selecting alternatives upon the state authorities. The
parallel, however, is imperfect. School boards have the general
power to adopt plans for assignment of their students; in desegregation cases the court has merely to free that power from
unconstitutional fetters in order to let it operate. In the school
finance case none of the Illinois officers named had power in
any sense to redesign the distribution of state money, whether

25. Office of the Superintendent of Public Instruction, Division of Finance
and Statistics, *1965 Assessed Valuations and 1966 Tax Rates in Descending
Order of Illinois Public Schools,* Circular Series A, no. 198, 1967.

26. The argument for "compensatory education for disadvantaged children"
was dropped in the jurisdictional statement before the Supreme Court. As an
alternative standard for judgment, however, the appellants offered nothing
more specific than the following language from Williams v. Rhodes, 393 U.S.
23, 30 (1968): "In determining whether or not a state law violates the Equal
Protection Clause, we must consider the facts and circumstances behind the
law, the interests which the State claims to be protecting, and interests of
those who are disadvantaged by the classification."

27. The use of plans is rooted in the holding in Brown v. Board of Education, 349 U.S. 294, 299 (1955), that the local authority has primary responsibility for solving the problem. See J. R. Dunn, "Title VI, the Guidelines and
School Desegregation in the South," *Virginia Law Review,* 53:42 (1967).

in regard to amount, proportion, or beneficiaries. Only the legislature can offer a "plan" which is anything like the guarantee required by the court. It is true that, in reapportionment cases, special commissions including state legislators from the two dominant parties were permitted to work out plans more or less under the court's eye, even though it always lay with the legislature as a whole to reject them.[28] But in most situations the constitutional principle (one man, one vote) to be satisfied by the plan was very narrow, and only two fundamentally partisan interests were at stake; any plan coming from a committee fairly representative of both parties would generally be acceptable to the legislature. In school finance cases no plan from a few bureaucrats, however highly placed, could in any sense substitute for the judgment of the legislature. What is necessary is not a plan but a statute. It is also unclear what the Illinois plaintiffs expected would happen in the interim before the plan. Taken literally, their prayer to the court required that the schools be closed.[29] It could have been safely predicted that they would not be closed, even if on appeal the Supreme Court had agreed with one of plaintiffs' meanings of the substance of the right.

The two California suits depart basically from the Detroit model.[30] Each complaint makes plain the central objection to the determination of quality by wealth, and each involves plain-

28. See, e.g., In Re Apportionment of State Legislature, 373 Mich. 247, 128 N.W.2d 721 (1964). See generally Comment, "Reapportionment and the Problem of Remedy," *U.C.L.A. Law Review*, 13:1345 (1966).

29. Amended complaint at 2–3, 13–14, McInnis v. Shapiro, 293 F. Supp. 327 (N.D. Ill. 1968), aff'd mem. sub nom. McInnis v. Ogilvie, 394 U.S. 322 (1969).

30. Serrano v. Priest, General Civil No. 93854 (Super. Ct., Los Angeles County, Calif., dismissed Jan. 8, 1969); Silva v. Atascadero Unified School District, General Civil No. 595954 (Super. Ct., San Francisco County, Calif., filed Sept. 26, 1968). The same approach is adopted in Guerra v. Smith, General Civil No. A–69–CA–9 (U.S.D.C. W.D. Tex., filed Jan. 28, 1969). The Guerra complaint adds the unique request for judicial creation of a metropolitan authority responsible for schools.

tiffs from districts with high tax rates and low wealth. The complaint in Serrano v. Priest in particular details the contrast between the wealth and the tax rates of the plaintiffs' districts and those of the wealthier districts of the state. Each, however, from the point of view taken here, suffers from the invocation of a constitutional standard of individual need and an allegation of race discrimination.

The future of these cases in the light of the McInnis decision is not easy to predict. Unless amended, those complaints which, like McInnis, fail to pull the issue of wealth discrimination into clarity can expect short shrift. In any event, the cases — with the possible exception of those moving toward the California Supreme Court[31] — are unlikely to be given much attention by any court below the Supreme Court of the United States. We have struggled here to suggest a proper approach to that court. If we are correct, this much at least seems clear: the court will insist upon a detailed understanding of how the system of any state discriminates against poor districts, and it will not be interested in vague exhortations to reform education. This may well suggest the abandonment of existing litigation and a fresh start featuring plaintiffs from districts with the lowest wealth and the highest tax rates, asserting the single principle that wealth shall not determine quality.

JUDICIAL STIMULUS AND STATE RESPONSE

Even assuming eventual success before the court, the variety of judicial prods, clubs, and carrots does not guarantee victory. They have in fact failed in the fourteen years since Brown to ameliorate significantly the effects of segregation.[32] On the

31. For a sense of the possibilities in California, see Department of Mental Hygiene v. Kirchner, 60 Cal.2d 716, 388 P.2d 720 (1964).

32. U.S. Commission on Civil Rights, Racial Isolation in the Public Schools (Washington, D.C., 1967), pp. 84–89; see Hobson v. Hansen, 269 F. Supp. 401 (D.D.C. 1967).

other hand, they have succeeded with incredible ease and dispatch in reapportioning legislatures.[33] Full explanation of the different results exceeds our purpose, but three points of comparison and difference between these two cases, and between each of them and the school finance case, are relevant for predicting response to a judicial holding along the lines of Proposition 1.

The difference in intelligibility of standards is surely one factor. Once the superstructure of explicit official segregation is removed, de jure racial segregation becomes so immanent and elusive that its existence for purposes of judicial action is problematical. Description of the beast may be possible but requires extraordinary elaborations of legal and social "science." The reapportionment standard requires little more than a judge who can do his sums. Proposition 1 lies somewhere between. Except for the relatively minor complications of variations in costs of educational goods and services the standard approaches in simplicity that standard employed in reapportionment. Even taking these complications into account, the problem is of a different order of magnitude from racial conundrums such as the injury to children from segregation. Legislative evasions would be relatively transparent (the "rational category" ruse is a possible exception we will discuss below) and can be described in financial terms which do not rely upon occult and popularly suspect disciplines. Having less wealth to devote to education is a considerably more concrete thing than having one's self-image eroded by segregation.

A second general point of comparison is community consensus or acquiescence. Brown evoked none in most states, and the federal courts were left to stand for years, largely without the aid of the political arms, struggling to wrest insignificant

33. See Phillip Kurland, "Equal Educational Opportunity: The Limits of Constitutional Jurisprudence Undefined," *University of Chicago Law Review*, 35:583 (1968).

victories from local guerillas. The reapportionment cases, on the other hand, liberated political forces whose self-interest was represented in the full implementation of the court's order. The groups whose self-interest will promote Proposition 1 are at least a substantial minority. The political alignment for reform will be no worse than rich district versus poor district, with the middle disinterested. The poor districts will have in their corner the full weight of the court and of every educational pressure group not representing the interests of particular districts. Evasions designed to continue the preference for rich districts can only mean prolonged judicial disruption of the entire system, to the injury of all. In this context it is reasonable to suppose that the disinterested middle also will be co-opted for the cause of reform. In short, a consensus for the court's mandate is very likely to materialize once the system is freed from its present political paralysis. In this context the resort to baroque legislative artifice to escape change is also unlikely. That resistance which is encountered from rich districts can be tempered by a careful selection of judicial remedies. Where an injunction against rich districts would seem inflammatory, the court may employ the more direct sanctions outlined above.

A third factor for comparison could be called the humiliation quotient, which is closely connected to consensus but should be thought of more in social than in political terms. We refer to the very visible and inflammatory characteristics of integration when compared, for example, with reapportionment. The Negro child who appears at the all-white school, even in the North, shows a capacity to focus Satanic energies. His visible presence alone unleashes all the aggressions of the insecure white whose self-respect is somehow put at issue. The fact may resist rational analysis, but, like Everest, it is there. No commitment to compensatory education, however great, could ever evoke the insane reactions attributable to a black face in the wrong place. Compared to this cauldron of emotions, reapportionment was a polite shuffling of impersonal counters in a parlor game of the politicians. The radical difference of reapportionment from racial integration did not spring from a difference in the significance of the stakes, but from the remoteness of this game from the interests, fears, and expectations of most men. It is doubtful whether most men today are aware that reapportionment has occurred; those who are seem indifferent.

Fiscal equity, like reapportionment, will produce emotional ripples of little consequence. No children will be bussed by it; no black and white bodies will be juxtaposed; no targets will be put into cross hairs. The movement of dollars is nearly invisible and quite incapable of stimulating anything worse than the passing malaise associated with military reverses and tax increases. It will be denounced by the residents of rich school districts and in ten years accepted as a natural phenomenon. Here and there, in those days, rich men will refer to it with pride as an example of how the states meet their social responsibilities.

Retaliation and the Rich

Suppose that the poor districts, the professionals, and their new allies from the middle districts somehow were all dominated in the legislature by the minority rich; the principal objective of the rich would be a fiscal facade seemingly neutral with respect to wealth and of sufficient rationality to pass the "classical" test of equal protection. The only promising chicane for this purpose is the employment for preference of seeming nonwealth criteria which in fact define the children of the rich.

The rich can be defined by their money, location, or culture. Use of the first as a classifying criterion to benefit their children would be invalid under any rationale of equal protection.

Use of the second we have already disposed of, with much labor. But suppose the state decided that all educational spending upon each individual child would be according to that child's "academic achievement" or "promise," and that selection of those with and without promise was by standardized tests of intelligence and achievement. It is a cultural fact that a strong positive relation exists between wealth of the family and the child's performance on such tests.[34]

As the scheme is stated here, it may seem a transparent dodge; but its vulnerability is by no means clear. Its rationality seems superficially unassailable no matter how pernicious it may be. Unlike the case of specific geographical boundaries, there is here a positive justification to be offered for the preference accorded members of this classification. It is a clear value choice of the legislature — and how can the reward and nurture of excellence be invidious?

Such a system, especially if the magnitude of the dollar differences between "gifted" and "nongifted" were significant, could present an extreme temptation to the court to abandon general standards in order to void gross inequities. One such easy but unpredictable judicial route would be ascription to the legislature of an invidious purpose: to prefer the rich. Or, the court may begin the seductive slide down the slope to a constitutional right either to uniformity in education or, worse, to expenditure according to need as the court defines that need. At that point the court would have pre-empted effectively the educational policy of the state.

One could argue that Proposition 1 itself voids this kind of relation between wealth and quality. The principle is not limited to explicit statutory connections; and in none of the "poverty" cases already decided have the rich been explicitly favored. Such an approach would be fairly moderate; there is no risk that it would forbid altogether a preference for gifted

34. See generally *Racial Isolation in the Public Schools.*

students. It would forbid it only where the de facto preference for wealth was not softened by other preferences, for example, for underachievement, blindness, retardedness. As part of a *system* of preferences, a program of special aid to the gifted would seem unassailable. But the argument against preferring gifted students is not particularly convincing in any case, because the state has such a strong, manifest, and essentially innocent interest in fostering excellence. There also is some question whether the de facto relation between wealth and "gifts" would be sufficiently close to be regarded as state action.

There would be other exits from the trap, such as Judge Wright's virtual annihilation of the existing testing devices as a basis for rational categories.[35] In support of this tour de force in *Hobson* we could offer what has already been said above about the fungibility of children, especially in the primary grades. The whole line of argument about the essential democracy of children seems especially pursuasive during what may become an antitechnological interlude in our history; indeed, these arguments may even be intrinsically correct. Still, one can be uneasy over sweeping results which depend for their rationale upon the superiority of the court's judgment, not only over the legislature, but also over most of the teaching and testing profession as well. And new tests will be devised.

We concede that all such attacks upon the rational category ruse have weaknesses, and there is little point in adding others of even greater dubiety. Although the most respectable argument is that regarding the inadequacy of tests, it is not one the Supreme Court will be anxious to adopt. A specific determination of the validity of each test would approach in magnitude the problem of judgment the court faces in ob-

35. Hobson v. Hansen, 269 F. Supp. 401 (D.D.C. 1967), and see generally Note, "Legal Implications of the Use of Standardized Ability Tests in Employment and Education," *Columbia Law Review*, 68:691, 734–743 (1968); Robert Rosenthal and Lenore Jacobson, *Pygmalion in the Classroom: Teacher Expectation and Pupils' Intellectual Development* (New York, 1968).

scenity cases without providing the redeeming qualities of diversion that obscenity surely possesses.

Perhaps we have dwelt upon what is in reality a minimal threat. It was assumed for purposes of argument that the political support for such an evasion was the "rich," but it is questionable whether even their enthusiasm could be predicted. The rich may produce more "gifted" children, but the mass of their children are not gifted unless the standards for that category are set so low as to incorporate great numbers of children of the poor. Setting the "gifted" standards low would have enormous negative consequences for the rich, probably including either vastly increased expenditures or such an unconscionable difference in expenditure between gifted and nongifted that it would surely be held constitutionally invalid (hang the rationale). In either case, large numbers of children of the wealthy would still be left out of the benefits of high expenditure and would suffer the burdens of low expenditure. It is utterly unrealistic to think that enclaves of opulence like those created by the district system as it now operates can be reproduced in effect on a nongeographical basis — the wealthy clearly live together more as rich than as smart, and the higher incidence of "intelligence" among their children is radically insufficient to serve as an organizing political principle capable of asserting its interest against opposition. And observe that opposition to such a systematic discrimination would include not only the groups hitherto noted, but also significant numbers of those wealthy who suspect that their children (or some or merely one of them) will not be among the favored. The rich may or may not believe in democracy for the mass of mankind; among their own children it could be quite another matter. These unfavored rich should qualify as the strong opponents of special educational advantages for children who would in fact be their most threatening social and economic competitors. In short: even the wealthy would not stand for preference of the wealthy.

We have assumed here that preference was offered to the *individual* "gifted" child. If instead the preference — the extra dollars — were awarded without strings to a district upon the basis of its average performance on tests or upon the number of "gifted" students it produced, matters would stand somewhat differently. The residents of rich districts might support such legislation. Of course, there would be grave doubt of its validity; such a collective preference surrenders the close link to the individual gifted student that provides the chief source of its rationality, and the system might on that ground fail the "classical" test. Furthermore, if the aim is to increase the incentive for academic achievement, the wrong means has been chosen — if it is the sole criterion of preference, at least — for it would encourage the further withdrawal of teaching talent from districts that need it most, and it would create the strongest temptation toward academic corruption in testing and/or test reporting.

The risk that such a device would be adopted seems minimal: quite aside from the fact that personal wealth and district wealth often fail to correspond, its implications would be politically intolerable. In effect, the children of every district would be lined up publicly by the state on its official merit scale to accept their portion of praise or humiliation in the form of dollars. It is not hard to imagine the reaction of the citizens of Chicago, New York, Detroit, or Los Angeles to such gross discrimination; to speak of political suicide would be unduly metaphorical. For states with large urban districts, the price of attempting such a system of preferences would be Armageddon. In more rural states, and especially in the South, the system would seem politically unattractive for the additional reason that wealth is more evenly distributed. The "rich" districts would have less advantage to gain, even if it were adopted.[36]

One should not conclude that preference for the gifted — the individually gifted — is not viable politically or judicially. The only point here is that such a policy is most easily defended as part of a balanced system of preferences. It may be ironic to prefer both superiority and inferiority, but the very sanity of the system lies in that incongruous balance in which society stimulates the excellent, cradles the unfortunate, and somehow in the process humanizes itself. There is room in a wealth-free system for as much "preference" as a state could wish, including special concern for the blind, deaf, retarded, and disadvantaged, plus all the categories of gifted from the eclectic genius to the one-talent specialist. Nor does anything in the Constitution bar experimentation, even where it means extra money for the students involved and less for others. It is hard, indeed, to think of any program or structure freely chosen by a disinterested educational planner that would offend the minimal standard we have proposed, because there is simply no sound educational reason for favoring the child according to the wealth of his parents or neighbors.

If the system is truly wealth-free, will the wealthy choose to retaliate by defecting to private education? We have argued

36. Here, as elsewhere, the available statistics are of limited assistance. National data is often reported only for governmental units, and not all school districts are "governments." This is true of the U.S. Bureau of the Census, *Statistical Abstract of the United States: 1968*, 89th ed. (Washington, D.C., U.S. Government Printing Office, 1968). However the extent to which school districts within a state differ in expenditures under existing systems is probably a fair predictor of the political strength in that state for continuing discrimination. In this respect the Southern states show a rather consistent pattern of smaller differentials than the rest of the country: "Many of these States are typical of the States in which the amount expended by the low-expenditure classroom units is not significantly lower than would be required to support the lower half of the classrooms at the State median expenditure level." F. W. Harrison and E. P. McLoone, *Profiles in School Support: A Decennial Overview* (Washington, D.C., 1965), p. 95.

that the answer to this depends a good deal upon the character of the system that emerges from the state legislative process and that, if they do leave, it will be principally because the legislature has decided upon inferior public education. It should be well within the power of the nonrich majority and the professionals to prevent such a decision. Further, it is possible to conclude that the response of the rich is irrelevant — that they already have defected. The residential clustering of the rich and the existing financing structure give to the suburban school system many of the qualities of a private school. If the wealthy should abandon such "public" schools in favor of private education, perhaps nothing will have been lost. Little political support for a high level of state subvention will have been jeopardized in such areas because little ever existed.

Clearly, the range and variety of legislative response in fifty states to the judicial establishment of Proposition 1 is unpredictable. That this is so is one of the chief strengths of the constitutional system proposed; the invalidation of wealth as a determinant of quality would operate, not to bind the states, but to liberate them from the iron law of privilege.

What can be foreseen is that battle lines in each state will be drawn sharply between local and central control of the levels of spending. Once Proposition 1 is established this division should no longer follow the old lines of self-interest, but should represent disinterested differences in philosophy of government. And such differences between the two camps will be trivial in comparison to the differences of both from the private school enthusiasts who may seek forms of family power equalizing.

Considering the multitude of potential compromises among these three basic styles, it is clear that the Supreme Court has the capacity to touch off an explosion of creativity in the structure of education. It is an opportunity that in importance can be compared only to the first flowering of public education in the nineteenth century. As then, our society is faced with a crisis of division. The potential factions are many and the lines of cleavage complex; in the decent education of children may lie the common adhesive.

Appendixes · Bibliography · Index

Appendix A · The State-nation Analogy to the District-state Picture

The variation among the states themselves mirrors the pattern of district variation within the states. One of the implications of this is that large-scale federal aid to education is needed if we are to achieve full national equalization. This, of course, is not our major concern, but national analysis can be helpful because it suggests by analogy what is happening within given states.

Among the states, as within the states, variation in expenditure per pupil is a product of the state's (1) task, the amount of educating to be done; (2) gross ability, the total public wealth available in dollars; and (3) effort, the interest and willingness of the people to tax themselves for schools (F. W. Harrison and E. P. McLoone, *Profiles in School Support: A Decennial Overview* [Washington: Government Printing Office, 1965], p. 96).

Task can be cast in terms of the number of classroom units that must be served; such units not only count pupils but also adjust for a variety of factors so as to derive a comparable measure of the educational burden faced in a great diversity of settings. The notion of *relative* task (which allows comparison between populous California and sparsely inhabited Wyoming, for example) can be measured by the number of classroom units to be served for every 1,000 in population. In general, a lower relative task is found where there are "lower birth rates, more private school attendance, restricted coverage of school attendance laws, more satisfactory attendance areas, and dense population" (Harrison and McLoone, p. 100). The national average is 7.73 classroom units per 1,000 population (as a guide, one can expect something like one unit for every 25 pupils). Here are the national extremes (in terms of units of 1,000 population):

Heavy		Light	
South Dakota	12.03	Rhode Island	5.81
North Dakota	11.17	New York	6.19
Oklahoma	10.66	Illinois	6.41

Another way of looking at relative task is simply in terms of the number of pupils in daily attendance per 1,000 population. The national average is 181; the national extremes follow.

Heavy		Light	
Utah	231	Rhode Island	135
Wyoming	226	New York	147
West Virginia	225	Illinois	149

It is evident from these task figures that a large variation exists in educational task to be accomplished. That is, having controlled for population differences among relevant units (here the states), one finds that public education systems still have highly different burdens.

Ability, as previously defined, can be measured by the property tax base (gross assessed valuation) or in other ways, for example, by total personal income. Ability alone is not directly helpful. Ability per educational task unit is helpful and is what we call

wealth throughout the book. Thus wealth can be measured by assessed valuation per classroom unit or, for example, by personal
income per classroom unit. It is a measure that serves as an ideal
comparative device — it tells us which education providers are rich
and which are poor. The great national variation in wealth is clear
below, where the national extremes are compared in terms of the
percentage that local wealth (state valuation per classroom unit) is
of national median wealth. With the national median 1.00, the
relation of median personal income per classroom unit to the national standard can be expressed:

High		Low	
New York	1.58	Mississippi	.44
Illinois	1.44	South Dakota	.45
Delaware	1.44	Arkansas	.49

With the national median again at 1.00, the same relation for
median property values can be expressed:

High		Low	
Illinois	1.44	Mississippi	.42
Nevada	1.43	South Carolina	.43
Texas	1.33	Alabama	.51

Two facts are now clear. The more important is the great variation — better than a 3-1 relationship — between richest and poorest states; the same or much worse can be expected regarding districts within a state. In addition, the difference in the two sets of
figures suggest that property valuation may not be a perfect indi-
cator of income, which is a matter discussed elsewhere in the
book.

Finally, effort is measurable by the percentage that funds spent
on education are of some measure of wealth. In terms of spending
as a percent of personal income, the national figure in 1959–60
was 2.79 percent. Compared here are the efforts, in terms of the percentage that current educational expenditure is of personal income,
of the high and low wealth states mentioned above.

Selected States

South Dakota	4.50
Mississippi	3.25
South Carolina	2.93
Alabama	2.83
Arkansas	2.80
Nevada	2.83
New York	2.77
Texas	2.69
Illinois	2.31
Delaware	2.26

Clearly, the poorer states, just like the poorer districts, are forced to make a greater effort than their sister states.

Appendix B · Cubberley's Search for a
Unit to Measure
Educational Task

In his central work, *School Funds and Their Apportionment* (New York: Columbia Teachers College, 1905, pp. 88–198), E. P. Cubberley sets out and evaluates the then existing task units chosen by the states as the criteria for apportioning and distributing money set aside for education. According to Cubberley, the task units in ascending order of propriety were:

(1) *Apportionment by Taxes Paid.* This grant-in-aid type of distribution actually exacerbates existing evils, giving more state funds to those localities able to raise more local taxes. It is also unrelated to task and claims merit only as the purest form of a "stimulation of local expenditures" policy of state aid. It is a uniform matching grant plan, in which the state considers neither what job must locally be done nor how much help is needed in doing it.

(2) *Apportionment by Total Property Wealth.* According to Cubberley, this method is better than the first. Taxes need not actually be raised by the poor districts in order for them to receive

state help. However, not only is there no incentive to maintain a good school under this method, but the criterion again is not related to the amount of educating to be done in the district.

(3) *Apportionment by Total Population.* This approach is a beginning, perhaps, but only the roughest (Cubberley found that the percentage of students to total population ranged from 11 to 28).

(4) *Apportionment by School Census.* In Cubberley's day, this was the most common method of distributing educational funds (38 states). The term "school census" denotes all children of compulsory school age in the district. Cubberley found several weaknesses in the approach:

(a) The percentage of children in actual attendance varied considerably among schools with an equal census. Cubberley saw that the number attending was a more appropriate guide to educational task. Under a census measure schools would get money for pupils they did not train: for example, one school could operate a kindergarten (noncompulsory) and receive no more state aid than a district with equal census having no kindergarten.

(b) Actual costs were related more to the number of teachers employed than to the number of pupils. Here for the first time is an appreciation of the importance of viewing task in terms of the dollar cost of that task.

(c) There was no incentive for the districts actually to provide facilities for all in the census or to encourage attendance; in fact, the opposite was likely to be true. Since the amount of state aid remained the same regardless of expansion of facilities, localities were encouraged to stagnate or even cut back. This is an early recognition that one must be concerned with the impact of the form of grant, that is, how it might alter behavior.

(5) *Apportionment by School Enrollment.* Enrollment, too, though a more sophisticated measure, was shown to be an imperfect measure of educational task. The relationship of first-day attendance (enrollment) to year-round attendance in school varies considerably from district to district. Cubberley further feared that schools might "pad" their enrollments in order to qualify for more aid without doing additional educational work. For the small country school that was disfavored by the school census method (since it of necessity had smaller classes yielding high teacher costs) this measure would be somewhat more favorable, as those schools traditionally

had lower enrollment to attendance ratios. Yet this is a rather backhanded way of adjusting for the problem.

(6) *Apportionment by Average Membership.* The average number of childen that the district could keep enrolled all year has also been used as the criterion for distribution. Naturally, since the artificial first-day membership is not utilized, this measure better reflects shifts in actual attendance because of dropouts (in Cubberley's day large numbers of students were likely to leave at harvest time or when the family needed money). However, this is only a better guide to what can be seen as true enrollment and is not yet tied down to the number of students actually being instructed. In Carroll County, New Hampshire, for example, Cubberley found that actual attendance in class ranged from 73 to 94 per cent of average membership.

(7) *Average Daily Attendance.* This measure finds expression in the following formula:

$$\frac{\text{total days attended by all pupils}}{\text{days school is open}}$$

It appealed to Cubberley because it is much better related to the educational task being performed than previous measures. Moreover, it appears to stimulate efforts to encourage attendance, whereas the other measures are at best indifferent. But according to empirical observation at Cubberley's time, several defects persisted:

(a) Small districts which perforce enjoyed low student-teacher ratios would be faced with relatively low attendance and hence less aid, even though their costs were as great as those of more densely populated districts.

(b) For large cities which attempted to lengthen the school term into seasons in which attendance was poor (summer, for example), the system was penal, resulting in less state aid for districts performing in a superior fashion from the standpoint of educational goals. Today's modern economic techniques could likely adjust for both these factors in a very acceptable way.

(8) *Aggregate Days Attendance.* This criterion for distributing state aid is identical to the former except that total days attended is not divided by length of the term; rather, the sum of all days attended by all students in the state is divided into the total amount

of state aid to be distributed. This yields the number of dollars per pupil per day that the state will distribute; then the aggregate days attended in each locality is multiplied by this figure to determine state aid to the district. As indicated above, under procedures in effect during Cubberley's time this was better for the localities which extended their school terms than was the average daily attendance (ADA) unit; not that they were preferred to districts with shorter terms (as their legitimate costs would mean that they spent the aid to support the longer term), but rather that the otherwise existing penalty was eliminated. Today, it is common to find both a special summer-school aid plan and a standardized regular school year; thus approaches numbered (7) and (8) are no longer meaningfully different.

(9) *Apportionment by District Basis.* Although some measure of daily attendance may well reflect task when districts are economically and socially similar, the more districts vary the more such other factors enter to distort the usefulness of this simple device as a comparative tool. In such circumstances, refined adjustments in aid formula might be desirable to account for these factors; hence the "classroom unit" concept used by the Office of Education. Of course, this begins to make clear that the whole concept of task is susceptible to a great amount of tinkering, much of it problematical. For example, does a child who elects to receive vocational education represent a greater task (in most cities more per pupil is spent in this area than in the academic course), and if so how much greater? Cubberley found that some such distinctions among districts made their costs differ and were not accounted for in the calculation of ADA. He felt they should be considered; therefore (for example — in order to crudely rationalize the extra burden of the sparsely populated districts), he suggested that perhaps some part of the state funds could be distributed on a district basis ($5,000 per district, for example).

(10) *Apportionment by Teachers Employed.* Cubberley's primary suggestion was the distribution of aid on a teachers-employed basis, as described in Chapter 1. Here was a criterion which, though it did not look directly to task, represented it in a seemingly useful way; after all, the teacher taught a class and that class was the task to be educated. It was at least a harbinger of today's "classroom unit" measure — but only part of it. Cubberley's measure recog-

nized the primary cost of education as teachers' salaries, and it reflected the then large problem of the real costs to smaller districts which had to maintain a basic faculty in spite of low attendance. But Cubberley's own warnings tell us at once to consider the impact of this criterion on behavior, as it is the kind of unit which can be altered by the district in response to the offer of aid; that is, if the state contributes to the district per teacher hired, the number of teachers hired may well increase, and more so in rich districts. In short, it is a revenue task unit. Unless such a differential response is desired, it is a dangerous thing upon which to apportion. Nonetheless, combined with the aggregate days of attendance criterion, the teachers-employed basis was thought by Cubberley to best compromise the opposing values in the distribution of state aid to education.

The real payoff in Cubberley's painstaking effort is that it so clearly demonstrates the vast complexity of weighing alternative criteria for a state aid plan and thus underscores the need for sharp and detailed analysis both of intended results and of predicted consequences. From an analysis of his proposals, it can be seen that Cubberley thought in terms of basing state aid upon the legitimate costs of education. His contribution was that of looking at the child both as a unit to be educated and one on which money is to be spent and then synthesizing these into a measure upon which relative state aid to the districts could be based.

Today, Cubberley's insights regarding cost variation tend to be given effect by more direct methods of cost accounting; as noted, aid can be distributed on the basis of "classroom units" (a district will get 1 unit for 30 regular pupils or 5 handicapped children, and so on) which are further weighted by extra cost factors like high transportation cost in sparsely settled districts. Moreover, many of Cubberley's specific concerns have been mooted by developments in education subsequent to his time.

Even so, new and subtle cost variations are continually being pointed out: for example, price level variation among districts, or the varying cost of inducing the same quality teachers to work for different districts. Thus the factor of evaluating the task remains a vital consideration today in any state-local financing formula.

Appendix C · Development of the Foundation Plan Myth

In spite of the fact that the foundation plan in operation is more holes than cheese, it has enjoyed an egalitarian reputation. Many or most states even call their state aid the "equalization" fund. As a premonitory exercise it is worth examining some of the rhetoric which may have contributed to this misbranding.

The *Report of the National Conference on the Financing of Education 1933* is a good place to begin (by the Joint Commission on the Emergency in Education, National Education Association and the Department of Superintendence, and published by Phi Delta Kappa, 1934). At the time of the report, professionals perceived two grave problems. One, of course, was the depression. The other was the fact that state school finance systems, which had failed to provide equal educational opportunity, had generally overstrained local tax sources. In response to these problems, the *Report* presented a program which apparently was accepted as a sound general approach by the leaders in the field and which is frequently cited today as the authoritative expression of professional education on the issue of equality of opportunity.

The *Report* adopts a "School Finance Charter," with various

474

planks. We will consider four, the first of which is titled "Educational Opportunity" and calls for: "Funds to provide every child and youth a complete educational opportunity from early childhood to the age at which employment is possible and socially desirable. This right to be preserved regardless of residence, race, or economic status and to constitute an inalienable claim on the resources of local, state, and national governments" (p. 9). The second plank calls for adequate revenues: "Equitable taxation. For the adequate support of all governmental activities, including schools, a stable, varied and flexible tax system, providing for a just sharing of the cost of government by all members of the community" (p. 9).

What these mean is unclear. They do not say that the state should insure that a child from a poor district can claim the *same* educational offering as one from a rich district. And the *Report* apparently does not mean that: on close reading, two later planks undercut the notion that the *child* has a claim to equality. "Community initiative. For every school district the right to offer its children an education superior to state minimum standards and to seek and develop new methods intended to improve the work of the schools" (third plank, p. 10). Thus, the districts are to be given leeway in regard to effort: if the parents make a greater effort, a better education is available to the children. The fourth plank deals with adjustment for wealth: "Equalization of educational opportunity. For every school district, sufficient financial support from the state to permit the maintenance of an acceptable state minimum program of education and to relieve the local property tax when this tax, upon which local initiative depends, is carrying an unfair share of the cost of government" (p. 10).

What is meant in practice to be achieved by these principles is not immediately evident from the surface. There is talk of equal opportunity, of state support, of equitable taxation, of a "complete educational opportunity" — ideas which seem necessarily to involve adjustments for effort and wealth and a careful watch over the actual offering. Yet the final plank, on close reading, encourages the state to establish merely a basic educational offering level (the minimum program — the foundation) guaranteed to all children, and then to subsidize districts so that all can provide this offering with the same effort. Any effort greater than that is "local initiative" and not part of the state concern. This, of course, is Strayer-Haig.

But the rhetoric consistently outstripped the program; it is not surprising that nonprofessionals were misled. Consider the eloquent pleas of the *Report* for state participation, equalization, and incentive which make the program appear such a prodigy:

> The first and most basic of the reasons arguing for the importance of state support rests in the long-recognized responsibility of the state for education. That this responsibility is undeniable is attested by constitution, statute, court decisions and custom. . . . The challenge for a more adequate and more equitable state system of school support is inherent in the very nature of the state's position. . . . Inequalities of education opportunity constitute a second compelling factor in urging the importance and necessity of state support for schools. In many states slight investigation will disclose great ranges and discrepancies in the ability of local districts to support schools. . . . Generally these inequalities of offering are enforced by an unevenness of financial ability per unit of need which can be overcome by nothing short of the equalizing auspices of the state (*Report*, p. 21).

According to the drafters, the logic of these principles "calls upon the state to equalize educational opportunity"; but when the other shoe dropped, the *Report* had limited such equality "to a reasonably satisfactory minimum" (p. 23). The rationale for this schizophrenia is the apparent dilemma posed by equality and subsidiarity: "Local self-government or local initiative has been so deeply imbedded in American governmental policy that it is an important force to be reckoned with in support of public education. American citizens are jealous of their rights, privileges, and opportunities in so far as local initiative is concerned. It is the American way of conducting public affairs for the common good" (p. 33).

Three years later, a publication of the National League of Women Voters entitled *School Finance and School Districts* (by K. A. Frederic; New York, 1936), reinforced the same non sequitur: equality of educational opportunity is the goal and the foundation program is, therefore, the solution:

> Long years of public discussion have brought agreement that free public education is essential to the well-being of a democ-

racy, that government has a right to tax the wealth of all to provide schools, that the state should offer all children equal educational opportunities, and that it can compel attendance for the period fixed by law. . . . The carrying out of these principles rests in large measure with local governments, but today it is recognized that larger governmental units with broader financial powers must equalize educational opportunity" (p. 1).

As usual, the caveat is added, "Equalization leaves room for local initiative where the community raises more than the minimum amount" (p. 27).

Ten years later, at the close of World War II, it was evident that the children of this country were receiving dramatically varied educational offerings. New sounds of alarm were heard:

America has long been regarded as the land of opportunity — of equal opportunity. . . . It is a shocking fact that millions are still denied the equal opportunity that is the inalienable right of American citizens. . . . America today is a land of enormous inequalities in educational opportunity. . . . The principal reason why the public schools of America do not provide equal educational opportunity is that their financing is shockingly uneven (J. Norton and E. Lawler, *Unfinished Business in American Education* [American Council on Education, 1946], pp. 2–4).

Rather than fully equalizing the offerings, however, the call was to bring all those districts which were then below the national median in educational offering up to that median. That doing so would leave these districts below "average" seemed to be overlooked.

In view of the widely adopted foundation program concept, the great range of offerings should have been a clue that, when the minimum state supported offering is low, extra local initiative is the rule. Eventually, the Education Policies Commission of the National Education Association and the American Association of School Administrators realized that something was drastically wrong. In 1962 it published *Education and the Disadvantaged American* (see, generally, pp. 11–36), which repeated all the equality slogans but also injected a new tone into the debate with an emphasis upon the culturally disadvantaged. The emphasis was expressed in new proposals for reform:

> Improvements would entail in most places, a considerable increase in per-pupil expenditures. But pupils with an unfair share of obstacles must be given a fair chance to overcome them. . . . Local and state governments must do their best to help the schools meet the higher expenditures. But the communities, rural or urban, most directly affected by the problem (having many culturally disadvantaged students) often encounter the most difficulty in financing a solution" (p. 36).

The Commission's answer, of course: federal aid. Leaning heavily on the needs for the disadvantaged, it abandons hope for state solutions. The principle seems to be that, since state systems are inadequate as historically structured, federal aid is necessarily and immediately implied. We find this another in a veritable jungle of non sequiturs that have dominated the field. We support federal aid for certain purposes — including compensatory education — but we are convinced that no federal program should be built upon the premise that state systems are incorrigible. A better starting point, even for federal aid, is a re-examination of state foundation programs to see whether their structure is responsible for much of the problem. If so, they may not be beyond redemption; and, there is the Constitution.

Appendix D · Relation of District-pupil Population to Offering and Effort in 119 Elementary Districts in Cook County, Illinois

In an effort to determine what effect, if any, sheer size of a district might have upon offering and effort, the following three tables were prepared, using 1964–65 data.

In Table D-1, there is only a slight tendency for the best offering (Q-1 down) to come from smaller districts and worse offerings from larger districts (Q-4 down). However, the figures may be affected somewhat by economies of scale which large districts sometimes enjoy (note that we deal here with size of district, not schools), so that the cost of education there may be less. And — which is the same thing — since we are using expenditures as a measure of good offering, large districts may be able to achieve real offering equal to

Table D-1

Cook County, Illinois, elementary districts: matrix of numbers of districts by offering and size (ADA)

| | | Offering | | | | |
		Q-1[a]	Q-2	Q-3	Q-4	Total
Size	Q-1[b]	5	9	7	9	30
	Q-2	7	8	6	10	31
	Q-3	8	6	9	5	28
	Q-4	10	6	9	5	30
	Total	30	29	31	29	

[a] Best.
[b] Largest.

those of small districts with less money. To the extent that we discover wealth or effort related to size, we should consider how that relationship affects our conclusion, above, that offering is clearly a matter of wealth and effort.

On this point, note that size was assumed to be a convenient and logical measure of the economies of scale among districts. It is by no means clear, of course, that such economies do exist in this sample of districts, or, if they do, that this yardstick effectively considers them. It is hoped that the related factors of inflation and cost of living variation, which also can make comparisons difficult, are not operating within the system here analyzed: the data is from one year only, besides which the geographic proximity of the districts certainly makes cost of living variations insignificant. Size of schools may have some minor effect, though large schools are by no means exclusive to large districts. The large school is itself merely one of the common "economies of scale," however, and we shall assume its distorting effect for, as we have seen, it can only be trivial in relation to the other factors.

Only to the extent that we find that poorer districts have bigger student populations is the economy of scale point relevant. If the economies exist, it cuts somewhat against our conclusion that poor districts really have worse offerings. (Of course, this assumes as neutral any impact on quality which might flow not from economic differences but from the size of the school population alone.) In fact, it is seen in the tables that wealthier districts do tend to be somewhat smaller (D-2). That is, of the wealthiest, only 3 are on

Table D-2

Cook County, Illinois, elementary districts: matrix of numbers of districts by wealth and size (ADA)

| | | Wealth | | | | |
		Q-1[a]	Q-2	Q-3	Q-4	Total
Size	Q-1[b]	3	10	10	7	30
	Q-2	9	5	6	11	31
	Q-3	6	5	5	12	28
	Q-4	11	9	9	1	30
	Total	29	29	30	31	

[a] Richest.
[b] Largest.

the big district list. And of the poorest districts, 7 are of the large size category and only 1 of small size, though most are in between. Thus, some minimal distortion from size might be at work.

Table D-3

Cook County, Illinois: matrix of numbers of elementary districts by effort and size

| | | Effort | | | | |
		Q-1[a]	Q-2	Q-3	Q-4	Total
Size	Q-1[b]	12	12	2	4	30
	Q-2	7	7	9	8	31
	Q-3	6	11	8	3	28
	Q-4	6	5	6	13	30
	Total	31	35[c]	25	28	

[a] Greatest.
[b] Largest.
[c] Many districts had an effort at the quartile dividing line and in this experiment were all put into Q-2.

On the other hand, what is it about size which cuts against our overall conclusions about wealth, effort, and offering? It is merely that to the extent that poorer districts have bigger student populations they can get, in terms of real offering, the same thing with fewer dollars (the measure we use here); but if that is so we should also expect that, when ranked by effort, the smaller districts would display greater effort than the larger ones. (Again, presumably because big school districts need fewer dollars to do the same job.) What we find, however, is clearly to the contrary (Table D-3). In reality, 24 of the 30 biggest districts are above average in effort and 19 of the 30 small districts are below average in effort. This relation strongly tends to discount size as of significant bearing. Although, all things being equal, size may be of importance, the magnitude of the variations in *wealth* is such that wealth overrides as the factor which correlates with offering, and the other calculations (effort having been shown not positively related to wealth) are pulled along by it.

Appendix E · Opinion of the Three-
Judge District Court in
McInnis versus Shapiro

Linda McInnis et al. versus Samuel H. Shapiro et al., 293F. Supp. 327 (N.D. Ill., 1968), affirmed per curiam without opinion 394 U.S. 322 (1969), Mr. Justice Douglas dissenting.

Before Hastings, Circuit Judge, and Decker and Marovitz, District Judges.

Decker, District Judge.

This is a suit filed by a number of high school and elementary school students attending school within four school districts of Cook County, Illinois, on behalf of themselves and all others similarly situated challenging the constitutionality of various state statutes dealing with the financing of the public school system.[1]

1. There is also a corporate plaintiff, Concerned Parents and People of the West Side, which was organized to improve the quality of educational facilities available to the citizens of an era within Chicago popularly known as "Lawndale."

Plaintiffs claim that these statutes[2] violate their fourteenth amendment rights to equal protection and due process because they permit wide variations in the expenditures per student from district to district, thereby providing some students with a good education and depriving others, who have equal or greater educational need. Plaintiffs claim to be members of this disadvantaged group.

To correct this inequitable situation, they seek a declaration that the statutes are unconstitutional and a permanent injunction forbidding further distribution of tax funds in reliance on these laws.

The defendants are state officials charged with the administration of the legislation which allegedly permits this discrimination.

A three-judge district court was convened pursuant to 28 U.S.C. §§ 2281 and 2284. Defendants then moved to dismiss the complaint (1) for lack of jurisdiction and (2) for failure to state a cause of action.

We conclude that we have jurisdiction. After examining the complaint, and studying the extensive briefs filed by the respective parties as well as the brief of the amici curiae,[3] we further conclude that no cause of action is stated for two principal reasons: (1) the Fourteenth Amendment does not require that public school expenditures be made only on the basis of pupils' educational needs,[4] and (2) the lack of judicially manageable standards makes this controversy nonjusticiable. After explaining the structure of the

2. Specifically, the students challenge the following parts of 1967 Ill.Rev.Stat. ch. 122: §§ 11-1, 11-6, 11-9, 18-1 through 18-4, 18-8 through 18-14, 20-5, 34-22 through 34-29, and 34-42 through 34-82, also questioned are ch. 122, articles 17, 19, and 32, and ch. 85 §§ 851 through 851.5d.

3. The following five organizations filed a brief in support of the complaint as amici curiae: American Jewish Congress, League of Women Voters of Illinois, South Suburban Human Relations Council, National Association of Social Workers, and Inter-Community Programs, Inc.

4. While the complaining students repeatedly emphasize the importance of pupils' "educational needs," they do not offer a definition of this nebulous concept.

Presumably, "educational need" is a conclusory term, reflecting the interaction of several factors such as the quality of teachers, the students' potential, prior education, environmental and parental upbringing, and the school's physical plant. Evaluation of these variables necessarily requires detailed research and study, with concomitant decentralization so each school and pupil may be individually evaluated. See pages 333 and 335, infra.

existing Illinois legislation, this opinion will discuss these two conclusions in detail.

I. Jurisdiction

The federal courts have jurisdiction over the subject matter of this controversy. As stated in Baker v. Carr, 369 U.S. 186, 200, 82 S.Ct. 691, 701, 7 L. Ed.2d 663 (1962):

> "Since the complaint plainly sets forth a case arising under the Constitution, the subject matter is within the federal judicial power defined in Art. III, § 2, and so within the power of Congress to assign to the jurisdiction of the District Courts." [5]

Similarly, the allegations do not present a political question because there is no potential conflict between coordinate branches of the federal government.[6] Both the equal protection and the due process clauses have long been used to scrutinize state legislative action. See, e. g., Williamson v. Lee Optical of Oklahoma, 348 U.S. 483, 488–489, 75 S.Ct. 461, 99 L.Ed. 563 (1955).[7]

II. The Financing of Illinois' Public Schools

The General Assembly has delegated authority to local school districts to raise funds by levying a tax on all property within the district. In addition, the school districts may issue bonds for constructing and repairing their buildings. Legislation limits both the maximum indebtedness and the maximum tax rate which localities may impose for educational purposes. In 1966–67, the approximately 1300 districts had roughly $840 per pupil with which to educate their students, of which about 75% came from local sources, 20% was derived from state aid, and 5% was supplied by

5. See also Bell v. Hood, 327 U.S. 678, 66 S.Ct. 773, 90 L.Ed. 939 (1946); Colegrove v. Green, 328 U.S. 549, 66 S.Ct. 1198, 90 L.Ed. 1432 (1946).

6. "[I]t is the relationship between the judiciary and the coordinate branches of the Federal Government, and not the federal judiciary's relationship to the States, which gives rise to the 'political question.' " 369 U.S. 210, 82 S.Ct. 708. See also Reynolds v. Sims, 377 U.S. 533, 84 S.Ct. 1362, 12 L.Ed.2d 506 (1964); Gomillion v. Lightfoot, 364 U.S. 339, 81 S.Ct. 125, 5 L.Ed.2d 110 (1960). But see Coleman v. Miller, 307 U.S. 433, 59 S.Ct. 972, 83 L.Ed. 1385 (1939).

7. See also Allied Stores of Ohio, Inc. v. Bowers, 358 U.S. 522, 79 S.Ct. 437, 3 L.Ed.2d 480 (1959); Brown-Forman Co. v. Commonwealth of Kentucky, 217 U.S. 563, 30 S.Ct. 578, 54 L.Ed. 883 (1910).

the federal government. Since the financial ability of the individual districts varies substantially, per pupil expenditures vary between $480 and $1,000. State statutes which permit such wide variations allegedly deny the less fortunate Illinois students of their Constitutional rights.

Article VIII, section 1 of the Illinois Constitution, S.H.A. requires the legislature to "provide a thorough and efficient system of free schools, whereby all children of this state may receive a good common school education." Accordingly, a state common school fund supplements each district's local property tax revenues, guaranteeing a foundation level of $400 per student. The common school fund has two main components: (1) a flat grant to districts for each pupil, and (2) an equalization grant awarded to each district which levies a minimum property tax rate.[8] The equalization grant is calculated on the assumption that the district only assesses the minimum rate. Total revenues from the state common school fund account for about 15% — 18% of all districts' income.

The local tax revenues per student which is necessarily generated by the preceding minimum rate[9] is added to the flat grant per pupil. If this sum is less than $400, the difference is the equalization grant. Therefore, every district levying the minimum rate is assured of at least $400 per child. On the other hand, if a locality desires to tax itself more heavily than the minimum rate, it is not penalized by having the additional revenue considered before determination of the equalization grant. Since the hypothetical calculation uses the same tax rate for all localities, the assumed revenue per child depends upon the total assessed property value in a district and the number of students. Thus, the equalization grant tends to compensate for variations in property value per pupil from one district to another.

Finally, numerous special programs, both state and federal, supply about 10% of the districts' revenues. This "categorical aid" is allocated for particular purposes such as bus transportation or assistance to handicapped and disadvantaged children. Plaintiffs do

8. Over 97% of the districts qualify for the equalization grant. The flat grant, accounting for about one-third of the state aid, is now $47 per elementary student and $54.05 per high school pupil.

9. Specifically, the qualifying rate is multiplied by the average assessed property valuation per pupil to obtain a minimum income from local taxation.

not challenge these programs, conceding that they are rationally related to the educational needs of the students.[10]

III. The Fourteenth Amendment: Equal Protection and Due Process

The underlying rationale of the complaint is that only a financing system which apportions public funds according to the educational needs of the students satisfies the Fourteenth Amendment.[11] Plaintiffs assert that the distribution of school revenues to satisfy these needs should not be limited by such arbitrary factors as variations in local property values or differing tax rates.

Clearly, there are wide variations in the amount of money available for Illinois' school districts, both on a per pupil basis and in absolute terms. Presumably, students receiving a $1000 education are better educated than those acquiring a $600 schooling.[12] While the inequalities of the existing arrangement are readily apparent, the crucial question is whether it is unconstitutional. Since nearly

10. For a more detailed description of Illinois' public school financing, see generally Task Force on Education, Education For The Future of Illinois, ch. VII (1966).

11. Although plaintiffs stress the alleged denial of equal protection, they seek relief resembling substantive due process. Surely, quality education for all is more desirable than uniform, mediocre instruction. Yet if the Constitution only commands that all children be treated equally, the latter result would satisfy the Fourteenth Amendment. Certainly, parents who cherish education are constitutionally allowed to spend more money on their children's schools, be it by private instruction or higher tax rates, than those who do not value education so highly. Thus, the students' goal is presumably a judicial pronouncement that each pupil is entitled to a minimum level of educational expenditures, which would be significantly higher than the existing $400.

12. These figures probably understate the national discrepancies. See, e. g., Levi, "The University, The Professions, and The Law—An Address," 56 Calif.L.Rev. 251, 258 (1968).

"The average current expenditures in 1965 for the East South Central states was 354 dollars per pupil in the primary and secondary public schools. The comparable figure was 732 dollars in the Middle Atlantic states. * * * These discrepancies also occur * * * between suburbs surrounding a single city. For example, the expenditure per high school pupil in a suburb to the north of Chicago is 1,283 dollars; in a suburb to the south of the city it is 723 dollars. The expenditure per elementary school pupil in a northern suburb is 919 dollars; in a southern suburb it is 421 dollars." See also National Education Association, Rankings of The States, 1966, page 51 (1966).

three-quarters of the revenue comes from local property taxes, substantially equal revenue distribution would require revamping this method of taxation, with the result that districts with greater property values per student would help support the poorer districts.

A. Social Policy

While the state common school fund tends to compensate for the variations in school districts' assessed valuation per pupil, variation in actual expenditures remains approximately 3.0 to 1, 2.6 to 1, and 1.7 to 1 for elementary, high school and unit districts respectively. Though districts with lower property valuations usually levy higher tax rates, there is a limit to the amount of money which they can raise, especially since they are limited by maximum indebtedness and tax rates. Plaintiffs argue that state statutes authorizing these wide variations in assessed value per student are irrational, thus violating the due process clause. Moreover, under the equal protection clause, the students contend that the importance of education to the welfare of individuals and the nation requires the courts to invalidate the legislation if potential, alternative statutes incorporating the desirable aspects of the present system can also achieve substantially equal per pupil expenditures.[13]

Illustrating how the school financing could be improved, plaintiffs suggest two alternatives:[14] (1) all students might receive the same dollar appropriations, or (2) the state could siphon off all money in excess of $ × per pupil which was produced by a given tax rate, in effect eliminating variations in local property values while leaving the districts free to establish their own tax rate.[15]

13. Thus, the students advocate a doctrine similar to the close scrutiny given laws which infringe First Amendment rights. See, e. g., Kevishian v. Board of Regents, 385 U.S. 589, 87 S.Ct. 675, 17 L.Ed.2d 629 (1967); N.A.A.C.P. v. Button, 371 U.S. 415, 83 S.Ct. 328, 9 L.Ed.2d 405 (1963).

14. Plaintiffs' suggestions arguably go no further than the upheavals recently created by bussing pupils and redrawing district boundaries in order to achieve racial balance. Except where localities attempted to avoid Brown v. Board of Education, 347 U.S. 483, 74 S.Ct. 686, 98 L.Ed. 873 (1954), however, these changes were accomplished legislatively rather than judicially.

15. For example, if a district only levied a 1% tax rate, it could keep only $400 per pupil, regardless of the absolute dollars produced. On the other hand, the state would also guarantee $400 per pupil to units imposing the 1%. At higher rates, such as 4%, the state would thus substantially aid districts with low valuations, deriving most of its funds from wealthy districts which produced far more than $400 per pupil by a 1% rate.

Without doubt, the educational potential of each child should be cultivated to the utmost, and the poorer school districts should have more funds with which to improve their schools. But the allocation of public revenues is a basic policy decision more appropriately handled by a legislature than a court. To illustrate, the following considerations might be relevant to a financing scheme: state-wide variations in costs and salaries, the relative efficiency of school districts, and the need for local experimentation.

As stated in Metropolitan Casualty Insurance Co. v. Brownell,[16] 294 U.S. 580, 584, 55 S.Ct. 538, 540, 79 L.Ed. 1070 (1935):

"[T]he burden of establishing the unconstitutionality of a statute rests on him who assails it * * *. A statutory discrimination will not be set aside as the denial of equal protection of the laws if any state of facts reasonably may be conceived to justify it."

And more recently, the Supreme Court declared that:

"[T]he Fourteenth Amendment permits the States a wide scope of discretion in enacting laws which affect some groups of citizens differently than others. The constitutional safeguard is offended only if the classification rests on grounds wholly irrelevant to the achievement of the State's objective. State legislatures are presumed to have acted within their constitutional power despite the fact that, in practice, their laws result in some inequality."

McGowan v. Maryland, 366 U.S. 420, 425–426, 81 S.Ct. 1101, 1105, 6 L.Ed.2d 393 (1961).[17] See also Salsburg v. Maryland, 346 U.S. 545, 552–553, 74 S.Ct. 280, 98 L.Ed. 281 (1954).[18]

16. In Metropolitan Co., the Court upheld a state regulatory statute which distinguished between domestic and foreign casualty insurance companies, finding that differences in the security and collection of claims against the two groups may have justified differential treatment.

17. Sunday laws were sustained even though First Amendment rights were involved and despite the availability of less onerous alternatives for providing a day of rest and recreation.

18. "We do not sit as a superlegislature or a censor.

*   *   *   *   *

"We find little substance to appellant's claim that distinctions based on

Tested by these standards, the existing school legislation is neither arbitrary nor does it constitute an invidious discrimination.[19] It therefore complies with the Fourteenth Amendment.

In the instant case, the General Assembly's delegation of authority to school districts appears designed to allow individual localities to determine their own tax burden according to the importance which they place upon public schools. Moreover, local citizens must select which municipal services they value most highly. While some communities might place heavy emphasis on schools, others may cherish police protection or improved roads. The state legislature's decision to allow local choice and experimentation is reasonable, especially since the common school fund assures a minimum of $400 per student.[20]

Plaintiffs stress the inequality inherent in having school funds partially determined by a pupil's place of residence, but this is an inevitable consequence of decentralization. The students also object

county areas are necessarily so unreasonable as to deprive him of the equal protection of the laws guaranteed by the Federal Constitution.

" * * * Territorial uniformity is not a constitutional requisite." 346 U.S. 550–552, 74 S.Ct. 283.

19. See also Allied Stores of Ohio v. Bowers, 358 U.S. 522, 527–528, 79 S.Ct. 437, 3 L.Ed.2d 480 (1959) (exemption of certain merchandise from state taxation upheld under the equal protection clause); Brown-Forman Co. v. Commonwealth of Kentucky, 217 U.S. 563, 573, 30 S.Ct. 578, 580, 54 L.Ed. 883 (1910): "If the selection or classification is neither capricious nor arbitrary, and rests upon some reasonable consideration of difference or policy, there is no denial of the equal protection of the law."

20. While condemning the present distribution system, plaintiffs concede the virtue of decentralization, as follows:

"Decentralized administration and decision-making are desirable for administrative and political reasons. A division of the state into local school districts is therefore necessary. The voters in any particular area are best able to weigh convenience, the desired degree of homogeneity in the student body, and other factors. These voters are the best able to draw school district boundaries. Once these boundaries are drawn, the administrators or residents of the district, being closest to the problem, are best able to determine the educational needs of the district's children. That decision takes the form of support for a certain tax rate. Sometimes, this decentralized decision-making in creating districts or in adopting a tax rate will result in insufficient distribution of educational services. When that occurs the state in recognition of its ultimate responsibility provides sufficient funds to purchase 'basic' education for each child. Four hundred dollars per pupil is the figure necessary to support a 'basic' educational program. Of course, any disadvantage is outweighed by the values of decentralized administration and decision-making."

to having revenues related to property values, apparently without realizing that the equalization grant effectively tempers variations in assessed value by using a hypothetical calculation. Furthermore, the flat grants and state and federal categorical aid reduce the school's dependence on local taxes. While alternative methods of distributing school monies might be superior to existing legislation,

> "To be able to find fault with a law is not to demonstrate its invalidity. It may seem unjust and oppressive, yet be free from judicial interference. The problems of government are practical ones and may justify, if they do not require rough accommodations — illogical, it may be, and unscientific. * * * Mere errors of government are not subject to our judicial review. It is only its palpably arbitrary exercises which can be declared void under the Fourteenth Amendment."

Metropolis Theatre Co. v. City of Chicago, 228 U.S. 61, 69–70, 33 S.Ct. 441, 57 L.Ed. 730 (1913).[21]

Plaintiffs also attack numerous details of the present legislative scheme, such as the uniform maximum tax rate for both elementary and high schools. Allegedly, high schools need more money than elementary schools; but the answer is the increased number of students attending high schools may provide the additional funds. Also, plaintiffs complain that the maximum tax rate for the City of Chicago is about half that for the remaining school districts. Since the city is so much larger than other districts, however, distinctive legislation is appropriate to adjust for potential efficiencies.[22] The maximum tax rates which plaintiffs object to were enacted to avoid another disaster such as that which struck certain localities during the Great Depression; the possibility of similar economic crises supports the statutory ceilings.

In each of the instances where particular statutory provisions have been criticized by plaintiffs we can find a legitimate legislative policy. Where differences do exist from district to district, they can be explained rationally. The charges made in the complaint fall short of demonstrating either an arbitrary exercise of legislative

---

21. Differential theatre license fees based on the price of admission, rather than on profit revenue, satisfied the equal protection clause.

22. See, e. g., Latham v. Board of Education, 31 Ill.2d 178, 184, 201 N.E.2d 111 (1964).

power or an invidious discrimination. Under these circumstances, there can be no denial of any Fourteenth Amendment rights.

Moreover, the legislature is constantly upgrading the quality of education. For example, the foundation level was recently revised from the 1965–66 level of $330 to the present $400. Also, the General Assembly has substantially consolidated the school districts, reducing the 11,955 which existed in 1945 to approximately 1,340 today. Recently a legislative study commission suggested that educational television be introduced in the schools and that the foundation level be raised to $435. See Report of the School Problems Commission No. 9, ch. I (1967); compare Report of School Problems Commission No. 7, p. 76–77 (1963).[23]

B. *Plaintiffs' Legal Precedent*

The complaining students rely upon recent Supreme Court decisions in the fields of school desegregation,[24] voting rights[25] and criminal justice.[26] Specifically, they contend that "equal educational opportunity," however that term may be defined, is constitutionally compelled because (1) state discrimination in education may not be based on color, (2) the state may not employ arbitrary geographical lines to establish electoral units within local governments, and (3) wealth may not be used to differentiate

23. In addition, the Task Force on Education, sponsored in 1966 by then Governor Kerner and the legislature's School Problems Commission, recently proposed a plan of state financial support whereby each elementary student would receive a minimum of $600 and each high school student $750. Task Force on Education, Education For The Future of Illinois, p. 113, 135 (1966). Compare McLure, A Study of the Public Schools in Illinois (1965).

24. See, e.g., Brown v. Board of Education, 347 U.S. 483, 74 S.Ct. 686, 98 L.Ed. 873 (1954); Griffin v. County School Board, 377 U.S. 218, 84 S.Ct. 1226, 12 L.Ed.2d 256 (1964).

25. See, e.g., Baker v. Carr, 369 U.S. 186, 82 S.Ct. 691, 7 L.Ed.2d 663 (1962); Reynolds v. Sims, 377 U.S. 533, 84 S.Ct. 1362, 12 L.Ed.2d 506 (1964); Avery v. Midland County, 390 U.S. 474, 88 S.Ct. 1114, 20 L.Ed.2d 45 (1968).

26. See. e.g., Griffin v. Illinois, 351 U.S. 12, 76 S.Ct. 585, 100 L.Ed. 891 (1956); Douglas v. California, 372 U.S. 353, 83 S.Ct. 814, 9 L.Ed.2d 811 (1963); Gideon v. Wainwright, 372 U.S. 335, 83 S.Ct. 792, 9 L.Ed.2d 799 (1963); Miranda v. Arizona, 384 U.S. 436, 86 S.Ct. 1602, 16 L.Ed.2d 694 (1966).

among criminal defendants if such discrimination is adverse to the indigent.[27]

But the plaintiffs' conclusion does not follow so readily from the preceding building blocks. The decided cases established significant, but limited principles. To illustrate, Brown v. Board of Education was primarily a desegregation case. Although placed in the context of public schools, it does not undermine the validity of Illinois' public financing. Similarly, Hobsen v. Hansen, 269 F. Supp. 401 (D.D.C.1967), struck down variations in expenditures because the classifying factor was race.[28] The holding in Douglas v. California, 372 U.S. 353, 83 S.Ct. 814, 9 L.Ed.2d 811 (1963), derived primarily from its criminal justice setting, rather than the poverty of the defendant. Moreover, Reynolds v. Sims, 377 U.S. 533, 84 S.Ct. 1362, 12 L.Ed.2d 506 (1964), strengthened citizens' voting rights because the Constitution specifically enfranchises all citizens equally, not as a result of general antipathy to historical geographical divisions.

Actually, there is little direct precedent because the contentions now presented are novel. But, the few relevant cases indicate that plaintiffs must resort to the legislature rather than the courts. The students are not deprived of their civil rights under 28 U.S.C. § 1343 because the asserted guarantee does not exist under the Constitution. LeBeauf v. State Board of Education, 244 F. Supp. 256, 260 (E.D.La.1965), held:

"There simply is no right, privilege, or immunity secured to these plaintiffs by the Constitution and laws of the United States being in any way denied by these respondents when they allocate and disburse funds * * * " [29]

27. See generally Kurland, "Equal Educational Opportunity: The limits of Constitutional Jurisprudence Undefined," 35 U.Chi.L.Rev. 583, 586 (1968).

28. Of course, if plaintiffs alleged that Illinois' legislation was designed to avoid the Supreme Court's racial desegregation decisions, they would state a cause of action. See Griffin v. County School Board, 377 U.S. 218, 84 S.Ct. 1226, 12 L.Ed.2d 256 (1964).

29. Although the primary thrust of the complaint was directed against local segregation, the court squarely confronted the question now before this court, sustaining state legislation which provided that:

"[A] large portion of the funds so allocated must be apportioned on a per educable basis, and the remaining distribution is made on a basis of equalization

Similarly, in Hess v. Mullaney, 213 F. 2d 635, 15 Alaska 40 (9th Cir. 1954), the Ninth Circuit upheld a property tax which returned a disproportionately small amount of funds to the taxpayers' locality.[30] Since this tax also supported the public schools, the plaintiffs' instant claim is analogous. See also General American Tank Car Corp. v. Day, 270 U.S. 367, 46 S.Ct. 234, 70 L.Ed. 635 (1926).[31] Compare Dean v. Coddlington, 81 S.D. 140, 131 N.W.2d 700 (1964); Sawyer v. Gilmore, 109 Me. 169, 83 A. 673 (1912); Orleans Parish v. State Board, 215 La. 703, 41 So.2d 509 (1949).[32]

IV. Lack of Judicially Manageable Standards

Even if the Fourteenth Amendment required that expenditures be made only on the basis of pupils' educational needs, this controversy would be nonjusticiable. While the complaint does not present a "political question" in the traditional sense of the term, there are no "discoverable and manageable standards" [33] by which a court can determine when the Constitution is satisfied and when it is violated.[34]

---

so as to provide and insure a minimum educational program in all public schools." 244 F.Supp. 258.

30. "It is argued that * * * in effect it [the taxation formula] amounts to an exemption from the tax of all this property within cities and districts * * *

            *   *   *   *   *

" * * * No requirements of uniformity or of equal protection of the law limit the power of a legislature in respect to allocation and distribution of public funds." 213 F.2d 639–640.

31. "We are not concerned with the particular method adopted by Louisiana of allocating the tax between the State and its political subdivisions. That is a matter within the competency of the state legislature." 270 U.S. 372, 46 S.Ct. 235. See Columbus Southern Railway v. Wright, 151 U.S. 470, 476–477, 14 S.Ct. 396, 38 L.Ed. 238 (1894).

32. Moreover the students are arguably complaining only about a property interest, rather than their personal liberty, so that the grievance does not fall within section 1343. With more money, plaintiffs could either attend private schools or move to a wealthy school district. See generally Gray v. Morgan, 371 F.2d 172, 174 (7th Cir. 1966). See also Abernathy v. Carpenter, 208 F.Supp. 793 (W.D.Mo. 1962), affirmed 373 U.S. 241, 83 S. Ct. 1295, 10 L.Ed.2d 409 (1963).

33. Reynolds v. Sims, 377 U.S. 533, 557, 84 S.Ct. 1362, 12 L.Ed.2d 506 (1964).

34. Illustrating the lack of standards, plaintiffs' original complaint sought to have this court "order defendants to submit * * * a plan to raise and

The only possible standard is the rigid assumption that each pupil must receive the same dollar expenditures. Expenses are not, however, the exclusive yardstick of a child's educational needs. Deprived pupils need more aid than fortunate ones.[35] Moreover, a dollar spent in a small district may provide less education than one used in a large district. As stated above, costs vary substantially throughout the state. The desirability of a certain degree of local experimentation and local autonomy in education also indicates the impracticability of a single, simple formula. Effective, efficient administration necessitates decentralization so that local personnel, familiar with the immediate needs, can administer the school system. As new teaching methods are devised and as urban growth demands changed patterns of instruction, the only realistic way the state can adjust is through legislative study, discussion and continuing revision of the controlling statutes. Even if there were some guidelines available to the judiciary, the courts simply cannot provide the empirical research and consultation necessary for intelligent educational planning.[36] As early as 1919 Mr. Justice Holmes explained that "the Fourteenth Amendment is not a pedagogical requirement of the impracticable." Dominion Hotel v. Arizona, 249 U.S. 265, 268, 39 S.Ct. 273, 274, 63 L.Ed. 597 (1919).

Plaintiffs have assumed that requiring expenditures to be related to the needs of the students will result in better education for deprived students without a corresponding decrease in the quality of education now offered by the affluent districts. The more money the latter districts must supply to the former, however, the less incentive the well-to-do will have to raise their tax rates. If the

---

apportion all monies * * * in such a manner that such funds available to the school districts wherein the class of plaintiffs attend school will * * * assure that plaintiff children receive the same educational opportunity as the children in any other district * * *."

35. Ideally, disadvantaged youth should receive more than average funds, rather than equal expenditures, so their potential can be fully developed. A rule coercing equal expenditures for all, especially if raised to a constitutional plane, would completely frustrate this ideal. See generally Kurland, "Equal Educational Opportunity: The Limits of Constitutional Jurisprudence Undefined," 35 U.Chi.L.Rev. 583, 591 (1968).

36. Compare Baker v. Carr, 369 U.S. 186, 282 & 323, 82 S.Ct. 691, 7 L.Ed.2d 663 (1962); Colegrove v. Green, 328 U.S. 549, 556, 66 S.Ct. 1198, 90 L.Ed. 1432 (1946); Coleman v. Miller, 307 U.S. 433, 454–455, 59 S.Ct. 972, 83 L.Ed. 1385 (1939).

quality of good public schools declines, affluent children have the option to attend private schools,[37] thus completely eliminating the need for the wealthy to raise taxes.[38]

V. Conclusion

The present Illinois scheme for financing public education reflects a rational policy consistent with the mandate of the Illinois Constitution. Unequal educational expenditures per student, based upon the variable property values and tax rates of local school districts, do not amount to an invidious discrimination. Moreover, the statutes which permit these unequal expenditures on a district to district basis are neither arbitrary nor unreasonable.

There is no Constitutional requirement that public school expenditures be made only on the basis of pupils' educational needs without regard to the financial strength of local school districts. Nor does the Constitution establish the rigid guideline of equal dollar expenditures for each student.

Illinois' General Assembly has already recognized the need for additional educational funds to provide all students a good education. Furthermore, the legislative School Problems Commission assures a continuing and comprehensive study of the public schools' financial problems. If other changes are needed in the present system, they should be sought in the legislature and not in the courts. Plaintiffs have stated no grounds for judicial relief, and this cause must be dismissed.

37. See Pierce v. Society of Sisters, 268 U.S. 510, 45 S.Ct. 571, 69 L.Ed. 1070 (1925).

38. Furthermore, the public schools' most acute financial crisis is in the large cities. But their struggles are only symptomatic of the overall decay of many urban centers. Despite the attempts of Congress and the state legislatures, the nation still does not have the solution to this degeneration, principally because there are not enough tax dollars to meet all needs. If the legislatures cannot solve these problems, surely the deep cutting edge of constitutional precepts is not the answer. Compare Avery v. Midland County, 390 U.S. 474, 88 S.Ct. 1114, 20 L.Ed.2d 45 (1968) (Mr. Justice Fortas' dissent).

Appendix F · Tables Cited in Footnotes

Table 1

National extremes of interdistrict spending variation: interquartile range of expenditure (dollars) per classroom unit, 75th to 25th percentiles

Low		High	
Alabama	632	Missouri	4,481
Utah	753	Michigan	4,274
West Virginia	755	Ohio	3,619

Source: F. W. Harrison and E. P. McLoone, *Profiles in School Support: A Decennial Overview* (Washington, D.C.: U.S. Government Printing Office, 1965).

Table 2

National extremes of interdistrict spending variation: Ratio of interquartile expenditure per classroom unit, 75th to 25th percenttiles

Low		High	
Utah	1.11	Missouri	1.87
New York	1.13	Michigan	1.68
New Mexico	1.13	Ohio	1.60

Source: Harrison and McLoone, *Profiles in School Support.*

Table 3

National extremes of interdistrict spending variation: ratio of expenditures per classroom unit, 98th to 2nd percentiles

Low		High	
Nevada	1.37	Missouri	3.96
Utah	1.42	Wisconsin	3.84
Louisiana	1.47	Michigan	3.49

Source: Harrison and McLoone, *Profiles in School Support.*

Table 4

Percent of all educational spending raised locally and by state via property tax: selected states

State	Total raised locally (all taxes)	Raised by local district via 1959–60 property tax	Raised by state via 1959–60 property tax
Arizona	53.4	53.4	6.8
Delaware	9.8	9.8	0.
Illinois	67.1	67.1	0.
Nevada	33.2	30.8	3.7
New Hampshire	85.1	80.0	.5
New York	54.2	54.2	0.
North Carolina	27.8	18.9	0.
Ohio	69.4	63.9	0.
Rhode Island	72.8	72.8	0.
Utah	50.4	45.5	8.2
United States	53.0	50.3	.6

Source: U.S. Department of Health, Education and Welfare, *Revenue Programs for the Public Schools in the United States, 1959–60* (Washington, D.C., 1960), p. 7.

Table 5

Property tax as a percent of income by income level

Households by income	Approximate range of income quartile (dollars)	Resident property tax as percent of income
Lowest quartile	Under 3,000	3.5
Second quartile	3,000–5,000	1.6
Third quartile	5,000–7,000	1.3
Highest quartile	7,000 and over	1.0
All households		1.3

Source: J. A. Thomas, *School Finance and Educational Opportunity in Michigan* (Lansing: Michigan Department of Education, 1968), p. 183.

Table 6

Federal aid for vocational education (dollars per student) in Michigan by district wealth

District valuation	Receipts from federal government
More than 14,000	2.15
9,000–14,000	1.84
Less than 9,000	1.31

Source: Thomas, *School Finance*, p. 203.

Table 7

Federal aid under Elementary and Secondary Education Act of 1965, Title I[a] (dollars per student) in Michigan by district wealth

District valuation	Receipts from federal government
More than 14,000	13.50
9,001–14,000	6.87
9,000 or less	55.47

Source: Thomas, *School Finance*, p. 204.
[a] For areas with high concentrations of children from low-income families and those experiencing learning difficulties.

Selected Bibliography

CASES

Abington School District v. Schempp, 374 U.S. 203 (1963).
Anders v. California, 386 U.S. 738 (1967).
Aptheker v. Rusk, 378 U.S. 500 (1964).
Baker v. Carr, 369 U.S. 186 (1962).
Baldwin v. Seelig, 294 U.S. 511 (1935).
Bates v. Little Rock, 361 U.S. 516 (1960).
Baxstrom v. Herold, 383 U.S. 107 (1966).
Board of Education v. Allen, 392 U.S. 236 (1968).
Board of Education v. Michigan, General Civil No. 103342, (Cir. Ct. of Wayne County, Michigan, filed Feb. 2, 1968).
Braunfeld v. Brown, 366 U.S. 599 (1961).
Braxton County Court v. West Virginia, 208 U.S. 192 (1908).
Brinkman v. Board, General Civil No. 69C246 (N.D. Ill. filed Feb. 6, 1969).
Brown v. Board of Education, 347 U.S. 483 (1954).
Buck v. Bell, 274 U.S. 200 (1927).
Burns v. Ohio, 360 U.S. 252 (1959).
Burruss v. Wilkerson, General Civil No. 68–C–13–H (U.S.D.C. W.D. Va., decided May 27, 1969).
Calder v. Bull, 3 U.S. (3 Dall.) 386 (1798).
Carrington v. Rash, 380 U.S. 89 (1965).

Cipriano v. City of Houma, 395 U.S. 701 (1969).

Columbus and Greenville Railway v. Miller, 283 U.S. 96 (1931).

Cox v. Louisiana, 379 U.S. 536 (1965).

Dean v. Coddington, 81 S.D. 140, 131 N.W.2d 700 (1964).

Douglas v. California, 372 U.S. 353 (1963).

Draper v. Washington, 372 U.S. 487 (1963).

Duncan v. Louisiana, 391 U.S. 145 (1968).

Edwards v. California, 314 U.S. 160 (1941).

Epperson v. Arkansas, 393 U.S. 97 (1968).

Eskridge v. Washington State Board of Prison Terms and Paroles, 357 U.S. 214 (1958).

Flemming v. Nestor, 363 U.S. 603 (1960).

Ginsberg v. New York, 390 U.S. 629 (1968).

Glona v. American Guarantee Co., 391 U.S. 73 (1968).

Gray v. Sanders, 372 U.S. 368 (1963).

Griffin v. Illinois, 351 U.S. 12 (1956).

Griffin v. Prince Edward County School Board, 377 U.S. 218 (1964).

Griswold v. Connecticut, 381 U. S. 479 (1965).

Guerra v. Smith, General Civil No. A–69–CA–9 (U.S.D.C. W.D. Tex. filed Jan. 28, 1969).

Hall v. St. Helena Parish School Board, 197 F. Supp. 649 (E.D. La. 1961).

Harper v. Virginia Board of Education, 383 U.S. 663 (1966).

Hess v. Mullaney, 213 F.2d 635 (9th Cir. 1954).

Hobson v. Hansen, 269 F. Supp. 401 (D.D.C. 1967).

In Re Apportionment of State Legislature, 373 Mich. 247, 128 N.W.2d 721 (1964).

In Re Gault, 387 U.S. 1 (1967).

In Re Skipwith, 180 N.Y.S.2d 852 (1958).

Interstate Railroad Co. v. Massachusetts, 207 U.S. 79 (1907).

Jones v. Mayer Co., 392 U.S. 409 (1968).

Kent v. Dulles, 357 U.S. 116 (1958).

Kramer v. Union Free School District No. 15, 395 U.S. 621 (1969).

Lane v. Brown, 372 U.S. 477 (1963).

Lassiter v. Northampton County Board of Elections, 360 U.S. 45 (1959).

Lee v. Washington, 390 U.S. 333 (1968).

Levy v. Louisiana, 391 U.S. 68 (1968).

Long v. District Court of Iowa, 385 U.S. 192 (1966).

Loving v. Virginia, 388 U.S. 1 (1967).

Lucas v. Forty-fourth General Assembly, 377 U.S. 713 (1964).

McCabe v. Atchison, Topeka and Sante Fe Railway, 235 U.S. 151 (1914).

McCollum v. Board of Education, 333 U.S. 203 (1948).

McDonald v. Board of Election Commissioners of Chicago, 394 U.S. 802 (1969).

McGowan v. Maryland, 366 U.S. 420 (1961).

McInnis v. Shapiro, 293 F. Supp. 327 (N.D. Ill. 1968), aff'd mem. sub nom. McInnis v. Ogilvie, 394 U.S. 322 (1969).

McLaurin v. Oklahoma State Regents, 339 U.S. 637 (1950).

McNeese v. Board of Education, 373 U.S. 668 (1963).

Meyer v. Nebraska, 262 U.S. 390 (1923).

Miller v. Korns, 107 Ohio St. 287, 140 N.E. 773 (1923).

Minersville School District v. Gobitis, 310 U.S. 586 (1940).

Missouri ex. rel. Gaines v. Canada, 305 U.S. 337 (1938).

Monroe v. Pape, 365 U.S. 167 (1961).

Morey v. Doud, 354 U.S. 457 (1957).

NAACP v. Alabama, 357 U.S. 449 (1958).

NAACP v. Button, 371 U.S. 415 (1963).

Pierce v. Society of Sisters, 268 U.S. 510 (1925).

Plessy v. Ferguson, 163 U.S. 537 (1896).

Prince v. Massachusetts, 321 U.S. 158 (1944).

Railway Express Agency v. New York, 336 U.S. 106 (1949).

Reitman v. Mulkey, 387 U.S. 369 (1967).

Reynolds v. Sims, 377 U.S. 533 (1964).

Rinaldi v. Yeager, 384 U.S. 305 (1966).

Rodrigues v. San Antonio Independent School District, General Civil No. 68–175–SA (U.S.D.C. W.D. Tex. filed July 30, 1968).

St. Helena Parish School v. Hall, 368 U.S. 515 (1962).

Sawyer v. Gilmore, 109 Me. 169, 83 A. 673 (1912).

Serrano v. Priest, General Civil No. 938254 (Super. Ct. for Los Angeles County, Calif., decided Jan. 8, 1969).

Shapiro v. Thompson, 394 U.S. 618 (1969).

Shelton v. Tucker, 364 U.S. 479 (1960).

Shepheard v. Godwin, 280 F. Supp. 869 (E.D. Va. 1968).

Sherbert v. Verner, 374 U.S. 398 (1963).

Silva v. Atascadero Unified School District, General Civil No. 595954 (Super. Ct. for San Francisco County, Calif., filed Sept. 26, 1968).

Sipuel v. Board of Regents of the University of Oklahoma, 332 U.S. 631 (1948).

Skinner v. Oklahoma, 316 U.S. 535 (1942).

Smith v. Bennett, 365 U.S. 708 (1961).

South Carolina State Highway Dept. v. Barnwell Bros., 303 U.S. 177 (1938).

Strauder v. West Virginia, 100 U.S. 303 (1880).

Sweatt v. Painter, 339 U.S. 629 (1950).

Tennessee Electric Power Co. v. Tennessee Valley Authority, 306 U.S.
    118 (1939).
United States v. Carolene Products, 304 U.S. 144 (1938).
United States v. Guest, 383 U.S. 745 (1966).
United States v. Hart, 382 F.2d 1020 (3rd Cir. 1967) *cert. denied*,
    88 U.S. 1851 (1968).
United States v. Holmes, 387 F.2d 781 (7th Cir. 1967) *cert. denied*,
    391 U.S. 936 (1968).
United States v. Jefferson Electric Co., 291 U.S. 386 (1934).
United States v. Johnson, 319 U.S. 302 (1943).
Webb. v. Board, General Civil No. 61 C 1569 (N.D. Ill. filed Sept. 18,
    1961).
Webb v. Board, General Civil No. 63 C 1895 (N.D. Ill. filed Oct. 23,
    1963).
Webb v. Board, General Civil No. 65 C 51 (N.D. Ill. filed Jan. 14,
    1965).
WHYY, Inc., v. Borough of Glassboro, 393 U.S. 117 (1968).
Williams v. Fears, 179 U.S. 270 (1900).
Williams v. Oklahoma City, 395 U.S. 458 (1969).
Williams v. Rhodes, 393 U.S. 23 (1968).
Williams v. Shaffer, 385 U.S. 1037 (1967).
WMCA v. Lomenzo, 377 U.S. 633 (1964).
Yick Wo v. Hopkins, 118 U.S. 356 (1886).

BOOKS, PUBLISHED AND UNPUBLISHED REPORTS, PUBLIC DOCUMENTS

Annual Educational Summary 1963–1964. Albany: New York State
    Education Bureau of Statistical Services, 1965.
Annual Report, 1965–66. Delaware Department of Public Instruction,
    Statistical Section. Dover: State Board of Education, 1966.
*Annual State Report on Local Government Finances and Tax Equal-
    ization*. Providence: State of Rhode Island and Providence Planta-
    tions, Department of Administration, Division of Local and Met-
    ropolitan Government, 1966.
*Arizona Annual Report of the Superintendent of Public Instruction,
    1965–66*. Phoenix: Office of the State Superintendent of Educa-
    tion, Division of Research and Finance, 1967.
*1965 Assessed Valuations and 1966 Tax Rates in Descending Order
    of Illinois Public Schools*. Springfield: Office of the Superintendent
    of Public Instruction, Division of Finance and Statistics, Circular
    Series A, no. 198, 1967.

Bailey, S. K. *Achieving Equality of Educational Opportunity*. The Ohio Foundation, May, 1966.

Becker, G. S. *Human Capital*. New York: National Bureau of Economic Research, 1964.

Benson, C. S. *The Cheerful Prospect: A Statement on the Future of Public Education*. Boston: Houghton Mifflin, 1965.

—— *The Economics of Public Education*. Boston: Houghton Mifflin, 1961.

—— *The School and the Economic System*. Chicago: Science Research Associates, 1966.

Benson, C. S., ed. *Perspectives on the Economics of Education*. Boston: Houghton Mifflin, 1963.

—— *Readings on the Economics of Education*. Boston: Houghton Mifflin, 1963.

Benson, C. S., and P. B. Lund. *Neighborhood Distribution of Local Public Services*. Berkeley: University of California Institute of Government Studies, 1969.

Bickel, Alexander. *The Least Dangerous Branch*. Indianapolis: Bobbs-Merrill, 1962.

Biennial Report of the Superintendent of Public Instruction. Carson City: Nevada Department of Education, Division of Finance and Retirement, 1966.

Bloom, B. S., Allison Davis, and Robert Hess. *Compensatory Education for Cultural Deprivation*. Chicago: Holt, Rinehart, and Winston, 1965.

Blum, V. C. *Freedom in Education: Federation Aid for All Children*. Garden City: Doubleday, 1965.

Bochenski, I. M., Alonzo Church, and Nelson Goodman. *The Problem of Universals*. Notre Dame: University of Notre Dame Press, 1956.

Brogan, Dennis. *The American Character*. New York: Alfred A. Knopf, 1944.

Burkhead, Jesse. *Public School Finance*. Syracuse: Syracuse University Press, 1964.

—— *State and Local Taxes for Public Education*. Syracuse: Syracuse University Press, 1963.

California Public Schools Selected Statistics 1967–1968. Sacramento: Department of Education, 1969.

Callahan, R. E. *Education and the Cult of Efficiency*. Chicago: University of Chicago Press, 1962.

Coleman, J. S. et al. *Equality of Educational Opportunity*. Washington, D.C.: U.S. Government Printing Office, 1966.

Committee on Educational Finance, ed. *Financing the Changing*

School Program. Washington, D.C.: National Education Association, 1962.

Comparison of State and Local District Contributions to School Financing. Carson City: Nevada Department of Education, Division of Finance and Retirement, 1966.

Conant, J. B. *Slums and Suburbs.* New York: McGraw-Hill, 1961.

Cost per Pupil in Average Daily Membership in Ohio's City, Exempt Village and County School Districts, 1966. Columbus: Ohio State Division of Computer Services and Statistical Reports, 1966.

Cubberley, E. P. *Public Education in the United States: A Study and Interpretation of American Educational History.* Boston: Houghton Mifflin, 1919.

———— *Readings in Public Education in the United States: A Collection of Sources and Readings to Illustrate the History of Educational Practice and Progress in the United States.* Boston: Houghton Mifflin, 1934.

———— *School Funds and Their Apportionment.* New York: Columbia Teachers College, 1905.

———— *State School Administration.* Boston: Houghton Mifflin, 1927.

Current Expenditures by Source of Funds, 1965–66. Raleigh: Office of State Superintendent of Public Instruction, North Carolina State Department of Public Instruction, 1966.

Current Expenditures per Pupil in Public School Systems: Urban School Systems, 1958–59. Washington, D.C.: U.S. Department of Health, Education and Welfare, circular no. 645 (1961).

Daly, C. U., ed. *The Quality of Inequality: Suburban and Urban Public Schools.* Chicago: University of Chicago Press, 1968.

Dewey, John. *Democracy and Education.* New York: Macmillan, 1923.

Drake, W. E. *The American School in Transition.* New York: Prentice-Hall, 1955.

Economic Report of the President, January 1964, together with the Annual Report of the Council of Economic Advisers. U.S. Office of the President. Washington, D.C.: U.S. Government Printing Office, 1964.

Economic Report of the President, January 1966, together with the Annual Report of the Council of Economic Advisers. U.S. Office of the President. Washington, D.C.: U.S. Government Printing Office, 1966.

Edwards, Newton. *The Courts and the Public Schools.* Chicago: University of Chicago Press, 1955.

Edwards, Newton, and H. G. Richey. *The School in the American Social Order,* 2nd ed. Boston: Houghton Mifflin, 1963.

Fesler, J. W., ed. *The 50 States and Their Local Government*. New Haven: Yale University Press, 1967.

Fiscal Balance in the American Federal System, vol. I. Advisory Commission on Intergovernmental Relations. Washington, D.C.: U.S. Government Printing Office, 1967.

Flanagan, J. C. *The American High School Student*. Technical Report to U.S. Office of Education, Cooperative Research Project 635. Pittsburgh: University of Pittsburgh Project Talent Office, 1964.

Frederic, K. A. *School Finance and School Districts*. New York: National League of Women Voters, 1936.

Freeman, R. A. *Taxes for the Schools*. Washington, D.C.: Institute for Social Science Research, 1960.

Friedman, Milton. *Capitalism and Freedom*. Chicago: University of Chicago Press, 1962.

Garber, L. O., and Newton Edwards. *The Law Governing the Financing of Public Education*. School Law Casebook Series, no. 8. Danville, Ill.: Interstate Printers and Publishers, 1962.

———— *The Law Relating to the Creation, Alteration, and Dissolution of School Districts*. School Law Casebook Series, no. 2. Danville, Ill.: Interstate Printers and Publishers, 1962.

———— *The Public School in Our Governmental Structure*. School Law Casebook Series, no. 1. Danville, Ill.: Interstate Printers and Publishers, 1962.

Gardner, J. W. *Excellence: Can We Be Equal and Excellent Too?* New York: Harper and Row, 1961.

Gross, C. H., and C. C. Chandler, eds. *The History of American Education Through Readings*. Boston: D. C. Heath and Co., 1964.

Hand, Learned. *The Bill of Rights*. Cambridge: Harvard University Press, 1958.

Harris, R. J. *The Quest for Equality: The Constitution, Congress, and the Supreme Court*. Baton Rouge: Louisiana State University Press, 1960.

Harrison, F. W., and E. P. McLoone. *Profiles in School Support: A Decennial Overview*. Washington, D.C.: U.S. Government Printing Office, 1965.

Hayek, F. A. *The Constitution of Liberty*. Chicago: University of Chicago Press, 1960.

Hohfeld, W. N. *Fundamental Legal Concepts as Applied in Judicial Reasoning, and Other Legal Essays*. New Haven: Yale University Press, 1923.

Illinois Amended State Aid Claim Statistics: Illinois Public Schools 1965–1966 School Year. Springfield: Superintendent of Public Instruction, Division of Finance and Statistics, Circular Series A, no. 196, 1967.

Illinois Education Association. *Common School Aid in Illinois*. December, 1963.

Illinois Education Association. *Lessons in Illinois Public School Finance*. February, 1952.

Illinois Public Schools Financial Statistics 1963–1964. Springfield: Superintendent of Public Instruction, Division of Finance and Statistics, Circular Series A, no. 176, 1965.

"Impact of Head Start" (draft). Westinghouse Learning Corporation, 1969.

Impact of the Property Tax: Its Economic Implications for Urban Problems. Joint Economic Committee, Congress of the United States, 90th Congress, 2d Session, 1968.

James, H. T. *School Reserve Systems in Five States*. Stanford: School of Education, Stanford University, 1961.

James, H. T., T. J. Alan, and H. J. Dyck. *Wealth, Expenditures, and Decision-making for Education*. Stanford: School of Education, Stanford University, 1963.

Johns, R. L., and E. L. Morphet, eds. *Problems and Issues in Public School Finance*. New York: Columbia Teachers College, 1952.

Joint Commission on the Emergency in Education, National Education Association and the Department of Superintendence. *Report of the National Conference on the Financing of Education, 1933*. Phi Delta Kappa, 1934.

Keach, E., R. Fulton, and W. Gardner, eds. *Education and Social Crisis*. New York: John Wiley & Sons, 1967.

Keppel, Francis. *The Necessary Revolution in American Education*. Stanford: School of Education, Stanford University, 1961.

Lakoff, S. A. *Equality in Political Philosophy*. Cambridge: Harvard University Press, 1964.

Levin, H. M., ed. *The Community School Controversy*. Washington, D.C.: Brookings Institution, 1969.

Lockhart, W. B., Yale Kamisar, and Jesse Choper. *Constitutional Law, Cases-Comments-Questions*. St. Paul: West, 1967.

McKay, R. B. *Reapportionment: The Law and Politics of Equal Representation*. New York: Twentieth Century Fund, 1965.

Mayer, Martin. *The Teachers' Strike: New York, 1968*. New York: Harper and Row, 1969.

Measurement of the Ability of Local Governments to Finance Local Public Services. Albany: University of the State of New York, State Board of Education, Bureau of Educational Finance Research, May, 1967.

Mort, P. R. *State Support for Public Schools*. New York: Columbia Teachers College, 1926.

Mort, P. R., and W. C. Reusser. *Public School Finance*, 2nd ed. New York: McGraw-Hill, 1951.

Mort, P. R., W. C. Reusser, and J. W. Polley. *Public School Finance*, 3rd ed. New York: McGraw-Hill, 1960.

Munse, A. R. *State Programs for Public School Support*. Washington, D.C.: U.S. Government Printing Office, 1965.

Musgrave, R. A. *The Theory of Public Finance*. New York: McGraw-Hill, 1959.

National Education Association, Education Policies Commission, ed. *Education and the Disadvantaged American*. Washington, D.C.: National Education Association of the U.S., 1962.

National School Finance Conference, Committee on Educational Finance, ed. *Long Range Planning in School Finance*. Washington, D.C.: National Education Association, 1963.

Netzer, Dick. *The Economics of the Property Tax*. Washington, D.C.: Brookings Institution, 1966.

Noble, S. G. *A History of American Education*. New York: Holt, Rinehart, 1954.

Norton, J., and E. Lawler. *Unfinished Business in American Education*. American Council on Education, 1946.

Passow, A. H., ed. *Education in Depressed Areas*. New York: Columbia University Teachers College, 1963.

Pennock, J. R., and J. W. Chapman, eds. *Equality: Nomos IX*. New York: Atherton Press, 1967.

Phelps, Edmund, ed. *Private Wants and Public Needs: An Introduction to a Current Issue of Public Policy*, rev. ed. New York: W. W. Norton, 1962.

Polley, John. *Variations in Impact of Municipal Government on Ability to Support Schools*. Albany: New York State Education Conference Board, Staff Study no. 3, 1961.

Public School Finance Programs of the United States, 1957–58. Washington, D.C.: U.S. Department of Health, Education and Welfare, 1958.

Puffer, R. N. "A Private Study," unpub. research paper. Office of R. N. Puffer, Northwestern University, 1967.

Racial Isolation in the Public Schools, vol. I and vol. II (appendixes). U.S. Commission on Civil Rights. Washington, D.C.: U.S. Government Printing Office, 1967.

Reconnection for Learning: A Community School System for New York City. ("Bundy Report.") New York City Mayor's Advisory Panel on Decentralization of the New York City Schools, 1967.

Revenue Programs for the Public Schools in the United States, 1959–60. Washington, D.C.: U.S. Department of Health, Education and Welfare, 1960.

The Rhode Island State School Aid Program: A Report to the Legislature. Providence: Rhode Island Special Commission To Study The Entire Field of Education, Rhode Island State Legislature, 1967.

Ribich, Thomas. *Education and Poverty.* Washington, D.C.: Brookings Institution, 1968.

Richardson, J. D., ed. *A Compilation of the Messages and Papers of the President, 1787–1887,* vol. II. Washington, D.C.: U.S. Government Printing Office, 1896–1899.

Riesman, Frank. *The Culturally Deprived Child.* New York: Harper and Row, 1962.

Roberts, Joan I., ed. *School Children in the Urban Slum,* New York: Free Press, 1967.

Rogers, David. *110 Livingston Street: Politics and Bureaucracy in the New York City School System.* New York: Random House, 1968.

Rosenthal, Robert, and Lenore Jacobson. *Pygmalion in the Classroom: Teacher Expectation and Pupils' Intellectual Development.* New York: Holt, Rinehart, and Winston, 1968.

Sears, J. B., and A. D. Henderson. *Cubberley of Stanford.* Palo Alto: Stanford University Press, 1957.

Sexton, P. C. *Education and Income.* New York: Viking Press, 1961.

Smith, Adam. *An Inquiry into the Nature and Causes of the Wealth of Nations,* 2nd ed., vol. I, J. E. T. Rogers ed. Oxford: Clarendon Press, 1880.

Smythe, A. H., ed. *The Writings of Benjamin Franklin,* vol. X. New York: Macmillan, 1905–1907.

A Staff Report: Measure of State and Local Fiscal Capacity and Tax Efforts. Washington, D.C.: Advisory Commission on Intergovernmental Relations, October, 1962.

State Aid to New York School Districts, 1965–66. Albany: University of State of New York, State Education Department, Bureau of Educational Finance Research, January, 1967.

State Programs for Public School Support. Washington, D.C.: U.S. Department of Health, Education and Welfare, 1965.

1965–66 Statistical Tables. Providence: Supervisor of Statistical Services, Rhode Island State Department of Education, 1966.

Strayer, G. D., and N. L. Engelhardt, eds. *State Support for Public Schools.* New York: Columbia Teachers College, 1926.

Strayer, G. D., and R. M. Haig. *Financing of Education in the State of New York.* New York: Macmillan, 1923.

Stuart, G. A *History of American Education*. New York: Rinehart, 1954.

Studies of Public School Support 1966 Series: Vital Issues in Public School Finance. Albany: University of State of New York, State Education Department, Bureau of Educational Finance Research, 1967.

Task Force Report: Crime and Its Impact — An Assessment. President's Commission on Law Enforcement and Administration of Justice. Washington, D.C.: U.S. Government Printing Office, 1967.

Thomas, J. A. "Efficiency in Education: A Study of the Relationship between Selected Variables and Test Scores in a Sample of the United States High Schools," unpub. diss. School of Education, Stanford University, 1962.

―――― *School Finance and Educational Opportunity in Michigan*. Lansing: Michigan Department of Education, 1968.

―――― "State Aid Formulas and Educational Finance in Illinois," paper presented at the University of Chicago, Dec. 11, 1964.

Tocqueville, Alexis de. *Democracy in America*, rev. ed. New York: Alfred A. Knopf, 1945.

Tumin, M. M. *Social Stratification*. Englewood Cliffs: Prentice-Hall, 1967.

U.S. Riot Commission Report. National Advisory Commission on Civil Disorders, 1968.

Utah State Board of Education Annual Report, 1965–66. Salt Lake City: Utah State Board of Education, Office of State Superintendent of Public Instruction, 1966.

Van den Haag, Ernest. *Education as an Industry*. New York: Augustus M. Kelley, 1956.

Vose, C. E. *Caucasians Only, the Supreme Court, the NAACP and the Restrictive Covenant Cases*. Berkeley: University of California Press, 1959.

Warner, W. L., R. J. Havighurst, and M. B. Loeb. *Who Shall Be Educated?* New York: Harper, 1944.

Weber, Max. *Protestant Ethic and the Spirit of Capitalism*. New York: Charles Scribner's Sons, 1956.

Weinberg, J. S. *State Aid to Education in Massachusetts*. Cambridge, Mass.: New England School Development Council, 1962.

Weisbrod, B. A. *External Benefits of Public Education: An Economic Analysis*. Princeton: Princeton University, Department of Economics, Industrial Relations Section, 1964.

West, E. G. *Education and the State*. London: Institute of Economic Affairs, 1965.

Wise, A. E. "The Constitution and Equality: Wealth, Geography, and Educational Opportunity," unpub. diss. University of Chicago, 1967.
——— Rich Schools, Poor Schools: The Promise of Equal Educational Opportunity. Chicago: University of Chicago Press, 1968.
Woollatt, L. H. The Cost-Quality Relationship in the Growing Edge. New York: Columbia Teachers College, 1949.

ARTICLES

Allen, F. A. "Griffin v. Illinois: Antecedents and Aftermath," University of Chicago Law Review, 25:151 (1957).
Anderson, C. A., and P. J. Foster. "Discrimination and Inequality in Education," Sociology of Education, 38:1 (Fall, 1964).
Anderson, J. W. "Poverty Stalks a Neighborhood," The Washington Post (Dec. 24, 1967), p. B1.
Berlin, Sir Isaiah, and Richard Wolheim. "Equality," Proceedings of the Aristotelian Society (London), NS, 56 (1956).
Bickel, Alexander. "The Original Understanding and the Segregation Decision," Harvard Law Review, 69:1 (1955).
Bikle, H. W. "Judicial Determinations of Questions of Fact Affecting the Constitutional Validity of Legislative Actions," Harvard Law Review, 38:6 (1924).
Bowles, Samuel, and B. M. Levin. "The Determinants of Scholastic Achievement — An Appraisal of Some Recent Evidence," Journal of Human Resources, 3:1 (1968).
Choper, Jesse. "The Establishment Clause and Aid to Parochial Schools," California Law Review, 56:260 (1968).
——— "On the Warren Court and Judicial Review," Catholic University Law Review, 17:20 (1967).
Cohen, David. "Defining Racial Equality in Education," U.C.L.A. Law Review, 16:255 (1969).
——— "Policy for the Public Schools: Compensation and Integration," Harvard Education Review, 38:114 (1968).
——— "The Price of Community Control," Commentary, 48, no. 1: 23–32 (July, 1969).
Coleman, James. "The Concept of Equal Educational Opportunity," Harvard Educational Review, 38:7 (Winter, 1968).
——— "Equality of Educational Opportunity: Reply to Bowles and Levin," Journal of Human Resources 3, 237 (Spring, 1968).
Comment, "Developments in the Law — Equal Protection," Harvard Law Review, 82:1065 (1969).

Comment, "Rational Classification Problems in Financing State and Local Government," *Yale Law Journal*, 76:1206 (1968).

Comment, "Reapportionment and the Problem of Remedy," *U.C.L.A. Law Review*, 13:1345 (1966).

Cox, Archibald. "Constitutional Adjudication and the Promotion of Human Rights," (foreword to "The Supreme Court 1965 Term") *Harvard Law Review*, 80:91 (166).

Deutsch, J. G. "Neutrality, Legitimacy, and the Supreme Court: Some Intersections Between Law and Political Science," *Stanford Law Review*, 20:169 (1968).

Dowling, N. T. "The Methods of Mr. Justice Stone in Constitutional Cases," *Columbia Law Review*, 41:1160 (1941).

Dunn, J. R. "Title VI, the Guidelines and School Desegregation in the South," *Virginia Law Review*, 53:42 (1967).

Dyer, Henry. "School Factors and Educational Opportunity," *Harvard Educational Review*, 38:38 (1968).

Foote, Caleb. "The Coming Constitutional Crisis in Bail," *University of Pennsylvania Law Review*, 113:959 (1965).

Franz, L. B. "The First Amendment in the Balance," *Yale Law Journal*, 71:1424 (1962).

Goldberg, Arthur. "Equality and Governmental Action," *New York University Law Review*, 39:205 (1964).

Horowitz, Harold. "Unseparate But Unequal — The Emerging Fourteenth Amendment Issue in Public School Education," *U.C.L.A. Law Review*, 13:1147 (1966).

Horowitz, Harold, and Diana Neitring. "Equal Protection Aspects of Inequalities in Public Education and Public Assistance Programs from Place to Place Within a State," *U.C.L.A. Law Review*, 15:787 (1968).

Jaffe, Louis L. "Was Brandeis an Activist? The Search for Intermediate Premises," *Harvard Law Review*, 80:986 (1967).

Jencks, Christopher. "Is the Public School Obsolete?" *The Public Interest*, no. 2 (Winter, 1966).

Jensen, Arthur. "How Much Can We Boost IQ and Scholastic Achievement?" *Harvard Education Review*, 39:1 (1969).

Kaplan, John. "Equal Justice in an Unequal World: Equality for the Negro — The Problem of Special Treatment," *Northwestern University Law Review*, 61:363 (1966).

———— "Segregation Litigation and the Schools — Part II: The General Northern Problem," *Northwestern University Law Review*, 58:157 (1963).

Kenney, J. F. "The Principle of Subsidiarity," *The American Catholic Sociological Review*, 16:31–36 (1955).

Kirp, David. "The Constitutional Dimensions of Equal Educational Opportunity," *Harvard Law Review*, 38:1 (1968).

Krause, H. D. "Legitimate and Illegitimate Offspring of *Levy* v. *Louisiana* — First Decisions on Equal Protection and Paternity," *University of Chicago Law Review*, 36:338 (1969).

Kurland, Phillip. "Equal Educational Opportunity: The Limits of Constitutional Jurisprudence Undefined," *University of Chicago Law Review*, 35:583 (1968).

———— "Equal in Origin and Equal in Title to the Legislative and Executive Branches of the Government," (foreword to "The Supreme Court 1963 Term"). *Harvard Law Review*, 78:143 (1964).

Levin, H. M. "The Failure of the Public Schools and the Free Market Remedy," *Urban Review*, 2, no. 7 (June, 1968), 32–37.

———— "What Difference Do Schools Make?" *Saturday Review*, Jan. 20, 1968, pp. 57–58, 66–67.

Lieberman, Myron. "Equality of Educational Opportunity," *Harvard Educational Review*, 29:167–83 (Summer, 1959).

Lusky, Louis. "Racial Discrimination and the Federal Law: A Problem in Nullification," *Columbia Law Review*, 63:1163 (1963).

McKay, R. B. "The Preference for Freedom," *New York University Law Review*, 34:1182 (1959).

Merriam, I. C., A. M. Skolnik, and S. R. Dales. "Social Welfare Expenditures, 1967–68," *Social Security Bulletin*, 31:14 (1968).

"The National Cost of Education Index — 1965–66," *School Management*, January, 1966, pp. 119–187.

"The National Cost of Education Index — 1966–67," *School Management*, January, 1967, pp. 120–126.

Neal, Philip. "*Baker* v. *Carr*, Politics in Search of Law," *Supreme Court Review* (1962).

Note, "Appellate Review of Primary Sentencing Decisions: A Connecticut Case Study," *Yale Law Journal*, 69:1453 (1960).

Note, "Discrimination against the Poor and the Fourteenth Amendment," *Harvard Law Review*, 81:435 (1968).

Note, "Equality of Educational Opportunity: Are 'Compensatory Programs' Constitutionally Required?" *Southern California Law Review*, 42:146 (1968).

Note, "The Equal Protection Clause and Imprisonment of the Indigent for Nonpayment of Fines," *Michigan Law Review*, 64:938 (1966).

Note, "Judicial Review of State Welfare Practices," *Columbia Law Review*, 67:84 (1967).

Note, "Legal Implications of the Use of Standardized Ability Tests in

Employment and Education," *Columbia Law Review*, 68:691 (1968).

Note, "Poverty and Equal Access to the Courts; The Constitutionality of Summary Dispossess in Georgia," *Stanford Law Review*, 20:766 (1968).

Note, "The Right to Nondiscriminatory Enforcement of State Penal Laws," *Columbia Law Review*, 61:1103 (1961).

Paterson, I. W. "Determinants of Expenditures for Education," *Canadian Educational Research Digest*, 7:84 (June, 1967).

Pollack, L. H. "Racial Discrimination and Judicial Integrity: A Reply to Professor Wechsler," *University of Pennsylvania Law Review*, 108:1 (1959).

Sager, L. G. "Tight Little Islands: Exclusionary Zoning, Equal Protection, and the Indigent," *Stanford Law Review*, 21:767 (1969).

Sizer, Theodore, and Phillip Whitten. "A Proposal for a Poor Children's Bill of Rights," *Psychology Today*, 2:3 (August, 1968).

Struve, G. M. "The Less Restrictive-Alternative Principle and Economic Due Process," *Harvard Law Review*, 80:1463 (1967).

Tussman, Joseph, and Jacobus tenBroek. "The Equal Protection of the Laws," *California Law Review*, 37:341 (1949).

Weaver, J. B., and S. W. Hess. "A Procedure for Nonpartisan Districting: Development of Computer Techniques," *Yale Law Journal*, 73:288 (1963).

Wechsler, Herbert. "Toward Neutral Principles of Constitutional Law," *Harvard Law Review*, 73:1 (1959).

West, E. G. "The Uneasy Case for State Education," *New Individualist Review*, 4:38 (1968).

Index